HAWAI'I POLITICS AND GOVERNMENT

*Politics and Governments
of the American States*

General Editor

John Kincaid
Robert B. & Helen S. Meyner Center
for the Study of State and Local
Government, Lafayette College

Founding Editor

Daniel J. Elazar
Center for the Study of Federalism,
Temple University

Editorial Advisory Board

Thad L. Beyle
University of North Carolina
at Chapel Hill

Diane D. Blair
University of Arkansas

Ellis Katz
Temple University

Charles Press
Michigan State University

Stephen L. Schechter
Russell Sage College

Published by the University of
Nebraska Press in association
with the Center for the Study
of Federalism, Temple University, and the
Robert B. & Helen S. Meyner Center
for the Study of State and Local
Government, Lafayette College

RICHARD C. PRATT WITH ZACHARY SMITH

Hawai'i Politics and Government

AN AMERICAN STATE IN A PACIFIC WORLD

UNIVERSITY OF NEBRASKA PRESS

LINCOLN AND LONDON

Manufactured in the
United States of America

⊛

Library of Congress
Cataloging-in-Publication Data
Pratt, Richard C., 1941–
Hawai'i politics and government :
an American state in a Pacific world /
Richard C. Pratt with Zachary Smith.
p.   cm.—(Politics and governments
of the American states)
Includes bibliographical
references and index.
ISBN 0-8032-3724-3 (cloth : alk. paper)
ISBN 0-8032-8750-X (pbk. : alk. paper)
1. Hawaii—Politics and government.
I. Smith, Zachary A.
(Zachary Alden), 1953–
II. Title.   III. Series.
JK9316.P73   2000
320.4969—dc21   99-33799
CIP

To Hasty and Debra Jean

CONTENTS

TABLES

JOHN KINCAID

Series Preface

The purpose of this series is to provide information and interesting books on the politics and governments of the fifty American states, books that are of value not only to the student of government but also to the general citizens who want greater insight into the past and present civic life of their own states and of other states in the federal union. The role of the states in governing America is among the least well known of all the 85,006 governments in the United States. The national media focus attention on the federal government in Washington DC, and local media focus attention on local government. Meanwhile, except when there is a scandal or a proposed tax increase, the workings of state government remain something of a mystery to many citizens—out of sight, out of mind.

In many respects, however, the states have been, and continue to be, the most important governments in the American political system. They are the main building blocks and chief organizing governments of the whole system. The states are the constituent governments of the federal union, and it is through the states that citizens gain representation in the national government. The national government is one of limited, delegated powers; all other powers are possessed by the states and their citizens. At the same time, the states are the empowering governments for the nation's 84,955 local governments—counties, municipalities, townships, school districts, and special districts. As such, states provide for one of the most essential and ancient elements of freedom and democracy, the right of local self-government.

Although, for many citizens, the most visible aspects of state government are state universities, some of which are the most prestigious in the world, and state highway patrol officers, with their radar guns and handy ticket books, state governments provide for nearly all domestic public services.

Whether elements of those services are enacted or partly funded by the federal government and actually carried out by local governments, it is state government that has the ultimate responsibility for ensuring that Americans are well served by all their governments. In so doing, all of the American states are more democratic, more prosperous, and better governed than most of the world's nation-states.

This is a particularly timely period in which to publish a series of books on the governments and politics of each of the fifty states. Once viewed as the "fallen arches" of the federal system, states today are increasingly seen as energetic, innovative, and fiscally responsible. Some states, of course, perform better than others, but that is to be expected in a federal system. Each state is unique in its own right. It is our hope that this series will shed light on the public life of each state and that, taken together, the books will contribute to a better, more informed understanding of the states themselves and of their often pivotal roles in the world's first and oldest continental-sized federal democracy.

Preface

The project began as a joint venture with Zachary Smith, with whom I enjoyed collaborating as coeditor on a book of original essays about political and policy issues in contemporary Hawai'i. Unfortunately, commitments at his new position on the faculty at Northern Arizona University did not permit him the time to remain fully involved in this effort, and part way through the first draft we agreed I would assume responsibility for its completion.

I am responsible for what is written here, but a number of people have helped make this manuscript better than it otherwise would be. They include Kehau Kealoha-Scullion, Dan Boylan, Harry Ball, Bob Cahill, Richard Kahle Jr., Neal Milner, Jima Rile, Jim Hall, and Randy Iwase. Peter Manicas of the sociology department and liberal studies program at UH Manoa deserves mention for the care with which he reviewed the entire manuscript and provided candid feedback.

The librarians at the Legislative Reference Bureau and the Department of Business, Economic Development, and Tourism always were able to promptly accommodate my requests for information. Earl Anzai, the director of the Department of Budget and Finance, was gracious in sharing information I requested, as was Chris Grandy at the Department of Business, Economic Development, and Tourism. A number of graduates of the public administration program chipped in to help me find things I otherwise would have missed. In our office, Trisha Kagawa good-naturedly bore the brunt of the detailed work needed to finalize the manuscript. Teri Matsuda stepped in to help when it was most needed.

One other person requires special acknowledgment. Deane Neubauer, faculty member in political science at the University of Hawai'i at Manoa, provided help and insight at a crucial point in the manuscript's development. He was willing to take the time to share his rich knowledge of Hawai'i's political life, despite having numerous other commitments. I could not hope for any more from a valued colleague.

Note on Spelling and Terminology

Hawaiian words use special notations to guide pronunciation. These are the glottal stop (*kahako*), signified by a reverse apostrophe and placed between letters, and the macron (*'okina*), a hyphen-like mark above a letter. The glottal stop is used to create a sound similar to the sound between the *oh*'s in the English *oh-oh*. The macron is placed over the vowels of Hawaiian words to make them longer and add stress.

Not much attention was given to these notations until there was a resurgence of interest in Hawaiian culture about twenty years ago. There has been a kind of unspoken argument about whether or not to incorporate these new spellings since then. Many places, the University of Hawai'i for example, have adopted the proper Hawaiian language spelling of the state's name (and dropped *Hawaii*), while many others have not.

This text uses the apostrophe to signify the glottal stop but does not employ the macron. Both of these decisions reflect technical capabilities, not preferences. Words that are predominantly Hawaiian, with the exception of well-known place names, are in italics.

In Hawaii it is more common to refer to individuals called *whites* on the mainland as *haoles* or, less commonly, as Caucasians. That practice is followed here.

Finally, it is the convention in Hawai'i to capitalize the word *islands* when referring to the Hawaiian Islands, as in "I live in the Islands." That practice has not been adopted here, following the stylistic preferences of the press.

HAWAI'I POLITICS AND GOVERNMENT

CHAPTER ONE

Change and Continuity

It is not hard, in the late 1990s, to stand on a street corner in downtown Hono-lulu or to drive through parts of suburban, Southern California–like Hawai'i Kai and imagine oneself in another part of the continental United States. Still, despite the dramatic growth since statehood in 1959, those impressions of complete assimilation into what residents commonly refer to as "the mainland" remain surprisingly bounded in comparison to the effect of other factors in shaping life in the state.

These factors include the islands' natural history and physical setting, their social and political evolution from an independent Pacific nation, the continuous overlaying of immigrant groups and their cultural patterns, cen-tralized public institutions and a distinctive political culture, and shifting re-lationships with outsiders. All of these, taken together, help to shape what is unique about Hawai'i as an American state and a Pacific society.

NATURAL HISTORY

The chain of islands that make up Hawai'i originate in a geological hotspot, one of 30 or 40 places on our planet where molten lava relentlessly forces its way up through the earth's upper mantle and crust. These thick upper layers have formed large, slowly moving sections, called Tectonic plates, that slide into and away from one another.

The Hawaiian Islands sit on the Pacific plate. Molten rock came up out of the Pacific plate as it passed across the hotspot over hundreds of thousands of years, the lava in many places rising above the ocean's surface. The plate's northwest movement resulted in a geological record that runs from north-west to southeast, starting below and east of the Aleutians and ending just inside the latitude that defines the tropics in the center of the Pacific. Where the continuous action of wind, rain, and waves have not yet eroded the lava formations below the ocean's surface, there remains what we know today as the Hawaiian Archipelago.[1]

The archipelago spans more than 1,500 miles and consists of 132 islands, reefs, and shoals.[2] Its northwestern reach, which ends 300 miles beyond Midway Island at Kure Atoll, is made up of low lying seamounts and atolls. Eight of the islands, starting with Kaua'i and moving southeast to the island of Hawai'i, are currently inhabited. They are at the most recently formed end of the archipelago and make up 99 percent of the state's land mass of 6,425 square miles.

The most northerly, and therefore the oldest, of these eight are Ni'ihau, Kaua'i, O'ahu, and Moloka'i. Their place in geologic time has left these four islands with the most eroded mountains, steepest cliffs—named *palis* by Hawaiians—and finest sand beaches. In stark contrast, Maui and Hawai'i, the most southerly islands, have far fewer fine-grained stretches of sand and are dominated by the often snowcapped dormant and active volcanoes that formed them: Haleakala, Mauna Kea, and Mauna Loa.

On Hawai'i, labeled the Big Island because it is 65 percent larger than the other islands combined, Kilauea volcano is active in long cycles of eruption. These outpourings send lava down its slopes to expand the county's physical jurisdiction. At the archipelago's most southeasterly reach, off-shore in the blue waters beyond this new real estate, one can witness the primal forces that created the islands. There, hundreds of feet below sea level, ocean-cooled lava piles layer upon layer to form what someday will be known as the island of Loihi when it too emerges above the surface.

Mountains, sub-tropical setting, and physical isolation are as significant as these primal geologic forces in the islands' natural and social evolution. Their location just below the Tropic of Cancer ensures a warm, moist climate year-round. Although temperatures may drop well below freezing on the volcano summits, at or near sea level temperatures range from lows around 60°F in the winter to highs above 90°F in August and September. The latitude and prevailing northeasterly winds combine with the moderating influence of the surrounding ocean to produce the lowest maximum daily temperature and the highest minimum daily temperature of any place in the United States.[3]

Mountains are sufficiently high to create clouds by causing the warm, moist air, pushed by the wind across the ocean's surface, to rise and then cool, ensuring a predictable precipitation pattern. Rainfall and accompanying erosion are heavier on the windward sides of each island, especially near the mountains. Rainfall averages as high as 440 inches on Mount Wai'ale'ale on Kaua'i, but more typically falls in the 60–120 inch range. On the leeward sides, mean rainfall is as little as nine inches in the "desert" areas, but is generally between 15 and 25 inches.

Finally of significance, the islands are among the most remote on earth.[4] Their physical distance from other land masses—2,400 miles from the American west coast, 2,700 miles south of Alaska, 2,700 miles north of Papeete, Tahiti, and 3,800 miles east of Japan—is unmatched by places better known for their isolation, such as the Galapagos. Such distances require any life that established itself on these islands to have been carried great distances on ocean or air currents, or to have been part of the supplies the earliest Polynesian settlers brought on their long ocean voyages.

Mountains, subtropical setting, and isolation mean that Hawai'i's natural history is one of gentle and even climate, excellent growing conditions across a range of environments, and the evolution of unique animal and plant life. When human beings arrived in the islands, they entered an environment that supported the most concentrated aggregation of different ecological zones in the world. These life-forms, although abundant and diverse, often were extremely vulnerable to new flora and fauna. As Richard Tobin and Dean Higuchi observe, "Isolation provided an evolutionary advantage, but it also created a high vulnerability to disruption . . . island species are limited in where they can go and how rapidly they can develop defense mechanisms."[5]

This vulnerability lead to plants and animals brought by historic and contemporary settlers encountering conditions very attractive for expansion, often with little resistance from the local flora and fauna. Abundance and fragility, ease and risk, became part of the islands' ethos, fostering an unresolved tension between desires to make use of them and fears that a unique environment will be irreparably damaged by human activity.

SOCIAL EVOLUTION IN AN ISLAND ENVIRONMENT

Successive waves of immigrants and visitors have come to the islands because temperate climate and natural beauty make them desirable places to live. The first immigrants are estimated to have sailed from the Marqueas in the South Pacific between the second and sixth centuries, A.D. More than a millennium later, before the arrival of non-Polynesians, their descendants lived so successfully off of the islands that their numbers had grown to a population that may have exceeded 800,000.[6] The relative ease of cultivating abundant land and sea resources, together with isolation from outside influences, left these inhabitants, like the flora and fauna, vulnerable. The Native population dropped catastrophically in the years after the islands were "discovered" by British explorer James Cook in January 1778, reduced by diseases to which Hawaiians had no immunities. By the 1870s, they had declined to less than 70,000, while those remaining had experienced massive dislocations.

The arrival of strong-minded missionaries and ambitious businessmen threatened the values of Native Hawaiian culture. Plantation owners transplanted laborers from Asia to support export agriculture. Later, dramatic changes in transportation technology reduced the islands' physical isolation. After statehood, these changes permitted millions of short-term visitors, so many that, on an average day in 1992, more than 1 in 4 people on Maui was a visitor.[7] Waves of new residents and visitors, similar to the repetitive cycles of Kilauea, simultaneously covered over earlier cultures and expanded the islands' cultural base—occasioning a great drama of cultural struggle, integration, and succession.

Being remote, mountainous islands separated by deep ocean channels has other significance for Hawai'i's institutions, culture, and politics. Remoteness reduced to a relative trickle those who would follow nineteenth-century western expansion and seek their new life in the islands. Missionaries and agriculturists did change the islands culturally and politically, but their numbers were relatively small; throughout the nineteenth century, the foreign Caucasian population numbered only a few thousand.

With two-thirds of its land mass on the mountainous Big Island of Hawai'i, and much of the rest made up of eroded slopes and steep ridges, only a finite amount of land is suitable for habitat or productive uses. The new arrivals' desire for arable land created a complex struggle in which a few large producers came to own or lease most of the attractive agricultural lands. The control and use of land was destined to remain a paramount issue in Island political life.

The non-nomadic Hawaiian life-style did not prevent outsiders' access to the lands they coveted, creating little motivation to isolate the Native population. Land claims could be dealt with through legal mechanisms, rather than placing the Native population in reservations. As a result Hawaiians, while having lost much of their land as well as its economic, social and cultural benefits, remained within the population. Co-mingling with the new arrivals, often through intermarriage, they changed the immigrants' outlook and culture.

Finally, even though the string of inhabited islands is only 300 miles long, with urban O'ahu and rural Moloka'i a cozy 25 miles apart, the channels are sufficiently wide and wind-blown to prevent easy crossings. Although integrated into one system of governance, the distinct character of each island society was already established. The consequence is that tensions remain between the push for integration that comes from the center of political power in Honolulu, and the desire for voice and differentiation that arises from the Neighbor Islands.

CONTEMPORARY SOCIAL, ECONOMIC AND POLITICAL CHARACTERISTICS

In 1959, the resident population, whose voters overwhelmingly approved becoming the nation's fiftieth state, totaled about 630,000. That population would become 770,000 by 1970, an increase of 21 percent. It would stand at more than 1.1 million in another twenty-seven years, making it the forty-first state in population size. Three of four residents lived in and around the state's capital of Honolulu on O'ahu, an island comprising about 10 percent of the state's land area.

About half of this population growth resulted from in-migration.[8] Much of this proliferation in turn, was triggered by the development of tourism and, to a lesser extent, the military's presence. Tourism's role in population growth reflects its dominant place in the post-statehood economy as well as the decline of sugar and pineapple. The plantation industries induced huge population increases in the years before and after annexation in 1893. Between 1986 and 1996, the acreage devoted to sugarcane production was reduced from 184,300 acres to 68,800 acres, and in 1999 pineapple passed sugar as the primary agricultural product. In 1922 approximately 9,700 tourists visited the islands to stay two or more nights, adding $4,400,000 to the economy. Almost 300,000 arrived in 1959 to spend $131,000,000. By 1997, those same figures would change to 6,876,140 visitors and $10.8 billion. In that year, a daily average of 157,810 visitors mingled with a resident population of about 1,100,100.[9]

Tourism, urbanization and military spending intensified demographic changes, especially on O'ahu and in urban Honolulu. In 1831, population still reflected the more even distribution that characterized Hawaiian society before Western contact. At that time, 22.8 percent lived on O'ahu, 35.1 percent on the island of Hawai'i, 32.1 percent on Maui and Lanai, and 9.2 percent on Kaua'i. These numbers had shifted somewhat by annexation at the century's turn, with O'ahu holding 38 percent of the new territory's expanding population of 154,000. Sixty years later, at statehood, following several decades in which the net population of the other counties declined, 79 percent resided on O'ahu. When O'ahu's congestion and high cost of living, especially housing, became a factor in the mid-1980s, population data began to reflect a modest shift back toward the Neighbor Islands. From a 1970 high of almost 82 percent of the population, by 1997 O'ahu dropped to just over 73 percent.[10]

Despite population increases and these recent shifts, there still are no urban centers on the Neighbor Islands remotely comparable in size to Honolulu. Using "census designated place" to permit the description of de facto cities and towns existing within the jurisdiction of county governments, Honolulu had a 1990 population of 377,059 while the largest Neighbor Island town of Hilo on the Big Island had 37,808.[11]

High land prices and trans-Pacific shipping always have made Hawai'i an expensive place to reside. The high cost of living has been an especially critical factor since statehood. Residents of only a few other places in the United States, such as the city of San Francisco or the state of Alaska, bear living costs at the same level. None combine Hawai'i's high expenses for basic necessities like housing and food with only slightly above average wage levels.

The 1972 budget for a four person family on O'ahu was 119 percent of the national average. By 1992 this had increased to almost 140 percent.[12] The figure dropped to 132 percent in 1997, the result of six years of economic stagnation. In comparison to the relatively high costs, in 1997 the per capita personal income for the state was 102 percent of the national average, a substantial decline from around 120 percent of the national average in the early 1970s.[13]

It is not surprising that economic issues are featured prominently in the concerns expressed by the state's residents in three surveys in 1976, 1986, and 1997 (table 1).

Employment concerns ranked first in all three surveys among problems cited, followed closely in two of the three years by high cost of living. Crime and education are companions to these economic concerns in all three surveys. Crime ranked sixth in 1976, rising to fourth in 1986 and 1997. This consistency reflects apprehensions about higher levels of violent crime as well as crimes against property, both of which have accompanied urbanization and the growth in tourism.

Table 1: Primary Concerns of Residents

Rank	1976	1986	1997
1	jobs	jobs	jobs
2	cost of living	traffic	cost of living
3	government costs	government infighting	education
4	housing	crime	crime
5	education	education	taxes
6	crime	housing	drug abuse

Sources: Greg Wiles, "Economic Woes Lie Heavy on Hawaii's Mind," *Honolulu Advertiser*, February 18, 1996, p. A-1; Robbie Dingeman, "Improving Education a Top Goal," *Honolulu Advertiser*, October 30, 1997, p. A-2.

There is a better basis for some of these concerns about crime than others. Hawai'i ranked forty-second in the nation in incidents of violent crimes per capita in 1997. In 1996, however, the state had the fourth highest rate of property crimes per capita in the nation. These data reflect an increase of 23.3 percent in reported violent crimes, and 39.6 percent in property crimes between 1984 and 1994, followed by a decline in almost every crime category after 1995.[14]

The overall decrease in crime during economic hard times is an interesting phenomenon. Researchers attribute it to demographic shifts as much as to effective public policies, better policing, or more jail time. There are relatively fewer people in the age groups most likely to commit crimes, a change that reflects the aging of the state's population. The median age in 1980 was 28.3. By 1997, it had increased to 35.7. It is projected to be 37.3 in 2020.[15] This shift has important implications not only for crime, but for the kinds of services, such as long-term care, that will be required in coming years.

Between 1974 and 1997, concern for the quality of education increased the most in importance to residents. Hawai'i's newspapers regularly document, sometimes with great fanfare, the poor performance of public school students, publishing Scholastic Aptitude Test (SAT) scores, the verbal results of which continue to be low compared to both national norms and local private schools. With equal regularity, upset parents and nervous legislators call for changes in funding, curriculum, or administration to improve learning, or at least test results. Some note that in 1994 the state spent about $5,620 per public school pupil in grades K-12, ranking it fifteenth nationally, that scores are improving, and that over 90 percent of students feel safe on their campuses. Others observe that there is an acute shortage of classroom space in some areas, while others have a surplus; that Hawai'i has the highest rate of reported racial and physical violence in its schools; and that, taking cost of living into account, in 1995 it paid public school teachers the least of all fifty states.[16] While this debate goes on, parents on O'ahu continue to send more than 16 percent of their primary and secondary school aged children to private schools, among the highest percentages in the country.[17]

The argument over education reveals a great deal about the state. One defense of the system's performance is that Hawai'i's lower scores are partially accounted for by the large number of residents for whom English is not the first language. In 1990, 14.7 percent of the resident population was born outside of the United States and its territories to non-American parents, an increase from 9.8 percent in 1970.[18] Another explanation is that the school system is centralized. Unlike more decentralized jurisdictions where results for some schools are not reported, scores from all schools are part of the state average.

Public education's monolithic structure reflects other aspects of contemporary Hawai'i: the high degree of centralization in governance and concentration in the economy.[19] Hawai'i has the smallest number of government units per population of any state in the union.[20] Consistent with this, in fiscal year 1993 state government received 80.8 percent of all state and local tax revenues, placing it second only to Alaska.[21] Also consistent, at 183 it has the small number of state and local elected officials among the fifty states, as well as the lowest rate of elected officials per 10,000 population.[22]

Yet government has a large presence in Island life. At 556 per 10,000 residents, Hawai'i ranked seventeenth nationally in 1994 on number of public employees. It ranked fourth on the size of state and local taxes as a percentage of personal income.[23] State and local tax revenue averaged $5,885 per person in 1993, the fourth largest nationally. Hawai'i was first in general sales and gross receipts per capita, second in alcohol beverage taxes per capita, and fifth in public utility and user taxes per capita.[24]

These data on tax burdens can be misleading, also owing to the state's centralized institutions. State government relies on general excise and use and general income taxes as its primary revenue sources. The excise tax is broad based, and is levied on most goods and services. The counties, on the other hand, obtain most of their income from the property tax. There are no jurisdictions below the county, and the counties in Hawai'i perform few of the functions common to them in mainland states, making property taxes among the lowest in the nation.

Marc Schulhof compared total tax burdens—property taxes as well as other revenue sources—in major metropolitan areas across the United States.[25] When he did this, he found that Washington DC and large cities in 36 states placed higher burdens on residents than does Honolulu. He might have added to this analysis a feature of Hawai'i's environment that very likely reduces the relative burden even further. The general excise and use tax comprise more than 40 percent of all taxes collected. For consumers, it is equivalent to a sales tax of just over four percent. This tax, therefore, is paid by the more than 7 million tourists who visit the state each year, the effect of which is to export part of the tax burden to non-residents. Some of the cities to which Schulhof made comparisons may have the same combination of sales tax and high number of visitors, but it is unlikely most do. It may be challenging to make the argument that Hawai'i's taxes are too low, but it is equally difficult to make the case that they are comparatively out of line.[26]

Approximately 80 percent of all spending by state and county governments is accounted for by the state. In fiscal year 1999, the state general fund, which is the repository of income and excise taxes, was the source of more than one-half of the $5.85 billion the state expected to spend. Other major sources are special funds, such as fuel taxes (about 20 percent); and federal funds (about 15 percent). The rest comes from trust and revolving funds.[27]

In 1998, state and local governments employed approximately 44,000 people full-time; the largest single group worked in K-12 public education and the University of Hawai'i system.[28] Public sector employment increased 44 percent between 1984 and 1994, a period during which the civilian labor force was growing by 26 percent and the resident population by 15 percent. After 1994, the number of public employees not related to education began to drop. In 1996, 51 percent of the public sector workers belonged to one of six unions, compared to 38 percent for the rest of the country.[29]

Japanese-Americans are a high but declining proportion of employees within public bureaucracies. Their total of 18,463 represented 43.9 percent of the state's full-time employees in 1984. By 1994, while still a plurality and over-represented relative to their proportion in the general population, Japanese-Americans had dropped to 17, 269, or 32.7 percent. Caucasians (6,643 to 11,585), Hawaiians and part Hawaiians (6,101 to 10,322) and Filipinos (3,492 to 6,777) had increased their presence in the same period.[30]

The centralized and consolidated system of governance is mirrored in economic affairs. Of the 4,110,996 acres that make up the inhabited and proximate islands of the state, over 24 percent, or 996,226 acres, were controlled by eight large estate landowners in 1997. That these eight estates control roughly 40 percent of all privately held land makes this even more dramatic.[31]

As suggested above, the goods and services economy is dominated by tourism which replaced, in a relatively short period, sugar and pineapple. Tourism was directly or indirectly responsible for about 76,000 jobs in 1970, a substantial but not overwhelming number. By 1991, this had become 250,900 jobs, approximately 44 percent of the civilian workforce for that year.[32] Tourist spending in 1995 accounted for between 25 and 30 percent of the state's total product, and more than 30 percent of its total tax revenues.[33]

The monolithic quality of the economy appears in other areas. Hawai'i consumers pay extraordinarily high prices to fuel their automobiles. The difference between a gallon of gasoline on the West Coast and O'ahu, where the prices are lowest, is usually about 40 cents. Mostly this appears to result from the fact that there are only two refineries. This virtual monopoly brought little protest until 1998. That year, after several inconclusive studies of the matter, in which the refiners argued the problem was that local consumers did not like to price shop, the state brought suit, charging price collusion.

RECURRING THEMES

Formal and informal power has been highly centralized from the time Hawai'i was a kingdom through its evolution into a constitutional monarchy, republic, territory and state. American states vary historically with regard to the degree of central authority, and it is inaccurate to characterize this centralization as unique. It is the case, however, that the evolution of Hawai'i's institutions began uniquely from a monarchy and followed a distinctive path.

Most government institutions in the United States evolved from local communities. The authority of larger jurisdictions—state and federal in particular—was superimposed on governments that were definitively and decisively local (although, of course, not necessarily democratic). Consistent with emerging liberal principles so influential in shaping political institutions in the United States, these developments often were greeted with deep-seated resistance, resistance that sometimes turned to violence.

Arguments about central versus local control were, over time, settled in favor of progressively greater degrees of central authority, something forecast by the replacement of the Articles of Confederation by the federal constitution, and later by the Civil War. The struggle to find an acceptable balance, both between the states and the federal government and within the jurisdictions making up a state, remained. This struggle continues today in various forms, a powerful issue in American political life.

Public institutions in Hawai'i evolved from the "top" down rather than the "bottom" up to an unusual and perhaps singular degree. Even though characteristics of traditional Hawaiian society distinguished it from the feudal systems of Europe and Asia, its hierarchical pattern of authority on each island resembled those systems. King Kamehameha' I's consolidation of his rule across the islands in 1795 brought a larger and more integrated system of governance within a traditional framework of obligations and responsibilities. The traders, missionaries and businessmen found it necessary to work within these arrangements to obtain their spiritual and economic goals. As time passed they found few incentives to devolve this authority. A centralized system served the interests of these emerging players, especially those associated with the plantation system. Plantation owners preferred to have jurisdictional autonomy in dealing with Hawaiians, and later with the tens of thousands of Asians who came as immigrant labor. For their part, the missionaries did not include among their goals the establishment of secular power in Native Hawaiian communities.

Centralized power and the interwoven fabric that developed to support it remain in place. Unless one counts the advisory role played by the system of Neighborhood Boards on the island of O'ahu, or the operations of the soil conservation districts, there are no levels of government below the county. As is made clear in chapter 10's discussion of local governance, the four county governments have fewer responsibilities and far less authority than analogous jurisdictions in other states, while state government has much more.[34] Primary and secondary education illustrates this. The responsibility for each rests exclusively with state government and, as further witness to the concentration of central authority, a single statewide school board makes policy.

Hawai'i's historic and contemporary politics, as is true for any complex community, is not made up of precise divisions or monolithic in-groups. Tensions are continual and occur throughout the system, infusing those who dominate its institutions as well as those who wish to do so. At the same time, groups have found enough common interest to predominate for long periods, and centralized authority, joined with other sources of power, has become a powerful source of influence over social and economic affairs.

Each historical period has produced an elite group able to establish a high degree of control over issues of primary concern to it. Prior to Cook's arrival and through the early years of the nineteenth century, the elite was made up of Hawaiian royalty, the *Ali'i*. The Native Hawaiian elite largely had been replaced by a network of businessmen by the end of the nineteenth century, who moved the islands into the orbit of the United States and then advocated its incorporation as a territory. That new elite dominated most aspects of life in the territory until after the Second World War. It was officially displaced from its base in elected office in 1954 by an emergent group made up primarily of Americans of Japanese ancestry. This group of second (Nisei) and third (Sansei) generation Japanese immigrants, operating through labor unions and the Democratic party, became the most recent holders of power.

The other side of this pattern of successive elite groups exerting tight control through centralized institutions is the constant arrival of those seeking a place in Hawai'i's society. Each in succession has been seen as outsiders by those who themselves were recently so defined, a dynamic familiar throughout much of the United States. The persistent unwillingness of elites to grant social, political, economic, and cultural standing to "outsiders" resulted in a build-up of pressure for change. When changes came, they were often abrupt, suddenly redefining who is privileged and powerful. Simultaneously each change has been followed by something that oddly resembles the old pattern of centrally controlled authority.

This pattern of powerholders changing places inside a centralized structure has been a feature of other parts of the United States and is not unusual. Its Hawai'i form is distinguished by the close connection with beliefs and symbols that orient people to the islands and their place in the world. It is a complicated, sometimes contradictory orientation, born of mixing values absorbed from traditional Hawaiian culture with American and Asian cultures; the sense of uniqueness and vulnerability brought by physical isolation; and identification with the natural splendor and congenial physical environment of the islands.

The sentiment of "aloha" encapsulates part of this orientation. Aloha signifies openness to and tolerance of others, either visitors or members of the same broad community. It is often coupled with a commonly expressed belief that Hawai'i is different from other places, perhaps most especially "the mainland." Openness and identity as someplace special, perhaps even unique, in turn co-exists with a sense of Hawai'i as fragile and vulnerable; a social and cultural space in need of protection from those who don't understand it, or who wish to exploit it.

These images of openness, distinctiveness, and vulnerability join with other patterns. Hawai'i often has relied on powerful "outsiders"—individuals, economic actors, or governments—to do what its own resources seemed unable to accomplish. This is illustrated by the king's use of foreign advisers, the importation of foreign labor, the embrace of federal presence through annexation and statehood, and more contemporary dependence on Japanese tourism and investment.

Though bringing benefits, the turn to outsiders always has required guarding against the loss of autonomy and identity. Thus, from another perspective the king's Caucasian advisers betrayed the Kingdom; annexation gave authority to people who lived far from the islands and knew little about their circumstances; foreign labor brought the prospect of take-over by people alien to Hawai'i and the United States; statehood meant uncontrolled development, promoted external takeover of major businesses, and further threatened a Hawaiian lifestyle; and Japanese investment resulted in foreign ownership of the state's key industry. Thus, to some observers external relationships contribute to a healthy evolution, while to others they produce the feeling that "Hawai'i is helpless on all fronts."[35]

A desire for respectability is linked to the tension between dependence and self-protection. Respectability means that despite its small size, limited resources, and physical remoteness, Hawai'i is not to be seen as inferior or out of the mainstream. It is equal to other parts of the nation and the world, even to those places that somehow seem to be the center when Hawai'i is the periphery.

The drive for equal standing fosters attempts to gain respect through the establishment of institutions sometimes hard to justify in terms of the state's history, culture, and resources. Examples range from the pre-statehood campaign to prove Hawai'i at least as democratic as any other place; to sports competition in which the state university's athletic teams fly back and forth across the Pacific in hopes of toppling larger and better funded competitors; and to schools of medicine and law publicly funded despite difficulty in supporting more basic education programs.[36] Each example reflects desires for a cosmopolitan projection while simultaneously seeking to preserve a cherished "localness." These commitments have an odd relationship, and it is no surprise that Honolulu is experienced by residents and visitors alike as an international city with small town characteristics.

Much of this complex orientation is revealed in the idea of "paradise," itself a tangled image of competing elements.[37] In an unfinished novel about Hawai'i, a place that during his six-month visit in 1866 made a lifelong impression, Samuel Clemens recalled the islands as "to this day the peacefullest, restfullest, sunniest, balmiest, dreamiest haven of refuge for a worn and weary spirit; they lie asleep on the waves, perpetually green and beautiful, remote from the work-day world and its frets and worries."[38] Elvi Whittaker, a contemporary anthropologist, identified it as a transcendent image Westerners have of a "bounty of things natural and beautiful, and somehow in accord with what is viewed as basic human nature."[39] A guiltless and unconditional surrender to sensuality is included in this projection, something not constrained by gatekeepers responsible for maintaining order in society and individuals.

Francine du Plessix Gray, a writer who spent a few months observing life in the islands in the early 1970s, saw something quite different. She found Hawai'i to be "profoundly hedonistic and provincial, a sugar-coated fortress, an autistic Eden, a plastic paradise in which the militarism and racism of the American empire are cloaked by a deceptive veil of sunshine and of flowers."[40]

For most residents, the idea of paradise speaks to relationships to the physical place and to one another. It points to what is sacred about where they live, and helps to explain their willingness to sacrifice as much as they do economically (a sacrifice referred to as the "paradise tax") to remain in Hawai'i.

To revere paradise, however, also opens the possibility that someone not raised in, or at least captivated by, the islands will not share in this meaning and, while still using the word, contribute to its loss. "Paradise" thus has a second meaning that does not evoke the sacred, but represents a tool to be used for economic gain or personal benefit. The perpetuation and commercial exploitation of a paradise myth faces residents with the same dilemmas as visitors on package tours. As Whittaker notes, "The paradoxes of the Hawai'i of the most recent quarter century reflect then the same profound tension between ecological paradise and commercial instinct that have been present in every phase of its history. The uncertainties currently visited upon a once idyllic Pacific isle could be equated with the fall from grace, with the paradise lost."[41]

These themes—the interplay of control, exclusion, and change in a highly centralized institutional setting, and in the context of the tension between an open community and a physically isolated polity struggling to control its relationship with outsiders—are woven through the chapters that follow. Among these themes, the role played by centralized authority in Hawai'i's evolution is pivotal. The ability of elite groups to operate outside of public view is a disincentive to develop processes which, with some consistency, incorporate broader public interests. The chapters that follow point to the ways in which Hawai'i's physical setting, historical patterns, political culture, ethnic characteristics, economic relations, and public institutions have sustained central authority. They also observe centralization's virtue's and vices, and consider how what has been valuable might be retained while evolving in the direction of a more open and differentiated polity.

This leads us to two questions about the state's future. Contemporary Hawai'i is experiencing significant pressures for change. These pressures include a shifting demographic make-up, the movement for some form of Native Hawaiian sovereignty, and restructuring of the local economy in response to global economic changes. How will these alter historic patterns? If earlier shifts put new players in the same centralized roles, is there reason to expect these forces to lead in the direction of less centralization and more pluralism?

The second question concerns the self understandings and identities of people living in Hawai'i. What will result from the tension between, on one side, pervasive social and economic transformations and, on the other, the historic desire to maintain Hawai'i as a special place? How well equipped are the state's public institutions and political culture to work through the challenges of that tension? What kind of paradise will remain?

CHAPTER TWO

From Kingdom to the Edge of Statehood

Hawai'i's past is woven of a complex tapestry of powerful individuals, popular voices, cultural interplays, institutional commitments, and critical events. This complexity means that the selection, representation, linking, and interpretation of these, that is, the creation of a "history," comprises something closer to the telling of a story than a reading of the data. It dictates what will be given attention and what will be ignored, and determines the meanings that will link what receives attention.

As is true in other places, multiple, often antagonistic stories connect people in this state to their past.[1] They may incorporate many of the same elements, but the meaning given to them varies widely. For example, a common nineteenth-century story, adopted mainly by white immigrants and their descendants, accentuated the role missionaries and energetic businessmen played in giving Native Hawaiians literacy, good morals, and a viable economic system.

A different story, told in the early post-statehood period by descendants of the Hawaiian Kingdom, portrayed Hawaiians as the victims of foreign ambitions, both religious and economic. Here, Hawaiian society was devastated before its people, generous and tragically innocent to the ways of outsiders, learned to protect themselves.

More recent stories, such as those created by the descendants of Asian immigrant laborers, a new class of educated Hawaiians, and revisionist historians, make it clear that the relationship between people and events is muddier and messier than any one perspective, especially one painted without subtlety, can capture.

Any story of the past must recognize an on-going dance of principles and interests; the conflict between actions that claim to have public significance and be public-regarding, and actions intended to serve a particularistic interest. It also must acknowledge that in Hawai'i, as elsewhere, it is difficult, perhaps impossible, to know which of these is motivating individuals and groups at any particular moment.

Finally, there is the continuous unfolding of contradictions; of actions that lead to outcomes different than individuals or groups wanted, but outcomes that in some way are embedded in how they went about dealing with the situations and structures they confronted. From this vantage point, the long struggle by an emerging Caucasian elite to establish a set of profitable business arrangements based upon export agriculture contained within it what they most dreaded: loss of control to the huge numbers of Asians they had imported to labor on the plantations. And the way descendants of those imported laborers infused their interests throughout centralized public institutions created a society that seemed uncomfortably like that from which they had been the liberators.

HAWAI'I THROUGH 1819

Many contemporary Hawaiians refer to themselves by their traditional name: Kanaka Maoli. Their earliest ancestor in the islands came from Polynesia. The first are thought to have come from the Marquesas by wind and paddle driven outrigger canoes, a distance of about 2,000 miles, arriving on the Big Island between 200 and 600 A.D.[2] A second migratory wave is believed to have come from the Society islands about 1200 A.D. These open ocean crossings over such long distances, together with the ability to make landfall on a small chain of islands, represent tremendous feats of navigation. The evidence of trips back and forth between the islands and the South Pacific further demonstrates the navigational sophistication among Hawaiians before contact with Western technologies.

Like other island groups throughout the Pacific, these were not integrated under one ruler but governed regionally by local chiefs. Within these regions society was organized by pie-shaped divisions of land (*ahupua'a*) that ran from the sea to the mountains. Each of these divisions, and their sub-units, was under the authority of someone loyal to the local chief (*konohiki*), and each offered their residents (*maka'ainana*) access to the range of life-sustaining ocean and land resources existing in these rich environments. Residents obtained protection by sharing a portion of their produce and labor with their chief. Unlike other social systems popularly labeled "feudal," commoners were free to migrate to another *ahupua'a* if they didn't like their present circumstances and they, in general, had longer occupational tenure than the chiefs, whose control of the land typically was redistributed at their leader's death.

Traditional Hawaiian society was more culturally diverse than stereotypic images suggest. In many locations communities were cohesive and fit our picture of Hawaiians as highly group-oriented, but in others people lived more solitary, or as Marion Kelly says, even individualistic, lives, having only occasional contact with neighbors or distant relatives.[3]

Traditional society also was relatively prosperous,[4] as testified by a rich array of games, music, and festivals and a growing population (estimated to have been between 300,000 and over 800,000).[5] Hawaiians were distributed rather evenly throughout the chain, contrasting starkly with later demographic shifts toward urban O'ahu.

The first authenticated contact by non-Polynesians with Hawaiians occurred in 1778. Captain James Cook came upon Kaua'i by accident in his search for the elusive northwest passage. In light of recent controversies over what Cook's visit meant to Hawaiians and subsequent development in Hawai'i, it is of interest that earlier contacts may have occurred.[6] Evidence suggests the Spanish might have been in the islands in the sixteenth century. More provocatively, because of events that later connected Hawai'i and Japan, others suggest that Japanese explorers reached the archipelago long before Cook.[7]

By the time Cook reached the islands, its most famous king, Kamehameha I, was on the verge of becoming the first warrior in the Pacific to unite a chain of islands under one ruler. Kamehameha was selective and strategic in his welcome of foreigners and in this manner he utilized them in bringing the island chain under his rule. He made use of the advice of sailors who had abandoned their ships as early as 1790, and over the years he was able to break the power of antagonistic chiefs by appointing a Caucasian man— John Young—governor of Hawai'i and others to official positions on various islands.[8] In contrast, from the beginning many chiefs saw foreigners as a threat and wanted them thrown out.

Many contemporary Hawaiians embrace Kamehameha I as a great warrior and a savvy leader; others regard him as a ruler who created shortsighted relationships with outsiders, and thereby began a process that would lead to the end of the kingdom and its people's culture. In this context, it is worth remembering that in the conquest of Native peoples on the American continent it was common for Caucasian men to be seen as promising allies against local enemies.[9]

Twenty-two-year-old Liholiho (Kamehameha II), successor to the throne in 1819, faced a difficult political situation.[10] Under the watchful eye of Ka'ahumanu, Kamehameha's most powerful wife, and, again with help from foreigners, he was able to maintain sufficient loyalty among chiefs to face down those challenging his rule. The challenge was partly based on continued resentment at Kamehameha I's aggressiveness in establishing his authority, and in part it was the first stages of a long, and unsuccessful, effort by some Hawaiians to prevent Caucasian foreigners from gaining more control over the islands.[11] The resistance to King Liholiho also emanated from his role, along with Ka'ahumanu, in overturning the *kapu* system, a system basic to the governance, society, and religious foundations of the islands. (For more on the place of the *kapu* system, see chapter 7.)

1820 THROUGH ANNEXATION TO THE UNITED STATES

While Hawaiian leaders were urging their people to abandon the old customs, developments were unfolding outside of the islands that would set the kingdom on a 80-year trajectory toward annexation as an American territory. Some New England seaboard Protestant missionaries were preparing to convince "the natives" that a new life awaited them in Christianity. A small, but growing, number of entrepreneurs and businessmen, primarily from the United States and Europe, were becoming interested in Hawai'i as a site for commerce. Finally, the islands' location in relation to developing commercial and diplomatic patterns meant Hawai'i was registering as an item of geopolitical interest for the United States, France, Great Britain, and Russia.

Missionaries and Businessmen

The arrival of missionaries and businessmen accelerated the transformation of Hawai'i. When missionaries appeared in 1820, one year after the formal casting-off of the *kapu* system, their primary task was the spiritual salvation of "natives." This meant "educating" and "civilizing" them, and often included the inculcation of work values and the principles of discipline, postponed rewards, and personal success. Coupled with this, missionaries believed that secure possession of land by Hawaiians was one means, and perhaps the only means available, of overcoming what they took to be native indolence.[12] The missionary's rationale was that people who had a vested interest in the use and preservation of property, and who could count on it not being taken away from them by capricious authority, would be more likely to put their energies into it. In this, the carriers of God's message were anchored in a liberal view of economic man and saw both the problem and the solution through its lens.

Missionaries frequently came into conflict with the emerging foreigner business class and attempted to restrain practices they judged to undermine what the Natives *should* be. Throughout the Pacific region, their fellow emissaries acted as a brake on the tendency of economic interests to appropriate resources with no regard to impacts on native populations.[13]

The conflict between missionary and trader was continuous during the first half of the nineteenth century, yet these groups also had much in common. Each was competing for control—the one of spiritual and cultural matters and the other of secular affairs. Moreover, both were exemplars of the West's emerging liberal, capitalist institutions.[14]

Missionaries and businessmen believed three things would lead to success against the stubborn realities that threatened their work in this island society:

1. developing the "latent industry" of the people and the natural resources of the land;
2. establishing a government along modern constitutional lines;
3. getting Hawai'i formally recognized as an independent nation[15]

Missionaries often began with few personal assets, gradually severed their ties with the mainland, and then acquired land for income or domiciles. By 1852, each of 36 Protestant missionaries had, on average, acquired 219 acres.[16] Many found their way to desirable property in the islands and, predictably, came to have an interest in control over it. Some went into business so that "after the first generation it becomes increasingly difficult to differentiate between [missionaries and traders] on the basis of either blood or sentiment."[17] Their prodigy frequently became wealthy, and later many were prominent among the elite Caucasians of Hawai'i.

Businessmen needed capital, land, and labor succeed in their endeavors. However, the key to everything they experimented in during the 1830s—rice, silk, coffee, sugar, flour, livestock—was to have a stable political environment. That, at least in the beginning, meant assuring the kingdom's independence and avoiding conflicts between the international powers.

Forces of Change

In 1840, Hawaiian land, from the perspective of Westerners, was "in large part idle and untouched—a promise and a temptation."[18] Already, foreign involvement in the islands was extensive and complex; Nation-states with influence in the Pacific—especially the United States, Britain, and France—all made evident their interest in the islands' future.

It was evident by this time that a precipitous decline in the indigenous population was occurring, dropping over 75 percent by 1832 and about one-third (47,508) that figure by the 1870s.[19] This catastrophic drop reflected the lack of resistance Hawaiians had to introduced diseases, most notably chicken pox, measles, the flu, and the venereal diseases (the latter made more devastating by Hawaiians' open sexual mores).

The seat of government, at first located in the whaling port of Lahaina on the island of Maui, was moved to Honolulu in 1845. A new palace was constructed for King Kauikeaouili (Kamehameha III), who had become king following the death of Liholiho. Responding to early pressures to Westernize institutions of governance, the chiefs had become involved in the precursors of legislative functions as early as 1825. The constitution of 1840 created the first popular representation in a legislative function.[20] (See chapter 5 for the evolution of the 1840 constitution.)

Culture and Class in Native Hawaiian Resistance

Accompanying these transforming forces were the objections and forms of resistance mounted by Native Hawaiians. Hawai'i is one of many places in the Pacific where king and chiefs found themselves having to deal with the economic and political interests of foreigners, but it is the only one where there was no physical struggle lead by local rulers against foreign intervention. Over time, however, the growing presence of foreigners; ever-expanding role of advisers to the throne, who the king made naturalized citizens; and increasing fears about disappearance of the Hawaiian people, all helped to create an active dissent, but a dissent that sought to work through government and its laws.

In the mid-1840s Hawaiian commoners (*maka'ainana*) organized a petition movement that, according to Hawaiian scholar Lilikala Kame'ekeihiwa, showed "a spirit to firmly resist any further foreign oppression."[21] Through the petitions, Hawaiians argued to their king and high chiefs (*ali'i nui*) that foreigners should not become naturalized and should not be able to purchase land, and that the *maka'ainana*, whose loyalty to the king and the kingdom were unquestioned, needed more time to adjust to the external threats mounting against them.

The king and the newly established legislature, made up of *ali'i nui*, each replied for the government, in essence disregarding the concerns expressed in the petitions. They responded that the services of some foreigners were needed in order to understand how to deal with the rest of them, and those most invested were more likely to have the king's interests as their own. Some suggested that resistance was being stirred up by discontented foreigners, and that it was not possible to avoid foreigners or foreign nations.

The exact reasons the commoners' voices were disregarded is still debated by historians. Kame'ekeihiwa argues that they were not heeded because, in their world, it was not the place of the *maka'ainana* to offer advice to those who, in the natural order of things, were responsible for their well being. In addition, by this time the king and *ali'i* had begun deferring to missionary reformers, who in essence became the advisers (*Kahuna*) on the right (*pono*) thing to do.[22]

Kehaulani Kealoha-Scullion, another Hawaiian scholar, believes that the protests were ignored not simply for reasons of cultural stresses and strains, but because the king and *ali'i* had come to have distinctly different material interests from the *maka'ainana* within the new political-economy. As their circumstances changed, they were less able, or less willing, to meet their traditional responsibilities.[23]

Transforming the Land

Events of the late 1840s shaped much of what would happen over the next 150 years. In rapid succession, land and labor systems were established to move Hawai'i away from a self-contained economy. These developments increasingly marginalized Hawaiians, while giving foreigners more power to shape the institutions of governance according to their own principles and interests.

Monarch and *ali'i* participation in conversion from a common-use system to a private property system was crucial to the pace and extent of these changes. Understanding why such participation occurred is important and remains controversial.

From a cultural perspective, the Calvinist missionaries encouraged Hawaiian rulers to see modifications in the land system as a way of reducing abuses of *maka'ainana* that occurred in the old society. Changing the land system "would be *pono* behavior, benefiting the *maka'ainana* and meeting their traditional duty to protect the society as whole."[24]

From another perspective, the agreement to change the land system reflected shifting interests within Hawaiian society. A new type of middle chief had appeared, positioned between the king and island chiefs (*M'oi*) and the *maka'ainana*. These chiefs asserted their permanent control of lands, once given to their temporary stewardship in exchange for loyalty, and some favored land inheritance over reversion to the crown.[25]

By the fourth decade of the nineteenth century, the king and *ali' i* had distinct interests in the economic benefits of property. Sandalwood exports to China had been a source of income until Island forests were depleted in the early 1820s. The crown needed a stable tax base to fund its growing responsibilities, while members of the *ali' i* and individual chiefs were looking for income to satisfy their new tastes or pay off their debts. Private property, which could be taxed, sold, or rented, was a means to increase their wealth.[26] Each party came to the position, during the complex negotiations that led to new rules governing land, that they could get what they wanted (e.g., capital, income, and sufficient security) without giving up control to foreigners, and while retaining their legitimacy.

The willingness to change the status of land also affected the influence of external forces. The same foreign relationships that lead to economic opportunity also brought threats. Foreign powers had created cause for concern for different reasons and at different times. In the years after Cook's arrival, foreign governments frequently intervened in response to the protests of mistreatment by their citizens residing in the islands. The kingdom was at a disadvantage in trying to limit access to property by foreigners because of uncertainty about its independence, especially from France, Britain and the United States.[27] From this perspective, dividing the land reflected the range within which the Hawaiian government felt it must act without inviting further reprisals.

The Mahele (meaning, to divide or share) was the instrument created to allot all lands between king, chiefs (landlords), and *maka'ainana* (tenants). The crown was reserved 984,000 acres (24 percent), the government obtained 1,523,000 acres (37 percent), and 245 chiefs were granted 1,619,000 acres (39 percent). An agreement, called the Kuleana Act, was added later to set aside 28,600 acres (0.8 percent) for commoner Hawaiians.[28]

After the Mahele, only small parcels of this land were secured by *maka'ainana*, who struggled to pay the necessary fees and complete required surveys by an 1855 deadline. Kame'ekeihiwa estimates that 9 percent of the population actually were awarded something, that many who did lacked the financial resources to purchase it, and that the average parcel was too small to farm.[29]

Jocelyn Linnekin argues that cultural factors were important in the outcome. She concludes that "The Mahele was never intended to effect a proletarian revolution or equalize the distribution of resources in Hawaiian society. The king and the chiefs had always controlled the most and best of everything—rightfully so in the indigenous cultural scheme—and the Mahele once again institutionalized their priority."[30]

The king and his Caucasian advisers, many of whom argued the cause of preservation of the kingdom against takeover by foreigners, were aware that those Native Hawaiians who did obtain fee simple land might sell it too cheaply, not having been educated or acculturated to private property.[31] Suggestions were made as to how to prevent this from happening, including having the king attach a cautionary note to each conveyance document. Nothing was done because, "There seems to have been a reluctance to impose any restriction upon the use which the individual proprietor might wish to make of his own property."[32]

This reluctance to adopt protections for Native Hawaiians from foreigners who were, often aggressively, seeking to control property and make their new export agriculture ventures less risky, left the indigenous people vulnerable to displacement from lands that their families had occupied for generations. A liberal principle had, as historian Ralph Kuykendall states it, left open the door "for the evil that would follow."[33]

The final stage in the land's transformation and the displacement of Native Hawaiians was the Act of July 1850. The legislature had passed a law in 1841 giving the governors of each island authority to lease land for periods up to fifty years. The new act permitted foreigners to acquire and sell land on the same terms as Natives. The law passed, despite strenuous objections from among Native Hawaiians and the king's advisers, including influential Caucasian adviser Gerrit P. Judd.

"Land" became "property" by passage of these acts. The constitution of June 1852—more liberal and less theocratic—noted the "inalienable . . . right of acquiring and possessing property."[34] Predictably, in its new status land fell rapidly under the ownership or de facto control of Caucasian businessmen. By 1862, an estimated three-fourths of all land was under the control of *haoles*.[35] By 1936, 15 years after passage of the Hawaiian Homestead Act of 1921 to restore Hawaiians to the land as small farmers, only 6 percent of the original 28,000 acres set aside for commoners through the Kuleana Act belonged to Native Hawaiians.[36] Little land ended up directly in the hands of Native Hawaiians, and that which was held for them often came to be used by others.

This historical transformation signifies land's importance in a finite island setting. Land and its control remain a central feature of political life in the state, and are among the most contentious of legal and policy questions. In contemporary Hawai'i, many residents still live on land that they only lease, and which they could eventually lose (see chapter 11).

Labor

On June 21, 1850, one month before the law permitting foreigners to own land, and six months after the Kuleana Act, came passage of "An Act for the Government of Masters and Servants." The act became the basis for a contract-labor system that would last until annexation. It allowed employers in the islands to bind foreign labor in contracts of up to five years. Heavy sanctions, including double service and imprisonment, were stipulated for a laborer breaking or inadequately serving the terms of the contract. Contractors could be, but rarely were, fined for violations, although unbridled abuse was episodically an issue, especially with the Japanese later in the century.

As early as the 1840s, the experimental plantations attempted to employ Native Hawaiian labor. This had worked with some success in the whaling business, the mainstay of the economy from the early 1820s through the beginning of its decline in the late 1850s. The local population, however, showed little interest in plantation labor.

Immigration policy in the islands had evolved in response to conflicting impulses over several decades. One was to supply emerging export agriculture, primarily sugar, but at first rice as well, with cheap, compliant labor. The other push was the crown's desire to replenish the islands' declining population. Immigrants were viewed by Hawaiians as tools for use in the new commerce or settlers expected to become integrated into Island society. The monarchy favored immigration because it saw its independence linked to a robust and stable economy. It tried to control the process by creating a board that established criteria for labor immigration, dealt with foreign powers on immigration matters, and set quotas.

The interests of planters and the Hawaiian monarchy overlapped on economic development, but diverged with regard to other matters. The type of laborer to import was an important point of dispute. The crown preferred people who were culturally similar ("racially cognate") and it wanted more females to help stabilize and re-build the population. The planters were more interested in securing an industrious and compliant workforce. In addition, as early as 1883, they felt that deliberately mixing "races" would increase their control over labor.

Attempts were made to use South Pacific Islander workers in the 1860s and again in the late 1870s. Clearly the most cognate, their lower motivation for work in highly disciplined settings, as well as their British orientation, displeased plantation owners, and only about 2,500 were brought in.[37] Europeans, another option given the crown's fondness for European culture, proved too costly to import and to compensate, although some, most notably the Portuguese, were brought in as foremen. Importation of Chinese labor began in 1852, and public concern was almost immediately expressed about the large number of single males. By the 1880s, previously diffuse concerns had shifted to unhappiness over the competition Chinese presented small businesses as they swiftly relocated from plantation to town upon the completion of their contracts. Many small businessmen looked for ways to end Chinese immigration or, at a minimum, prevent their movement off the plantations. Their proposals were countered by the planters' dependence on replacement and expansion labor, and by others arguing that liberal principles of fair treatment should apply to the Chinese.[38] In November 1890 the legislature passed "An Act Relating To Restricting Chinese Immigration," which allowed immigration of Chinese laborers only if they remained on the plantations.[39]

The first attempts to use Japanese labor occurred in 1868, just after shortages created by the American Civil War put sugar on its long trajectory as the dominant export business. They were brought in without the Japanese government's permission, and when 40 returned home and complained about the working conditions, their importation ended for another eighteen years.[40]

In January 1886, after years of attempts by the Hawaiian government, Japan and Hawai'i signed a labor convention. The policy, whose singular focus on the conscription of Japanese led to between 125,000 and 180,000 laborers coming to the islands between 1886 and 1924, was driven by several factors.[41] Principal among them was the planters' increasing desperation to find sufficient labor to expand production while creating a labor pool sufficiently large to prevent the rise of wages; Japan's depressed agricultural economy; the Japanese government's unwillingness to have Japanese and Chinese mixed together;[42] local concern over the large numbers of Chinese who were coming to the islands; and failure to attract or retain the kind of labor the planters and the government might have agreed to be most desirable. Given these complexities, agreement on the importation of Japanese labor was facilitated by redefining them culturally. In talks preceding the Japan-Hawai'i labor convention, the kingdom's representative argued the similarity of the two peoples, while playing to Japanese-Chinese historic antagonisms.

Only a few planters, however, showed sensitivity to the cultures of immigrant laborers. Such sensitivity might have brought recognition that Japanese, to a much greater extent than Chinese, possessed orientations to authority and loyalty that, if respected and nurtured, might have given Japanese plantation laborers more of what they wanted. Instead, in the nearer term, many would be dissatisfied with and rebel against the conditions they found, despite some attempts by their home government to assure good treatment and provide for medical and educational services.

Over time the Caucasian elite increasingly viewed Japanese laborers as a menace: a threat to Western ways of doing things and, ultimately, to their control of the islands. The last concern would prove prescient. It also contained some irony. Less than a hundred years later, the descendants of these same Japanese, now dominant in Hawai'i government, would be accused of the very elite behavior said to characterize those who feared their takeover in the late nineteenth century.

Economic Ties

Nineteenth-century economic policy was firmly based on promoting a viable, stable economy in order to retain its independence. This, however, placed the kingdom in a fundamental dilemma. Economic development meant the community of foreign business interests grew larger and more powerful, exerting greater influence over policy and institutional development, and eventually enabling foreign interests to act on their shared belief that an autonomous sovereign was unacceptable.

The demand for Hawai'i sugar had subsided by the end of the American Civil War in 1865, and its producers worried about a continued, stable return on their capital. By the early 1870s, an extended recession set in, and planters collectively saw only two options for increasing their chances of success: find a duty-free market, or join the American political system. Differences of opinion about these strategies would divide planters and other foreigners until annexation.

Several factors in the early 1870s converged to push Hawai'i toward a treaty of reciprocity. Agricultural interests were becoming more desperate; changing relations between France, Britain, and the United States made it harder for the two European powers to prevent the assertion of American hegemony over the islands; Washington was becoming more interested in having a Pacific outpost; and, in the context of American politics, a territorial status for Hawai'i was not a likely choice.

The decision to enter into a reciprocity agreement with the United States was a difficult one for the Hawaiian government. King Lunalilo, the first popularly elected Hawaiian monarch, refused to sign a completed agreement in 1872. Lunalilo's last-minute rejection demonstrated the monarchy's continued ability to resist the growing power of the planters. His successor, King David Kalakaua, worked hard for the agreement of reciprocity that finally took effect in August 1876. He, like many monarchs preceding him, believed that economic strength and stability were crucial for national independence.

It is ironic then that the economic boom that followed reciprocity also brought greater internal threats to the government's sovereignty. By the 1880s, the *haole* business class, consisting by then of the men who ran the rural plantations and professionals and businessmen who lived primarily in Honolulu, was much stronger. Its members worked harder to decrease the king's power while increasing their own. They forced a showdown with King Kalakaua in June 1887 over legislation and appropriations they disliked, resulting in revision of the existing constitution. Under terms of the "Bayonet Constitution," the "goal of universal suffrage, brought to the islands by the Americans, had been abandoned."[43]

Voting for certain legislative offices became subject to income and property qualifications. In a society in which Caucasians were a small minority (in 1890 non-plantation labor Caucasians comprised about 7,000 of a population of 90,000), these restrictions disenfranchised much of the king's support among Native Hawaiians.[44] The elites also were able to write rules allowing the cabinet and upper house—the House of Nobles—to constitute a governing majority, in effect enabling property to out-vote popular representation.

King Kalakaua signed a renewal of the Reciprocity Agreement in November 1887. The revision included a clause he had previously refused to consider, ceding Pearl Harbor to the exclusive use of the United States. The changing boundaries of American national interests, which hereafter would intermingle with local interests in a complex, conflicted, but expanding web, made this remarkable natural harbor, with its narrow, highly defensible entrance, an American outpost.

Political Control

The Bayonet Constitution could not dissipate the tension between King Kalakaua and his Caucasian adversaries. His critics formed a political party, named the Reform Party. Through it they attempted to organize and articulate their interests in the legislature. Native Hawaiians, supported by some *haoles*, created the National Reform Party focused on revision of the 1887 constitution.

When King Kalakaua died in January 1891, his sister, Lili'uokalani, ascended to the throne determined to reverse the erosion of authority experienced by the monarchy. She began by appointing Hawaiians and part-Hawaiians to posts previously held by foreigners. She then proposed that the government raise revenue through a lottery and by licensing the opium "clubs" already existing among the Chinese. She went further in January 1893 and prepared to promulgate a new constitution that would restore the crown's control over the House of Nobles while giving suffrage to official subjects, thus limiting the influence of non-subject foreigners.

The queen's actions were intolerable to many members of the *haole* elite. Earlier some had formed a Committee of Safety, which later became the vehicle for overthrowing the monarchy. Membership consisted of Caucasians, mostly Americans, but with some nationals from other countries.[45] Despite their small numbers, those involved in the coup were able to end Lil'uokalani's rule and establish a republic in a bloodless overthrow: one royalist policemen was wounded in the leg.

The success of the revolutionaries resulted from the queen's decision to avoid bloodshed, and perhaps from Hawaiians' predisposition to avoid violence in favor of compromise and negotiation. It also was helped by a display of American military hardware on behalf of the insurgents, an exhibition ironically reminiscent of Western technology's role in Kamehameha I's ability to consolidate his rule a century earlier.

President Grover Cleveland sent a representative to assess the situation and, based upon this detailed report, concluded that the overthrow had been unwarranted and illegal. The queen waited for months for a signal to resume her office and reclaim her country, while members of the new provisional government hoped their message would find sympathetic ears. William McKinley's ascent to the presidency changed things dramatically. Thereafter the ambition to include Hawai'i within the country's expanding sphere of influence took over.

Hawai'i's new rulers quickly consolidated their positions. Citizens of the republic were required to pledge their loyalty and disavow a return to the monarchy. Voting carried property and income qualifications. The previous decades' inchoate movement toward institutional decentralization was reversed in favor of "an uncommonly strong central government with very large powers in the hands of a few."[46] At the same time, because the new government was composed mostly of the descendants of missionaries, it was affected by their social values. These served to temper the harsher provisions of the Masters and Servants Act, promote policies that would make small amounts of land available to individuals, and placed an increased emphasis on public education.

Toward Annexation

Talk of annexation had begun among the business community in Hawai'i earlier in the nineteenth century. Such conversations were associated with hopes of entering a duty-free market to promote Hawai'i's growing commercial ties with the U.S. economy, especially with the west coast. Hawaiian monarchs, attempting to navigate the increasingly dangerous shoals of both domestic and international politics, had struggled with the annexation question for decades.

External and internal circumstances affecting the possibilities of annexation had changed by the mid-1890s. The United States had become the dominant power in the Pacific while the influence of Britain and France declined. American foreign policy had come to be driven partly by difficulties in the domestic economy, and partly by the transition from an agrarian to an industrial society. Both contributed to a search for foreign markets. This search in turn congealed a new foreign policy constituency interested in the use of national power to protect investments and markets.[47] Hawai'i inevitably was of interest to this constituency and affected by this de facto policy.

The rising *haole* elite, though only a fraction of the population, had become economically—and politically—more powerful, and more socially vested. Yet the sugar growers experienced in the 1890s a severe economic crisis, precipitated by the McKinley Act of April 1891. This act dissolved the protections of reciprocity by abolishing all duties on imported sugar and giving American producers a $0.02 per pound advantage. The act forced many in the sugar industry to rethink their historic commitment to the principle of independence, and made annexation and its accompanying non-foreign status for Hawai'i much more attractive.[48]

Native Hawaiians were overwhelmingly against annexation, no less than they were against overthrow of the queen.[49] They had little official say on this question so fundamental to their future, though, because the rules established by the Caucasian oligarchy for governance of the republic excluded their direct participation. Their leaders mounted a petition movement to show Congress and the President their united opposition to an American takeover.

The U.S. Congress twice between 1894 and 1898 did fail to produce the two-thirds majority needed to approve a treaty of annexation. The Spanish-American war, however, fostered both American expansion into the Pacific region and a concrete need for an outpost in that region it could control. In July 1898, with no referendum in the islands and through a simple majority in the American Congress, Hawai'i became a territory of the United States.

ANNEXATION TO WORLD WAR TWO

American territories have moved to statehood in response to differing circumstances and at differing paces. For California, it happened almost immediately after Western settlement. Nevada took four years. In the cases of New Mexico and Arizona, 63 years passed between territory and statehood, several years longer than the islands. Puerto Rico, or course, has not yet made the transition.

Hawai'i's more than one-half century territorial period was characterized by a distinct set of issues. These issues—the maintenance of centralized authority, struggle for control of land, and the changing politics of cultural differences—emerge from its earlier history and color the dynamics of the state today.

Centralized Authority

From the perspective of the oligarchy that had successfully overthrown the kingdom, the challenge after annexation was not how to dominate the economy, but how to control social and economy policy through government. The sugar business came to be controlled by agencies, called factors, that created wealth by doing things that often could not be done by the plantations themselves. These services included ground and sea transportation of crops, loans, equipment and supplies, insurance, and utilities. Because the plantations required these things all the time, the agencies made money constantly, largely unaffected by the cyclical profitability of the plantations.

The vagaries of the sugar market often left plantations cash-poor. Consequently, the factors gradually were able to acquire or assert de facto control over the plantations and the industry. By 1910, what came to be called the Big Five factors—Alexander and Baldwin, Castle and Cook, Hackfield and Co. (later American Factors after its German-owned assets were seized in World War I), Theo. Davies and Co., and C. Brewer and Co.—controlled 75 percent of the sugar crop. Twenty-three years later, in 1933, they controlled 96 percent. By then, they also had taken over pineapple production, an industry that since its origins in the nineteenth century had become the second largest in the territory.[50]

Unlike in many places in the American West during this time,[51] there was no struggle for control among the rich in Hawai'i, primarily because of their common interest in resisting internal and external threats to their positions. Cooperation on behalf of economic and cultural interests was common in the islands and led to extensive ties among members of the economic elite.[52] One observer suggested that "the nepotism in Hawai'i's capitalist circles was unparalleled in any other area in the United States."[53]

This social integration reflected business connections that touched all parts of the economy, including the key elements of shipping and banking. Noel Kent quotes a public official who in 1937 observed that: "Everything that comes into the territory comes through a large corporation. The independent businessman who attempts to enter business here immediately finds that even nationally advertised lines from the mainland are tied up by the Big Five."[54]

Clearly, the problem for the local elite was not economic control but dominating the levers of government and its policies. Annexation presented a difficult question to the business oligarchy and the missionary groups advocating Americanization of the islands: how to maintain control at home within the umbrella of the United States Constitution. In particular, American laws threatened to extend suffrage to Native Hawaiians and the descendants of immigrant labor.

Several years elapsed between the decision to admit the islands in 1898 and the implementation of the Organic Act which established rules of governance for the new territory. During this period, Washington lobbyists for the *haole* oligarchy argued forcefully that the vote should be restricted to those who could demonstrate their ability to participate in governance. They depicted Asians as having mixed loyalties, and imbued with cultural values antithetical to self-government. Native Hawaiians were portrayed as children unable to exercise civic responsibilities, or even to know their own best interests. Sanford Dole, the first territorial governor and a man less hostile than some to Native Hawaiian concerns, wondered, "What if all the natives and the Portuguese can vote without being perfectly responsible simply because they are grown up?"[55]

Despite their apprehensions about the perils contained in electoral participation, political principles about broader representation prevailed, at least for males. As the historian Gavan Daws observes, "There were things about the American political tradition too important to discard because of peculiarities in Hawai'i's local condition."[56] Enfranchisement of non-Caucasians represented another important step in playing out the contradictions begun when members of the emerging plantation elite elected to import tens of thousands of laborers to achieve their business goals. The force of these principles would give control over the instruments of government to the sons and daughters of immigrant laborers a half-century later.

In the shorter run, however, the local elite was able to do something about its most fundamental problem, namely, that at the time of annexation Native Hawaiians constituted more than two-thirds of the electorate. In the 1901 legislature, the first as a territory, they controlled 73 percent of the seats, much more than at the end of the monarchy when they already were able to frustrate the wishes of the *haoles*.[57]

Native Hawaiians, together with some dissident *haoles*, formed the Home Rule party to articulate their interests and cultural values. To reduce its power, the *haole* elite relied on a relationship with a Hawaiian of royal lineage popular among Native Hawaiians.

Jonah Kalaniana'ole Kuhio had been made an heir to the throne by the unwed Queen, Lili'uokalani. When those against whom he previously had fought courted him to run as a Republican delegate for Congress in 1901, Kuhio agreed out of concern that something must be done to curb rising Asian influence, and from a desire to distribute land and money to his people. His words and actions once again reflected a belief held by some Hawaiian leaders before him. As social historian Lawrence Fuchs put it, "He would join [the *haoles*], but not to serve them. Rather he would use them for the benefit of the Hawaiian people. He would force them to give Hawaiians jobs and land."[58]

Kuhio's success had the effect of reducing the threat Native Hawaiians posed to *haole* interests. The personal allegiance of Native Hawaiians to Kuhio turned their politics into passive withdrawal or into the election of Republican majorities to the legislature. The patronage that Kuhio was able to offer also helped. Some of it was private, facilitated by his connections with the business elite. Kuhio was re-elected ten times between 1902 and 1922. The Republican dominance of electoral politics, allowing the *haole* elite efficient control of the government, prevailed until the middle of the century.

The elite in the early twentieth century found its needs best served by a structure that gave authority to the territorial government while minimizing the role of the counties the Organic Act had forced upon them (see chapter 10). Its members had no interest in establishing other, potentially uncontrollable, jurisdictions, such as cities and towns.

By World War II, the apparatus of Hawaiian government ironically bore a remarkable resemblance to that of the former Kingdom. It seems accurate to describe the situation as it had been characterized in 1903 by Edward Dole, the attorney general of Hawai'i. "There is a government in this territory which is centralized to an extent unknown in the United States, and probably almost as much centralized as it was in France under Louis XIV."[59] The difference, of course, was that it now reflected new interests.

Land

The transition to a private property system gave plantation owners access to huge amounts of land. In 1890, three-fourths of all land owners were Hawaiian, but three of every four acres belonging to private owners were used by *haoles* or their corporations. By 1909, fully one-half of all privately owned land was controlled by *haole* corporations.

By the turn of the century, the indigenous population's declining physical and cultural position had become obvious to everyone. As Daws put it, "The Hawaiian had all but ceased to be a person; he was defined as a problem."[60] This re-labeling, from subdued to endangered, spawned a movement to find ways to prevent the extinction of Native Hawaiians. Efforts centered on re-patriating Hawaiians to the land, so central to their cultural worldview, as the way to save them.

Beginning a few years after annexation, Delegate Kuhio, seeing repatriation to the land as a way to save his people, sought support in Washington for federal direction. At the same time, the local elite felt threatened by the prospect of major demands being made on land currently in sugar, especially because their leases on more than 200,000 acres of government land would expire over the next years.[61] The *haole* elite, again, had created a situation of dependence on outside forces, in this case federal policy.

The interests of the sugar industry and Native Hawaiians appeared to coincide on one key issue: neither wished to extend homestead opportunities to outsiders. This shared view provided the impetus for the Hawaiian Rehabilitation Act of 1920. The symbolically important part of the act allowed individuals of more than one-half Hawaiian blood to apply for low-cost, ninety-nine year leases on small pieces of land. These parcels were intended to restore their agrarian pursuits with their allocation overseen by a Hawaiian Homes Commission. The work of the Commission on behalf of Hawaiian homesteading would be paid for from lease rents of other land. Yet, the act

initially made less than 200,000 acres available to 20,000 potentially qualified Hawaiians.[62]

The act's less prominent provisions eliminated that part of the Organic
Act restricting corporations from owning more than 1,000 acres. (This restraint previously had been bypassed by forming multiple corporations.) The
Rehabilitation Act thus lessened corporate vulnerability to internal or external changes in the political climate. The act also excluded from homesteading acreage already used for cultivating sugar, along with forest reserves and
land already occupied by homesteaders.

A main problem with the act and the implementation decisions that followed is that it offered for homesteading land that no one else had been able
to make productive. Existing leases of valuable tracts were protected while
agricultural interests with investment capital were permitted to acquire
others on a fee basis. In addition a large percentage of Hawaiian Homes
Commission Lands came to be leased to sugar and pineapple interests.[63]
Consequently, only a few of the homestead applications were acted on because of the land's unsuitability or the absence of a supporting infrastructure
in water or electricity.

By 1930, Caucasians controlled only 633 of 5,669 "farm units," yet
leased or owned 2,579,733 acres, more than sixteen times that for Hawaiians, forty-five times that for Americans of Japanese Ancestry, and 140 times
that for Chinese.[64] Over the next thirty or so years the plantations would benefit enough from low lease costs, low taxes, and long-term security to maintain a high return on capital, in some cases consistently more than 10 percent.[65] By contrast, in the 1990s, thousands of qualified Hawaiians still were
wait-listed for homestead lands.

Ethnic Diversity

The provisions of the Organic Act ended the system of contract labor in effect since the passage of the Master and Servants Act of 1850. Contract labor
could no longer be imported; the act also canceled all existing contracts. The
sugar industry confronted the problem of keeping workers in the islands.
Laborers could return to Japan, which many had done over the years, or
move further east in search of work on the American mainland. By 1907,
40,000 had in fact left Hawai'i, recruited by agents whose employers offered
wages two times the local rate to meet the labor shortage that existed in
places like California.[66] By the early 1930s, industry officials had begun im-

porting large numbers of Filipino laborers, the group whose members would constitute the third and final wave of immigrant labor.

Perhaps the most serious problem facing the planters was that, even if they did find ways to keep workers on the plantations, the Japanese and, later, Filipinos could use their new legal status to make demands for higher wages and better working conditions. They responded in a number of ways: recruiting uneducated, illiterate and, they presumed, more docile workers; asserting authority over workers in ways that reduced disobedience or shows of independence; using the police to enforce vagrancy laws on those who left a plantation, but had not yet established themselves in other work; charging mainland recruiters fees as a disincentive; and passing laws that officially restricted employment in public jobs while relying on informal agreements to reduce access to work in the private sector.[67]

These methods were augmented by a strategy of deliberately separating the labor force by race. This strategy is not unique to Hawai'i. It was, for example, employed during the same period in mining communities in the American West to prevent the development of unions.[68] In the islands, it had been done in the years preceding annexation. In 1883, the Planters' Labor and Supply Company, a body which represented planters in trying to influence government immigration policy, articulated a strategy that would be followed with great success until the 1930s: "We need [Portuguese] especially as an offset to the Chinese; not that the Chinese are undesirable—far from it—but we lay great stress on the necessity of having our labor mixed. By employing different nationalities, there is less danger of collusion among laborers, and the employer, on the whole, secures better discipline."[69] Recruitment promoted a mix of cultural groups that might be aligned against one another—sometimes within and sometimes between national groups.

Perhaps the clearest manifestation of this de facto policy is seen in wage practices that consistently differentiated between racial groups for the same kind of work. Wages overall in Hawai'i were higher than for plantation work in other parts of the world, but in 1902, Caucasians doing skilled work got $4.22 per day, while Hawaiians received $1.80, Portuguese $1.69, Chinese $1.22, and Japanese $1.06.[70] Even among those who supervised field laborers—called *luna*—there were large differences. In 1910, *haole* (mainly Portuguese) *luna* received a monthly salary of between $87.54 and $96.03 while Japanese got between $31.52 and $31.95.[71]

Between 1852 and 1946 almost 500,000 men, women, and children were brought to Hawai'i as part of labor migrations.[72] The number of Japanese, which had been 61,000 in 1900, was 109,000 in 1920 and would reach

158,000 in 1940.[73] The Filipino population, virtually non-existent in 1900 and only 21,000 in 1920, would reach 52,000 by 1940.[74]

In 1930, persons of Asian ancestry accounted for 64 percent of the population, though only 26 percent of adult citizens.[75] Much more to the point, in 1920, 3 of every 100 voters were Japanese. This had become 8 of 100 by 1926, but by 1936 it was 1 of every 4.[76]

These methods, however, only postponed what had been set in motion by the importation of labor and closer integration with the United States. The changing composition of Island society and the political opportunities the new rules offered immigrants and their off-spring inevitably fed the forces that culminated in a dramatic shift in power holders. The first signs that the groups plantation owners and managers wished to control would not be prevented from asserting their own interests came soon after annexation, in the form of demonstrations of labor unrest and later organized strikes. The strikes, confined to single ethnic groups until the 1930s, were often bitter, with owners accusing organizers of being motivated by personal greed, foreign nationalism or, later, communism; and strikers contending that they were being denied their basic rights as well as fair treatment. Sometimes the demonstrations were violent, as in the strike of 1924 in Hanapepe on Kaua'i in which 16 Filipino strikers were killed and 60 more were given four-year prison sentences.

Despite these recurring protests, coming primarily from the plantations, labor was not successfully organized in the islands until collective action was legalized for dock workers under the National Labor Relations Act of 1935. Upheld by the courts in 1937, the act gave birth to formal labor unions, the most notable of which would be the International Longshoreman's and Warehouseman's Union (ILWU). The ILWU started its work along Hawai'i's docks, but immediately after the Second World War turned its attention to the plantations.

The union movement of the late 1930s promoted class consciousness and racial cooperation. This undermined the divide-and-dominate strategy employed by plantation owners. In April 1937, the last strike organized on the basis of an ethnic group took place on Maui. A strike in 1939 in Hilo on the Big Island was the first successful effort by organizers to mobilize by class rather than ethnicity. Called the "Hilo Massacre" because fifty workers were injured in a sit-down strike on the docks, it became a rallying cry directed at overturning the *haole* oligarchy. In 1941, the Castle and Cook Company, a member of the Big Five, became the first large employer to sign an agreement with a union. ILWU membership increased from 900 in 1944 to

30,000 in 1947.[77] The union had completely organized Hawai'i's docks and moved deeply into both sugar and pineapple plantations by 1946. In that same year, a failed attempt to bring in thousands of laborers from the Philippines to break a strike signaled the demise of the old strategy of plantation owners and caused Harry Bridges, the national head of the ILWU, to proclaim to Jack Hall, the key figure at its Hawai'i chapter, that "Hawaii is no longer a feudal economy."[78]

Assimilation

Accompanying these political and social changes were new policies and attitudes toward assimilating Asians into Hawai'i society. In the late nineteenth century, a growth in Asian immigration had been matched by an increase in resistance to their presence; Chinese and Japanese immigration was restricted. By the 1920s, however, the idea of integrating Asians into Hawai'i society began to gain support.

It should be recognized that integration promoted changes in identity among immigrants as well as local residents. Thousands of Japanese had returned earlier to Japan upon expiration of their contracts. After 1907, this became harder because of the rising cost of living in Japan and the Gentleman's Agreement. Going home now brought less economic pay-off as well as the likelihood of never returning to the islands. These factors gave impetus to the process of settling and acculturation and meant that, gradually, Asian immigrants and their descendents would identify with America, a shift in orientation symbolized by the thousands of picture-brides who came to reside in Hawai'i before Japanese immigration was further restricted in 1924.

Local residents' views of Asian immigrants became more complex. Some who initially had defined the Japanese as inferior in almost every way now came to see them as constituted of racial and cultural endowments—no humanitarian tradition, highly focused energies, group solidarity, secrecy—that made futile any resistance to their takeover.[79] Others felt the Japanese and other Asians were here to stay and that the real challenge was to help them and their off-spring to adopt American values and practices.

The primary vehicle for assimilation was public education. By 1920, one-half of all children in the public schools were Japanese.[80] There were poignant struggles within the Japanese community over respecting the traditions of the culture and the homeland rather than adopting the practices of the new society, and over the wisdom of being more accepting, respectful, and thankful versus being aggressive in seeking to redress grievances, but there was also consensus in demands for good education for the next generation.

THE WAR AND ITS AFTERMATH

World War II started for the United States on December 7, 1941, at Pearl Harbor, a location so important in joining Hawai'i to the United States seventy years earlier. A military governor replaced the territorial governor within twenty-four hours of the attack. At times, over the next four years, the number of troops stationed in Hawai'i greatly exceeded the civilian population.[81] Residents grappled with the loyalty of the territory's most numerous racial group for much of the war.

The power of the local elite, held together for half a century, was severed at this time, and when civilian authority was restored after the surrender of Japan, it would prove impossible to re-establish. Several factors contributed to this failure. One was sugar's declining importance. Between 1930 and 1959, the year of statehood, the number of plantation workers had dropped from about 50,000 to 15,000.[82] This change reflected the effects of mechanization as the industry attempted to reduce its costs and remain competitive against international sugar producers. It also showed the slipping position of sugar in the territory's economy relative to military spending and, soon, tourism.

Another factor was the continuing evolution of the imported labor force. A number of Chinese had, by the late 1940s, become successful in finance and real estate, breaking a Caucasian monopoly in these fields. The unions organized other racial groups that had come later and taken different paths to assimilation. Even though the membership of the ILWU—the most powerful of them—already was declining, a decline that would cause its leaders to organize the tourist industry, the union remained a potent force. In 1949, a strike of 2,000 longshoremen tied up the islands' economy for 178 days, demonstrating how much the elite's strategies of containment had come apart.

The war itself lead directly to a third reason that the *haole* business elite failed to re-assert itself. Although some first and second-generation residents of Japanese ancestry were interned on the mainland during the war, by its end, others had been permitted to fight for the American cause. Members of the 442nd Regimental Combat team, composed of draftees and National Guardsmen, and the 100th Battalion, composed of volunteers, fought exceptionally hard and courageously. They returned to the islands at war's end, less insular in outlook, more adamant about their status as citizens, and armed with the resources of the GI bill. As one veteran later wrote in eulogy to his World War II comrade: "We went to war all young and eager, and came back home older and wiser, and now we saw it was our turn to labor hard and long, to change the world for all who will come later. And so we went to war again, this time with books and laws and pens, to help the weak and poor belong, the same as all the rich and strong."[83]

Daniel Inouye is a good example of this group. A graduate of McKinley Public High School in central Honolulu, a school locally famous for the post-war Japanese-American leaders it produced, Inouye lost an arm in combat. He left a long hospital recovery only to find himself a decorated veteran standing in the door of a barbershop in Oakland, California, being denied a haircut because he was "a Jap." He used federal money to go to law school in Washington DC and returned to the islands to help form the new Democratic Party. Later, symbolizing the changes about to visit the islands, he would become the state's U.S. senator, like many of his contemporaries, having gone from loyal immigrant to dissident to powerful insider.[84]

Inouye's rise reflects where Hawai'i was going and where it had been. His career will come to stand for a new inclusiveness, and a place at the table for those who had none. It will also signify changing relations of power from one group to another.

He will come, at the same time, to represent a new center of power that, for many, will itself seem exclusive. In helping to bring Hawai'i into the next stage of its future, he will find it very hard to escape those forces that we have seen shape its past.

CHAPTER THREE

Cultural Relations and Political Culture

The preceding chapter illustrates that both cultural dynamics, in the form of differing worldviews and ethnic group conflicts, and political-economic dynamics, in the form of class relations and the linkage between wealth and power, have played important roles in shaping political life and public institutions. That is no less true today, and often it is difficult to know which of the two is more influential or, for that matter, whether political-economic events are shaping cultural patterns, or cultural patterns are shaping political-economic outcomes.

It is also true that Hawai'i's contemporary political life is oriented by a distinctive political culture that is, simultaneously, highly progressive and like a traditional, Old Boy dominated, southern American state. The rich ethnic fabric and dominant political "style" are inter-woven, each reflecting historical forces described in the previous chapter. What emerges from this interweaving affects virtually everything that happens in Hawai'i.

REVOLUTION AND STATEHOOD

By the late 1940s, the direction of the long- and short-term forces made change likely, and it occurred dramatically in the fall of 1954. The Democratic party, virtually invisible in the five decades before the war, gained control of the legislature and began to use the apparatus of government to alter the direction of social and economic policy. Referred to in subsequent years as the "Revolution of 1954," this election previewed the power of a party that re-created itself by appeal to groups marginalized under the preceding regime.

The "revolution" gathered support from disaffected Hawaiians and part-

Hawaiians, Chinese, Portuguese, and Filipinos, but it was overwhelmingly based in the numbers, loyalty, and solidarity of second and third generation Japanese Americans. The new Japanese-American leaders were "of modest means, progeny of the plantations, distrustful of the entrenched wealth of the few."[1] The torch bearers of a new social agenda, they vanquished the Old Guard of the Republican party as well as its "new" wing, whose members had, by the 1950s, recognized the necessity of advocating social policies with broader appeal.

Democratic control over statewide elected offices was not complete until 1962. In that year, increased voter turn-out helped elect John Burns the first Democratic governor and re-captured the state Senate, temporarily regained by Republicans in the 1960 election. The party of the *haole* business class rapidly declined and then disappeared as an effective political force, overwhelmed by the new alignment of electoral players. Between 1962 and 1996, Republican candidates did not come close to controlling either house of the legislature, and did not win the governorship. The sole Republican representative was Hiram Fong in the U.S. Senate, ironically one of the new Chinese entrepreneurs who helped to break the economic power hold of the Caucasian elite.

John Burns was the architect of this coalition of former outsiders. In his earlier career as a Honolulu police officer during World War II, he was assigned surveillance duties over Japanese-Americans, people authorities suspected might pose a security threat in any conflict with Japan. Burns' contacts with individuals in the Japanese-American community fostered a sympathetic familiarity that led him to champion social causes, such as the reform of the territory's labor and education policies, with which they, and others who felt excluded, could identify.

Electoral success also paved the way for one of the major targets of Burns and his allies: statehood. A statehood proposal first had been introduced in the federal Congress in 1921, and in 1947, 1950, and 1953, statehood bills had passed the House of Representatives, but not the Senate. The *haole* elite, with some notable exceptions, had opposed these attempts, arguing that Hawai'i society was not ready for it. Statehood was overwhelmingly favored by Japanese-Americans. Other groups, especially Hawaiians, were ambivalent or negative.[2] To achieve statehood, its proponents had to defuse Cold War-era charges that the islands were run by Communists who controlled the labor unions. Burns and his allies successfully won control of the party from the powerful International Longshoreman's and Warehouseman's Union (ILWU) in the late 1940s and early 1950s. He pushed for statehood after being elected territorial delegate to Washington in 1956, arguing forcefully that subversion simply was not an issue.

Advocates for statehood also had to contend with mainland fears of a "Japanese menace," anxieties reflecting prejudices in America that earlier produced exclusion laws for Chinese and Japanese and had been refueled by World War II. Rather than play down the issue, or argue defensively, Burns contended that Japanese-Americans, by cultural values as well as demonstrated loyalty during the war, had shown themselves to be the best kind of citizens.[3] In June 1959 voters in the former Kingdom opted overwhelmingly for statehood.

Change and Non-Change After Statehood

In the years following the Revolution of 1954, legislatures passed, governors signed, and courts upheld a remarkable stream of policies shaping social and economic life, measures that stood in sharp contrast to the narrower definitions of government's responsibility held by earlier regimes. (For more on the scope of these policies, see chapter 6.)

In terms of how wealth and power were concentrated in the islands, however, these changes could be seen as more appearance than reality. Where sugar earlier had dominated the economy, tourism came to account for one-third of the state's income. Where there had been a one-party political system dominated by Republicans, the Democrats now occupied all but a few seats in the legislature. Where there had been a monarchy and then a territorial plutocracy, there was now a centralized system of government that rejected most forms of local representation and only grudgingly gave powers to the four counties. Where Caucasians had had interconnections that enabled them to dominate, now it was Japanese-Americans who had an unspoken closeness, made deals with business interests that had been their enemies, and filled expanding state offices with people from whom they expected loyalty as a primary value.

By the late 1960s, one disenchanted member of the 1954 Revolution dejectedly noted, "Now they have a slice of the pie and they are getting fat . . . Hawaii has gone full circle, from the closed society of the plantation days to a new closed society run by the Burns clique."[4]

Social and political life seemed to be headed in two directions, both consistent with the islands' historical legacy, but hard to reconcile with each other. One path was toward greater institutional openness and a more pluralistic system with multiple centers of power and policies intended to solicit broader public involvement. The other path was the familiar combination of

Table 2: Hawai'i Population by Ethnic Background, 1996

Total Unmixed	673,178	55.6%
Caucasian	254,421	22.2%
Japanese	233,435	20.3%
Chinese	35,682	3.1%
Filipinos	114,717	10.0%
Black	16,314	1.4%
Hawaiian	9,118	0.8%
Total Mixed	466,381	40.6%
Part-Hawaiian	228,010	19.9%
Non-Hawaiian	238,371	20.8%

Source: The State of Hawaii Data Book, 1997, p. 43. Data are derived from the State Department of Health, Health Surveillance Program. The table does not list the least numerous ethnic groups.

privileged insider relationships that reward loyalty and punish dissent, use centralized authority to serve specific interests, and promote economic activity at the expense of community integration and self-determination.

The ethnic and intercultural mosaic of the islands, and the political culture that has been formed around that mosaic, have helped shape both of these directions, permitting them to exist as parallel futures, in tension with one another.

ETHNIC CULTURES SHAPING HAWAI'I'S POLITICAL CULTURE

Contemporary Hawai'i society displays a remarkably rich diversity of cultural groups whose origins are outside of Western traditions. Within this setting, no group, including Caucasians, holds anything approximating a numerical majority (see table 2). In addition, Hawai'i is much less affected by the two minority groups that have had a dramatic influence on communities and cultural relations elsewhere in the United States: Blacks and Hispanics. The islands' ethnic relations and politics contain very little of their history and concerns, or of the responses of other groups to them.

Hawaiians

There is no consensus on the total number of contemporary Hawaiians. Variations originate in the counts for those with a mixed ethnicity that includes some Hawaiian lineage, rather than those who are pure Hawaiian. The U.S.

Census Bureau doesn't recognize persons of mixed race and simply asks respondents to designate their ethnicity. The state Department of Health's Health Surveillance Survey, which appears to be the most accurate, bases its counts on information collected on family histories.[5]

There were about 140,000 Hawaiians living in Hawai'i in 1990, according to the 1990 census. About one-third of the national total of 211,000 lived outside of the state on the mainland. Approximately one-half of these resided in California.[6] Within the state, by the federal census of 1990, Hawaiians comprised 12.5 percent of the population and were the fourth largest ethnic group after Caucasians, Japanese, and Filipinos.

The Health Surveillance survey for the same year found 205,000 Hawaiians in the state, which at 18.8 percent of residents was the third largest group. There is considerable variation in their distribution across the islands. Slightly less than half of the 8,711 pure Hawaiians, but two-thirds of the 196,387 part-Hawaiians, lived on O'ahu, where they constituted 16.1 percent of the population. The Big Island had the second largest number, but, at 28 percent, the highest proportion of its population. On both Kaua'i and the Maui county islands of Maui, Lanai and Moloka'i Hawaiians constituted about 25 percent of population.

Contemporary Hawaiians do not fare well on major social indicators, a sad distinction shared with other Native peoples in America. In 1990, they showed the highest poverty rate of any ethnic group (14.1 percent), as well as having the fewest (13.6 percent) with family incomes of $60,000 or more.[7] They comprised more than one-third of all prisoners in the state in that same year.[8] Forty-six percent of all juvenile drug-related arrests in 1992 were Hawaiian.[9]

In health, Hawaiians and part-Hawaiians have had the highest or higher than average incidence of a range of chronic diseases, such as cancers, hypertension, and diabetes.[10] They have not performed as well as other ethnic groups in primary and secondary education, and fewer have gone on to college or obtained professional degrees.

These indicators do not always mean what they appear. Many Hawaiians have chosen an alternative lifestyle, and what is defined by an official statistic as poverty is, for some, a positive choice to live a rural, less commodity-based lifestyle. At the same time, these data signal some conflict between Hawaiian cultural values and mainstream society, a conflict contributing to their social and physical marginalization.

Although traditional Hawaiian culture was not monolithic, in general it valued affiliation and the maintenance of group harmony.[11] Relationships for most Hawaiians had primacy, especially, but not exclusively, their family and kinship relations. Generosity and gift giving were important ways of affirming the importance of relations. Possessions served relationships rather than relationships being a vehicle for obtaining more possessions, and prestige and personal gain at the expense of others, especially those in the community, were not usually regarded as valuable.

Attachment to the land played a crucial role in this pattern. The relationships that made up Hawaiian communities and Hawaiian society were dependent on a shared caring for and participation in the land's abundance. In addition, of course, the land was the basis of material livelihood and the patterns of exchange supported that livelihood.

The qualities underscored in Hawaiian culture were significant in shaping how outsiders encountered one another. Because Hawaiians remained in the midst of a society being formed from successive waves of ethnic migration, their culture provided continuity for the "secondary culture" that developed where these waves met.

At the same time, despite its significant influences as a base culture, and not withstanding efforts of the indigenous population to resist domination by foreign values, the integrity of Hawaiian culture was continually undermined by social and political marginalization and a market society's pervasive embrace of competitiveness.[12]

Many Native Hawaiians experienced a social, cultural and political awakening after statehood. Resistance to the loss of yet more land in the post-statehood development explosion also attracted the sympathy and support of non-Hawaiians, often newly arrived, who worried about changes in their adopted home. By the 1970s, organizations of activist Native Hawaiians had begun to proliferate throughout the state.[13] Dramatic, highly publicized confrontations occurred over the following years between groups of Native Hawaiians and their supporters, and development interests.

The awakening included a resurgence of Hawaiian language; greater interest in a Native perspective on the history of Hawaiian people; the flowering of traditional cultural practices, such as music, hula, and building and sailing outrigger canoes; and the appearance of educated, articulate spokespersons for Hawaiian causes. An increasing number of individuals of Hawaiian ancestry began to refer to themselves by the traditional term *Kanaka Maoli*.

By the 1990s these discrete threads had woven into a movement to create

a stronger Hawaiian identity and a vibrant Hawaiian culture. The movement's appeal and power rested in several places, but, understandably, the
most important was in relation to land issues.

Chinese

About 46,000 Chinese were imported for field labor between the early 1850s
and annexation. To a greater extent than either the Japanese and Filipinos,
who in succession would be the planters' choice as sources of labor, the most
common response of the Chinese to plantation life was not protest, but to
leave it as soon as possible.[14]

Most Chinese immigrants were unskilled farmers from Kwangtung prov-
ince in southern China. It is not surprising, then, that upon leaving the plantations, many first tried other forms of farming, especially growing rice. Although successful for a time, competition from California, and sugar and
pineapple's insatiable appetite for land, soon made rice cultivation unten-
able. The Chinese then turned to the city to start laundries, restaurants, and
other small businesses. About one-fourth of the population of the city of
Honolulu was Chinese by the time the republic was annexed to the United
States in 1898. Forty years later, on the eve of World War II, 80 percent of the
population of Chinese ancestry lived there.[15]

The city afforded Chinese opportunities to form networks of support
groups and communities. The earliest phases of their immigration had been
beset by internal divisions, reflecting the absence of a national identity—
China was not then a nation, but an arena of rival warlords—and the history
of clan differences. These divisions did not last, in the way they would later
for Filipino immigrants in Hawai'i.[16] Their future was in the islands. As their
Hawaiian and *haole* antagonists in Hawai'i turned attention to the Japanese
influx, Chinese support groups focused on achieving success in education
and business, becoming less defensive and exclusive.

By the 1930s, the Chinese, more than any other immigrant group, had integrated themselves successfully and acquired characteristics associated
with being American.[17] They had adopted English, become Christians,
learned American politics, and become successful in business. The Chinese
passed Caucasians in median male income by $108 per capita in 1950. This
lead increased to $1,447 by statehood in 1959.[18] Chinese businessmen were
among the first to take advantage of the lessening of the economic grip of the
Caucasian elite after the Second World War. They invested aggressively in

land, finance, and the tourist-driven airline industry, and then used their wealth and influence to support the 1954 Revolution.

These successes reflected successful adaptation of cultural heritage to new circumstances. Among Chinese-Americans in Hawai'i, education was highly respected, and their cultural tradition valued traits necessary to success in business: thrift, diligence, family solidarity, and the desire to improve one's social status. Over time, they created a financial infrastructure of banks and investment firms independent of the *haole* elite. Education, combined with opportunities created by money, enabled many to enter professions and white-collar work.

Perhaps equally important, by the first decades of the twentieth century the Chinese social presence was viewed differently than the Japanese, whose strong group ties and seemingly incomprehensible cultural rules alarmed Caucasians and Native Hawaiians. Chinese-American commercial success met little resistance from the ruling elite because "they accepted the social order as it was without trying to change it."[19]

Filipinos

Some Filipinos participated in the 1954 Revolution, although most brought neither leadership nor resources to it. This reflects the fact that they immigrated later and experienced a slower rate of movement away from low-status occupations than either the Chinese or the Japanese. In 1960, almost 60 years after they began arriving in the islands in large numbers, and 30 years after their in-migration peaked, the proportion of Filipino men classified as laborers was more than three times that of all other males.[20]

Because of the Philippines territorial status, only those serving in the United States military were eligible for citizenship through naturalization, a factor slowing their social and political integration. The passage of the Philippines Independence Act altered their status from nationals to aliens, and, in 1946, Congress passed an act allowing naturalization for those who wanted it.

Filipino immigrants to Hawai'i were predominantly Tagalogs, Visayans and Ilocanos, the latter being by the far the largest in number as well as the poorest and least educated. These groups originate in different parts of the Philippines, and are culturally and linguistically distinct. Their differences, which have remained a source of conflict and division within the Filipino community in Hawai'i, were utilized by planters to combat the organization of labor slowdowns and strikes by Filipino labor leaders.[21]

Filipino plantation workers were overwhelmingly young males, unmarried or without their families. Most planned to return to their *barrios* with the status and wealth they'd accumulated. By 1935, more than 58,000 had gone back, but those remaining stayed single for a much longer time than either their Japanese or Chinese counterparts.[22] The male to female ratio had been reduced to 131 to 100 by 1970, but in 1930 it was 975 to 100.[23]

These circumstances and characteristics influenced the adaptive strategies Filipinos used to integrate into their adopted society, and the opportunities they were able to create. An absence of older males cost the community leadership, and the young had no guidance in a culture that traditionally deferred to elders. Large numbers of lonely, unattached males in small plantation towns created social problems; their clustered visibility contributed to reputations as unsavory characters or sexual menaces.[24]

Forced bachelorhood also meant that families were not started and no second generation begun in a culture that relies heavily on the family as the basis of pooled resources. Normally, in Filipino culture, an individual's status is tied to the family's standing. Individuals are expected to accept decisions, commonly rendered in the form of male authority, within a family. In social and economic life, the Filipino family's obligations and opportunities for assistance extend matter-of-factly to what most Caucasians would think of as distant relatives.[25]

Finally, the success of Filipinos in Hawai'i society was affected because education played a lesser role in their adaptation strategy than it had for the Chinese and Japanese. Fewer opportunities, in combination with the first generation's low levels of education, resulted in the highest illiteracy rate of any group in the islands.[26]

Portuguese

The first organized group of Portuguese laborers arrived in 1878. By the 1890s, their number had risen to approximately 11,500. They were favored by the owners and managers of plantations because they were European and Christian, arrived committed to remaining in the islands, were in general less socially and economically ambitious than the Japanese or Chinese, and some spoke English.[27]

The elite did not give Portuguese the status of, Caucasians from Scotland, England, Germany, or the United States, despite being seen as Caucasian Europeans. They came, therefore, to occupy a unique position in the social and economic order. Their poor backgrounds, lack of education, and willingness to accept assignments without protest, made them desirable to plantation owners. Owners and managers rewarded them with less menial work because they were "white"; the Portuguese dominated the *luna* role, equivalent to a first-line supervisor, overseeing the work of an Asian workforce. In that role, they were paid more than members of lower status ethnic groups, even when the latter held identical positions.

The gap between the Portuguese and non-Caucasian *luna* was less than the differences in rewards and status that separated the Portuguese from the *haole* elite. This incongruity between privilege and exclusion meant that Portuguese often felt it necessary to display their superior standing to Asians in order to secure their own ambiguous position.[28]

As Europeans, the Portuguese were eligible for naturalization and for homesteading, both of which assisted their assimilation. However, their ambivalent ethnic status as not "fully" Caucasian left them marginalized with little or no access to established sources of capital. Like other affiliative immigrant groups, especially the Japanese and Chinese, they joined together to accumulate savings for use in their own community. Received Portuguese culture, however, did not emphasize the importance of success in urban commerce or promote upward mobility nearly to the extent of the Chinese, or even the Japanese, and, in combination with their small numbers, the Portuguese remained a less economically and politically powerful group.

Japanese

Japanese immigrants and their progeny were the most numerous and influential of the ethnic groups. Just as successful Chinese businessmen illustrate the Chinese story in the islands, U.S. Senator Daniel Inouye's rise to power through public office reveals a great deal about his ethnic group's experience.

Inouye displayed, from his earliest years, the loyalty and respect often found in first-generation immigrants. In the pre-war period, he joined a close-knit group of Japanese-Americans troubled by how they would fit into Hawai'i's society. In this period he shed traditional respect for authority and became known as a "barefoot radical." The war interrupted whatever direction his discontent might have taken, and in its aftermath, he was transformed from barefoot radical to the most popular elected figure in the islands. He would retain his deep commitment to equal rights, be the object of tremendous loyalty from Japanese-American voters, and remain closely connected to the friendships of his formative years.

The discontent that energized Inouye's drive to gain power on behalf of his and other ethnic groups might originate in part from an error Theon

Wright attributes to the *haole* elite: not understanding who the Japanese were. As Wright puts it, the oligarchy "did not feel it necessary to worry about the characteristics or customs of the field laborers."[29] They wanted to see Japanese immigrants as compliant and cognate, and remained insensitive to their values, styles, and ambitions. Had the owners and managers taken time to understand Japanese culture, an alliance might have been forged at least in the short term that worked better for both sides.

The 70,000 to 90,000 Japanese contract-laborers brought to the plantations were primarily farmers from southern Japan.[30] Their cultural values tended to emphasize cooperation, duty, and the maintenance of appropriate appearances. Though differences existed, their culture also nurtured deep pride in the superiority of things Japanese, emphasizing the importance of protecting its essence. Japanese immigrants were not the only ones to establish newspapers and create a network of schools to preserve their culture and language, but they did this much more extensively than other groups. Marrying a non-Japanese was considered a dishonor, which slowed the process of assimilation.

Participation in an interwoven system of obligations between the members of families, villages, and nation was a central ideal of Japanese traditional culture. Relationships were hierarchical, and the system contained a strong authoritarian component. Each person was expected to know his or her place in the reciprocal relations among unequals. Morally correct behavior consisted of keeping the distinctions clear, in knowing one's place, and in not violating the "natural" social order.[31]

Japanese immigrants to Hawai'i did not have to overcome the internal tensions relating to place of origin or clan affiliation, as had the Chinese and the Filipinos. Japan was already a unified nation with a strong, indigenous central authority, and common respect for and protection of its national symbols overwhelmed internal differences. That unifying allegiance, often focused on the emperor, worried many Caucasians who saw them as unable to be Americanized.

Although there were fewer internal group differences, the new social environment challenged Japanese cultural values and created conflict over assimilation. It presented a dilemma that divided the immigrants over the proper way to adapt to their new homeland.[32]

Many Japanese found plantation life extremely disappointing. Workers generally were treated with neither respect nor sensitivity, a stark contrast to the promises contained in agreements between the nation of Hawai'i and the Japanese government. They occupied the bottom rung on the social ladder from the beginning, receiving the lowest pay for the most menial work.[33] The cultural dilemma this created was that their deeply ingrained sense of duty and respect for the established order predisposed them to accommodate and live with this new social hierarchy, while their pride and need to protect from debasement the essence of things Japanese pushed them to reject these same conditions.[34]

As time passed and more Japanese identified Hawai'i as their home, and as their low wages threatened the prospects for new families, two distinct orientations emerged. One group opposed any public dissent that might bring shame on Japan or the Japanese by suggesting a lack of humility or an absence of gratitude. This group adapted to the paternalistic system of the plantation with less visible stress. The second group was increasingly affected by ideas about rights and equality, American values that reinforced their disaffection. For them, the planters were undemocratic and un-American, and this betrayal justified, even made a matter of duty, the use of whatever means they had to defend themselves and their future. This is the sentiment that led the Japanese to organize the first of many strikes in the islands in 1909. Coming along later, Daniel Inouye would embody some of this legacy.

Japanese integration into Hawai'i society was highly differentiated, determined by the relationship between traditional culture and the new setting. Where there was compatibility, such as in the emphasis on education and occupational mobility for men, assimilation could be accommodated. Other areas, like intermarriage and women's roles, remained sites of resistance.[35] Emphasizing individual achievement and commercial success less than the Chinese, they instead sought acceptance in their adopted land, some signal that they were a respected part of the social order.[36] Many would enter government bureaucracies and the public school system over the years, pulled there by the high regard accorded education and service. In the post-statehood years, both of these institutions would be dominated by Japanese Americans.

CULTURAL RELATIONS IN HAWAI'I

Virtually every aspect of private and public life is permeated by this mix of cultures and the "secondary culture" created in reaction to their meetings. The values and traditions that constitute each group; adaptations their members have made in forming social, economic, and political lives amidst conditions Hawai'i presented to them; struggles to maintain their cultural identity; and evolving relationships with one another are the milieu for social life and have shaped Hawai'i's political culture.

The Tenor of Contemporary Ethnic Relations

Contemporary relations between ethnic groups in Hawai'i are neither paradise nor facade, but simply work better than in most other places. The islands are a noteworthy, and perhaps even unique, instance of multiethnic harmony in the United States. As put by someone who has spent years doing research on ethnic issues, "Although no ethnic group is free from discrimination in Hawai'i, the extent of relentless racism is less than in the mainland United States. Islanders pay more attention to the feelings of other ethnic groups."[37]

Numerous indicators support this conclusion. There are, relatively speaking, few well-defined ethnic districts in the state, even though ethnicity remains an important part of people's lives.[38] Many more were transitional and have disappeared, blending into the social landscape. The best known of them, downtown Honolulu's Chinatown, lasted for a number of decades, but had virtually disappeared prior to recent restoration efforts. Even at its height, it held a smaller Chinese population than its counterpart in San Francisco, despite Honolulu's larger Chinese population.

A broader mixing of ethnic groups throughout residential areas takes the place of clearly bounded, culturally homogenous enclaves, an interweaving the sociologist Andrew Lind earlier pointed out would make busing impossible as a strategy for remedying any differences in the quality of education.[39] A high rate of inter-group marriage parallels this, the proportion having increased steadily during the twentieth century. Mixed-ethnicity couples accounted for 11.5 percent of all new marriages in the period 1912–16, but by the 1950s this had grown to 32.8 percent and by the years 1975–77 had reached almost 40 percent.[40] This, in turn, has led to a high proportion of multiethnic families: in the late 1970s, 30 percent of the civilian population reported itself as belonging to two or more cultural groups. By 1992, this had become 37 percent.[41]

Occupational mobility in the post-World War II period also has been high. Three ethnic groups whose members came to Hawai'i as immigrant laborers—the Japanese, the Chinese, and the Koreans—exceeded Caucasians in median income as early as 1970.[42] With respect to representation in public office, the electorate has not only elected Chinese-Americans, Japanese-Americans, part-Hawaiians, and Filipino-Americans as their governor, mayor, and representatives to Congress, but the state legislature and county councils are also generally multi-cultural.

Historic social patterns and contemporary economic conditions help to explain this high degree of intermingling and acceptance among cultural groups. The historic openness of Hawaiian people to foreigners is an important factor. Openness was reflected in generosity and trust shown strangers and in Hawaiians' willingness to inter-marry and make outsiders part of family.

This orientation was powerful because it occurred in combination with the new arrivals' adjustment to indigenous culture: immigrants tried not to remain permanent outsiders in a land with a strong Hawaiian social and cultural presence. As Wayne Wooden noted about Caucasians, "because [their rise to power] evolved *within* the existing social structure, established by the Hawaiians themselves, . . . the evolutionary (as opposed to revolutionary) nature of this transition saw maintenance of a society that kept a distinctive 'Hawaiian' style and tone."[43] In the long run, this process had the effect of establishing a tone of tolerance, a tolerance that resisted efforts by planters to divide ethnic groups.

Post-statehood economic development also has had a positive effect on ethnic group rapport. The connection between economic conditions and cultural relations is subtle and disputed, some arguing that ethnic conflict is primarily a disguised class issue.[44] Whatever the contribution class differences make to ethnic conflict, there is little doubt that the expanding post-World War II economy eased potential frictions. Even though the economic success of immigrant groups differed markedly—the Japanese, for example, were much more successful than the Filipinos, and the Chinese more than both— the differences occurred in a context where conditions for all immigrants (though not Native Hawaiians) improved, or seemed about to do so.

Threats to Cultural Harmony

A fragility haunts Hawai'i's cultural relations, despite strong ethnic pluralism and high degrees of occupational, residential and family ethnic intermingling. Crises have regularly interrupted the prevailing movement toward greater ethnic equality.[45] These occurred in the agitated voices of prominent citizens decrying the dangers of "multi-racialism"; the conflict-ridden mobilization of Asians into a labor movement; or the calls for internment of Americans of Japanese ancestry during the Second World War. Today, it is not uncommon to attribute outbursts of fighting in the public schools, confrontations between youth gangs, and violent assaults on individuals to ethnic resentments. These crises of tolerance reflect Hawai'i's delicate balance separating the movement toward equal standing from steps toward exclusion. Anticipating this, Lind concludes that the apparent lack of ethnic tension in the islands provides "no magical formula for exorcising the evil spirits or racial discord and distrust in other parts of the world."[46]

The degree to which present relations are based on a superficial tolerance or a deeper acceptance of cultural differences is difficult to know. It is clear, however, that even if relations are formed of something substantial, they are not immune to erosion. Two factors create the potential for higher levels of disharmony.

One is the movement by Native Hawaiians to reverse the processes that cost them their culture and their land. The same openness Hawaiians showed toward the groups displacing them accelerated their own decline. Land issues now are at the center of their grievances. Attempts to obtain sovereignty or redress may be handled by Hawaiians with the same degree of generosity and accommodation characteristic of them in the past. However, land has been elemental in the state's politics, and attempts to re-claim specific property from those who occupy or use it might bring explosive reactions. The frustration felt by Hawaiians, together with the feeling of threat other groups may experience, could exacerbate long-simmering conflicts, promoting ethnic divisions.

The second factor threatening ethnic harmony is the state's economic future. The post-statehood period was one of almost unbroken economic expansion until the late 1980s, when the tidal wave of Japanese investment in the tourist industry and housing subsided and the mainland economy entered recession. The factors leading to expansion had evaporated by the mid-1990s. In their place was a combination of high living costs, out-migration of residents to cheaper locales on the mainland, the sugar industry's demise, little success in finding a viable alternative to heavy reliance tourism, and ever greater dependence on decisions made in the global economy.[47]

If there is continued economic decline, or if, as some predict, Hawai'i's economy "recovers" by producing a two-class society of well-paid professionals and poorly paid service workers, it will happen to some of the sons and daughters whose immigrant parents were the beneficiaries of post-statehood growth, and to Hawaiians, Filipinos, and other groups already frustrated by their sense of exclusion.

POLITICAL CULTURE

The state's distinctive contemporary political life and public institutions have been described and explained by conflicting, often stereotypical, interpretations. One view, that might be called "ethnic domination," gives expression to the worst fears of early-twentieth-century Americanists, who worried about an Asian takeover.[48] Central to this interpretation is the penetration of Hawai'i's political system by recent immigrant groups, most notably Americans of Japanese ancestry. Japanese-Americans are perceived to be close-knit and loyal, primarily to one another, excluding other groups and foreclosing on commitments to a broader public interest. Politics is depicted as an amalgamation of life under the Liberal Democratic party of Japan and a South American *junta*, with power closely held by the ruling group and access denied to most others.

Another interpretation of Hawai'i's political life, "political assimilation," rejects ethnicity as a dominating feature, instead focusing on the islands' emergence as an American polity. This view suggests that, after long periods of monarchical and plutocratic rule, Hawai'i became a multi-centered, democratic political system in the years following the 1954 Revolution and statehood.[49] Assimilation is considered to be based heavily on inclusion of a diversity of ethnic groups into the corridors of power. It includes the embrace, by those holding power, of nationally adopted principles of good government and public responsibility—such as due process, open accountability, broad-based citizen input, and rule-driven bureaucracies.

These portraits of the islands' political life contain kernels of truth. In a few short years after the 1954 Revolution, government offices, both elected and administrative, were disproportionately filled by Americans of Japanese ancestry, a development some felt was anti-democratic and exclusionary. Evidence supporting the political assimilation perspective can be found in Hawai'i's adoption of model government standards and procedures, such as in administrative law and the penal code, from national templates; the success of the public school system in socializing large numbers of immigrants to the norms of democratic politics; and the impact of mainland Caucasians who migrated in the islands after statehood.

Local Culture and Political Culture in Contemporary Hawai'i

Power was not as monolithic in the years following the Democratic Revolution of 1954 as it had been during the time of the Caucasian elite. The elite had dominated both government and business, while the new regime could claim only the public sector. Command of government, of course, meant control of public policy and access to the good-paying, white-collar jobs from which most non-Caucasians had been excluded. Nevertheless, exclusion from the activities of the business world in a growing economy would represent a serious constraint. To consolidate power, and to signify their new-found status, occupants of the emerging power structure made connections with the *haole* elite that dominated commerce, men quick to recognize their own interest in working with the new powerholders.[50]

These connections, however, were not what came to orient the newcomers' politics at a more fundamental level. That was done by something more consistent with their ethnic traditions and historical experience in the islands, something capable of sustaining the network of relationships that would advance their own public values *and* their growing interest in maintaining newly found power. That something was embodied in "local culture," an outlook and set of values that has meanings special to the islands and the state's political culture.

The phrase "local," as seen on clothing apparel sold by mainstream retailers in the islands, emerged in the 1990s as a popular but ambiguous and ironic symbol of protectiveness about Hawai'i in the face of perceived threats from urbanization, in-migration, growing numbers of tourists, and an expanding consumer life style.[51] Not much earlier, "local" carried a more specific, and often divisive, connotation, distinguishing Hawaiians and other non-Caucasians from mainland or mainland-appearing Caucasians.

These meanings are commodified or abbreviated signposts for something deeper: a shared identity that was forged in the state's past and became powerful in its present. Michael Haas and Peter Resurrection argue that immigrant groups had to build an ethnic self-understanding that resisted assimilation into the distinctive, non-mainland culture of the islands. One sociologist referred to this process as "becoming like one another in a mutual interchange, rather than becoming like the target and dominant people among whom immigrant groups have gone to live, in a one-way process."[52] Jonathan Okamura points out that this accommodation occurred in the midst of an Island society "distinguished by a wide cleavage between the *haole* planter and merchant oligarchy on the one hand, and the subordinate Hawaiians and plantation workers on the other."[53] These social facts meant a new culture was forged from the tensions that accompany collective subordination. Second-class status lead to closer social relations between groups, as well as a shared awareness of their common "subject" status.[54]

Haas and Resurrection argue that the sensibility of such a local culture captured the imagination of the post-statehood generation as the basis for a

new unity.[55] A state of mind and a certain lifestyle, it protected many traditional, working class, agricultural, and less commercial values embedded in
the immigrant cultures, holding these values up against the challenge of
business culture. It also excluded mainstream Caucasians and symbolized
the end of their domination. In doing these things, local culture became both
subtle and significant, its historical and cultural circumstances making it
powerful.

Local culture uses a mix of cultural and ethnic distinctions to mark the
differences between the newly influential groups and those previously dominant. As cultural values, these differences are expressed as "local" styles of
cooperation, loyalty, and consensus-making, versus mainland styles of aggressiveness, competition and achievement. In ethnic terms, local culture distinguishes non-Caucasians from Caucasians, the latter embodying, in their
"non-localized" form, discredited or threatening values and lifestyles.[56]

By creating an unspoken, but well understood, line between Insiders and
Outsiders, this distinction became a means for establishing and maintaining
power. In the post-statehood period, much social, and ultimately political,
power came to be based on informal relationships that pervaded public institutions and public decisions, relationships infused by a shared sense of what
is proper and what needs protection.

The amalgamation that is local culture contains a strong moralistic orientation to political life.[57] It is born of social values found in the Asian and
Pacific immigrant cultures that make it up, as well as shared historical experiences of subordination in a plantation-based society. This is revealed in
public policies, created after the mid-1950s. These policies expressed the
sense of injustice that had accumulated over the preceding decades and reflected the vision of a more integrated, egalitarian Hawai'i society, including
the positive role public institutions, especially state government, could play
in shaping it. (For a review of these policies, see chapter 6.)

Local culture also contains a strong traditionalistic strain that rejects more
open and pluralistic forms of politics. Laws, rules, and official procedures—
the formal, rationalized mechanisms that, in principle, dictate what gets
done—compete with the priority given to informal relationships and common, group-based understandings. These relationships dictate that much of
what in many other American states may be fixed and predictable is, in
Hawai'i, the subject of on-going negotiation among well-acquainted insiders. This, in turn, creates an environment in which official behavior can
be seen, on one hand, as appropriate and desirable loyalty or, on the other, as
self-serving, corrupt, or simply aimed at maintaining power.[58]

Local Political Culture and Denied Power

Sheer numbers and high motivation, in combination with in-group reciprocity and exclusivity, resulted in Americans of Japanese ancestry dominating the groups that replaced the white-business coalition after 1954.[59] As a consequence, the way in which Japanese-Americans approached public and political affairs reveals a great deal about Hawai'i's post-statehood political culture.

Land politics is a good place to see this. In 1959, the year of admission to statehood, eleven private landowners held 30 percent of all land and 52 percent of all private lands, a direct legacy of the struggle over land that had taken place in the previous one-hundred years. The Bishop Estate, the largest of these, by itself controlled 16 percent of all private land in the state, and 22 percent on the island of O'ahu.[60]

The 1954 Revolution accomplished a great deal with respect to social policy. Land reform was considered essential to building a just society. Growing needs for housing made this even more urgent. Using government's authority to open up access to land had been among the most important goals of most of the new Japanese-American leaders. Once in power, however, they accomplished little real land reform. They failed initially because of the resistance of Republicans held-over in office, but in the longer run because of how their orientation to the complexities of political life affected their focus and commitments.

The New Democrats passed tax policies making it more costly for the large estates to sit on their land, an early accomplishment. This change created an incentive for land's development. As development intensified, many Japanese-Americans formed groups—called "*hui's*"—to pool their resources and make investments.[61] Frequently these associations of individuals with long family and personal histories were networked to others who worked in government and administered land policy.

The Land Use Commission was a frequent site of insider negotiation in the 1960s and 1970s. The New Democrats established the Commission in the late 1950s to oversee a statewide land-use system, one of the first such systems in the United States. Its purpose was to guide land development in orderly, publicly beneficial directions. The land use system placed land throughout the state in one of several categories, some categories permitting commercial development, others being protected for agriculture, and still others set aside for conservation. The Commission had authority to change particular holdings from one use to another by dispensing variances from established plans. *Hui* connections to Land Use Commission members allowed them to initiate or predict land zoning action in ways that led to enormous returns on investment.[62]

The authors of an extensive and detailed study of land transactions and land politics in this period believe that the new leaders "could probably have done far more than they did to shake up the big landowners." However, they recognize the conflicting forces that operated on them and are tolerant of why it didn't happen.[63]

Cindy Kobayashi MacKey's review of the how Japanese-Americans handled land reform leads her to a different conclusion. Using the data painstakingly gathered by George Cooper and Gavan Daws, she notes that, by 1970, 27 Democrats and Democratic appointees had solidified ties to major landholders, and that 18 of these 27 were Japanese-Americans. To MacKey, this signifies that the leaders of the new Democratic party had switched from the principles of land reform to an in-group taking part in land.[64]

The competing intentions and practices of Japanese-American leaders are also expressed in another important arena. After statehood, many came to believe their ideals and their own cultural position was under siege, threatened by demographic shifts for which their policies of development had helped set the stage.

A look at these demographic changes makes the problem clear. In the first decades of the twentieth century, Caucasians in the islands were outnumbered by Japanese by as much as 2 to 1, but by 1960 their numbers were even, with both groups representing about 32 percent of the population. As a result of the post-statehood influx of U.S. Mainlanders seeking residence in the prosperous fiftieth state, Caucasians soon became the most numerous ethnic group.[65]

John Burns and the Japanese-Americans who worked closely with him, while committed to ethnic equality and openness, also worried that outsiders, especially this growing influx of Caucasians, would overwhelm the islands. In *Catch a Wave*, an analysis of Burns' 1970 campaign for governor, Tom Coffman described a revealing incident involving a key Burns adviser, Bob Oshiro.[66] The campaign was against Tom Gill, member of a long-time Island family and embodiment of an activist government, by-the-rules, equal-treatment approach to public issues.

With Burns trailing badly in the election's early stages, Oshiro explained to campaign workers why winning the election was so important. He drew on a chalk board in foot-high letters the acronym WASP, followed by an arrow going westward to a circle that represented the islands. Less worried about the negative effects of rapid growth against which Gill was campaigning, Oshiro made it clear that his commitment to Burns came from concern that his children's "distinctive cultural heritage"—both his own culture and the blended local culture in which they lived—would be overrun by the arrival of Caucasian Outsiders.[67]

Andrew Hiroshi Aoki makes a more contemporary case for the need to protect the stabilizing qualities of local culture. A member of the generation following Oshiro, he too is concerned that the influx of aggressive individualism from the mainland, by overwhelming the qualities of local culture, will reduce the power of "local people" and rob Hawai'i of what is special in its private and public life.

For Aoki, these qualities are the primacy of the extended family; gift-giving; conflict avoidance and consensus-making; self-restraint, discipline and shame; loyalty, obedience and willingness to follow; openness to others and integration.[68] He suggests that, in order to protect them, "New systems of participation must be designed for local styles to counter an access bias that favors practitioners of non-local culture." In particular, local people must learn to take more initiative in participating in public affairs if they are to protect their way of life, but without giving up the other qualities of local culture: "traits of verbosity, wealth, boldness, and nerve need not be required for participation to be effective."[69]

Standing not far behind Oshiro's and Aoki's concern for protecting Hawai'i's blended culture and the groups that make it up is the issue of who is, and who should remain, authentically "local." It is an issue because, in dominating the groups asserting so much influence over the state's public institutions, Japanese-Americans create the potential for a backlash from the growing numbers who see them as a new elite.

Jonathan Okamura and other observers argue that Japanese-Americans have dealt with the backlash potential by downplaying their position and power, defining Hawai'i as a special place that needs their protection from outsiders, affirming their ties to other marginalized groups, and in general "emphasizing the local dimension of their ethnic identity."[70] Consistent with this, Japanese-American powerholders rarely flaunt their power. Their dress, language, and behavior generally conceal, sometimes to an extreme degree, their connections and ability to get things done.

The Continuing Evolution of Local Culture

By the late 1970s, many of the Japanese-American leaders of the Revolution of 1954 either had come to occupy highly visible positions of power, or passed from the scene. These changes tested the ability of local culture to continue to define the islands' political culture. The appearance of a movement known as "Palaka Power" demonstrated its continued strength as well as its ability to evolve.

Palaka Power refers to a point of view shared by a group that formed before the 1978 Constitutional Convention. Adherents united around its ideas and, during the convention, several of them obtained influential positions. The best known would become John Waihe'e, who catapulted into the lieutenant governorship in 1982 and governorship in 1986. As was true for others in this network who stayed in public life, the 1978 "Con Con" was the triggering event in Waihe'e's political career, and Palaka Power was the set of mobilizing beliefs that created his power base.

"Palaka" refers to a checkered cloth worn by Hawaiians, plantation workers, and dock workers. As a symbol, it provides a link to the non-*haole* common people who overthrew the Big Five and created a new society.[71] It stands for the strong fabric that protected those groups against forces that conspired to take away the unique culture formed by common social-political history. "Like the Palaka cloth that protected our people against the wind, sun, dust, and the *luna's* [plantation foreman] whips, Palaka Power will protect the people's interests at the Convention."

The new threats against which the Palaka Power group formed included erosion of the vision that had inspired the Revolution of 1954; the arrival of powerful mainland businesses, transnational corporations, and media, all of which are likely to exclude "local people"; the rise of religious conservatives attacking the unions that had given power to working people; and "liberals."

Given that liberals tend to be identified with, among other things, the struggle against discrimination, one would expect Palaka Power members concerned about their social position to align themselves with liberals. Their unwillingness to do so is instructive. Part of the answer lays in cultural and social class differences; liberals were seen to be mostly upper middle class and Caucasian. It also rested on the sense that liberals were arrogant because they thought themselves smarter than "local people," and naive because they didn't realize the consequences of their proposals.

For those in the Palaka Power network, evidence of this undesirable orientation to politics was found in liberal proposals for terms limits; restrictions on the number of bills that could be introduced during a legislative session; and referendum and initiative. Each of these were believed to disadvantage the common people of Hawai'i, with whom Palaka Power members resonated. These proposals, if passed into legislation, would give power to business interests and the media, against whom the average person couldn't compete, while taking it away from legislators, whose position and closer ties to local concerns enabled them to provide protection.

Palaka Power is an evolution of Hawaiian political culture, responding to the changing times while continuing to blend local culture's moralistic and traditionalistic orientations. It is moralistic in the commitment to use public authority to serve a broader community of underrepresented interests. It is traditionalistic in its protection of historic, shared values and in a deep reluctance to open up the political process to those who may not understand or share those values.

Like other galvanizing beliefs, and remindful of the post-statehood experience of the new Japanese-American leadership, the extent of Palaka Power's ability to shape the behavior of its adherents once they attained power was problematic. As governor, John Waihe'e appeared to move far from its commitments. He was commonly perceived, by the end of his eight years in office, as having sold out to specific commercial interests and individual political corruption, and to have been a relentless promoter of Japanese investment at the further expense of what remained "local" in Hawai'i.

His successor, Ben Cayetano, will be important in determining the next evolutionary turn of local culture, as well as its future influence. He is not as close to the network that supported previous governors. For years he was part of a dissident group critical of the leaders of his own legislative party. Moreover, he is faced with new pressures to reduce the size and cost of government and grow the business sector. Still, his ties to local culture run deep, from his childhood experience in Kalihi, an area that is made up heavily by the descendants of Asian and Pacific immigrants, to the people he feels most comfortable with today. As his wife put it at the beginning of his second term as governor, "He wants to leave behind that he was able to lead the state through this transition, without changing the values that make Hawaii so special."[72]

Changing Orientations to Political Culture

Several factors suggest an individualistic orientation to political culture may come to play a more important role in the state's future then it has in the past.

One is the recent growth of Caucasians as a proportion of the total population. Although often viewed as one common ethnic group, Caucasians are highly heterogeneous with respect to background, values, and attitudes.[73] They originate from a variety of European countries, and come from politically and subculturally distinct parts of the United States. Like other ethnic groups, they incorporate differing social class origins.

Despite these variations, ethnic groups with European roots share much that is important, placing relatively greater emphasis than Asian and Pacific cultures on personal achievement and the development and use of individual abilities. Relationships per se are not as central because there is less of an expectation that a person's interests will defer to group concerns. Change is given a higher value than preservation, because it allows individuals to pursue new experiences and creates more opportunities for success. Added to these basic ingredients, in the face of perceived exclusions created by local culture, Caucasians are more likely to turn to commercial relations and to the ideology of the impartial market to establish themselves socially.[74]

The gradual breakdown of Hawai'i's extensive networks of family and informal relationships is another factor contributing to a more individualistic political culture. These relationships, illustrated today by the way in which the high school a person attended creates a life-long social, political, and business web, attach people to one another in a network of familiarity and reciprocating obligations. Despite their resiliency, such networks are likely to become harder to maintain, and therefore less significant, under the atomizing pressures of urbanization and consumer culture. These pressures may make other, non-Caucasian immigrant groups seeking power and status, such as the Filipinos, more individualistic in outlook than they have been in the past.

The continuing erosion of the Democratic party's unifying mission is the last element. In the years after the "Democratic Revolution," the party's platform was a focal point for action, but its sense of mission and ability to maintain adherents has declined significantly. In the wake of this collapse of common purpose, party members have carved out their own individualized campaign agendas and legislative concerns, viewing public office in more self-referential terms. (For more on this point, see chapter 6.)

Political culture in Hawai'i is complex, and evolving. Its strong moralistic dimension gives authority to public-regarding values and energizes the desire to use public institutions to alleviate social inequities. This orientation co-exists with a strong traditionalistic side that justifies in-group control, relies on government to solve problems, and discounts an involved, deliberative public. This synthesis creates a pattern unusual, and perhaps unique, in the United States.

The continuing evolution of political culture is relevant to the most important issues facing Hawai'i. Pressures toward a more individualistic culture should lead in the direction of greater pluralism and more democratic practice. On the other hand, "the market" has its own politics, and its workings, often starkly, produce winners and losers. One result could be greater displays of a public-disregarding self-interest, higher levels of social and economic inequalities, and a diminishing role for public institutions in ameliorating the worst consequences of these disparities. Which, or to what extent, one of these comes to pass will be influenced by, among other things, the vitality of the economy, the course of the Native Hawaiian sovereignty movement, developments in the relations between ethnic groups, and changes in local culture. How all of these factors will influence prospects for the state to experience, for the first time, governmental institutions embodying both public values *and* openness, provides a context for the rest of this book.

CHAPTER FOUR

Hawai'i's Relations with the Outside World

Hawai'i's relationships with the rest of the nation have been characterized by a deep uncertainty, derived from competing internal interests and needs, about how to establish a proper balance with outsiders. Many territories and states have struggled in defining their relations with the federal government and other states. The islands' distance from the American mainland, in combination with domestic contests for control of a once-sovereign nation, helped give their relations a distinctive character.

Those in power have long recognized that outside assistance is needed to support economic enterprise and provide legitimacy for local authorities. Yet too much outside influence might look like or lead to interference, threatening the distinctive policies local decision-makers believe are required by the particularities of their circumstances. The federal government's relationship to the state's indigenous people has changed from the time it was instrumental in the overthrow of the Hawaiian nation. In its current role, federal programs provide assistance to Hawaiians and Hawaiian initiatives. At the same time, the part the federal government will play in the efforts of Hawaiians to redefine their place in contemporary Hawai'i society remains unclear.

International relations are also complicated and troubled. Although associations within the American union have been of great importance, Hawai'i's attention is constantly drawn to relationships outside the nation, probably more than any other state. By cultural heritage, contemporary economic inter-penetration, the long-standing interests and desires of some of its most influential citizens, and its native peoples' movement toward self-determination, Hawai'i is connected to the Pacific and Asia to a remarkable degree.

HAWAI'I'S NATIONAL AND REGIONAL RELATIONS
DURING THE TERRITORIAL PERIOD

Two years after annexation, Congress voted to designate Hawai'i as an "incorporated territory," a status entitling it to eventual statehood. Advocates for territorial status had eliminated this option during the annexation debates to make Hawai'i more palatable to ambivalent legislators. The new designation reflected a national interest, formulated in the nation's centers of power, prevailing over strong regional dissent. The regional dissent remained, however, throughout the territorial period.

Although earlier objections to association with Hawai'i were heavily based on southern concerns about economic competition, racial concerns were important too. Objections became more racially based once Hawai'i became a territory eligible for statehood. Such objections were heard in other parts of the country but, as Roger Bell points out, "during the sixty years of territorial rule that followed annexation, Southern Congressmen dominated all efforts to deny Hawai'i's diverse peoples equality under statehood."[1]

Hawai'i's economy was virtually absorbed into the United States during the territorial period. By 1914, more than 95 percent of Hawai'i's exports went to the United States, rising to almost 97 percent in 1933.[2] One observer of Hawai'i society, writing in the 1930s, noted that "Hawai'i's economy has been so largely contingent upon the political programs evolved at Washington that news from the capital is always received with special interest in the islands."[3] The most critical news, of course, concerned policies that might affect King Sugar.

Hawai'i's sugar quotas relative to American states were reduced by passage of the Jones-Costigan Act in 1934. This act had the effect among local decision-makers of making the pull of statehood more powerful than the push of fears of takeover by Asians poised to obtain the right to vote. Outside of Hawai'i, as relations between Japan and the United States deteriorated during the 1930s, many Americans feared that the Japanese in Hawai'i would remain loyal to their homeland in any potential conflict. This expectation caused a drop in support for statehood in Congress at the same time it was increasing in the territory.

Japanese-Americans' loyalty during the war diminished some of these fears, but a familiar regional pattern re-established itself. The opposition of southern representatives in Congress was a primary factor in Hawai'i's exclusion from the union between 1945 and 1959.[4] Their reasons combined concern about the loss of southern autonomy from giving more congressional votes to their social enemies, with deep differences about race relations. James Eastland, a powerful Democratic senator from Mississippi, stated on the Senate floor that Hawai'i statehood would mean "two votes for socialized medicine, . . . two votes for government ownership of industry, two votes against all racial segregation, and two votes against the South on all social matters." Senator Price Preston Jr., a Democrat from Georgia, observed that statehood "makes citizens with equal rights with you and me of 180,000 Japanese."[5]

It is hard to overstate the role played by America's ambivalent and contradictory orientations to ethnic and cultural diversity in United States-Hawai'i relations during the territorial period. Sectional fears, concentrated in, but by no means confined to, the South, about an Asian presence, "Japanization" of the islands, and uncertain Asian loyalties were balanced against the perceived importance of individual rights, social equality, and national commitments to self-governance and avoidance of colonies. These latter principles eventually prevailed, but only in combination with the nation's strategic military interest in Hawai'i, bringing federal policies that would help to reshape Island society. Support of equal access to public education as a vehicle for developing active citizens was crucial among these policies. Many of the non-Caucasians who came to dominate the system of governance after statehood had benefited from primary and secondary education, and then from the GI Bill after the war.

Territorial Uses of the Federal Government

From the vantage point of the interests dominating the local economy and Hawai'i politics, relations with the United States should accommodate the needs of a robust export economy in agriculture, while selectively applying the principles of constitutional democracy. Serving the economy involved the maintenance of favorable trading arrangements and fiscal support. Political accommodation meant accepting those principles of governance that would not jeopardize control over Native Hawaiians or, later, containment of the growing population of Asian immigrants and their off-spring.

The local elite was remarkable in molding a federal presence around these desires.[6] It supported a descendent of the Hawaiian royal family to be a delegate to Congress, for more than two decades using him to increase federal expenditures for maritime and military infrastructure and to promote favorable immigration policy. Of perhaps greater importance, the elite's members kept the territorial governor within their sphere of influence.

Under the Organic Act, the governor, appointed by the president, was much more powerful than counterparts in mainland states. The power resulted from being locally unimpeachable; the direct control of hundreds of appointments; a veto over individual items in appropriation bills passed by the territorial legislature; the authority to suspend the writ of *habeas corpus* and to place any part of the territory under martial law; and from having jurisdiction over a wide administrative scope, including health, welfare, highways, and public works.[7]

Prior to World War II, most of the men who were territorial governors had previously held important positions in or around the sugar industry. Their policies reflected those connections. Whether chosen by Democratic or Republican presidents, there were few differences in the way Hawai'i's territorial governor's chose to balance the federal presence.

POST-STATEHOOD FEDERAL RELATIONS

Statehood brought many economic benefits. Hawai'i continues to get more than its "fair' share of federal monies. In 1997, the U.S. per capita federal expenditure was $5,263, but in Hawai'i it came to $6,963. This amounted to each resident getting $1.32 for every dollar he or she paid in federal taxes, ranking the state fifth nationally.[8] Breaking this down to include what Hawai'i taxpayers contributed as well as what they gained, in 1994 each resident paid $4,685 per person in federal taxes, about 107 percent of the national average. For that, they received $6,017 per resident, or 125 percent of what on average went to other states. This means that, for that year, Hawai'i residents showed a net gain of $1.17 for every dollar they paid in taxes, tying them for seventeenth place.[9]

The state received approximately $7.0 billion from the federal government in 1997. This was a little less than eight times what it received twenty-five years earlier (not taking inflation into account). Within federal spending categories, it was second nationally in per capita spending on salaries and wages, fifteenth in grants to state and local government, twentieth in procurement, and thirty-first in direct payments to individuals (e.g., social security). Reflecting changes in the form of federal monies but stability in the relative amount received, thirteen years earlier the state was sixth in per capita federal expenditures, ranking first in spending on salaries and wages, twenty-first in procurement funds, thirty-first in grants to state and local governments, and thirty-fifth in direct payments to individuals.[10]

Federal dollars are an important part of Hawai'i's state government budget. In 1995 federal grants constituted 19.1 percent of the state's operating revenue receipts, the largest revenue category after general excise and income taxes. Federal funds are expected to total $890 million, or 15.2 percent of state appropriations, in fiscal year 1999.[11]

These data make evident the continuing importance of the federal role since statehood. They also point out that, as is true of other states, local dependence on federal resources did not abate with the transition from territorial status. Hawai'i, like other places in the west, has made extensive use of federal assistance to underwrite an economy that always seemed fragile. Like those other places, although to a lesser degree and for different reasons, the help has been a cause of tension.

Areas of Federal Impact

Forty years ago, by far the most important federal activities were those affecting export agriculture, especially sugar. Places like Cuba and the Philippines, in the post-statehood years, presented intense competition for Hawai'i's producers of export products. Rising labor and land costs required development of highly efficient operations, and forced reliance on federal policies that, in essence, maintained prices at a level below which Hawai'i sugar could not be profitable. In recent years, these policies have provided a steadily declining subsidy, less than most owners and investors feel is needed to justify continuation. Total acreage devoted to sugarcane dropped from 205,000 to 68,800 between 1982 and 1996.[12] Since then, several of the remaining producers have ceased production or radically scaled back operations. Sugar is no longer grown on the islands of Hawai'i and O'ahu. It is unlikely that sugar producers will continue to be successful in their appeals for federal help in a national policy environment more critical of the value of agricultural price supports.[13] Sugar will, as a consequence, continue to diminish as a factor in the local economy, and the impact of federal agricultural policy, though not absent, will be much less important than in the past.

It is military spending that gives the state a high rank in the relationship between federal taxes paid and federal dollars received in the 1990s. In 1997, approximately 38 percent of all federal expenditures in the state came from the U.S. Department of Defense. In that same year, Hawai'i was second nationally in per capita defense expenditures, in comparison to its rank of thirty-ninth for all non-military spending.[14]

Hawai'i is a part of the national pattern of spending more defense dollars on states along its geographical perimeter;[15] unlike other perimeter states, it is not a recipient of contracts for technology development. Much military-related expenditure is due to the same reason behind American interest in the island nation in the nineteenth century: the state's strategic location in relation to Asia and the Pacific. This passive attraction has been supplemented by the effectiveness of the state's Congressional delegation, particularly that of long-term Senator Daniel Inouye, in promoting Hawai'i as a recipient of military funds.

According to a study by the National Commission for Economic Conversation and Disarmament, in 1994 Hawai'i obtained $3.3 billion in military monies. That figure represents a net gain of $1.7 billion over spending before downsizing began, equivalent to receiving $1,442 per person more in military spending than residents paid in taxes.[16] The study confirmed that most states experience a net loss from a military presence, something they term "Pentagon Burden." In contrast, Hawai'i was third behind Virginia and New Mexico (and the District of Columbia) among the fifteen states that take out more than they put in. Moreover, within that group of fifteen it is probable that Hawai'i and Alaska are the most affected because of their smaller economies. This is especially so because of a bill introduced by Senator Inouye in 1986 that requires Defense Department contractors in Hawai'i and Alaska to hire local contractors when the unemployment rate in those states is below the national average.

The proportion of total federal spending in Hawai'i that goes through the Department of Defense has dropped from about 52 percent in 1988 to 38 percent 9 years later. Nevertheless, it remains the second largest source of income in the state, though well behind that deriving from tourism.[17] Though smaller than it used to be, the Pearl Harbor shipyard is still one of the largest civilian employers in the islands.

The Department of Defense, in addition, controls a large amount of land, either by direct ownership or leasehold. This amounted to almost one-quarter million acres in 1992. On O'ahu, by far the most densely populated island, the Department of Defense owned or leased 21 percent of the land, all of which is highly prized in terms of both monetary value and the potential for alternative uses.[18]

Airline and ocean shipping regulation, highway construction, immigration policy, telecommunications policy, and disaster assistance are other areas of special importance in the state-federal relationship. Dependence on air transportation, transpacific as well as inter-island, makes the regulatory environment for that industry significant. Tourism's reliance on a large number of attractively priced seats means concern about federal aviation policy can reach the level reserved for sugar policy earlier in the century. Scheduled airlines serving the islands were estimated to have a total seat capacity of almost 9.3 million in 1996, down from a high of nearly 12 million in 1991.[19]

The number of airlines and the variety of their routes is of special interest. In 1996, the state-run Honolulu International Airport was the nineteenth busiest in the United States, handling more than 24 million passengers and generating an average monthly revenue of about $20 million. Its duty-free revenues, which generate millions in tax income for state government, were second only to London's Heathrow.[20]

The Airline Deregulation Act of 1978, which reduced carriers and routes nationally, has had parallel affects in the islands. By 1990, United airlines served 27 percent of those coming to Hawai'i, more than double its nearest rival.[21] This raised concerns among elected officials about an absence of meaningful fare competition or alternatives in case of a strike. (In 1985 a United Airlines strike threatened to curtail tourism radically and heightened anxiety about dependence on a single carrier.) At the same time, the two dominant intrastate airlines have attempted, with some success, to use federal rules to preclude competition from smaller operations or national companies. In 1993 and 1994 those carriers waged a long, costly fight to prevent establishment of a third inter-island airline, citing complicated federal rules about percentage of foreign ownership. The airline finally began business, but failed after a short time.

The Jones Act was passed by Congress in 1920 to develop and protect a merchant marine that could be the basis of an American shipping industry and a resource in time or war. The act specifies that cargo shipped between two U.S. ports must be carried on American ships. Today, 75 years after its passage, the policy serves to protect a shipping industry that cannot compete with low-cost foreign lines.

Hawai'i imports about 90 percent of what its residents consume, and more than 95 percent of that comes to the islands by sea. The Jones Act today contributes heavily to the fact that Hawai'i has only two shipping companies: Matson Navigation Company, a subsidiary of former Big Five Hawai'i firm Alexander and Baldwin, and Sea-Land Service, Inc.. Matson does most of the business, coming to the islands with four large container vessels each week.

Local opponents of the Jones Act, who are part of a national coalition whose members want it repealed or at least amended, argue that the outdated policy raises costs to consumers and results in less efficient shipping practices. Their estimates vary, but generally conclude that Hawai'i consumers pay thousands of dollars more for products than they would cost in a more competitive environment. Jones Act proponents counter that it gives stability to Hawai'i's sea life line and keeps jobs in the United States and the islands that otherwise would go abroad. They also contend that the primary reason foreign shippers have lower costs is their immunity from the safety, health, and environmental regulations that most Americans support.

The state's Democratic representatives have supported the act. Republican candidates have repeatedly tried to make the presumed burden of the Jones Act a reason to vote for them. Voters have shown little interest in these arguments, and the act is unlikely to be substantially changed in the near future.

Hawai'i has a total of about 4,100 miles of highways, less than one hundred of which are designated national freeways. Federal spending on highway construction has been important to the state's economy despite these small numbers. The third of three "interstate" freeway segments on O'ahu, labeled H-3, was completed in 1998 at a total cost of about $1.2 billion, 95 percent federally funded. This is a substantial amount of money in an economy the size of Hawai'i's. It was also an expenditure critical to the viability of the local construction industry.

The impact of federal spending on ground transportation is reflected in efforts that culminated in the early 1990s to build a fixed rail rapid transit system in the downtown Honolulu corridor. Promoted by the city and county administration since 1972, and with $700–800 million in federal support later secured by Hawai'i's congressional delegation, the county council narrowly rejected the project after an extensive and bitter debate. Apart from fundamental disagreements about the viability of the proposed system as an affordable solution to traffic congestion, its defeat was widely viewed as a blow to the economy because no other major, federally assisted capital projects were on the horizon.

The federal role in telecommunications has been significant for the islands. Prior to the advent of satellite communications, Hawai'i was linked to the United States mainland by cable, but line charges were very high, adding to the state's physical and social isolation. Up through the early years of satellites, the absence of economic competition together with the historic pattern of differential Hawai'i-U.S. rates served to keep the charges to users artificially high.

Over time Senator Inouye was able to employ his influence through the federal communications bureaucracy to begin a process of rate equalization with the rest of the country, a process that today finds Hawai'i's rates reflective of the marginal rates for distance charges that apply in other parts of the country.. This relative parity stands in stark contrast to the rest of the Pacific Islands, which continue to endure extremely high long distance telecommunication charges. Many policy makers see rate equalization as significant in the economic vitality of the islands, and essential to any role it might play in international commerce.

Between 1950 and 1995 the populated islands of the chain experienced seven major hurricanes, four after 1978. In November 1982, hurricane Iwa struck Kaua'i and parts of rural O'ahu with recorded gusts of 117 miles per hour. Property damage was estimated to be $245 million. Slightly less that ten years later, in September 1992, Iniki rampaged across the center of Kaua'i with peak recorded winds of 143 miles per hour, causing almost $2 billion in property damage. Despite some complaints about the timeliness and appropriateness of responses, there is little question the federal role in emergency relief and recovery assistance was crucial to the survival and short-term recovery of communities whose resources had been stretched to the breaking point.

Finally, federal policies governing the number of immigrants and their rights as workers and citizens historically have been crucial in the economic and political life of the islands. Contemporary in-migration is unlikely to equal the nineteenth-century influx of plantation labor. Nevertheless, between 1970 and 1990 the foreign-born population increased from 9.8 to 14.7 percent of residents, with 133,735 of 162,704 coming from Asian countries.[22] Because foreign in-migration accounts for such a substantial proportion of population growth in the islands, any changes in federal policy would have an important impact on population size as well as cultural make-up.

Tensions in State-Federal Relations

Many states, especially since the 1970s, have had conflicts with the federal government over its attempt to leverage nationally adopted social policies through rules attached to the use of federal funds. This has been much less of an issue in Hawai'i, with some important exceptions. The state's social policies, reflective of the political culture dominant since 1954, are often compatible with, or more ambitious than, federal initiatives. As a consequence, even with the 1990s combination of the state's poor fiscal status and declining federal funds, conflicts have been minimal over discrimination, the rights of members of ethnic minorities, the desirability of welfare assistance, the provision of maximum unemployment benefits, the adoption of work-place health and safety standards, or access to health care.

Illustratively, in workplace health and safety and access to health care, the state has designed policies that go well beyond federal government requirements. State government elected to administer occupational safety and health regulations, and offers one of the most generous compensation packages of any state for work-related injury or illness. In health care, Hawai'i was the first to try to provide near-universal access to services, coming to this well before serious consideration of such an option at the national level.

Some conflicts do occur. One developed not long after statehood. During the 1970s, the state came up the loser to the federal Constitution in the area of population control. Governor George Ariyoshi proposed restricting residency out of concern that the dramatic population growth that followed statehood would outstrip available resources, in the process altering what was special about Island culture. While the issue he addressed was, and remains, a critical one for the state, his administration's response was incompatible with membership in the federal system. (See chapter 11 for further discussion of the population issue.)

The military's role is another source of tension. Boosterism for military spending has been a constant in the islands, but so has public concern over suspected storage of nuclear weapons at Pearl Harbor; the impact of large numbers of single military men on local communities, especially through bar culture and prostitution; cost-sharing with respect to the additional burden of accommodating military dependents in public schools; and the impact on the physical environment.[23]

Other conflicts take place at a less generic level and involve disputes about the specific federal or state actions and decisions. The end of the Cold War brought questions about the continued possession by the military of lands no longer seen as essential to national defense. The Admissions Act of 1959 and the Conveyance Procedures Act that followed in 1963 require that lands ceded to the federal government at annexation be returned to the state when no longer needed for military purposes.

These questions raised the divisive issue of who will obtain future use of any lands returned to the state. For example, in 1999 the Navy will deactivate Barbers Point Naval Air Station, which sits on 2,000 acres of prime land in a new urban corridor on the island of O'ahu. Governor Waihe'e created the Barbers Point Naval Air Station Redevelopment Commission to make recommendations on its use after the closure. The commission's work became the focus of highly contentious hearings and intense lobbying by citizens groups, aviation interests, and commercial operators before an agreement was reached, a scenario likely to be repeated for other prime pieces of real estate controlled by the military.

The allocation of federal monies to construct the H-3 freeway on O'ahu illustrates another kind of conflict. First planned in 1963 and expected to cost $93 million, a long and bitter struggle delayed its completion until 1998, by which time the final cost was more than 13 times the original estimate.[24] Federal appropriations were justified by connecting two military bases sixteen miles apart on opposite sides of the island. Proponents, represented by the state's Department of Transportation and strongly supported by construction interests, argued the new highway would reduce traffic congestion in the urban corridor, support the state's economy, and avoid having to build an even more expensive rail system being promoted by the mayor of the City and County of Honolulu. Opponents invoked federal environmental impact requirements while contending the required route spoiled two of the island's few remaining undeveloped valleys, violated historic Native Hawaiian cultural sites, did little to decrease traffic congestion, and promoted growth in a part of the island that heretofore had been outside of commuting range from the urbanized leeward side.

Federal laws can be a source of conflict with state agencies, usually involving the implementation costs of those laws. Laws governing sewage treatment are a good example of this. The City and County of Honolulu argued for years, eventually successfully, that the unique capacity of the ocean for cleansing should exempt taxpayers from the expense of tertiary treatment. The state was not as successful in another area. It lost its argument that the housing of prisoners did not violate federal standards of fair treatment, and was forced to spend a great deal of money to implement a settlement.

A conflict in the human services field shows how important the state's inability to meet federal standards can be. In 1993, parents brought a class action suit against the state, accusing it of failing to provide adequate educational and mental health services for children with special needs or disabilities. The basis of the suit was two federal laws, the Individuals with Disabilities Education Act and the Vocational Rehabilitation Act, and the funding associated with them. U.S. District Judge David Ezra dismissed the state's argument that it was providing adequate services to these children, given existing resources. A federal master and monitor were appointed to oversee implementation, over a five-year period, of what came to be called the Felix Consent Degree. The decree stipulates that the state identify all children with special needs and provide appropriate educational and mental health or related services by June of the year 2000. Apart from the millions of dollars spent on court proceedings, the outcome has a significant impact on how social services dollars and personnel are allocated within the state at a time when both are in short supply.

Federal and local law-enforcement authorities work together in a number of areas. Cooperating to reduce the state's large, but illegal, marihuana industry has been one of the most visible. Another, the federal investigation of public corruption in state government, has produced a less clear relationship between state and federal officials. Between 1991 and 1996, agents from the Federal Bureau of Investigation initiated at least five investigations of potential illegality involving elected or appointed officials. Two focused on the sitting president of the state Senate and his predecessor, and one probed workings of the powerful Land Use Commission. Another investigation jailed the head of the state's Office of Environmental Quality Control. A well-connected member of the Democratic party, he was sent to prison for distributing public funds to phony environmental consulting firms run by his friends.

For those who applaud this role, it is justified by the level of political inbreeding and pubic corruption in the state and represents the only hope for remedy. For example, in 1994 the F.B.I.'s Honolulu agent-in-charge offered his opinion that, "Public corruption is Hawai'i's number one crime problem."[25] For many local officials, however, it represents an uninvited and unnecessary form of surveillance, one likely to be abused by federal officials themselves, or by individuals in the state who can use those officials for a personal agenda.[26] For example, while many applaud the Internal Revenue Service's investigation of the Bishop Estate's tax free status, others see it as a way to reduce the control of Native Hawaiians over their own affairs.

The Prospects for State-Federal Relations

Officials in any state as thoroughly Democratic as Hawai'i have reason to be concerned about their prospects during a period of Republican ascendancy in the federal Congress.[27] They can expect the policy climate to change and less federal dollars to surface for programs to which they are committed, such as education and health care. In addition, no matter what the climate, their representatives have been bumped off their positions of power on legislative committees in the House and Senate.

In the short and long term it is likely the state will do fairly well, although there undoubtedly will be some losses. The main reason for this expectation is the role of military spending. Most Republicans and some conservative

Democrats may be hostile to many social and environmental policies, but most also have, if anything, a greater commitment to spending for defense. Nothing short of a drastic revision in strategic planning is likely to harm Hawai'i fiscally, simply because of its geographic location.

The base closings that followed break-up of the Soviet Union illustrate this. The National Commission for Economic Conversion and Disarmament estimated that forty-one states would suffer economic losses, some fairly dramatic, as a result of decisions made by the base closing commission and accepted by the President Bill Clinton. Only five of the nine expected to benefit would gain more than Hawai'i, and Hawai'i was predicted to end up with about 3,000 new jobs.[28]

The state's congressional delegation is another reason Hawai'i is likely to do well. Their power lies primarily in voters' habit of re-electing federal representatives, the same pattern that has made a number of southern congressmen powerful. Senator Inouye illustrates this. First elected to the House in 1960, he joined the Senate in 1962. He now is one of that longevity-honoring body's most senior members. A nationally known figure because of his role in the Iran Contra hearings during the Bush administration, his legislative stature was indicated by symbolic mention as a vice presidential choice in presidential campaigns. He was chair of the important Armed Forces Appropriations Sub-committee until the Senate was re-organized after the 1994 elections, leading a national columnist to observe that he was "a principle holder of purse strings for defense spending."[29]

A change to minority party status unquestionably cost Inouye some power; there is no substitute for a committee chair. At the same time, his knowledge of the rules, network of relationships, and reputation as an inside player who has respected, and often protected, other members of The Club regardless of party, suggest he will continue to be effective.

Barring a change in the habits of Hawai'i voters, even an extension of Republican power to the presidency is unlikely to mean that Senator Inouye, together with the rest of the low-turnover delegation, will cease to be successful in competing for federal monies. This projection is supported by the fact that in 1998, when military construction spending nationally dropped, Hawai'i was allocated a record amount of $249 million.

RELATIONS WITH OTHER REGIONS AND OTHER STATES

Hawai'i's intra-national economic rivals have not been its nearest neighbors in the post-statehood period, but locations throughout the country that competed for military expenditures, tourists, and technology development companies.

Within these strictures, the state's primary subnational identity and most relevant comparisons are with the western region of the country, for reasons of both physical proximity and economic ties. Economic relations first were established by sugar, followed after the War by tourism. In 1994, for example, well over one-half of all visitors to Hawai'i from the U.S. mainland came from the Pacific and Mountain states; over one-third came from California alone.[30]

In statistical comparison to these western states, Hawai'i is first in the number who successfully complete high school, but ninth in primary and secondary school spending per capita; sixth in per capita spending on corrections activities, and seventh in the number of serious crimes reported per 100,000 population; twelfth in infant deaths per capita, but first in per capita spending on health and hospital services; fourth in federal aid per capita, first in per capita personal income, third in state and local government spending per capita, and last on an index of state solvency.[31]

Perhaps of more significance and substance, the Hawaiian state government has established a number of compacts with western states to help it do what size and isolation prevents. The WICHE agreement between public universities, which permits students easier access to educational programs not available in their own state, has been one of the most visible of these. In 1995, governors of 14 Western states including Hawai'i, agreed to develop Western Governors University, a degree-granting program that provides access to courses using the internet and other distance learning technologies.[32]

HAWAI'I IN THE ASIAN AND PACIFIC ARENAS

Many states participate in some form of international relations in an era of globalized business and the penetration of national economies by transnational companies. Some, like Hawai'i, promote these relations and fund trade-promotion offices in foreign countries.

A few states, such as California, do a larger total volume of business with Asian and Pacific countries, but Hawai'i is distinguished by its history of political, cultural, and economic connections. This history and these contemporary patterns are consequences not only of location, but also of outlook and worldview.

Foreign Investment

Prior to the 1970s, the only substantial foreign investments were the 1958 opening of a Japanese-financed department store and, in 1963, purchase of two Waikiki hotels for $20 million.[33] In the mid-to-late 1970s, and again in

1982, the state experienced two "mini-booms," each dominated by the Japanese. A huge buying spree in real estate resulting in approximately $10 billion of investment, with 1990 alone totaling $3 billion, took place between 1986 and 1990. During this period, the buying pattern shifted from longer term corporate investment to hotels, apartment buildings and condominiums, and houses. Sixty percent of the purchases were on O'ahu. Foreign investment in Hawai'i real estate by 1990 was estimated to represent 12 percent of the total value of all real property in the state, including 18 percent of all commercial properties, and 16 percent of all apartments and condominiums. Foreign investors were estimated to have underwritten about 30 percent ($3.2 billion) of the total residential real estate transactions in the state from 1986 to 1990.[34]

The size of the boom relative to the state's economy was remarkable. That it was almost exclusively fueled by Japanese investment is equally noteworthy. Japanese spending went from about $150 million to $1 billion in 1985, spurred by the "bubble economy" in Tokyo real estate, the U.S-Japan trade surplus, declining value of the dollar relative to the yen, and openness of Hawai'i property to purchase by non-Americans.[35] Between 90 and 95 percent of all foreign real estate purchases were made by Japanese in the years 1986 to 1990. Their investment in Hawai'i property from 1985 to 1993 added up to almost $19 billion, a figure equal to 24 percent of all Japanese investment In the United States. This level of spending was second only to California's 33 percent of the total, and ahead of New York's 16 percent, despite the enormously greater size, populations, and wealth of those states.[36] As a result, in addition to the fact that Japanese capital accounts for most of Hawai'i's foreign investment, by the end of 1990 more than 60 percent of all hotel rooms and 43 percent of total visitor-plant inventory were Japanese owned, together with 28 of 46 existing private golf courses, and 16 of 24 of those under construction.[37]

Hawai'i is a small state, and the rush of Japanese yen was highly visible, creating more controversy than anywhere else in the country. With so little land—the state totals just over 4 million acres—and a large proportion of it controlled by state and federal governments and a few private estates, the influx of buying power had a major impact, in the process pointing again to the centrality of land in the state's political and social life. Reflecting this, large jumps in housing prices, commonly more than doubling, occurred between 1986 and 1990. Escalating property values were reflected in higher property taxes; and governmental revenues increased.[38]

A March 1990 survey of attitudes toward Japanese investment captured public concerns about these and other impacts. In a sample of 409 residents, 64 percent labeled themselves as "friendly" to the Japanese (with 86 percent of Japanese Americans making this statement) and 59 percent indicated their sense that Japanese investment is good for the state. At the same time, 41 percent did not trust the "political motives" of Japanese nationals, 67 percent thought the Japanese didn't care about Hawai'i "except as a place to play or make money," 69 percent felt there should be restrictions on land sales to foreigners, and 46 percent thought Hawai'i was on the verge of becoming a colony of Japan.[39]

Concern about Asian and Japanese takeover made its way into statements of some public officials. The most notable was the mayor of the City and County of Honolulu. In a highly publicized November 1989 speech, Frank Fasi quoted a Hawai'i historian who had suggested the state was finally meeting its ambition to be the crossroads of the Pacific by becoming the place where "the suburbs of Tokyo meet the suburbs of Los Angeles." The mayor went on to argue that "almost every American-style thing we have that is upscale and desirable" is becoming owned by the Japanese, and that "we local people are left with the remainder."[40]

It is hard to dismiss these comments as simple racism, although they may have contained elements of it.[41] Rather, they were part of an election strategy for a man ambitious to be governor whose power base lay in those non Japanese-American groups the survey showed to be most concerned about Japanese power.

What had been a heated issue declined in importance by the early 1990s, not because the Japanese owned much less of Hawai'i, or housing costs had declined appreciably, but because the buying spree was over. Japanese firms began selling or attempting to sell properties, especially hotels and resorts, after the rapid expansion of their economy ended in 1990. Nationally, by 1993 they were offering, foreclosing on, or internally restructuring $17.6 billion in properties. In that same year Hawai'i became first in the disinvestment process, affecting 28 percent of total Japanese purchases in the state.[42]

Japanese investment had disappeared as a public problem by 1995, invisible next to concerns about state government deficits, cut backs in services, and the need for more revenue and less spending. Statements about hoped-for increases in arrivals of higher paying Japanese tourists began to appear amidst the growing economic turndown, along with wishes from public officials for a return of Japanese investors, perhaps supplemented by Koreans or Taiwanese. These soon became a chorus, drowning out the earlier voices of complaint. In this changing tide the state was tied to its deep economic involvement in the East, but caught in its historic ambivalence about what that involvement means.

Hawai'i as a Pacific Society

After the middle of the nineteenth century Hawai'i was something of a show-piece, "an example of what could be done in the way of independent government by native Polynesians when assisted by right-minded foreigners."[43] As this statement suggests, early internationalism had two sources, apart from whatever special sensitivities to the external world may come from living on islands. One was the vision of the nineteenth-century missionary and business elite of the islands as the Pacific commercial leader and a global model for multicultural societies.[44] The other was the ambitions and aspirations of the Hawaiian nation's leaders.

In the 1870s and 1880s King Kalakaua attempted to make Hawai'i the center of a Pacific confederation, "a Polynesian empire . . . with Hawaii as the ruling island group."[45] Walter Murray Gibson, the King's Hawaiian-speaking Prime Minister and Minister of Foreign Affairs, was a strong advocate for Hawai'i, helping to send ambassadors throughout the Pacific in response to his belief that, "Hawai'i holds the first position among the native states in the Pacific, and should recognize a duty as attaching to that position."[46]

The first elected Democratic governor, John Burns, used his 1962 inaugural address to re-state this historic theme: His state should fulfill its destiny as the "hub of the Great Wheel of the Pacific," endorsing what he frequently expressed as a duty to promote a Pacific community of nations.[47] The International Development Assistance Program, started in 1967 and later renamed the Office of International Relations, was one manifestation of the state government's role in establishing Pacific linkages. The program explored the possibility of development assistance programs for the Pacific, as well as commercial ties under its initial mandate. The 1970 Governor's Conference on the Year 2000, a portion of which focused on establishment in the Pacific of a sense of community equivalent to that found among the North Atlantic nations, is another demonstration of the government's role.[48]

Hawai'i's internationalism has been a complex mix of cultural values, principles of globalism, and commercial interest. Paul Hooper notes that post–World War II activities raise questions about "how much of this talk is inspired by a genuine sense of internationalism, and how much is rhetorical flourish used to decorate a more traditional concern for ordinary profits."[49]

One prominent advocate for Hawai'i's Pacific role embodies this complexity. A. A. "Bud" Smyser, a well-known editor of one of Honolulu's two daily newspapers, argued in 1989 that Hawai'i must become a "Geneva-type international place" by turning to more non-tourist international activities. Such a role would permit the state to preserve its physical environment, maintain the "aloha spirit," create greater economic prosperity, and make use of its unique culture and Pacific location.[50] Smyser suggested that, to become an international center, the state, among other things, become the hub for air travel and communication, international meetings, Pacific agriculture and aquaculture, international sports competition, health research and fitness, military and diplomatic activities in the Pacific, and educating Asia and Pacific students.[51]

As the islands' historic international orientation has mixed interests and ideals, it also has been strongly elitist in character, a trait not changed by the post World War II involvement of government and educators.[52] None of the internationalist movements were popularly initiated, and none were sustained by grass-roots support.

The most recent embodiments have, however, changed this. The Pacific Voyaging Society was founded in 1973 to promote traditional Polynesian ocean navigation skills. Three years later the first outrigger canoe, named *Hokule'a*, sailed from Hawai'i to Tahiti and back using stars, winds and tides to reach its destinations.[53] A number of boats were built and navigators trained after that, a process that culminated in the spring 1995 convergence of a fleet of outrigger canoes from Pacific nations and cultures at three places in the eastern South Pacific and Hawai'i. This celebration, coming after hundreds of years of separation between Pacific peoples, brought an outpouring of interest throughout the state, suggesting the state's Pacific identity is changing.

Paralleling this, but distinct from it, the emergence of a Native Hawaiian renaissance and sovereignty movement has connected large numbers of Hawaiians with other colonized and displaced Native peoples. These have included not only American Indian tribes, but also Alaskan and Canadian Indians, New Zealand Maori's, and Pacific Islanders. If efforts to shape some form of Native Hawaiian nation are successful, and if that success is aided by connections with other Native peoples, especially those in the Pacific, then it is likely that Hawai'i's identity as a Pacific society will move in directions that earlier ventures in commercialism and multiculturalism may not have foreseen and could not have accommodated.

THE FEDERAL GOVERNMENT AND NATIVE HAWAIIANS

Native Hawaiian-federal relations take place at two levels. One is in the provision of assistance to improve health, increase access to education, and revitalize culture. Analogous to funds allocated to American Indian tribes, in 1994 the state received $79 million in federal monies for a range of services and projects.[54] These allocations have been facilitated by the work of Senator Inouye, until 1994 chair of the Indian Affairs Committee, a "temporary" committee established in 1977 whose life he has been successful in continuing.

At another level, the matter is not about the funding of specific remedial policies and programs, but the role the federal government will play in relation to Native Hawaiian claims. Congress, in the twentieth century, has offered some support for efforts to deal with the consequences for Hawaiians of their loss of land and national sovereignty. The Hawaiian Rehabilitation Act and its land trust, set up in 1920 for the official purpose of repatriating Hawaiians to their lands by means of low cost, long-term leases, embodied the mixed meaning of the federal role.[55]

The act stipulated that individuals who were at least one-half Hawaiian would receive long-term leases of farm land for $1 annually. Subsequently, however, many lands were leased, rented, or exchanged to non-Hawaiians, leaving very little good land for homesteading. These developments became a focal point of questions about whether in practice a higher priority was being given to privileged non-Hawaiian users. In the light of this, a federal-state commission reviewed the homelands program in 1983 and made 134 recommendations for change. These included allowing beneficiaries to sue the state and federal governments for breaches of the trust, swapping land for parcels more amenable to homesteading, and putting $250 million of state and federal money into infrastructure improvements. Few of these were done, or done to the extent recommended.

By 1997, 6,428 families, among the tens of thousands eligible, had been placed on land, the vast majority in residences. The waiting list totaled almost 16,000, and many had been on it for decades.[56] Although administered by the state since Admission, the frustration of thousands of Hawaiians has been a collection point for holding the federal government, participant in the overthrow and rule-maker for the trust, partially responsible.

When Hawaiian activism evolved in the 1970s and 1980s a small island not far off the coast of Maui became a rallying point for those frustrations. Kaho'olawe's size, location, and lack of contemporary inhabitants had made it a convenient bombing site for Navy pilots, a purpose for which it was used in the post World War II period. The island's besieged beauty and array of cultural sites resonated with people of Hawaiian ancestry awakening to their inherited culture and the assaults made on it.

The quest to "Save Kaho'olawe"—to have the bombing stopped and the island returned to Native Hawaiian control—became the work of a small group whose efforts gained momentum. This group's work was helped by support from the congressional delegation, including Senator Inouye, who expressed sympathy for the circumstances of contemporary Hawaiians. Further facilitated by the end of the Cold War, the "Save Kaho'olawe" Ohana had become the official Kaho'olawe Island Conveyance Commission by January 1991. The island came under the control of the Kaho'olawe Island Reserve Commission in January 1994. Operating as a program within the state's Department of Land and Natural Resources, the commission's tedious work of munitions removal and restoration was supported by millions of dollars in Department of Defense funds.

The Kaho'olawe settlement was an important step in the coming of age of a Hawaiian movement, but it did not resolve relations between Hawaiians and the federal government. The twin issues of admission of responsibility for an illegal act committed against a sovereign people, and what follows from that admission, are at the center of that evolving relationship. In 1993, junior Senator Daniel Akaka, a part-Hawaiian, introduced a resolution in commemoration of the 100th anniversary of the overthrow of the Hawaiian Kingdom. Public Law 103–150, approved by both houses and signed by President Clinton, reviews the history of the overthrow, makes reference to the dramatic apology of the President of the United Church of Christ for its role in the overthrow, and then offers the federal government's own "acknowledgment and apology." This statement acknowledges that the fall of the kingdom "resulted in the suppression of the inherent sovereignty of the Native Hawaiian people" and then "apologizes to Native Hawaiians on behalf of the people of the United States for the overthrow of the Kingdom of Hawaii on January 17, 1893 with the participation of agents and citizens of the United States, and the deprivation of the rights of Native Hawaiians to self-determination."[57] The resolution's final words are a disclaimer that follow a definition of Native Hawaiians as any descendent of someone living in the islands prior to Captain Cook's arrival in 1793. The disclaimer is that "Nothing in this Joint Resolution is intended to serve as a settlement of any claims against the United States."

This resolution, of course, can be read differently. In one interpretation, the words are an act of atonement and admission of moral responsibility that reconciles the federal government with an aggrieved people. This atonement and reconciliation might help resolve issues Native Hawaiians have with the state. In another interpretation, this language officially commits the federal government to Native Hawaiian independence by accepting responsibility for an injustice done to a sovereign people.[58]

Senator Akaka, noting that differing interpretations had created conflicts among Hawaiians after the resolution's passage, stated that "I look at the apology resolution as the first step toward healing, not creating new barriers. It is all a matter of perception."[59] Which perception prevails is significant. As a result of Supreme Court decisions in the 1830s, Native American tribes were formally designated to be distinct political societies, free from state control while remaining subordinate to the will of Congress. There are now hundreds of tribes deemed capable of managing their own affairs and occupying the often-conflicted status of "domestic dependent nations," that is, autonomous governments within the legal structure of the federal government. In addition, during the Nixon administration the official policy of the federal government toward Native Americans changed from wardship to self-determination. Rather than working to assimilate tribal peoples into American society—a policy referred to as "termination" since it would end in the disappearance of distinct tribes—their movement toward self-governance now would be supported.[60]

This policy has had little impact on Native Hawaiians because under federal law they are a "racial group" rather than a distinct political society for whom the federal government has a trust responsibility. Thus, on the one hand Hawaiians receive health and educational benefits through the same congressional committees and programs as other Native peoples, but on the other the federal government has not supported their independence or self-determination. To the extent that the apology resolves this contradiction in favor of a trust relationship that supports movement toward Native Hawaiian self-governance, it will act as a catalyst for other steps. Some of those steps have already been taken.

Two years after the apology statement, Congress passed the Hawaiian Home Lands Recovery Act, introduced by Senator Akaka and Representative Abercrombie. The act required the federal government to identify properties taken from the home lands trust without compensation, calculate the income lost to the trust, and then provide as compensation federal properties that have no potential for generating income.

The first exchange agreement was completed in September 1998 when the Department of Hawaiian Home Lands accepted the Navy's proposal to turn over, in July 1999, more than 900 acres, estimated to be worth between $70 and $90 million. The agreement is compensation for 1,350 acres taken by executive order from the Department of Hawaiian Home Lands during the territorial period. The federal government may continue to use thousands of acres of homestead lands at Lualualei and Waimanalo on O'ahu and Kalaupapa on Moloka'i in return for what it has given back.

The agreement is facilitated by the fact that, as with Kaho'olawe, the end of the Cold War has made these lands less strategically important for national defense, and less justifiable to the Department of Defense. The facilities on much of the land to be exchanged, such as the 586 acres at Barbers Point Naval Air Station or the 167 acres at the Omega Tracking Station, are being closed or greatly reduced. The lessened inconvenience to the federal government, however, does not diminish the compensation's significance. Unlike those previously set-aside for homesteading, these are desirable lands in desirable locations, and often include road, electricity and water infrastructure.

Of at least equal importance, the act and the compensation signify federal movement toward re-defining its relationship with Native Hawaiian in the same terms as other Native people's. Senator Inouye, speaking at the agreement ceremony attended by Secretary of Interior Bruce Babbitt, referred to a section of the Lands Recovery Act that mentions "the government's special trust relationship" to Native Hawaiians, and declared "What I want is a clear, definitive acknowledgment by the Justice Department that Native Hawaiians are Native Americans."[61]

Consistent with this sentiment, the federal Western Pacific Regional Fishery Management Council proposed in August 1998 to create allotments for bottom fishing in an area of the northern Hawaiian archipelago. The proposal specifies that 20 percent of the permits issued in the zone around Necker and Nihoa seamounts will go to individuals who can trace their lineage to 1776. The 20 percent figure is based on the estimated proportion of people of Hawaiian heritage currently in the total population.

This is the first special access to fishing resources granted to Hawaiians, and by itself does not mean much. The total value of catch in the zone was less that $450,000 in 1996. However, if the proposal is accepted by the Department of Commerce and made into law, it will be, as one proponent of fishing rights for Hawaiians observed, "the key to opening the door for other fisheries."[62] Equally significant, the set-aside will be another way in which Native Hawaiians have gained ground in receiving from the federal government the compensatory treatment accorded other Native groups, and an instance in which some who are not Hawaiian will experience, in a historically significant reversal, a sense of loss.

CHAPTER FIVE

Constitutional Development

Hawai'i's constitutional story is generally similar to what occurred in other states yet necessarily also stands apart because it is the only state that evolved from a constitutional monarchy. That remarkable period saw constitutions written and then abandoned as part of the struggle over what kind of society Hawai'i would become and who would control it.

Hawai'i's story is also distinct, though not unique, because its statehood constitutional history began so recently and, consequently, the form into which it will evolve has had less time to be established. Still, even in its span of less than fifty years it is possible to detect patterns. What began as a relatively brief, framework-setting document has become much more specific and detailed, its provisions at times appearing more legislative than constitutional.

The capacity of constitutions and constitutional provisions to transcend the political climate that produced their adoption is what renders them fundamental documents. Whether or not a particular constitution has that capacity is always a question. Because Hawai'i's constitution mandates its re-examination on a regular basis, the challenge of resolving tensions between provisions that are broad or specific, and between preservation and adaptation, can be expected to be a periodic source of both stress and creativity.

THE SOCIAL AND POLITICAL FUNCTIONS OF CONSTITUTIONS

Constitutions are defined in a variety of ways. Some describe them simply as the basic law of a government. Often this definition is expanded to include the fundamental principles that determine the structure and function of government, both written and unwritten.[1] Constitutions in the United States contain a bill of rights and a description of a government's structure and functions.

Carl J. Friedrich, a well known constitutional scholar, identified five general attributes of constitutions: philosophical (they lay out values and aspirations), structural (they posit governmental structures), legal (they frame laws), documentarian (they are documents of a society at a given historical moment), and procedural (they stipulate how government should proceed.)[2]

Constitutions also may be viewed as efforts on the part of polities to solve various fundamental and recurring problems, many of which are sufficiently common to seem universal. Failure to solve these problems can plunge society into the chaos of civil war.

One such problem is the issue of membership: who shall be considered a citizen and who shall not? This has been an issue through much of Hawai'i's history, and looms as a central problem in decisions surrounding Hawaiian sovereignty.

Another basic constitutional problem involves issues of succession. How shall one political regime succeed another? Prior to the modern constitutional age—which begins with the so called "glorious revolution" in Britain in 1688 and takes full force with the advent of the U.S. constitutional efforts in the American colonies, including the Articles of Confederation —many, perhaps most, wars had their sources in dynastic conflicts over succession to the throne. Republics were distinguished in part by their efforts to develop a public and regularized process of succession sufficiently legitimate for the basic rule structure not to break down with the death of a powerful and/or popular leader.

Constitutions also embody decisions on how governance is to be organized: will there be a centralized and unitary set of powers, or should public authority be dispersed and decentralized? The history of constitutional analysis, from Aristotle forward, is rich with advice about various mechanisms and structures of governance and administration.

A related set of debates about how power will be inscribed in the constitutional framework concerns issues of representation. Some scholars place representational issues at the center of the constitutional calculus, along with questions of succession, because these issues determine who "gets to play" in the processes of government. Conflicts over representation have occurred throughout Hawai'i's history, and now re-appear, among other places, in relation to creating more local government.

Finally, by its provisions and assumptions, a constitution signals the basic relationship of various societal sectors. For example, is property to be privately held, and, if so, when may the state restrict its uses? Is the government to have the authority to intrude in private wealth relations, and if so, to

Table 3: The Constitutions of Hawai'i

Year of Adoption	Name of chief promulgator	Major characteristics	Reasons for Change
1840	Kamehameha III	Bicameral legislature; Supreme Court; Bill of Rights	*Haole* pressure to produce a more "American Constitution"
1852	Kamehameha III	Universal suffrage, annual elections to lower house; repeals property qualifications for voting	King's desire to restrict the democratic character and enhance power of monarch
1864	Kamehameha V	Restricts suffrage, extends power of monarch vs. legislature, unicameral legislature	Pressure from *Haole* advisors and others to limit power of monarch
1887	Bayonet Constitution	Restricts power of the Monarch to act without legislative concurrence	Replaced by Republican Constitution upon overthrow
1893	Constitution of the Republic	Created a republic with governor elected by legislature	Replaced by Organic Act with Territorial Status
1900	Organic Act	Written and passed by U.S. Congress to govern Territory	Abolished by pre-statehood Constitution whose sole purpose was to gain U.S. admission
1950	Hopechest Constitution	Modeled after other U.S. state constitutions. Creates strong chief executive	With minor modifications became the first state Constitution upon statehood
1959	Statehood Constitution		First official statehood constitution
1968	Constitutional convention	Addressed voter reapportionment. Proposed 23 amendments, among them dropped literacy requirements	Changes reflect delegate consensus and voter ratification
1978	Constitutional convention	Creates Office of Hawaiian Affairs; 18 year olds can vote	Changes reflect delegate agreements and voter ratification
1986	Vote on Constitutional convention	Voters reject constitutional convention	

Year of Adoption	Name of chief promulgator	Major characteristics	Reasons for Change
1996	Vote on Constitutional convention	Constitutional convention vote is ambiguous because of spoiled ballots	Supreme Court rules that voters did not approve a convention
1998	Vote on Constitutional convention	Voters reject constitutional convention. Strong opposition from groups concerned that convention will be taken over by single interest coalitions	

what extent? If there are constituent units within a polity, what is to be their relationship—with each other, and with the central government? What will be the rights of individuals against the state? How will the forms of organized religion be recognized? In nineteenth-century Hawai'i the Protestant, Catholic, and Mormon churches fought among one another for exclusive access to the islands, sometimes attempting to use the authority of the kingdom's government in support of their cause.

CONSTITUTIONAL EVOLUTION IN HAWAI'I

Hawai'i's constitutions may be seen through two lenses, one appropriate for a process of nation formation under the Kingdom of Hawai'i, the other relevant to the challenges of territoriality and statehood. Each, however, reflects the political realignments and political culture present at particular points in the history of the islands. As influential actors have changed—from kingdom through to statehood—this basic document of governance has been altered to reflect a shifting blend of principles and relations of power.

Hawai'i has had, by a generous counting, eight constitutions, with the last, the statehood constitution of 1959, being amended by constitutional conventions in 1968 and 1978 (table 3).

The initial period of constitutional development culminated with the writing of the constitution of 1840. Although this was the first official and formal definition of government powers in the islands, the framework for a constitution-based government of some kind had been prepared during the previous two decades.

Prelude to the First Constitution

Government was autocratic under King Kamehameha I. It was complex in structure, but representative of the institutional fluidity that characterized the islands before and after their unification. In a pattern recognizable throughout Polynesia, Kamehameha I ruled through a Council of Chiefs, even though his authority was nearly absolute. The king shared power with the *kuhina-nui,* a sort of chief executive officer or regent, whose primary purpose was to advise the king and to provide symbolic representation to the people. The *kuhina-nui* was the highest ranking female in the kingdom. Established by Kamehameha I, the *kuhina-nui* was significantly strengthened under Kamehameha II and Kamehameha III. By 1838, political authority was divided between the king, the *kuhina-nui,* and the Council of Chiefs.

During the 1820s and the 1830s a convergence of economic, cultural, and religious forces generated governmental and constitutional reform. Much of the early pressure for constitutional codification lay in the conflict that developed between the monarchy and the Catholic Church. Ka'ahumanu, the *kuhina-nui* under the first three Kamehamehas, was a powerful leader and personality during her period of influence. Later in her life, she also became a close friend of the Protestant missionaries and herself a strong Christian.[3]

Ka'ahumanu exercised her influence at various times either to restrict or to remove Catholic priests from the islands. Because these were most often French subjects, her acts sparked conflict with their government, culminating, after Ka'ahumanu had passed from the scene, in the French extracting by threat an agreement from Kamehameha III to protect the rights of Catholics. The French also used this occasion to induce the king to sign an additional agreement several days later that limited his ability to prosecute French subjects. To round off this constraint on Hawaiian sovereignty, the agreement limited the duty the kingdom could place on imported French wines and brandies.[4] In 1836, the British also secured agreements protecting British subjects. Although legally ambiguous, these agreements were assumed to provide some protection for the property used by British merchants, and thereby ensure stable trade relations.

The Hawaiian chiefs were, by the 1830s, coming to realize that they could benefit from better, more consistent guidance on political and economic matters. In 1836, the chiefs asked their American friends to send them "a teacher of the chiefs in what pertains to the land, according to the practice of enlightened countries," specifically the subjects of economics and political science.[5] Protestant missionary William Richards was recruited for the task after some searching, and, beginning on July 3, 1838, gave daily lectures to the

chiefs on matters of politics and economics. Through 1838 and the first part
of 1839, the king, *kuhina-nui,* chiefs and advisors, under Richards' influence, developed the Declaration of Rights and Laws of 1839. Some have
called the 1839 declaration the Hawaiian Magna Carta, for it was the first
voluntary concession of rights to his people by the king.

The Declaration of Rights and Laws of 1839, which was embodied in the
constitution of 1840, provided a number of protections that would look familiar to people from Western political, and religious, traditions. The document reads, in part:

> God hath made of one blood all nations of men, to dwell on the face of the
> earth in unity and blessedness. God has also bestowed certain rights alike on
> all men, and all chiefs, and all people of the lands.
>
> These are some of the rights which he has given alike to every man and ev-
> ery chief, life, limb, liberty, the labor of his hands, and the productions of his
> mind.
>
> God has also established governments and rule for the purposes of peace,
> but in making laws for a nation it is by no means proper to enact laws for the
> protection of rulers only, without also providing protection for their subjects;
> neither is it proper to enact laws to enrich the chiefs only, without regard to en-
> riching their subjects also; and hereafter, there shall by no means be any law
> enacted which is inconsistent with what is above expressed, neither shall any
> tax be assessed or any service or labor required of any man at variance with the
> above sentiments.
>
> These sentiments are hereby proclaimed for purpose of protecting alike,
> both the people and the chiefs of all these islands, that no chief may be able to
> oppress any subject, but that chiefs and people may enjoy the same protection
> under one and the same law.
>
> Protection is hereby secured to all persons of all the people, together with
> their lands, their building lots and all their property, and nothing whatever
> shall be taken from any individual except by express provisions of the laws.
> Whatever chief shall perseveringly act in violation of this Constitution shall no
> longer remain a chief of the Sandwich Islands and the same shall be true of all
> governors, officers, and all land agents.[6]

The Constitution of 1840

The first written constitution was completed in 1840 by King Kamehameha
III and his chiefs, with the help of their Western adviser, and was signed by
the king and his *kuhina-nui*. Through it the kingdom moved formally toward

constitutional monarchy. The constitution codified existing governmental agreements and practices, including the Declaration of 1839 and a hereditary House of Nobles (or Council of Chiefs). It created a bicameral legislature by adding an elected House of Representatives (or House of Commoners) although there was no guidance on how many representatives would sit in the House or how they were to be elected. The constitution did stipulate that the two houses could sit together or separately, and that any laws they passed must be approved by a majority of each house and signed by the king and the *kuhina-nui*.[7]

In the fall of 1840, after the signing of the constitution, the chiefs convened in council in Lahaina and passed the first election law. They set seven as the number of members in this new House of Representatives, declared that voting for representatives would consist of letters of nomination addressed to the king, and decided that the person named most frequently in these letters would be an Island's representative.[8]

The constitution of 1840 provided for freedom of religion, the right to a lawful trial, and the right against self-incrimination. It also created a supreme court to settle increasingly common and complex legal disputes. The court was composed of the king and the *kuhina-nui*, with four additional judges to be appointed by the House of Representatives.

Although the 1840 Constitution was a codification of existing practices and did not fundamentally alter the authority of the king, *kuhina-nui*, or the chiefs it did reflect political and social changes occurring in the islands. Autocracy was slowly giving way to a tri-part government based on ancient Hawaiian customs, particularly royal ownership of the land. Kamehameha I, II, and III firmly believed they had not transferred rights to land in their ongoing negotiations with foreign traders. The foreigners as well as some part-Hawaiian businesspersons assumed or hoped otherwise and soon began applying pressure for reforms to provide greater security for the properties they used. These influences, along with the input from American missionaries knowledgeable about their homeland's constitutional and commercial practices, are what lead to the incorporation of familiar Western principles in the Constitution of 1840.

The Constitution of 1852

The new constitution's inability to establish a system of government capable of adapting to the changes taking place in Hawai'i's political and economic life became apparent during the 1840s. A number of amendments attempted to bring it up to date, but, as seen by historian Ralph Kuykendall, the constitution did not "allow sufficient freedom for the political growth of the country."[9] Unlike the first constitution, which was written by the king and his chiefs, the initiative for change this time came from the new legislature. The legislature proposed a commission, and in 1851 approved three commissioners, to be appointed by the king, the House of Nobles, and the House of Representatives, for the purpose of making recommendations on the kingdom's constitution.

The commissioners were instructed to provide their recommendations for revision to the 1852 legislative session. The recommendations were written primarily by the *haole* Supreme Court Chief Justice William Lee—the commissioner put forward by the House of Representatives—and reflected his "American and democratic point of view."[10] The proposed revisions resulted in an almost entirely new document. The commissioners presented their proposals early in 1852. After being heavily amended, they were approved by the legislature and signed by the king on June 14, 1852.

The constitution adopted in 1852 displayed two sources of external influence. Kuykendall saw that it particularly revealed "the influence of American political ideas" in its sense of an expanded suffrage.[11] It also, however, was much influenced by R. C. Wylie, an admirer of the British constitution, whose primary contribution to the continuing discourse on Hawaiian constitutionalism was the principle that the constitution may be abrogated by the sitting monarch.[12]

The new constitution expanded the Bill of Rights, and membership in the House of Nobles changed from being hereditary to lifetime appointment by the king. The three branches of government, which previously had been only partially separated, now were defined more clearly in relation to one another, thus placing greater checks on the actions of the monarch.

The addition of universal male suffrage was an important change that would prove to be a source of constitutional strife. Beginning in 1852, men 20 years of age or older could participate in annual elections for the House of Representatives. Ownership of property was no longer a requirement for voting. These were surprisingly liberal provisions compared with constitutional developments in other nations during the same period.

The 1852 constitution also dictated that all revenue bills, those requiring the raising or spending of money, originate within the House of Representatives, adding fuel to the potential fire of conflicting interests in Hawai'i society. Two years before, in 1850, the legislature passed and the king signed a law stipulating the use of secret ballots. The secret ballot, universal male suffrage, and the power of the House of Representatives to originate revenue bills subsequently placed the greatest constraints on the king and his advisors.

During the 1850s, the House of Nobles frequently was in conflict with the popularly elected House of Representatives, as was the king, especially over money matters. These conflicts led the king and his advisors to conclude that the House of Representatives needed some kind of check or restraining influence put upon it.[13]

The Constitution of 1864

When King Kamehameha V ascended the throne in 1863, he opposed the universal suffrage provisions, advocating property qualifications for voters as well as members of the House of Representatives. (On this issue, see also chapter 6.) At a more basic level, he believed that "the prerogatives of the Crown ought to be more carefully protected . . . and that the influence of the Crown ought to be seen pervading every function of government."[14]

The constitution of 1852 had been amended several times before July 7, 1864, the date the new king assembled a constitutional convention. Made up of the king, the 15 members of the House of Nobles, and 26 elected delegates, the 1864 convention's charge was to focus on correcting some of the "excesses" of democracy in the 1852 constitution. By the middle of August, this body was dead-locked. Its members could agree on a literacy requirement for voting, but the elected delegates would not accept a property qualification, and the king and nobles could not tolerate its absence.[15]

In response to the impasse, the king dissolved the convention, abrogated the constitution of 1852, and declared that he would provide a new constitution. Kamehameha V stated, in a revealing speech given to explain his actions:

> As I said the other day, this [voting] is not a right belonging to the people, as some here have said. I have told you, and my ministers have also told you, that in other monarchical countries, suffrage is limited, and it is thought that the possession of property is proof of industry and thrift, therefore in those enlightened countries it is said that class who possess property are the proper persons to advise the representatives in the regard to the necessities of government, and the poor, lazy, and ignorant are debarred from this privilege.
>
> It is clear to me if universal suffrage is permitted, this government will soon lose its monarchical character . . . I make known today that the constitution of 1852 is abrogated. I will give you a constitution.[16]

The king met with his advisers, together with Supreme Court Associate

Justice George Robertson, for several days after his announcement, during which time the nation was not governed by a written constitution. The new constitution was presented on August 20, 1864, when King Kamehameha V signed it and declared Hawai'i's third constitution the fundamental law of the land.

The constitutions of 1852 and 1864 were alike in many respects, but their differences were also significant. The office of *kuhina-nui* was abolished, and the House of Nobles and House of Representatives were combined into a legislative assembly. The king was no longer required to seek the advice and counsel of the chiefs, or nobles, and he acquired the authority to veto the new chamber's legislation. The cabinet became directly subject to the will of the king.

The constitution of 1864, of course, withdrew from the principle of universal suffrage, forcing a settlement on the heated deadlock of the unsuccessful convention. The vote now was predicated on a property qualification of real property valued at $150, or an income of $75 per year. Additionally, voters born after 1840 were required to demonstrate an ability to read and write.[17] Overall, the Constitution of 1864, a more simplified document, substantially strengthened the authority of the king by changing the constituency basis of the legislature and permitting him to act more forcefully in his executive capacity.

The Bayonet Constitution of 1887

The role played by *haoles* in the life of the Hawaiian nation continued to expand in the period after the 1864 constitution. Economic and political relations were changing in response to the consolidation of sugar as the islands' primary production crop. These changes affected implementation of the constitution of 1864, sowing seeds of social conflict that led ultimately to the Bayonet Constitution.[18]

By the 1880s, the business community, composed overwhelmingly of American and British *haoles,* had grown unhappy with King Kalakaua, a skillful politician, popular among Native Hawaiians, who had assumed office in 1874. The legislature, in turn, was dominated by Native Hawaiians whom the *haole* business community felt were not responsive to their interests. Several proposals advanced by the legislature for the benefit of the whole of the population were considered "extravagant and wild" by the business community.

Members of the *haole* elite perceived themselves increasingly to be the source of the kingdom's wealth—and tax revenues—and were determined to realign political structures to match their increasingly dominant economic power. Merze Tate observed that "The capitalist class long had been apprehensive over the absence of representation of their capital in the legislative assembly and their inability to control appropriations . . . with the unprecedented prosperity and industrial expansion incident to reciprocity, the disparity between invested capital and political power became more pronounced, for American capital in Hawaii increased more rapidly than did the American population."[19]

These conflicting interests and points of view led to a constitutional crisis and the so-called Bayonet Constitution of 1887. The Hawaiian League, a collection of planters' interests and paramount organizer of the crisis, was willing to brush aside the legal niceties surrounding imposition of the new constitution, believing desperate times required desperate solutions. A new cabinet was appointed—made up largely of League activists—and it set about writing a new document.

Working day and night, they quickly drafted a new constitution and convinced King Kalakaua he must sign it on July 6, 1887. For Lorrin Thurston, one of its primary architects, "Unquestionably the Constitution was not in accordance with the law; neither was the Declaration of Independence from Great Britain. Both were revolutionary documents, that had to be forcibly effected and forcibly maintained."[20]

The constitution stripped the monarchy of important sources of authority. Cabinet members would still be appointed by the king, but could only be removed by a vote of the majority of the legislature or upon conviction of a felony. The legislature now could override an executive veto. The king remained the commander in chief of the kingdom's military forces, but those powers could be exercised only with the consent of the legislature.

A bicameral legislature was restored, with both houses being elected. Membership of the House of Nobles was increased from twenty to twenty-four. No longer appointed by the king, they were required to own taxable property worth $3,000, or to have an income of not less than $600 per year, requirements that, given the economics of the day, ensured that only substantial men of property would be selected. More modest property qualifications were also required of candidates for the House of Representatives, who needed to own real estate worth at least $500, or have an annual income of at least $250.

Defining electoral constituencies with a comparable class bias, the financial requirements to be a member of the House of Nobles also were put in place to qualify to vote in elections for nobles. This stipulation virtually assured that the upper house would be controlled by *haoles*, Native Hawaiians being unable, for the most part, to meet the property requirements. Finally, the framers of the constitution of 1887 revealed their growing apprehension about the political threat from their own imported labor force, permitting voting rights to be exercised by male residents of Hawaiian, American, or European birth or descent, but not by Chinese or Japanese.

The Failed Constitution

Queen Lili'uokalani, who came to power in 1891, was not satisfied with the constitution of 1887, and sought to return power to the monarchy. Her feelings became broadly known and in an effort to "be ready to act quickly and intelligently, should Lili'uokalani precipitate the necessity by some move against the Constitution," a small group of *haole* businessmen with significant investments in the islands formed the Annexation Club.[21] The constitutional crisis erupted in the first days of 1893 as the queen prepared to proclaim a new constitution that would restore many powers of the monarchy, in particular permitting the monarch to act in various arenas without legislative concurrence. As the queen wrote later, "Let it be repeated: the promulgation of a new Constitution, adapted to the needs of the times and demands of the people, has been an indisputable prerogative of the Hawaiian monarchy."[22]

At the point the new constitution was to be promulgated, two of Lili'uokalani's new cabinet members, with loyalties to the business community, refused to sign the document. Her opponents were quick to act. The crisis quickly escalated and by the 17th of January, the Committee of Public Safety proclaimed the monarchy dissolved, took over the government building, and announced that a provisional government would run the country under the leadership of Sanford Dole until annexation by the United States. Under protest, the queen yielded to the forces allied against her. In her statement she said, "to avoid any collision of armed forces and perhaps the loss of life, I do this under protest, and impelled by said force, yield my authority until such time as the government of the United States shall, upon the facts being presented to it, undo the action of its representatives and reinstate me to the authority which I claim as the Constitutional sovereign of the Hawaiian Islands."[23]

The queen had, in fact, temporarily surrendered to the United States government—not to the revolutionaries.

A New Government

The provisional government applied for annexation to the United States, but this request was denied after an investigation ordered by President Cleveland. The investigation concluded that the queen represented the lawful government of the Hawaiian Islands and that the monarchy should be restored. The provisional government ignored this recommendation, instead authorizing a constitutional convention on March 15, 1894. Sanford Dole, in a letter to the American political scientist John W. Burgess, requested advice on setting up a government that had a strong executive, an upper house with limited membership, and other characteristics designed to keep it "out of the control of the irresponsible elements."[24] Participation in this constitutional convention was limited to Hawaiians, and Americans or those of European birth and descent who were twenty years of age, or taxpayers, and had been residents for a year. The primary objective of this scheme was to limit the participation of Asians and Hawaiians. The new constitution was adopted without popular vote, and on July 4, 1894, the Republic of Hawaii was established.

The new government included a bicameral legislature, a governor appointed by the legislature, a cabinet and council of state, and a judiciary. Property requirements were retained as a voting qualification for members of the upper house. In addition, literacy requirements, introduced in the United States as part of the Jim Crow laws designed to disenfranchise black voters, were imposed, requiring demonstration of literacy in either Hawaiian or English. Chinese and Japanese persons were not allowed to become citizens, unless they were born in Hawai'i.

The Organic Act

On July 7, 1898, President McKinley, Cleveland's successor, signed a joint resolution of Congress authorizing U.S. annexation of the islands. It provided that a special commission made up of five people be appointed by the president and charged with drafting an Organic Act for the new territorial government. The five commissioners included two U.S. senators, one member of the House, and two Hawai'i residents—Sanford Dole and Walter Frear, Supreme Court Justice and businessperson, a "*haole* elite representative par excellence."[25]

The commissioners worked on the Organic Act for roughly two months, submitting their draft to Congress in December 1898. American statutes gave the Organic Act the status of the fundamental law for the territory, which meant, in effect, that Congress could alter Hawai'i's government and its relations with the rest of the Union. Constitutional authority had not only passed from the monarchy; in the course of seven years it had come to reside partially in an external authority. The Organic Act was passed by Congress on April 30, 1900, and when President McKinley signed it on June 13, Hawai'i officially became a territory of the United States.

The Organic Act retained many of the central elements that were part of previous Hawaiian constitutions. A citizenship provision permitted all persons who were citizens of Hawai'i on August 12, 1898, to become citizens of the Territory of Hawai'i and the United States. By this provision, the approximately 40,000 Hawaiians and part-Hawaiians living in the islands became citizens, but the vast majority of Chinese and Japanese immigrants did not. Income and property requirements for voting were eliminated by the Congress, overturning the commission's recommendation to retain them. Literacy requirements, however, were retained and specified speaking, reading and writing in either English or Hawaiian. Eligible voters had to be U.S. citizens, 21 years of age, and male.[26] Consequently, immigrant Asians were disenfranchised and barred from territorial politics, as they had effectively been kept out of the public life of the kingdom and republic. The Organic Act provided that Hawai'i would elect and send a non-voting territorial delegate to the U.S. House of Representatives.

Although the territorial legislature would be elected, the governor of the new territory, as well as the territorial secretary, supreme court and circuit court justices, were to be appointed by the president of the United States with the advice and consent of the Senate. The territorial governor was a constitutionally strong officer. The governor was given veto power over legislation passed by the territorial legislature, including a line-item veto. The governor, was, furthermore, not popularly elected and unimpeachable, which meant that local opinion could be ignored at will. And, whoever occupied Washington Place was handed the major tool for building political loyalty: patronage. The territorial governor was provided the power to make the myriad appointments characteristic of mayors and county officials throughout the United States.

As noted previously, in many ways these executive powers exceeded those of the American president. The territorial governor could, for example, suspend the writ of habeas corpus and impose martial law in any part of the territory. The fiscal powers of this office were perhaps the most extensive in the United States; in addition to the line-item veto, the governor could extend legislative sessions if requested appropriations were not forthcoming.

Government authority remained centralized in Honolulu, as it had been for the previous fifty years. This centralization was fully evident in the Organic Act, which placed under the direct power of the territorial governor residing in Honolulu most of the activities normally assigned to counties in other United States jurisdictions.[27]

CONSTITUTION FORMING AND STATEHOOD:
THE HOPE CHEST CONSTITUTION

The period spanned by implementation of the Organic Act and maturation of the movement toward statehood was, as related in chapter 2, defined by issues surrounding centralized authority, land, and ethnic diversity. The constitutional dimension lay in the work, successful after several failed efforts, to develop a document capable of gaining congressional support for admission to the union.

In 1949 the territorial legislature passed an act for a convention to write a constitution that could be used to persuade Congress that Hawai'i was ready for statehood. Fifteen other territories seeking admission had modeled state-like behavior prior to this, and later Alaska would do the same.[28]

The legislature specified that 63 delegates should be chosen, and 243 candidates filed to run for the spots available. Interest in the election was high. Both major parties endorsed non-partisan candidates, and 79 percent of registered voters cast ballots in the second of a two-stage process. The elected delegates came from diverse occupational and ethnic backgrounds, though both professionals and Caucasians were over-represented. Of the 63 delegates, only 5 were women.[29]

The convention assembled in April and completed its work in July. After approval by the legislature, the proposed document was given to the voters, who approved it by a ratio of more than 3 to 1. The 1950 Constitution—which came to be known as the Hope Chest Constitution—became, with a few minor changes, the state's new constitution when statehood came in 1959.

The document produced by the 1950 convention was short compared to other state constitutions, and contains about 14,000 words. Its brevity and commitment to laying out frameworks and general principles was consistent with thinking about constitution-making then current among experts, which was not surprising since "proponents of statehood deemed it important to their cause to have a proposed Constitution incorporating the latest thinking about good government."[30] The ability of its drafters to avoid details and focus on what seemed essential brought praise for the product. It set, according to the National Municipal League, "a new high standard in the writing of a modern state constitution by a convention."[31]

Much that is familiar in the United States Constitution, its Bill of Rights for example, and other states constitutions is found in the 1950 constitution. It also incorporated parts of the Organic Act. Its noteworthy progressive provisions included establishing a voting age of 21, one year below that in most other states; rejection of segregation in any state military organization; the short ballot; and commitments to the federal Native Hawaiian homesteading program and to trust obligations.

The literacy requirements of previous constitutions were retained—these would not be removed until the 1968 constitutional convention. Reflecting the temper of the times, the 1950 convention had duly considered the reforms of the initiative, referendum, recall, and a unicameral legislature, and rejected them all—thereby seeming to set the limits of the delegate's enthusiasm for democratic reform.

The constitution provided for managerial efficiency by limiting the number of executive agencies to 20 and concentrating power at the top—in the governor's office. This stroke of public administration enthusiasm would prove a significant challenge for the new state government a few years later. The sometimes haphazard arrangements of the territorial period required a considerable re-working of departments, boards, and commissions to put in place the more restrictive categories of the new state government model. As a consequence, the first order of business for the charter state administration in 1960 was a massive reorganization.

The constitution created a merit-based civil service system. In addition, although the 1950 document did not recognize collective bargaining for public employees—this was added later—they were given the right to organize and make their grievances known. Workers in the private sector were accorded a constitutional basis for organizing and bargaining collectively.

Two features of the 1950 constitution especially reflected the political culture of the islands and the times in which it was written. First, it continued the tradition of highly centralized government, now on the state level. Under the Hawaiian Kingdom, the Republic of Hawaii, and the Organic Act governing the territory, local governments played a very limited role in governance. Although the 1950 constitution authorized counties to adopt charters, subject to guidelines set by the legislature, the content of these charters, and the ability of county governments to raise revenues, required legislative approval (see chapter 10).

Centralization is evident in the organization of the state executive branch. The 1950 constitution provided for the election of two state officials, the governor and a lieutenant governor, the latter having little authority. Most of the departments were given single heads appointed by the governor, the governor was given authority to reapportion the lower house and to appoint, subject to legislative approval, judicial officers.

The budget authority given the governor also served to place that office in a pivotal role in the policy process. The governor would directly supervise the Department of Budget and Finance, the most powerful department in state government. The governor also would retain the line-item veto, subject to being over-ridden by a two-thirds legislative majority. Perhaps the most important budgetary power would rest in the governor's authority to withhold appropriated funds from departments. This power, over the years, has permitted the governor to establish budgetary priorities virtually on his own authority, at times thwarting legislative intent. (The significance of the budgetary process for the Hawai'i governor is examined in detail in chapter 8.)

The second feature, characteristic of the times, was loyalty oaths. When the delegates convened the United States was in the midst of a campaign against a perceived communist menace. This climate of suspicion, along with the need to look at least as "American" as people on the mainland, affected the convention's work from the beginning.[32] Richard M. Kageyama resigned in its early stages, stating that he did not wish to imperil the work of the convention since he earlier had testified to membership in the Communist party before the House Un-American Activities Committee. Shortly after that the delegates set-up a special committee to investigate whether another member, Frank G. Silva, should retain his seat after his refusal to testify under oath before the same House committee. Although he argued that his refusal was a matter of principle, and not a cover for communist party membership, the delegates voted 53 to 7 to expel him. The governor appointed delegates to the two vacant positions.

The presence of Hawai'i's powerful trade unions and highly visible Asian immigrant population underscored the delegates' need to propose rules for governance that left unquestioned allegiance to the United States. Consequently, the 1950 constitution prohibited from public office or employment anyone belonging to an organization advocating the overthrow of government by violence or force, and required that all public officials take a oath of loyalty.

CONSTITUTIONAL REVISIONS

The Hope Chest constitution contained an unusual provision regarding future constitutional conventions. It stated that amendments may be made either by constitutional convention or by the state legislature—with voter approval. In accordance with this, it directed the legislature to submit periodically to voters for approval the question, "Shall there be a convention to propose a revision of or amendment to the constitution?" Should the legislature fail to do this within a ten-year period, the question would be placed on the ballot by the lieutenant governor.

Constitutional Conventions

Voters have approved two constitutional conventions, in 1968 and 1978, and rejected three others since the islands achieved statehood.

Reapportionment was the motivation for the 1968 convention.[33] In 1964 the United States Supreme Court held, in *Reynolds v. Sims,* that representation in both chambers of a state's legislature must be based upon the principle of one person-one vote. The Hawai'i Attorney General decided that both the house and senate were apportioned unconstitutionally, but the Supreme Court decided that only the rules for the senate were invalid. The court asked the legislature to solve the problem, and the governor attempted to help it do so, but legislators were not able to reach agreement.

During the same period, the federal district court reached a similar conclusion regarding the senate's rules. This court instructed the legislature to devise an interim plan, but also to place on the ballot the question of a constitutional convention to establish a permanent districting plan. The court declared that if, for some reason, the convention failed to adopt a reapportionment plan, or to adopt one that met the one person-one vote principle, it would take on that responsibility.

Despite the governor's argument that the legislature should deal with the reapportionment problem, two-thirds of those voting in the November 1968 election approved formation of a convention.

The legislative act establishing the 1968 con con, as it came to be called, increased the number of delegates from 63 to 82. The number of candidates grew from 243 in 1950 to 378 in 1968, but participation in the election dropped from 79 to 45 percent of registered voters.

Representation at this convention was dominated by legislators, not surprising given the main item on the agenda. Forty-five incumbent legislators from the 76 member legislature filed as candidates, and 37 were elected. Their number, combined with five previously elected representatives, gave them a 51 percent majority.

The backgrounds of the delegates reflected aspects of the political landscape besides the apportionment problem. In 1950, 30 percent of the delegates were of Japanese ancestry, while by 1968 this figure had increased to 46 percent. Reflecting the same forces, the proportion of Caucasians declined from 43 to 27 percent. Filipinos and Koreans appeared for the first time. Although delegates are formally nonpartisan, observers estimated that the 1968 convention was dominated by Democrats, while 18 years earlier the reverse was true. And, in 1968 Richard Kageyama, who the first time around had resigned because of his appearance before the House Un-American Activities Committee, was present as a delegate.

Reapportionment issues occupied much of the work of the delegates. House districts were now to be developed on the basis of an average of 4,966 registered voters each, while Senate districts numbered 10,130.[34] (For more on the significance of this issue, see chapter 9.) Delegates looked beyond devising this immediate formula for realigning districts and adopted a system for reapportionment every eight years that took this responsibility away from the governor. The convention recommended, and the voters approved, the appointment of a bipartisan nine-member reapportionment commission that would convene to recommend districting changes consistent with shifts in the registered voter base in the islands.

The delegates worked on other issues beside apportionment. Most of these constituted what Norm Meller called "pruning and grafting," and did not touch on the philosophy or purpose of government. Others, however, were more significant.[35] Included in this group was the right of public sector employees to bargain collectively and strike, a stronger protection against the state's invasion of privacy, the legal representation of indigent defendants, and the shift to annual 60-day legislative sessions.[36] The 1968 constitutional convention also eliminated the long-standing English or Hawaiian literacy requirement, thus extending the voting privilege to many older immigrants who lacked formal schooling.

Altogether, the 1968 convention adopted 23 amendments—22 of which were approved by Hawai'i voters. The single amendment that failed would have extended voting rights to 18 year olds, a provision that would be adopted in 1978.

Another important outcome of the con con, one which would be seen again in 1978, is its role as an incubator and springboard for public figures. Among those who participated in the convention and later became important public figures statewide were Nelson Doi, a future lieutenant governor; Nadao Yoshinaga, a powerful figure in the legislature and Democratic party; Frank Fasi, long-time mayor of the City and County of Honolulu; Pat Saiki,

United States Representative and candidate for governor; and George Ariyoshi, lieutenant governor and governor.

The legislature placed the question of a second constitutional convention
before the voters in a special election in November 1976. Three out of four
thought it a good idea, but not due to a specific issue that needed to be re-
solved. Instead, their support was based on a more general feeling that a periodic review makes sense, as well as the result of promotion by single issue
groups that wanted to use the convention to give constitutional standing to
their views.[37]

The legislative act establishing the convention increased the total number of
delegates to 102, up from 63 in 1950 and 82 in 1968. Even though the number
of candidates increased substantially again, this time to 697, the turnout of
registered voters to elect delegates continued to drop, falling to 35 percent.[38]

The composition of the 1978 convention was distinctly different from its
predecessor. One stark contrast was in the number of state legislators. Where
more than one-half of legislative incumbents had run for delegate in 1968,
only two did this time. They both were elected, and when combined with
two others who once had held office and one sitting member of the city council, the total number of individuals with legislative experience was only five.

These delegates were different in other ways as well. In comparison to
both previous conventions, they were younger; less professional; and, when
30 women were elected, much more diversified with respect to gender.

The ethnic backgrounds of the delegates remained relatively stable, despite the other changes.[39] Japanese Americans were the largest group, followed by Caucasians. The number of part-Hawaiians increased over 1978, a
significant shift that both reflected the early stages of Hawaiian activism and
had a direct impact on the convention's work.[40] African-Americans (2) and
Samoans (1) were represented for the first time.

The delegates extensively debated the initiative, referendum, recall, and
a unicameral legislature, and defeated all four. They did, however, reach
agreement on 116 amendments that covered every article of the existing state
constitution, and produced two more. All of the proposed changes were approved by voters in November 1978. Most were cosmetic, technical (what
some refer to as constitutional housekeeping), or superlegislative in character, the latter serving to move the Hawai'i constitution away from the lean
form in which it originally was cast. Others, however, had greater significance. Many changes reflected the concerns of the Palaka Power majority, a
loosely knit group who saw themselves protecting Island culture, local people, and Hawai'i as a special place (see chapter 3).

The revised constitution included a tax review commission, established a statewide water resources agency, protected agricultural land, gave local governments authority over real property taxes, limited the governor and lieutenant governor to two consecutive four-year terms, adopted the open primary, placed limits on government expenditures, gave the university somewhat greater autonomy, and required the state to share the costs of programs mandated to the counties.

The more unusual provisions guaranteed each resident a clean and healthful environment, and committed government to greater openness. The bill of rights added a specific right to privacy. For Hawaiians and Hawaiian culture, the Office of Hawaiian Affairs was created as a semi-independent state agency that would control ceded lands income, the Hawaiian homes program was strengthened, Hawaiian was designated as an official language of the state and Hawaiian culture was required to be taught in public school classrooms, traditional and customary practices were protected, and the Hawaiian language state motto received constitutional status.

Like its predecessor, an important by-product of this convention was the public careers it began or enhanced. Eighteen of the delegates had run for and been elected to the state legislature as of 1992.[41] The most notable of these was John Waihe'e. A new star at the convention, he was elected to the house, then served as lieutenant governor and governor.

Rejecting a Convention

The required question of whether to form a new convention appeared on the ballot in 1986 and, perhaps because of all the work completed in the 1978 convention, failed substantially to gain an electoral majority. There were no advocates for it, no specific issues had emerged that needed to be addressed, newspaper editorials expressed opposition, and the public was generally disinterested.[42]

The decision was much closer ten years later when 163,869 voted "yes" for a 1998 Convention, 160,153 voted "no," and 45,245 ballots were returned blank or spoiled. The state attorney general interpreted the constitutional language to mean that more than 50 percent of those voting must be in favor, not counting blanks or spoiled ballots, and that a convention had been authorized. The state Supreme Court, however, agreed with a lawsuit brought by the Hawai'i State AFL-CIO, which had been against a convention, and which argued that all ballots must be counted. Since only 44 percent who voted had favored the convention, it was again defeated.

A number of legislators, representatives of groups, and individual citizens expressed disappointment at this outcome. They foresaw an opportunity to revisit proposals not passed in the two previous conventions, such as conversion to a unicameral legislature, or adoption of statewide initiative and referendum. Some had looked forward to dealing with specific issues they had unsuccessfully championed through their elected representatives, such as same-gender marriage.

The postponement was good news to Governor Cayetano, who expected a convention to require more than $12 million in a time of fiscal austerity. Beyond its expense, he believed the effect of the work done in 1978 had been to complicate government and add unnecessary regulations, burdens against which his administration now had to struggle to improve efficiency and increase economic activity.[43] Others felt that the rough and tumble of a convention was not the right place to address many of the sensitive issues that would come up there.

The question of a constitutional convention appeared again on the November 1998 ballot. Continuing changes in the social climate of the islands had heightened concerns among a number of groups that the convention would be taken over by highly motivated and well-organized single-issue groups. The concerned groups included labor unions, worried that privatization would be advanced and the scope of negotiable issues narrowed; the League of Women Voters, who argued that, among other things, religious right groups would try to give constitutional standing to their special views on abortion and same-gender marriage; and Native Hawaiians, who suspected that it would be an opportunity to reverse some of their gains on ceded lands questions. The Office of Hawaiian Affairs spent more than $160,000 in a media campaign against a convention.

On November 3, 1998, the proposal to hold a constitutional convention was overwhelmingly defeated by voters. Rejection of a year 2000 convention means that at least 25 years will pass before the constitution is again considered for revision by a popularly elected body.

Legislatively Proposed Changes to the Constitution

Although there has been no constitutional convention since 1978, the amendment process has continued through the other means established for its revision by the Hope Chest constitution: legislatively initiated amendments that must be ratified by popular vote. Most proposed revisions introduced into the legislature do not pass, but once passed the majority of the fifty-two amendments that have been presented to voters have been adopted.[44] Ratification has occurred despite the fact that, as Anne Feder Lee points out, proposed amendments are usually accompanied by little public education. This reflects the fact that no instructions for such education apply to legislatively-initiated amendments, which must only be published four times in a newspaper. Ironically, a 1980 constitutional provision that originated in the legislature requires all amendments proposed by convention be presented in full text to voters, and accompanied by a program of public education.

The November 1998 election provides an interesting, though not typical, example of the legislative constitutional amendment. Three same-sex couples went to the Department of Health in 1990 to apply for marriage licenses. When, as expected, the department interpreted the relevant Hawai'i statute as denying them a license, the couples decided to take the matter to court. Their case was rejected by the state circuit court in September of 1991, and they appealed.

On May 5, 1993, the Hawai'i Supreme Court ruled in *Baehr v. Lewin* that, absent the demonstration of a "compelling state interest," same-sex couples could not be prohibited from entering into a civil marriage. As the court saw it, such a denial would be in violation of their right to equal protection under the Hawai'i state constitution.[45] The couples were not awarded marriage licenses, but the case that earlier had been dismissed in circuit court was reinstated there. (See chapter 7 for an interpretation of this decision.)

The Supreme Court's judgment set off a flurry of activity, in the islands and in other parts of the country. A number of states passed legislation invalidating in their states same-sex marriages lawful in another jurisdiction. Many others added their state to those already having legislation specifically outlawing same-sex marriages. The federal Congress, in 1997, passed the Defense of Marriage Act to define "marriage" as the union between a male and female for the purposes of applying federal rules and regulations.

In Hawai'i, the 1994 legislature decided to remove any discretionary ambiguity from the statute that the Department of Health uses to decide who may obtain a valid marriage license.[46] The new language specified that in addition to being 16 years of age, unrelated, exercising free choice, not married to another person, possessing a license from the state, and without a "loathsome" disease unknown to the other person, a marriage "shall be only between a man and a woman."

The same legislature also established a Commission on Sexual Orientation to study the issue. The Commission submitted its report in December 1995, recommending that the legislature either legalize same-sex marriage or authorize a domestic partnership arrangement that would give same-sex couple benefits that belong to married couples.

The legislature that met in 1996 was unable to pass bills either proposing a constitutional amendment to ban same-sex marriage or legalizing "domestic partnerships." (See chapter 9 for the impact of this issue on the legislature.) In December 1996, state circuit court judge Kevin Chang rejected the argument being made by the state that it had demonstrated a compelling state interest to deny marriage licenses to same-sex couples. He ordered the state to issue marriage licenses to same-sex couples pending the state's appeal to the Supreme Court.

The 1997 legislature again considered the issue, which had become increasingly volatile and divisive. Legislators now were under additional pressure to act because of the likelihood that the Supreme Court's would rule against the state.[47] This decision would make Hawai'i first in the nation to legalize same-sex marriage.

A compromise was reached in which the senate proposal for "reciprocal benefits" for non-married couples, and the house proposal for a constitutional amendment limiting who may marry, both were passed. The reciprocal benefits law applies to people who have a significant personal relationship with one another, and provides them some of the benefits accorded a married couple. These benefits include joint participation in health plans, authority to make health care decisions, and the right of a surviving partner to an elective share of a decedent's estate.[48]

The constitutional amendment that appeared before voters for ratification in the November 1998 election read as follows: "Shall the constitution of the state of Hawaii be amended to specify that the Legislature shall have the power to reserve marriage to opposite-sex couples?" The amendment's wording was intended to create constitutional authority for the legislature, rather than the courts, to decide the question, while satisfying the court, including potentially the federal Supreme Court, that a fundamental violation of due process or privacy rights had not occurred.

The amendment drew a great deal of national and local attention. Nationally, groups concerned about the outcome sent substantial monies to those supporting or fighting the proposal.[49] Locally, two groups, "Save Traditional Marriage" and "Protect Our Constitution" were the focal points of a heated, sometimes mean-spirited, contest for voter support. Those in favor of the amendment argued, primarily, that both commonsense and tradition made it clear that marriage applied to only a man and a woman. Those against mainly urged that, by using the constitution to place restrictions on a specific group, this amendment debased Hawai'i's constitutional tradition and could place other rights, such as abortion, in jeopardy.

Public opinion surveys showed most Hawai'i voters were not comfortable with the idea of homosexual marriage. It was not surprising, therefore, that the overwhelming majority of those running for elected office declared their intention to vote for the amendment. This included both gubernatorial candidates. Almost without exception, those who came out against were running in safe districts, unlikely to hurt by their position. The major exception to this was the Democratic candidate for lieutenant governor, Mazie Hirono, who, after what she described as soul-searching, declared she would vote "no."

Those favoring creation of an amendment to allow the legislature to restrict marriage to a man and a woman won by more than two to one. The margin of the victory was surprising, as most expected a closer outcome.

Consistent with the reality that even constitutional amendments must be implemented and interpreted, the meaning of the vote and the future of this issue remains unclear. Governor Cayetano stated, in a post-election television interview, that he would urge legislators in the 1999 session to pass a more generous reciprocal benefits package, one that would give same-sex couples all of the important rights and benefits of married couples. His statement partly reflected challenges that had halted implementation of some of its provisions. In particular, five large employers argued that they should not have to pay benefits to domestic partners since the new law violates the federal Employee Retirement Income Security Act.

Some of those who fought for the amendment reacted angrily against either fixing or strengthening the domestic partnership act, claiming that the voters had spoken with a clear voice against the gay lifestyle. Others, on the opposite end of the spectrum, suggested that the matter inevitably would appear again before the Supreme Court since the new amendment, once applied, would be found to be fundamentally in tension with other provisions of the state constitution.

Hawai'i's constitution began as a concise document, although its focus is less sharp as a result of many amendments. The power of the executive has been retained, and there is clear constitutional attention to resources and social issues. Local government has been strengthened somewhat by constitutional provisions.

There is an ambiguous message about citizen participation in the constitutional process. Both con cons have produced substantive as well as superficial changes. On the other hand, the value of this direct citizen role seems to have come into question. Conventions have been rejected three times, the most recent resoundingly defeated. There has been wide-ranging opposition, including governors, labor unions, Native Hawaiians, and even advocates of citizen participation.

It may be that these concerns are temporary, and that more time must pass before enough people are satisfied that constitutional work again needs to be done. Better economic times will make cost less of an issue. Nevertheless, ambivalence about what will happen when citizens are convened for these weighty purposes appears to be lurking behind the rejections. In the end, these questions are about the extent to which Hawai'i's citizens collectively view themselves as able to balance the need to protect a document that embodies the broad rules of the game for life in Hawai'i, with the power to continuously transform those rules.

CHAPTER SIX

Public Participation and Political Parties

The primary role of political parties in the United States is to create broad policy agendas that pull together coalitions capable of winning elections. When one party is so dominant that electoral success is assured, its focus is apt to shift toward maintaining its dominant position as a gatekeeper to power and resources.

This describes the subtle but significant changes in the Democratic party during its forty-five year hegemony in Hawai'i. No second party has provided serious competition. The only significant opposition has been factions within the organization itself. The Republican candidate for governor in 1998 came within about 5,000 votes out of more than 400,000 cast of winning, but this near-success did not extend beyond that office to the state legislature.

In the fall 1994 elections, Republican candidates won four of nine county council seats on the Island of Hawai'i, one of the state's five elected bodies. These Republicans were able to create a council majority by forming a coalition with the single Green Party member. This could foreshadow a shift in Republican prospects at the local level, but it is noteworthy that this is only the second time since statehood that Republicans have controlled a legislative body anywhere in the state. Four years later, after the 1998 election, the council was composed of six Democrats, two Republicans, and one Green. In the words of a former chair of the Hawai'i Republican party, "There may be a two-party system in Hawai'i, but the Republican Party isn't one of them."[1]

As the years have passed, diverging purposes and abuses of power replaced the social convictions that inspired the 1954 Democratic Revolution. These changes threaten the loyalty of supporters, even when that loyalty is based upon ethnic affinity and shared culture. They also put the legitimacy, or at least relevance, of parties, and voting, under stress. The Republican party has contributed to these developments by its continued inability to adopt a platform that captures the imagination of Hawai'i voters.

VOTER ORIENTATIONS TOWARD PUBLIC INSTITUTIONS

Beginning in the 1950s, consistent with the idealism accompanying the shift to Democratic party rule and the implementation of its social agenda, Hawai'i's public institutions were accorded comparatively high levels of legitimacy. By the 1970s and early 1980s, however, surveys consistently found about one-half of voters disapproving of how the state legislature did its job. The work of county councils, the elected bodies closest to citizens, were viewed somewhat more positively.[2] The mid-1990s brought more indications that the widespread voter disaffection prevalent on the American mainland was appearing in Hawai'i's attitudes toward representative government.[3]

Perceptions of public corruption and bureaucratic self-servingness in recent years underscore citizens' sense that public institutions do not meet reasonable standards of fairness, efficiency, and responsiveness. Fifty-two percent of registered voters contacted in an August 1998 survey thought government in Hawai'i "basically dishonest," an increase of six percent from 1993. Fifty-one percent expected this to be about the same as other states, but 23 percent thought it worse.[4] A 1994 survey showed that 78 percent of those registered to vote believed a notorious instance of tying non-bid contracts to campaign contributions was typical of how the City and County of Honolulu operated.[5] A Honolulu newspaper, comparing these results to mainland voter attitudes, noted that its reporters "find the same sense of alienation and powerlessness as people shake their heads, shrug their shoulders, throw up their hands and refuse with disgusted grunts to talk about public issues."[6]

These data, and accompanying interpretations, are indicative more than conclusive. Yet, they support other more anecdotal evidence that attitudes toward public institutions are shifting away from the high regard, or at least sense of usefulness, they were accorded from the mid-1950s to the 1980s. Dovetailing with the state's political culture at that time, government was viewed as a vehicle for correcting social wrongs and providing economic opportunities for non-Caucasians.

Today the effectiveness and integrity of government is a public issue. Although this may not add up to what one National Public Radio commentator described as the "undifferentiated peevishness" characteristic of American voters in the 1990s, it does create uncertainty in the outlooks which join voters, parties and government.

Voting Patterns since Statehood

Less than 50 percent of those registered actually cast ballots in the pivotal 1954 election. This difference probably reflected, more than anything else, pessimism about having an impact on a regime so securely in power for so many years. Victories in the 1954 races dramatically increased the proportion who voted, to almost 90 percent of those registered in the 1956 and 1958 elections.[7]

Voter turnout, measured both as number of eligible registered and number registered who vote, has declined over the 40 years since statehood. In 1959, 93.6 percent of registered voters turned out to cast ballots.[8] The 1998 election brought 68.6 percent to the polls, only slightly better than the 1996 turnout when the poor turnout was attributed partly to heavy rain on election day. Hawai'i dropped below the national average for presidential elections after 1985. In the presidential election of 1992, the islands' were 8 percentage points below the fifty state average of 68.2 percent for proportion of eligible citizens who registered, ranking it 49 among the 50 states. In the same year Hawai'i was about 6 percentage points below the national figure of 61.3 percent for those eligible who actually voted, placing it in 48th position.[9]

These figures mean that in the islands, as in other places, a shrinking percentage of the population is deciding elections, with the winners basing their mandate on a decreasing portion of the electorate. This is dramatized by the 1994 governor's race,. It involved three major candidates, and was won by Democrat Cayetano with 35 percent of the votes cast, which translates to just 14 percent of those eligible to vote.

Some have speculated that shifts in registration and voting patterns may be related to the state's economic performance. Data collected over a thirty-year period by a local bank showed an association between variations in real personal income and voter turn-out. Specifically, annual declines in income of 1 percent were associated with 1.35 percent increases in voter participation in a subsequent election.[10] The continuing decline in voter participation during the extended economic downturn of the 1990s does not seem to support this explanation.

Differences in participation among ethnic groups, in particular between the higher rates for Japanese-Americans and the lower rates for Caucasians, are a more important factor. A 1988 survey of attitudes toward political participation among Honolulu residents reported that Japanese-Americans labeled themselves "interested in politics" about twice as often as non-Japanese-American respondents (23.8 percent vs. 12.2 percent) and described themselves to be slightly more active in electoral activities other than voting (31 percent vs. 25 percent).[11]

It is evident that Japanese-Americans register and turn out to vote at much higher rates than other groups. Although it is hard to be precise because of the changes in reporting rules noted previously, this is corroborated by both impressionistic information and election research. One researcher, familiar with variations in voting participation across ethnic groups, observed at the conclusion of one of his studies that, "voters of Japanese ancestry in Hawai'i consistently have the highest turnout rates of any demographic group that I have ever seen anywhere."[12]

In contrast, Caucasians registered to vote in the islands have a lower average turnout than many other groups. This appears to be the result of factors normally associated with lower participation, namely younger age, greater social instability, and less education. Caucasians, because of their in-migration, have replaced Japanese-Americans as the most numerous demographic subgroup. These new arrivals are more likely to be younger, renters, and less educated, all characteristics associated with lower voting turnout.

In short, while Americans of Japanese ancestry are the most active in electoral politics, their numbers are decreasing relative to Caucasians, a group whose members participate at a lower level. This has led to an overall decline in voter participation rates.

POLITICAL PARTIES

In her book on Arkansas politics, Diane Blair describes the state's Democratic party as, "a mere holding company under whose name all candidates sought office" and the Republicans as "somewhere between an esoteric cult and poised for plunder."[13] Her statement aptly describes political parties in Hawai'i. Democrats dominated elected office for more than forty years, the only exception being county mayors, especially the mayor of the City and County of Honolulu. During this period of one-party hegemony, the Republican party was marginalized as an institutional force, a loyal opposition whose primary visibility is the statesperson-like posture assumed by those few repeatedly elected from safe legislative districts.

In another way, however, Blair's observation is less relevant to Hawai'i's situation. Although Hawai'i has had one-party rule since the turn of the century the history of party dominance in southern states, like Arkansas, is much longer. The conditions that formed the modern Hawai'i Democratic party do not go back into the nineteenth century. Instead, they can still be experienced as echoes of the fervor that accompanied the party's 1950s emergence. Those echoes remain in the memories, and in the political oratory, of living public figures. In the 1990s, however, their message must compete with the misuses and abuses that come from holding power too completely, for too long. Today the Democratic party's mission is alternatively a banner to cover what abuse has occurred, and a beacon held out as the direction for recovery.

One commentator observed that Hawai'i has an "oppressive Democratic Party that has to find its way back to its roots, and a weak and dying Republican Party which needs to abandon its."[14] The Democratic party struggles to recover, or recreate, its purposes and maintain long-term loyalties, and the Republican party works to attract candidates who can weave together coalitions capable of winning elections. Both operate in the context of forces, both national and local, that threaten the role of parties in the political system, something examined later in this chapter.

Rules Governing Parties

Hawai'i nominates its candidates for office through direct-election primaries. State election laws formally obligate a party member to "carry out the provisions and pledges of the party platform," but this is hard to enforce, especially in a situation of one-party dominance where individuals of all persuasions believe only one label offers any hope of being elected.

Before 1949, election laws permitted a blanket system in which an individual could vote for any candidate in the primary. An open primary system was adopted that year as part of the drive to statehood. One party or the other had to be selected, the effect of which was to show Congress there were strong parties in the territory.[15] A closed system was instituted in 1968 to strengthen parties by preventing "raiding," the practice of switching parties in the primary in order to help nominate the opposition's weaker candidate for the general election. In 1978, voters approved a return to the open primary system, something adopted in that year's constitutional convention as compensation to those delegates who had lost in their fight for initiative and referendum.[16]

Hawai'i's statewide party organizations, like most other states, are decentralized, featuring state conventions to which party members are elected from precincts. State chairs and other officers are elected at the party conventions and, because of the informal organizing which occurs, typically represent the most powerful elected officials in the party.

Supporters must present the lieutenant governor's office with signatures equal to at least one percent of the registered voters, 150 days before the primary, for a party to place candidates on the ballot. A party's candidate must receive at least 10 percent of the general election vote to re-appear on the ballot in the next election. Several "third parties" have succeeded since statehood in getting on the ballot for a range of offices. In one case, the party was the creature of a specific individual, Honolulu mayor Frank Fasi, who chose to run outside the two major parties. More commonly, they reflect specific policy and value orientations. The Independents for Godly Government party ran candidates in 14 races in 1976, while the People's party had candidates in four. These subsequently disappeared. The third party with the greatest staying power is the Libertarian party. In recent elections it has been joined by the Green party, both obtaining a small percentage of total votes cast.

Historical Perspectives on Parties

Nothing resembling political parties developed in the islands until the reign of King David Kalakaua in 1874. Over the next 20 years, prior to the overthrow of the kingdom, they existed as relatively unstable organizations with shifting memberships, and acted as the rallying points for individuals and groups opposed to or in support of the monarchy.[17] None survived into the territorial period by the same names-Reform, National Reform, Liberal, Hawaiian Patriotic League, Native Sons of Hawaii—although there was continuity in the coalitions they represented.

Native Hawaiians were eager to reassert control after Hawai'i became a territory, and new rules created the means. The Organic Act declared, in defining citizenship, that all persons who had been citizens of the republic on August 12, 1898, automatically were accorded that status in both the United States and the territory. Since Hawaiians and part-Hawaiians had been citizens, their population of approximately 40,000 was the electoral majority, and virtually all Asians, slightly larger in number, were excluded.

The Home Rule party became the focal point for a range of interests revolving around restoration of the nation of Hawai'i and defeat of the power of businessmen and missionaries. Formed in 1900, its rallying cry was "Nana i Ka ili" [Look to the skin] and Queen Lili'uokalani, the deposed monarch, addressed the first convention. Home Rule candidates won the special elections held that year, sending its leader, Robert Wilcox, to Washington as territorial delegate and winning control of the local legislature. Despite this early victory, the party accomplished little in comparison to its ambitions and disappeared by 1912.

The early electoral success of the Home Rulers alarmed territorial Republicans, the party most representative of missionary and business interests. The voting rules of the Organic Act created, from their perspective, a situation that might demolish all of the work done to form a responsible system of governance and a stable economy.[18] To prevent this, the *Haole*-Business leadership acted through the party to court the loyalty of Hawaiians, endorsing Prince Jonah Kuhio as territorial delegate from 1902 to 1922, and offering patronage to Hawaiian community leaders over the next 30 years. This strategy proved highly successful, netting control of both the territorial legislature and congressional delegate. By 1923, Republicans held 44 of 45 legislative seats. They also sent 5 of the 7 delegates who served in Washington between 1902 and 1954.

The Republican party reflected the ideals and interests of the group that dominated Hawai'i society from the turn of the century to the 1950s. Despite its long hold on power, few internal factions developed. Instead, a colonial sense of common purpose emerged, focused on the need to protect against a perceived common danger. The party also incorporated a shared orientation toward political culture. This orientation mixed ideas about the appropriateness, or necessity, of their ruling position with obligations to protect their image of Hawai'i society and advance Western values. The party endorsed federal tariff policies that supported sugar and pineapple while business maintained control over labor at home. It accepted the power of the large, landed estates, relied on volunteerism and a sense of noblesse oblige to deal with social problems, and expressed concern about the "plight of the Hawaiians" without committing public resources to help remedy that plight. Worry about the growing number of Asians, especially Japanese-Americans, lurked behind Republican policy as the century wore on. As more Asians became citizens by birthright, the party made some attempts, largely unsuccessful, to court them.

A cross-section of mainlanders organized the Hawai'i Democratic party in 1902. For the next half-century, its ability to counter-balance the Republican elite was severely limited by an absence of an independent economic base: most of its members worked for someone else.

Limited access to financial help made it hard to overcome the tremendous advantage Republicans had through businesses, plantations, and churches to gain access to voters. Some opportunities presented themselves over this long period, especially in two elections of Democratic territorial delegates and in the appointment of Democratic governors by national Democratic administrations. These were, however, episodic and created no enduring institutional base to build upon.

Labor union organizers who came to the islands from the mainland shortly before World War II helped to persuade potential voters they might actually gain political power. Successful strikes in the post-war years confirmed this, and it became clear that support for, or at least tolerance of, the Republican Party was eroding. Republican attempts to attract Japanese-Americans failed, making it a virtual certainty that these new voters would be Democrats.[19]

A bitter struggle occurred for control of the emergent Democratic party in the late 1940s and early 1950s. One contestant was the now powerful unions, especially the International Longshoreman's and Warehouseman's Union (ILWU) that had successfully organized the waterfront and plantations. The other was a group whose members saw themselves continuing to be second class-citizens. Future governor Jack Burns and a core of Japanese-American supporters were at this group's center.[20]

Burns and his allies were afraid that domination of the party by the ILWU and its leader, Jack Hall, would ruin the party's chances for broad-based support and, later, for attaining statehood. Charges that the union was controlled by communists, an opinion voiced aggressively by the business community, the newspapers, and the Republican Party, underscored this concern.

The House Un-American Activities Committee (HUAC) traveled to Honolulu to hold hearings in the summer of 1953. This high-profile event gave the communism issue even more attention. By putting union leadership in jail and detracting from the legitimacy it had built-up in organizing plantation and dock workers, the Smith Act trials that followed the hearings played a key role in determining who would control the new Democratic party, and how radical its policies would be.[21] The Burns coalition was able to take charge of the party organization in early 1954. Hall and the ILWU were inherently more sympathetic to new Democrats than to either new or old Republicans, and had no other platforms by which to represent their positions. Though defeated within the party, the union proved crucial in delivering votes for the "Revolution of 1954" election.

Political Parties after 1954

Political scientist Norman Meller, writing just after the 1954 elections, reflected on the previous half-century of Hawai'i's one-party reign and gave expression to a common opinion: "A virile two-party system in Hawaii now seemed assured."[22] It did not happen, of course. Since 1954, and especially after 1962, when the governor's office was won by Jack Burns, the Democratic party has dominated the state. Its candidates have controlled, with the two exceptions noted in the introduction to this chapter, the county councils and have ruled the state legislature. Illustrative of this period, in the 1976 legislative elections, 22 of 27 House districts were designated "Democratic" or "Heavy Democratic," 3 "Republican," and 2 "marginal Democratic." In the 1980 election the Republicans offered no candidates in 13 of the House districts classified as "Heavy Democrat." Democrats have been especially strong on the more rural Neighbor Islands in statewide races for Congress and the governorship. The Democrats took over what once had been Republican party strongholds, based on control of the plantations, and reversed the mainland pattern in which Democrats generally do best in urban areas. Signs that this 40 year-old pattern might be changing did not appear until the 1998 election, when the Republican gubernatorial candidate won Maui and the Big Island.

The new Democrats came to power with the mission of changing the policies of the Republican regime, a purpose reflected in the party platform for the first Democratic majority. The platform's commitments were unusually specific.[23] They promised laws more sympathetic to labor, decentralization of authority to the counties, greater commitment to public education, tax reform, an economic development program that benefited more people, salary increases for public employees, and a break-up of the land monopoly.

This mission guided a remarkable body of policy from the mid-1950s. During this period:

- the tax system was made more progressive;
- more money was allocated to public secondary and higher education, and tuition was lowered in the state's university system to make it among the cheapest in the country;
- the property tax system was revised and lands held by large estates were taxed at higher rates, creating more revenue to fund social programs and forcing more productive uses;
- one of the nation's first state-wide land use planning systems was put in place;
- the owners of large parcels of land were forced, by powers of eminent domain, to sell to single dwelling-unit homeowners living under long-term leases that stipulated that upon expiration the houses they built or purchased would be forfeited to the land owner;

- shorelines were defined as the public domain and public access to them was protected;
- a system was established to treat water as a publicly managed resource;
- generous workers compensation rules where adopted to cover job-related accidents and illness;
- the rights of public employees were affirmed by an amendment that made public sector unions a provision of the constitution;
- public monies were utilized to provide basic automobile insurance for welfare recipients.

Consistent with all of this, Hawai'i was the first state to adopt the Equal Rights Amendment to the federal Constitution, to establish a statewide Ombudsman, to pass abortion rights legislation, and to have a constitutionally established Ethics Commission applicable to state employees, officials, and members of boards and commissions. It was first to create mandatory pre-paid medical care for employees and, later, tried to see medical coverage was provided for all residents. Its legislature was the first to support Cesar Chavez's boycott of grapes. The death penalty was abolished in 1957. In 1994, it adopted one of the most far-reaching gun control laws in the nation. And despite its reliance on tourist dollars, in 1996, Hawai'i remained one of only two states that permitted no gaming of any kind.

The Republican party has not been a viable opposition since the late 1950s, owing to its small numbers, poor infrastructure, and absence of a policy agenda capable of attracting coalitions of voters. The party's few successes reflect the particulars of situations—the personality of a Republican candidate for governor, the ineptness of a Democratic opponent, or the socio-economic profile of an election district—rather than attraction to Republican positions.

The depth of its problems are illustrated by their candidate for the United States Senate in the November 1998 election. The primary was won by Crystal Young, an astrologer whose political experience consisted of writing handwritten letters to office holders, advocating legislation to annex Baja California, prevent organ theft from homeless people, and remove the mountains surrounding the Los Angeles basin to reduce smog. The chair of the Republican Party observed that "Someone had to win the primary and she did, and whatever she's doing, she's doing on her own and we are unable to help her out in any way."[24]

Absence of an effective opposition party does not signify a complete absence of competition. It does mean that, like the legislative party, the most important competition has occurred within the Democratic party. Almost from the beginning the Democratic core group began to splinter into factions. The most powerful of them, surrounding the figure of John Burns, remained in control of the Democratic party. The founding group's direct inheritor was George Ariyoshi, Burns' hand-picked lieutenant governor. That mantle in turn was picked up by John Waihe'e, Ariyoshi's lieutenant governor. It was only with the 1994 election of Waihe'e's former Lieutenant Governor, Ben Cayetano, who traveled to the Governorship through a different wing of the party, that the power of the original group was significantly reduced.

Frank Fasi, an outspoken former Marine who for a short time in the 1950s was a member of the new Democrats, created one of the early splinter groups. Fasi quickly became unhappy with what he perceived to be the excessive power wielded by those at the party's center. Continuing at first to operate as a Democrat, he was elected mayor of Honolulu in 1968, a platform he subsequently used to challenge the "Democratic establishment." Later, he became a Republican, then an Independent, and finally formed his own party, all directed primarily at unsuccessful attempts to gain the governorship. In the process, Fasi developed a loyal following, labeled "Fasicrats," who shared his view of being outsiders in relation to the Democratic establishment.

Another faction was formed by individuals who wished to reform the party. Tom Gill was a principal figure in what came to be called the "liberal wing." Member of a long-time island family, he was elected O'ahu chair of the Democratic Party in 1952 and 1954 and won a seat in the state House 1958. Gill defied John Burns by successfully defeating his choice for Lieutenant Governor in 1968. He then lost twice in bids for the Governorship, both times running as the person who could recover the party and government from control by a self-serving in-group. He never sought public office again after 1974, although he did make a bid for Democratic party chair in 1998.

Patsy Mink is also in the party's liberal wing. She is a Japanese-American who disagreed with the ruling faction and, like Fasi and Gill, created her own loyal constituency. Mink was elected to the state legislature in 1956, then served twelve years in the Congress until losing in a run for the U.S. Senate in 1976. She then spent six years on the Honolulu City Council. Defeated for governor and mayor in the Democratic primaries, she was reelected to the federal House in 1990.

Other dissident factions have congealed, often in the state legislature. In the 1980 session, for example, Democrats loyal to the most powerful faction formed an alliance with Senate Republicans to form a ruling majority making other Democrats the de facto minority. One of this minority's most visible members was future U.S. Representative Neil Abercrombie; another was future Governor Ben Cayetano.

These dissident factions inside the party failed to create a permanent organizational base. They shared a focus on procedural concerns, as distinct from substantive policy. There are, of course, important disagreements about policy issues. Tom Gill offered clear alternatives in the areas of housing, transportation, and economic development when he ran for governor in 1970 and 1974. However, the issues that define these individuals and groups as outsiders to the party's center are largely about procedural matters, and particularly about openness. Dissident factions consistently have called for less in-group dominance of policy positions; more open management of party affairs, including finances; and, in general, a loosening of control over the party apparatus.[25]

One-party domination and intra-party disputes emphasizing process rather than policy have had important consequences for political life. Party labels cease to be an effective way to decipher what a public figure represents. Unlike the years following statehood when the positions of Democratic candidates reflected a coherent program easily distinguishable from traditional Republicans, a wide range of perspectives share the label "Democrat." People who otherwise might be Republicans become Democrats in order to win, and, until Richard Port's arrival in 1994, there was little public discussion of substantive differences within the party.

George Ariyoshi illustrates this homogenizing effect. The fiscal conservatism evident throughout his public career, including his years as governor from 1972 to 1986, would have permitted, or forced, him to be a Republican in another setting, but never was, at least visibly, an issue within the Hawai'i Democratic party.

FROM RADICALISM TO STATUS QUO

The post-war Democratic party did not succeed on two of the most passionately articulated and far-reaching elements of its platform: the decentralization of government authority and land reform. In 1999, no jurisdictions below the level of county have authority to respond to desires for local control. Moreover, state government only begrudgingly has yielded additional powers to the counties. With respect to land, the large estates remain, many residents are leaseholders on estate lands, and many legitimate Hawaiian claims are unmet. Illustrative of the early shift away from the land revolution called for by the party in 1954, in 1958 then-legislator and future governor, George Ariyoshi, cast the deciding vote against a land-conversion bill, even though the state's largest land trust, the Bishop Estate, had been excluded from its provisions.

One explanation for the deradicalizing of the party's mission is the different perspectives held by the reformer speaking from outside of public office and the office holder. Victorious reformers must get bills passed and policies implemented, and will soon begin to think about what needs to be done to stay in office. Impassioned reformers everywhere often become defenders of the status quo.

Another explanation is found in the socialization experienced by members of Hawai'i's reform group, a socialization that changed the sense of their own history. The public school system through which many passed focused immigrants' attention on the importance of upward mobility and individual success. Socialization also was influential because most of the activists were second-generation Americans. Being raised in the context of American culture, even though it was mediated by local culture, altered the values that earlier had defined their ethnic group.

Finally, there are the consequences of success. It is harder for Democratic party leaders to be radicals because they have solved some of the social ills that galvanized them years ago. They no longer can attack, for example, an exclusive educational system, or demand that workers be given protections. Both of these goals have been accomplished, and it is far different to call for a moderate increase in spending for public schools, or the maintenance of workers' compensation, than it is to address forcefully what seems to be a basic injustice.

The original radicalism's diminishment does not mean the party's mission was unimportant. The list of policy achievements cited above convincingly argues the contrary, while pointing to the pervasiveness of a moralistic political culture within the party. Still, over time, the energizing and consensus-making power of that mission declined, to be replaced by an emphasis on individual deal-making, serving more narrowly interested constituencies, and preserving power, all associated with a more traditionalistic political culture.

Misuses of public authority are closely connected to the rise of deal making. One investigative reporter discovered that over 90 percent of the architects and engineers appearing on the list of contributors were with firms receiving non-bid contracts worth millions of dollars during one or more of the previous four years.[26] Such evidence is not conclusive, but there is no question of the public perception that this and other forms of corruption have occurred.

Deal-making among ad hoc groups has gained in direct proportion to the absence of an overriding purpose uniting party members. The party's umbrella is commonly viewed as a restraint rather than an advantage, and many Democratic candidates and representatives have come to see themselves as more effective on their own. The focus on retention of power per se continues, however, and although the mission no longer is the purpose for having power, the benefits of holding it continue.

The Struggle for the Party

The 1,000 or so delegates sent to the 1994 Democratic party convention from precinct elections went against leadership and elected businessman Richard Port as state chair. Port ran on a platform to open up the party's organization to new voices and new positions, arguing that is the path to revitalization and social relevance. He worked to enlarge and diversify the number of people who participated directly in party affairs from the time of his election. He took an unheard of step after the 1996 legislative session and criticized House and Senate leaders, both Democrats, for not acting in ways he thought consistent with the Party's public responsibilities.

Port retired suddenly and unexpectedly in September 1996, creating an internal struggle for the vacated position. His replacement, in a 31–28 vote of the party's central committee, was former city council member and mayoral candidate Marilyn Bornhorst. Bornhorst was a compromise between the traditional and reformist wings that now had faced-off against one another. A realtor sympathetic to the concerns of small businesses, during her term she also was publicly critical of party leadership, in this case what she saw as the big business slant of the governor's economic development task force.

Bornhorst decided not to run for re-election in 1998, which triggered a fight over the party's identity. It was between two party veterans, Tom Gill and Walter Heen, who both had held elective office in the state legislature and were well-known in the party. Gill represented the liberal wing that had lost out to Burns loyalists in earlier fights for the party, a wing that had not held power until the election of Richard Port. He called for efforts to be more open, less interest group dominated, and clearer about what distinguishes Republicans from Democrats today.[27] Heen was the centrist who had lost to Bornhorst two years earlier when the liberal candidate bowed out and threw her votes to Bornhorst. He argued that the Republicans "smelled blood," and that the Democrats had to become more unified if they were to retain the governor's mansion at Washington Place.

The race between Heen and Gill for party leadership contained, in addition to the different wings they represented, another dimension. Heen had served as a substitute associate justice on the Supreme Court, and dissented from the majority's opinion that rejected the state's arguments against issuing marriage licenses to gay couples. Gill, on the other hand, was chairman of the Commission on Sexual Orientation that had recommended same-sex couples be allowed to marry, and was active in a local organization trying to defeat a constitutional amendment that would permit legislators to ban same-sex marriages.

Given the support of Heen by party leaders, as well as their concerns that Gill's position on same-sex marriage would cost them among the majority of voters unhappy about the idea, it is not surprising that in May 1998 the delegates elected him to a two-year term as party chairman.

THE STRUGGLE FOR WINNING COALITIONS

The 1998 statewide elections offer insight into the strategies the Democratic and Republican parties will employ to construct coalitions capable of winning elections, and into the likelihood of real two-party competition. Governor Cayetano appeared to win the 1994 election only because the vote was split between three candidates in the general election. As a result, many expected the next election to produce the first Republican governor since 1960, perhaps along with substantial changes in the balance of seats in the state legislature.

Republican candidate Linda Lingle offered a formidable challenge. She was first elected to the Maui county council in 1980, then re-elected four times. Lingle became the youngest mayor in Maui's history in 1990 and was returned to that office in 1994. The state slid into an economic slowdown during her administration, but the island of Maui continued to do well in tourism and job development. By the time she began her run for the office of governor in 1997, she was 44 years old, poised, and articulate. Although only a half a generation younger than Governor Cayetano, her appearance and demeanor seemed much closer to the growing number of younger voters who might not see the world in the same way as those in the Democratic party establishment.

Polls showed Lingle running ahead of Cayetano by as much as 20 percent in the months before the September primary. This was nothing unusual, as almost every Democrat had run well behind their Republican opponent in the early stages of gubernatorial campaigns. It was unusual, however, when tens of thousands of Democrats crossed-over in the open primary to vote for her. This was especially so given the conjecture that cross-over might be by loyal Democrats to vote for Lingle's primary opponent Frank Fasi, who was expected to be easier for Cayetano to defeat. The campaign seemed very different indeed when polls showed Lingle still ahead by 8 points one week before the general election.

Despite all these signs, the election was narrowly won by Cayetano, who got 49.5 percent of the vote compared to Lingle's 48.2 percent. There were no changes in the number of seats held by each party in the legislature, although Democrats came close to gaining one in the House. Four long-term Democrats failed to be re-elected, and their rejection seemed a sign of voter discontent. Each, however, was defeated by a Democratic challenger in the primary.

What happened here? One response is that the final outcome is somewhat different than the vote tallies in the individual races. Although the vast number of seats were won by huge majorities, Senate and House contests were closer in this election than at any time in recent memory. Three were decided by less than 500 votes. Another response is that the Republicans had some bad luck. The candidate they expected to seriously challenge Representative Neil Abercrombie for the United States House, part-Hawaiian businessman Quentin Kawananakoa, withdrew for personal reasons before the primary. In the race for governor, the Republican candidate whom Lingle defeated in the primary, well-known party switcher Frank Fasi, took the unusual step of urging his supporters to vote for Cayetano in the general. All of these suggest that time is on the side of the Republicans, and in future elections they will fare better.

Still, after 45 years of dominance, in an economy that has made Hawai'i residents anxious for more than six years, with many signs of voter discontent, and running a Democratic candidate for governor not known for his personal charisma or voter appeal, what can explain this?

Despite the fact that Lingle was ahead until the last few days, approximately 20 percent of potential voters remained undecided until the last moment. It is most likely that these were individuals who normally would vote Democrat, but they appeared to be caught between their traditional loyalties and a desire for change. Several factors may have influenced them to turn to the Democrats.

It was clear that, by the time of the general election, the American public had become disaffected from the efforts of Congressional Republicans to impeach President Clinton on the basis of the work done by Special Prosecutor Kenneth Starr. Those efforts served to remind ambivalent Hawai'i Democrats of their fears of what Republicans stand for. This reminder was reinforced by the presence of Lingle's running mate for Lieutenant Governor, Stan Koki. Koki, a local businessman with legislative experience, was strongly identified with the Christian right wing of the Hawai'i Republican party. That wing embraces positions on issues such as abortion and public school sex education that make most voters in Hawai'i very uneasy. Lingle attempted to downplay Koki's place on the ticket, and to identify only with the business experience he would bring to her administration. This was difficult, especially in the face of the strength that Mazie Hirono, Cayetano's Lieutenant Governor, brings to this campaign, and the clear message that they are running as team.

The problem presented by Lingle's running mate points to another, longer-term factor that helps to explain the Republican failure to win ambivalent voters. Just as Lingle had to ignore some of Koki's positions, she felt she had to ignore much of what Republicans typically stand for—reduce government's size, shift tax policy to favor businesses and corporations, question environmental regulations that harm economic development—in order to have any hope of forging a winning coalition.

To do this, she crafted a campaign message that, from the beginning, made it clear she had few disagreements with Cayetano. She stated repeatedly that their platforms were very similar, signaling to voters that they could trust her not to come to office with an agenda to overturn what Democrats had accomplished. What she did stand for, in contrast to policy differences, was effectiveness. She would be able to get things done, and her record on Maui was cited to testify to that. The downside of this for her was that she was unable to be very specific about what it was she would be doing, a vagueness that began to cost her as the campaign wore on.

The demands of positioning, of course, do not present themselves to Lingle alone. Cayetano has shifted to stands that seem closer to what many Republicans would embrace, such as decreasing taxes on corporations and reconsidering the role played by public sector unions. Despite doing this, however, he was able to embrace most of the things for which Democrats have stood across several decades, and to run effectively on the theme that the current status of the economy is less important than the differences in values that separate Democrats from Republicans, and him from Lingle.

Many observers suggested that if Republicans captured the governorship, and made gains in the legislation, a revolution would occur which equaled the change that took place in 1954. This was used, in part, to mobilize campaign workers against the dangers of loss or toward the prospects for victory. It also reflected an authentic belief that this was an election in which "real change" would occur in Hawai'i politics.

A Lingle victory would have meant something, especially if it had been accompanied by changes in the legislature. Its meaning, however, would have been far less than what the word "revolution" implies. The Democratic party came to power in 1954 with a social agenda that included land use reform, labor rights, better access to education, and an end to ethnic discrimination. No similar level of commitment energized the Republican campaigns of 1998. Even though they were almost successful in the governor's race, the Republican party, whatever it may look like in the context of Hawai'i's current traditionalistic and moralistic political culture, has not shown up yet.

ETHNICITY'S ROLE IN VOTER IDENTITY

Chapter 3 describes Hawai'i as a system of ethnic relations that seem to work better than other places. At the same time, tension exists as groups try to assimilate into local society while retaining their cultural identity. It is relevant, in that context, to consider the importance of ethnicity in determining how individuals vote or offer loyalty to parties.

In 1967, Andrew Lind, a sociologist and student of the islands' social relations and cultures, observed that "Nowhere else under the American flag has there been such an experiment in political democracy involving such a large portion of voters of Asian ancestry."[28] Almost no one dismisses ethnicity as a factor in the state's political life, but the results of that experiment are judged differently. One perspective is that ethnicity generally plays a minor role in electoral behavior.[29] Another suggests it is a significant, but generally denied, force shaping election strategies and outcomes.[30]

The latter perspective is corroborated by some compelling evidence. Data from surveys taken during two-way gubernatorial races confirm potential voters' tendency to support individuals from their own ethnic group. In 1974, George Ariyoshi led 5–1 among Japanese-Americans over a Caucasian candidate, Randolph Crossley, who in turn led 2 to 1 among Caucasians. In 1978, Frank Fasi, a Caucasian, led 5 to 1 among members of that ethnic group, while Ariyoshi was ahead 3 to 1 among Japanese-Americans. In 1994, more than one-half of Filipino voters surveyed indicated they would support the state's first Filipino contender for governor, Ben Cayetano.[31]

In an earlier study, Michael Haas empirically compared three models used to describe ethnic politics in different parts of the country in the 1980s.[32] One, labeled assimilation, sees ethnicity disappearing as a factor in political life as groups strive to become part of mainstream society. Another, integration, is defined by political behavior that retains patterns of segregation or separatism. Haas concluded that the third, cultural pluralism, characterized Hawai'i. Here, ethnic groups engage in bloc voting as a means of controlling elections, bettering their economic position, or improving the status of their culture. Haas suggested that of the five primary ethnic groups in the state, Filipinos and Japanese-Americans have shown the most ethnic solidarity, Caucasians next, and Chinese and Hawaiians the least.

A History of Denial

There *appears* to be good evidence of ethnicity's importance in voter identification. There is little disagreement about whether people who run campaigns *think* that it matters. Why then is it "the 'little secret' everyone in Hawai'i knows about but few speak frankly about"?[33] Dan Boylan suggests the denial is of relatively recent vintage.[34] As noted earlier, at the turn of the century members of the Home Rule coalition urged Hawaiian voters to "look to the skin." Republicans in turn were very explicit in using Hawaiian candidates, most notably Prince Kuhio, to lure Hawaiian voters, a strategy they successfully utilized as long as the native population remained an electoral majority.

The denial of ethnicity's role began in the 1930s. Americans of Japanese ancestry, who were increasing rapidly in number in the electorate, were taught that Good Americans—which they dearly wanted to be seen as—did not vote along racial lines. This was reinforced, first by the fear and suspicions of the Second World War, and later by the need for the islands to appear ethnically integrated in order to obtain statehood. The denial of ethnic campaigning and voting was furthered by the reality that no one group constituted a numerical majority in the post-statehood period. The consequence, according to Boylan, is that, as in other parts of America, "democracy and ethnic voting mix well," but in Hawai'i their connection is denied publicly while practiced regularly.

Some argue this attention comes primarily in close elections, but it is difficult to imagine campaigns which strategists and many voters do not see as having at least the potential to *become* close. If that is true, there will always be an incentive to cultivate ethnicity as a way of deciding.

The 1998 election illustrates this mixture. Incumbent governor Cayetano saw himself vulnerable on the economy, and his strategists agreed that he has in for a tough race. They decided an emphasis on values would permit him to point to the social programs the Democratic party stood for since the 1954 Revolution, but they had an added feature. That feature was to identify him with "local people" and "local culture." While usually not stated explicitly, which would run the risk of losing votes from groups that saw themselves as targeted, the values theme underscored that Republican challenger Linda Lingle is a mainland-born Caucasian who transplanted as an adult and never fully figured out how things really work in the islands.

This message was delicately crafted in television campaign commercials in which non-Caucasians repeatedly answer "I'm not stupid" or "I am not stupid" to proposals attributed to Lingle about the economy or other issues. The phrase played on well-known stereotypes of Caucasians as being too aggressive, too self-centered, and, above all, too patronizing to non-Caucasians.[35] The intention of this message was to distract voters from those substantive issues where Lingle had an advantage, to the style and emotional arena where Cayetano could score. When they succeeded, they got the response articulated to a reporter by one voter: "Lingle might offer something new. But with Cayetano, he seems to be more in touch with local people."[36]

Election results indicate that ethnicity was a factor in voters' decisions, although it is hard to know ethnicity's weight compared to social class and party. There are 51 House of Representative districts in the state. Census data revealed that 29 of these had Caucasians as the largest ethnic group. Lingle won 21 of these 29 in 1998. Cayetano, on the other hand, won handily in districts with Filipino and Japanese-American pluralities.

The Future of Ethnic Participation

As expected, ethnicity's future role in Hawai'i's political life is controversial. For some, most notably the sociologists Andrew Lind and Lawrence Fuchs, the latter the author of the influential social history *Hawaii Pono,* it will gradually decline in importance. This will happen as the state moves inexorably toward being fully integrated culturally and fully developed as a liberal polity.

For others, ethnic politics' future is less clear. Boylan sees conflicting forces pushing in each direction.[37] Two, demography and incumbency, lead in the direction of its diminishing importance. Demographic change is reflected in the gradual diluting of immigrant ethnic groups by inter-marriage and the arrival of greater numbers of Caucasians whose identity is less connected to ethnicity. The advantage incumbents have in holding onto public office discourages attempts on any basis, including ethnicity, by others to succeed in electoral politics.

On the side of seeming to strengthen ethnic politics is the continued immigration to the state from Asia and the Pacific; the emergence of a Native Hawaiian political movement; and the decline of political parties. Each new immigrant group will repeat the struggle to find its place, and the historical lesson suggests that each will rely on ethnic solidarity for help. Within the state, Native Hawaiian groups have made it clear they wish to define their own social and economic future, in the process gaining enough power to restore and protect their culture. This emphasis may cause non-Hawaiians, concerned about the impact of Native Hawaiian gains, to look to their own group's history of injustices and struggle as a way of protecting their future.

Finally, there is the decline of parties as a source of political identity. Increasing distance from the galvanizing period of the 1954 Revolution, the power of the media to enable candidates to bypass party mechanisms for fund-raising and getting information to voters, and the failure of major parties to create an agenda that resonates with voters, may all work in concert to decrease parties as a source of political identity. If that occurs, then it is possible the commonalties of history, values, and outlook provided by ethnicity may be a more important, although less public, substitute. Parties will exist in this future, perhaps primarily as devices for organizing legislative bodies, but voters will be formed into winning coalitions under the strong influence of ethnic affinities

The conflicted picture of ethnicity's future role was captured in the three-way race for governor in the 1994 election. During the campaign, Democrat Ben Cayetano, the eventual winner, used Filipino newspapers and radio stations to target Filipino voters. Although this is his ethnic group, Filipinos were an important constituency to shore up. Frank Fasi, a Caucasian candidate running in a party of his own creation, had spent his years as mayor of Honolulu carefully, and successfully, cultivating the Filipino vote through highly visible appointments in his administration. While denying they were catering to a politics of ethnicity, during the gubernatorial campaign Fasi and his Filipino wife told members of that group it would be, in their opinion, an act of betrayal to vote for another candidate.

The Japanese-American vote also was critical to Cayetano in piecing together a winning coalition. Polls revealed that Caucasians were leaning disproportionately toward Fasi, and Cayetano's Republican opponent, Pat Saiki, was a Japanese-American daughter of immigrant laborers. Campaign strategists expected Japanese-Americans to be torn between their attraction to Saiki for cultural reasons and their historic antipathy to the way the Republican party had treated people of her parents' generation.

The picture was further complicated by Cayetano's running mate for lieutenant governor. Mazie Hirono is also a Japanese-American, but had been born in Japan and come to the United States with her mother. This meant she shared none of the local intergenerational history, and her power to draw local Japanese Americans was unclear.

Finally, apparently to attract the substantial number of voters identifying themselves as part-Hawaiian, Cayetano boldly declared during the campaign that he would not occupy the governor's mansion, known as Washington Place. Instead, he would turn it over to Hawaiian groups as a act of atonement.

As is true for previous elections, it is difficult to know on what finally produced the outcome of the 1994 campaign. The kind of self-portrait each candidate attempted to create through carefully crafted television documentaries was important, and ethnicity also surfaced here. Just when Fasi's anti-Establishment message seemed on the verge of carrying him past front-running Cayetano in the polls, his campaign aired an expensive and instantly controversial advertisement depicting his opponents "morphing" into one another and then into a man he claimed is the "godfather of organized crime" in the islands.

After airing the advertisements, support for Fasi fell rapidly in the polls, and he eventually came in second. Using an ethnic politics perspective, one can conclude that Fasi's mistake was to change a Japanese-American and a Filipino-American into someone part-Hawaiian, thereby alienating people in all of these groups. The ad may, moreover, have raised the specter of aggressive, sometimes vindictive, campaigning for which East Coast Italian politics has a well-known reputation. Perhaps Fasi simply stepped past Hawai'i voters idea of how people should relate to one another in their Island community.

THE FUTURE OF PARTIES IN HAWAI'I

Hawai'i's Republican party has been unable, over the last forty-five years, to distinguish itself from the role played in the *haole* oligarchy and, at the same time, form coalitions capable of winning elections. Although they made a start on it in the 1998 election, Republicans have built neither an effective organization nor a grass roots operation. Distinctly Republican positions that resonate with a broader segment of the electorate have not been developed or articulated. Party candidates generally have failed in their appeal to Hawai'i voters, constrained in part by the fact they are overwhelmingly Caucasian.

Republicans will be challenged to devise a more compelling public philosophy. Office holders and candidates alike argue that there is too much government and too much regulation of business, and rely heavily on the generalization that restoration of a viable two-party system is in everyone's interest. To have broader appeal, their philosophy must be more compatible with the islands' strong moralistic and traditionalistic subcultures, while still accommodating mainstream party supporters who want to restrain government's role in favor of greater reliance on market solutions. It also will need to manage the intra-party conflicts created by a well-organized Christian right, many of whose positions do not play well in a setting as ethnically and socially tolerant as Hawai'i.

Despite Republican ineffectiveness, changing demographics and the length of time Democrats have been in power seem likely to present some opportunities. Caucasians are an increasing proportion of the population, and they are more inclined to vote Republican. In addition, Neighbor Island growth is dramatic, and Republicans may be identified as the means to devolve authority from O'ahu and establish more local control. Perhaps reflecting these opportunities, the Republican Party reported that between 1992 and 1997 party membership increased from 9,000 to 38,000. Perhaps equally significant, in the 1998 open primary Republican candidates received votes from about 160,000 residents, in comparison to 123,000 cast for Democrats. This contrasted with the pattern of the previous 16 years, when Democratic candidates attracted more than twice as many voters to their primary as all other parties combined.[38]

The Democratic party must rediscover itself to maintain its position. The legacy of 1954 can no longer sustain loyalty, a fact of life acknowledged in the gubernatorial campaigns of 1994 and 1998 when Democratic candidate Ben Cayetano repeatedly acknowledged that, "We've been given one last chance."

Several issues, each connected to the Democratic party's reformist roots, are especially relevant to the quest for renewed purpose. They are, however, a potentially volatile package, offering revitalization of the party as well as the threat of intra-party conflicts.

It may not be reasonable to hold any party, or any leader, responsible for the downturn that began in the early 1990s without also assigning responsibility to forces beyond the control of the state. Nevertheless, the party will have to support policies that at least appear to contribute to economic revitalization. Since contemporary neo-liberal thinking about what "works" involves offering corporate tax cuts, reducing the size of government, cutting welfare benefits, and reducing the cost companies must pay for labor fringe benefits, such as health care, Democrats will need to give these serious attention. The problem for the party is, of course, that these approaches are at odds with the core values that created the 1954 Revolution, and sacrificing them may leave the party with no distinctive appeal.

Active assimilation of the most recent immigrant groups is critical. Filipinos are a case in point. In the short run, especially with a Democratic governor who is a Filipino-American, they may see the Democratic Party as a natural ally in the struggle for a place in Hawai'i society. In the longer term, however, maintaining the loyalty of Filipinos, as well as other groups, means those who have run the party will need to relinquish some of their control over its machinery.

Promotion of more decentralized forms of governance, an important tenet of the 1954 party platform, also is important. As the state and its far-flung islands grow in population and complexity, more citizens express frustration with the performance of a public system so heavily concentrated in Honolulu. Responding by offering greater local control may help to defuse this, but it also may require giving up the power and resources that have come from commanding the levers of a centralized state.

Balancing the claims of Native Hawaiians against the interests of core supporters is another twin-edged issue. While sympathy unquestionably exists among party leadership for the injustices done to Hawaiians, going very far toward redress may threaten followers. This is likely to include the party's Japanese-American core, especially because land issues are involved here.

Japanese-Americans have remained loyal to Democratic candidates. A 1988 survey of eligible voters in Honolulu found that 70.6 percent of Japanese-Americans supported the Democratic party, in comparison to 35.7 percent for other groups. Equally important, at that time there was very little difference between younger and older respondents.[39] (It is also noteworthy that Japanese-Americans put more weight on party as a basis for voting than either local non Japanese-Americans or mainlanders.)[40] However, as the Japanese-American community continues to change under the disintegrating pressures of urbanization and the passing of its founding leaders, the Democratic establishment cannot assume their loyalty will remain at a level that counterbalances the less certain allegiance of other groups. For many, the 1998 election for governor hinged on whether younger Japanese-Americans would decide to vote for a candidate who, like them, did not have their parents' historical experience and who was more like them in generational terms.

Finally, there is for the Democratic party the larger challenge of finding an energizing public philosophy. Just as today's Republican party argues that one-party dominance is a common enemy, a half century ago, the Democratic party was animated by shared opposition to the *haole* elite. That focus helped to create strong organizational discipline. Defeat of the Republican party destroyed this common-threat basis for solidarity, contributing to internal factions.

Some Hawai'i Democrats may find a new mobilizing threat in community-destroying economic growth and the increasing influence of outsiders who disregard what is special about the islands. The party could establish itself as the gatekeeper for values and lifestyles under siege, dedicated to policies that balance change with protection, in the process joining forces with the strong preservationist elements of the sovereignty movement.

Such a public philosophy is consistent with the traditionalistic and moralistic threads woven so deeply through the islands' political culture and the Democratic party, and creates a potential to identify with concerns of a wide range of contemporary voters. However, it also may drive a wedge between the party and its pro-development supporters. Those who benefit most directly from economic growth and participation in the world economy, many of whom materially support the Democratic party and its candidates as the only show in town, are likely to reject this orientation as against their own financial interests.

Hawai'ian Parties in a National Context

Any analysis of Hawai'i political party futures cannot ignore the larger context of American politics and the role of parties in it. If the most basic function of parties is to form coalitions capable of winning elections, then the purpose of party competition is to maintain a system responsive to public concerns while providing sufficient discipline to prevent abuse by current office-holders. Even if such competition returns to Hawai'i for the first time in approximately one-hundred years, how much it will matter to most voters?

In one of many analyses of the discontent Americans express toward politics and political parties, E. J. Dionne Jr. argues that the ideological battles fought by the national parties have disaffected voters.[41] While candidates are struggling to win support on symbolically charged issues like abortion, same-sex marriage, prison release, or the pledge of allegiance, voters are struggling with their financial future, the loss of their communities, and their children's inadequate education. Results of a 1994 survey conducted by the Times Mirror Center for People and the Press corroborate a disconnection between party issues and voter concerns. Based on how they positioned themselves, respondents formed clusters of orientations having little to do with the way the major parties organize issues or attempt to create working coalitions.[42]

Prospects for a realignment of parties may be lower in Hawai'i than in parts of the mainland. Voters are more likely to try a second party before they think seriously about a third. Still, the same structural forces that nationally lead in the direction of decline in the institutional significance of political parties are present in the islands.[43] The direct links between special interest funders and candidates are among these forces, as is the power of television to afford visibility to anyone who can pay the price. Both of these decrease candidate and elected official dependence on the party, and give it fewer ways to build and maintain allegiance to a common policy agenda.

A comfortable compatibility seemed to exist for many years between Hawai'i's blend of traditionalistic and moralistic political culture and the Democratic party. As the political culture, the Democratic party, and the institution of political parties continue to change, it is worth pondering what might emerge to guide and give legitimacy to the state's electoral process.

CHAPTER SEVEN

Courts, Values, and the Law

The judiciary in Hawai'i—the state courts—reflect the combination of novelty and familiarity that characterizes much of what is found in Hawai'i. Organizationally quite similar to state judiciaries found throughout the United States, there is a great deal about the Hawai'i judiciary's history and outlook that is unique to the islands.

Consistent with the political culture that it both reflects and creates, it is the Hawai'i Judiciary's orientation to legal policy that has most distinguished it from counterparts in other parts of the country. In many ways, the Hawai'i courts, symbolized by sober and serious people attired in black robes, have been, in relation to most of their colleague's elsewhere, quite radical. That radicalism originates in efforts to blend principles from traditional Hawaiian society with more conventional Western-oriented legal philosophy. Its greatest impact is on the meaning given to property rights.

The Supreme Court of William Richardson has gone to the greatest lengths to fuse into Hawai'i law the traditions and cultural values that historically most distinguish the islands. The courts that have followed appear to be less interested in following this path, and their comparative conservatism may reflect changes in the social and political landscape as well as the personalities of the particular justices.

THE BUSINESS OF THE COURTS

The administration of justice is big business, a fact of modern life throughout the United States. Even in a small state like Hawai'i, it costs almost $90 million, or 1.5 percent of the states total appropriations.[1] It is useful, therefore, to note the various roles which courts the courts are asked to fill, and the costs associated with filling them.

The courts in Hawai'i, and probably in general, have at least five general functions.[2]

(1) Guardian of Constitutional Rights. The United States Constitution and all state constitutions specify individual rights in relation to the exercise of public authority. A major responsibility of state courts is to pass judgment on an unending series of cases that pit the government's desire to take action on behalf of some public good against the protection of individual constitutional rights. These conflicts occur in a variety or arenas. Hawai'i's political culture has meant that in many of these areas—the uses to which property may be put, access to public information, the rights of employees, and the obligations of the state to the disadvantaged—the state's authority to act on behalf of what is perceived as an overriding public interest has been affirmed more than in most other places.

(2) Dispute Resolution Mechanisms. Many view the resolution of thorny conflicts as the primary responsibility of courts. In addition to dealing with these conflicts in ways common to judicial processes everywhere in the United States, the Hawai'i courts have been national leaders in the utilization of alternative dispute resolution (ADR) techniques, such as mediation, to help litigants find remedies outside the formal legal process.

(3) Government Agency. The courts function as a government agency by providing various social services, such as family-court support and guardianship, and as the administrator of the various functions required to make the courts work. For example, the Supreme Court contains within its structure such entities as its capital improvements program (to build and maintain court facilities), the Children's Advocacy Center, the Commission on Judicial Conduct, an Internal Audit Office, the Adult Probation Administration, the Public Affairs Office, the Law Library, the Telecommunications and Information Services Division, and the Office of Public Guardian.

The Judiciary is an independent branch of government by constitutional provision. The monies it receives are not part of the budget put together by the governor, and budget requests are acted upon directly by the legislature. This fiscal autonomy from the executive branch is highlighted during budget crises when the governor, acting through the Department of Budget and Finance, can restrict or withdraw the funds of state departments, but may only "request" that the two independent departments, the Judiciary and the Office of Hawaiian Affairs, follow suit. As each makes clear, they are under no legal obligation to do so.

Table 4: Appropriations by Branch, 1995

Branch	Percentage	Appropriations
Executive	96.64%	$3,193,572,474
Legislative	0.66%	21,900,117
Judiciary	2.70%	89,129,443
Total		$3,304,602,034

The Judiciary utilizes about 2.7 percent of the total state budget. In fiscal year 1995 that amounted to approximately $90 million. Table 4 displays appropriations by branch.

(4) Subsystem of the Legal System. As the foregoing suggests, much of the business of the Supreme Court is to create and maintain standards for professional conduct within the legal system by licensing attorneys, making judicial appointments, and disciplining lawyers and judges. In Hawai'i, many of these functions are carried out by the Judicial Selection Commission, the Office of Disciplinary Counsel, and the Commission on Judicial Conduct.

(5) Agent for Change. Courts have the capacity, through their decisions, to become powerful agents for change in virtually all social and economic arenas. In the islands, the courts have been pivotal in crystallizing the values and defining the policies that shape Hawai'i society. Whether the issue is determining if the state has provided adequately for incarcerated or medically needy people, establishing the traditional rights of Native peoples, or the state's obligation not to discriminate in setting rules for who may marry, the courts have played a pivotal role.

HISTORICAL DEVELOPMENT

Before to the arrival of Europeans, the islands were ruled by the king and Ali'i nui, (high chiefs) whose word was law. The "laws" were based on custom and tradition, and they embodied what Hawaiians referred to as *kapus*. The *kapu* system in some ways served the role played by contemporary judiciaries by maintaining order in the light of existing societal rules and thereby enforcing Hawaiian ideas of justice.

Kapus were things that were physically dangerous, restricted, prohibited, forbidden, and to be avoided. In traditional Hawaiian society, many individuals and physical objects were held as *kapu*. Priests, chiefs, and their belongings were *kapu*. Should the shadow of a lesser person fall upon the house, clothing, or other possession of a great chief, that person was put to death. Women ate separately from men, and could not have certain foods suggestive of male power.[3] *Kapus* regulated fishing seasons, planting methods, and the disposal of human waste. Individual trees, such as the *'ohi'a lehua* tree, could be considered *kapu* because the tree was not only the manifestation of the god Kúka'óhi'alaka, but also because it happened to be the tree of choice for canoe builders.[4]

Kapus were designed to protect not only the chiefs but, due to the belief that one who came in contact with a chief would become contaminated with supernatural power, they were fashioned in a way that protected the chief's subjects as well. The net result was, in the words of George Hu'eu Sanford Kanahele, "by and large a very well ordered, practical and efficient world . . . in effect, the whole *kapu* system, with its rules and penalties, was an elaborate codification of laws governing interpersonal relationships as well as those between gods and human beings."[5]

The *kapu's* collapsed for a variety of reasons. Important among these was the sight of foreigners, especially visiting sailors, routinely breaking prohibitions without consequence; the acts committed by the chiefs and warriors during Kamehameha's conquest of the islands; and the demoralizing affects of epidemic diseases, against which no Hawaiians spiritual adviser (*kahuna*) could offer protection.[6]

Young King Liholiho, influenced heavily by Ka'ahumanu, the late king Kamehameha's most important wife, formally abolished the *kapu* system in the early part of November 1819. This occurred at a feast at Kailua on the Big Island, to which were invited important chiefs and several foreigners. The king and Ka'ahumanu deliberately made a show of breaking eating taboos during the feast. When it was over, the king ordered that religious sites— *Heiaus*—be destroyed and idols burned.

Although this was done from one end of the kingdom to the other, many people refused to abandon the *kapu* system and, while outwardly joining with the king, secretly clung to their traditional idols. This meant that the new Western-oriented court system for resolving conflicts, maintaining order, and gaining justice had to be overlaid on a strongly held, but harder-to-see, alternative system.

The First Western Court System

The first formal judicial system with some Western characteristics was established by the constitution of 1840, which created a "Supreme Court" that consisted of the king, the *kuhina-nui,* and four other judges appointed by the representative body within the bicameral legislature.[7]

The 1840 constitution included several rights for citizens of the Hawaiian nation. Among these were the freedom of religion, the right of redress for injury, the right to a lawful trial, and the requirement that no one sit as a judge or juror in their own case, or in the case of someone closely connected to them.

The Supreme Court acted as an appellate court. District courts were created on the several islands, and island governors appointed their judges. This constitution also created a system of tax courts and tax judges. The tax judges were appointed by the king and the *kuhina-nui* and given responsibility for assessing and collecting taxes, as well as hearing cases arising under the tax laws or between landlords and tenants. The decisions of tax judges could be appealed to the governor and to the Supreme Court.[8]

The first criminal code was produced in 1850, and in 1852 a new constitution modified the judiciary somewhat by replacing the Supreme Court created by the constitution of 1840, as well as the superior court established by the Third Organic Act in 1847, with a supreme court made up of a chief justice and two associate justices. The new constitution also gave the legislature power to adjust the number of judicial circuits, with the stipulation that there be no more than eight, or fewer than four. All judges of courts of record were appointed by the king for life or for good behavior, and district justices were appointed by the governors for a term of two years.[9]

The judicial system created by the 1852 constitution, and to a lesser extent by the constitution of 1840, reflected many of the dominant characteristics of judicial systems in the United States, then and today. Provisions for amending the constitution, the authority of the Supreme Court vis-à-vis the inferior courts, the method of judicial selection for the inferior courts, and the relationship of the courts to the chief executive—in this case the king—were drawn from the model dominant in several states, something which continues to the present. As chapter 5 pointed out, these provisions reflected the growing influence of foreign advisors.

The Territorial Court System

The territorial Organic Act of 1900 brought the federal territorial court system to the Hawaiian Islands. Under the Organic Act, judges were appointed by the president of the United States. It was common from 1900 until statehood for vacancies in Hawai'i's territorial courts to take two or more years to be filled. The primary qualifications, through most of the period, for appointment to a judgeship were social and political connections, and prestige. As a consequence, some magistrates had little or no formal education in the law and experience in judicial procedure. Territorial courts were funded by county governments, and because of the countys' scarcity of resources, they often were understaffed, procedurally disorganized, and in need of repair.[10]

FORMAL COURT ORGANIZATION

As with other basic aspects of what would later become Hawai'i's state government, the 1950 Hope Chest laid out the court system adopted in Hawai'i's 1959 constitution. That system is made up of the Supreme Court, an intermediate Court of Appeals, a Land Court, Tax Court, the circuit courts, and district courts. Consistent with other ways in which Hawai'i is centralized, there are no county or municipal courts.

The Hawai'i Supreme Court

The Hawai'i Supreme Court consists of the chief justice and four associate justices who serve ten-year terms and must retire at age 70. As the final appeals court and the highest court in the state, the Supreme Court develops rules of procedure that have the force and effect of law for all the state courts, and may reprimand, suspend, discipline, or remove state judges.

The case load of the Hawai'i Supreme Court more than doubled from 1975 to 1980, going from 988 to 2,013.[11] Growth has been relatively constant since the 1980s, with some variation. For example, 1985 had a level roughly equal to 1993, whereas 1990 was the lowest during the period 1985–95. During the 1996–97 court year, 822 primary cases were filed with the Supreme Court, an decrease from the 940 filed two years earlier. The court also saw 2,440 supplemental proceedings filed, almost the same as the earlier period.[12]

The Intermediate Appellate Court

Hawai'i is one of the relatively few states that has an Intermediate Appellate Court. The Intermediate Appellate Court has concurrent jurisdiction with the Supreme Court and essentially takes some of the case pressure off of the Supreme Court. Created in 1980, the three-judge Court of Appeals hears matters assigned to it by the chief justice. Like the Supreme Court, its appointees serve ten-year terms and must retire when they reach age 70.

The Hawai'i Appellate Court resulted from the action of the 1978 Constitutional Convention that considered and rejected expanding the size of the Hawai'i Supreme Court. Then sitting Chief Justice Richardson argued that an intermediate appeals court should be established to relieve some of the case load burdening the Supreme Court. Justice Richardson also argued that overcrowding the state Supreme Court docket was causing unnecessary delays.

During 1994–95, the Intermediate Court of Appeals was assigned a total of 220 primary cases from the supreme court. During that year the intermediate court completed 29 percent of its total caseload, or 158 cases.[13]

Circuit Courts

Trial courts in Hawai'i are organized into four judicial circuits, one for each county. Interestingly, these bear designations First through Fifth—the Fourth Judicial Circuit having been merged with the Third in 1943. The First Circuit includes the City and Country of O'ahu and the Hansen's disease settlement of Kalawao on Moloka'i. This Circuit is comprised of 21 districts, each presided over by a Circuit Court judge, fourteen District Court judges, ten Family Court judges (including a Circuit Court judge who serves as a senior Family Court judge), and twenty-nine per diem judges, ten of whom serve the Family Court. The Second Circuit is made up of the County of Maui, which includes the islands of Maui, Moloka'i (excluding Kalawao), and Lana'i. This much smaller circuit is served by three Circuit Court judges, three District Court judges, two Family Court judges, and eight per diem judges.

The Third Judicial Circuit covers the Big Island, divided into districts for Hilo and Kona. Somewhat smaller than the Second Circuit, it has three Circuit Court judges, three District Court judges, two Family Court judges, and six per diem judges. The Fifth Judicial Circuit covers the County of Kaua'i (including Kaua'i and Ni'ihau) with one Circuit Court judge, two District Court judges, and three per diem judges.[14] All jury trials are held in the Circuit Courts, which have general jurisdiction in both criminal and civil cases. Circuit Court judges are given ten-year terms upon appointment by the governor with the consent of the Senate. They too must retire at age 70.

Other responsibilities of the Circuit Courts include probate, guardianship, and criminal felony cases, civil cases where the contested amount exceeds $20,000 (they share concurrent jurisdiction with district courts in non-jury civil cases in the amounts of $10,000–20,000), mechanics' liens, naturalization proceedings, and misdemeanor violations transferred from the District Courts for jury trials. The Circuit Court case-load peaked in 1984 at almost 55,000; in 1996–97 it was 43,429.[15]

The Land Court, Tax Appeal Court, and Family Courts are within the Circuit Courts. The Land Court has original jurisdiction over issues within the state involving title to land, easements, or rights to land. The Tax Appeal Court hears real property tax assessment appeals and other matters pertaining to real property taxation. The administrative judge of the First Circuit Court, under the direction of the Supreme Court chief justice, assigns all Tax Appeal Court and Land Court matters to the appropriate judge or judges of the First Circuit Court.

Family Courts, established by statute in 1965, have exclusive original jurisdiction over a variety of offenses and conflicts concerning children and families. Hawai'i's Family Courts have the widest jurisdictional reach of any such courts in the country.[16] Their stated goals are "resolving family disputes in a timely, economical, and therapeutic manner using the least restrictive alternatives."[17] In 1996–97, the Family Court had a total case load of 89,824, of which it concluded 53,330 cases.[18]

The Family Courts are heavily invested in alternative dispute-resolution and educational techniques as vehicles for both problem solving and incidence reduction. Reducing domestic violence is the court's stated top priority. The court also runs an extensive array of programs, structured by each circuit, to deal with the particular juvenile and adult matters that fall under its jurisdiction; examples include the Juvenile Intake and Family Crisis Services Branch, and the Child and Youth Services Branch within the First Circuit.

District Courts

Finally, there are the District Courts. The District Courts have jurisdiction over civil matters in which the amount of dispute is $10,000 or less, criminal offenses that are punishable by fine or imprisonment of one year or less, and violations of county ordinances. District Courts are organized on the same basis as are the Circuit Courts—that is, into one of four circuits. Unlike the other judges discussed in this chapter, District Court appointments are made by Hawai'i Supreme Court justices for terms of six years. Once the responsibility of county governments, District Courts became the responsibility of the state in 1966. The reforms of that year, through the Family Court Act, also united the Juvenile and Domestic Relations Courts.[19]

POLITICS AND JUDICIAL APPOINTMENTS

Judges are appointed by the governor with the consent of the majority of the state senate in many states. Three states—Connecticut, South Carolina, and Virginia—have most of their judges selected by a majority vote of the state legislature. Others, notably Alabama, Arkansas, Illinois, Mississippi, New Mexico, North Carolina, Tennessee, Texas, and West Virginia, have partisan elections for all judgeships. Thirteen states have nonpartisan judicial elections, a progressive reform most often found in the Midwest and West.[20]

In 1978, Hawai'i adopted the "Missouri Plan" or "merit system" of judicial selection. Merit systems were designed to remove partisan politics from this aspect of courts and, in the process, improve the quality of state court justices. The merit system was proposed and rejected by the 1968 Constitutional Convention, then debated and accepted by the next convention in 1978, with ratification by voters in that year's general election.

The Judicial Selection Committee

Article VI, Section 4 of the Hawai'i Constitution provides for a Judicial Selection Commission to participate in appointments to the state's Supreme Court, Intermediate Appellate Court, and Circuit Courts. The Judicial Selection Commission consists of nine members, two appointed by the governor, two each appointed by the president of the Senate and the speaker of the House of Representatives, one appointed by the Supreme Court chief justice, and two appointed by members in good standing of the Hawai'i State Bar Association. Only one of the governor's, and none of the chief justice's, appointees may be an attorney, nor may more than four commission members be attorneys. Commission members are, theoretically, apolitical and are prohibited from taking an active role in election campaigns. No commissioner may be considered for a judicial appointment for three years after his or her service on the Selection Commission.

When there is a vacancy in the courts, it is advertised and nominations are invited. The Selection Commission screens candidates through lengthy questionnaires, and by examining any police records, credit records, and the Tax Office. For each vacancy on the Supreme Court, the Intermediate Appellate Court, and the circuit courts, the commission gives the governor a list of six names from which to choose. Vacancies in the District Courts are filled by the Supreme Court chief justice from a list of six individuals recommended by the commission. All appointees must be confirmed by the Hawai'i state Senate.

Prior to implementation of the Judicial Selection Commission in 1980, judges were appointed by the governor with the advice and consent of the Senate. District Court judges were appointed by the chief justice of the Supreme Court. William S. Richardson, a former lieutenant governor during the Burns administration, became chief justice of the Supreme Court, serving from 1966 to 1982 and exerting a major influence on the Hawai'i court system. Chief Justice Richardson and then-Governor John Burns used what Jim Wang has called the "Burns Method" of judicial selection. The "Burns Method" was personal and informal. Richardson "personally conferred with prestigious law firms and bar associations in the selection process."[21]

It is interesting to note that many who were champions of judicial selection reform in the 1950s when territorial judges were appointed by the president came to accept the system of partisan appointment when the context was local politics under statehood. Carol S. Dodd observed that, "By 1968, the power of those early party building Democrats was unchallengeable, and the move to dilute gubernatorial authority for judicial appointments sputtered along disjointedly."[22]

Partisanship in the Appointment Process

Although merit systems are intended to improve the quality of the state court justices and take unbridled partisanship out of judicial selection, it would be naive to think that politics can be removed from such an important function. In Missouri, the first state to adopt this method of judicial selection, an earlier study provided little evidence that merit criteria had improved the quality of justice.[23] In Hawai'i, suggestions of the persistence of centralized, in-group, and partisan influence in the selection process remain a nagging concern.

For most of the period since statehood, judicial appointees in the islands have tended to be Democrats. It has been common for appointees to have prior partisan service, either through participation in the electoral campaigns of others, or as candidates or office-holders themselves. In addition, a relatively large number are Americans of Japanese ancestry.

Under Hawai'i's current system, the requirement that judicial nominees be confirmed by the Senate is designed to put a check on the governor's judicial appointment powers. In fact, in Hawai'i, the Senate has rarely rejected the governor's recommendations. Given the enduring control of the legislative and executive branches since statehood by Democrats, this is not surprising.

A case occurred in 1993 that may prove the rule. The Senate refused to confirm Governor Waihe'e's nominee, Sharon Himeno, to the Supreme Court. Himeno had no judicial experience, but did have the advantage of being the wife of Warren Price, who served as attorney general for most of the Waihe'e administration. She also was the daughter of a local businessman influential in the Democratic party—Stan Himeno.

The public outcry over this nomination of a seemingly under-qualified but highly connected person to the highest judicial office was punctuated by newspaper allegations of possible misdoings by the Himenos in real estate dealings involving the state's employee retirement system. Although formal charges never were made, the prevailing mood in the state, and certainly in the legislature, seemed to signify that this level of overt cronyism was beyond the pail, and the nomination was rejected. The highly visible rejection of an important nomination by a legislature dominated by the governor's own party was a rare event.

In summary, it is difficult to say whether judicial selection in Hawai'i is any more or less partisan than in any other state. Some states, New Jersey and Illinois come to mind, have a rich tradition of searching for one or another mechanism to de-politicize judicial selection, with limited success. Consistent with its political culture, Hawai'i is probably farther away from the end of the continuum at which behavior toward the judiciary is marked by highly explicit norms of political separation, and nearer, but not at, the end where politicization is routine.

POLITICS AND POLICY IN THE HAWAI'I COURTS

While Hawai'i's judicial history is unique, and aspects of the court structure, notably the Intermediate Appellate Court and separate Land and Family Courts, are not commonly found in other states, it is the rulings of the Hawai'i Supreme Court that set it apart.

Judges are not neutral observers of their worlds. They are part of society and involved in a political process. They are influenced by interest groups, other branches of government, and the partisan disputes of their communities. Stated differently, all courts do far more than settle disputes arising out of the application of existing law, and are an important part of the public policy making apparatus.

The question of just how state courts are affected by the political milieu is difficult to answer, in part because the exercise of influence is subtle. Moreover, both the influencers and the targets of influence differ on when it has occurred.[24] Some studies of judicial behavior in state and federal courts suggest that political party affiliation makes a difference in judicial rulings, with Democratic judges being more inclined to support organized labor and the poor than Republican judges. Other studies have found that judges' decisions are influenced by ethnic and religious ties.[25] There also is evidence that state supreme courts are more likely, when compared to federal courts, to uphold the constitutionality of their own state's laws. This outcome is unsurprising given the likelihood that state Supreme Court justices will reflect the political culture of their state and policy orientation of the governors who appointed them.[26]

In Hawai'i, the court's referencing of the political environment is affected by a constitutional provision that permits the state's attorney general, the administration's highest ranking legal officer, to request Supreme Court "advisory opinions" in advance of an actual case or controversy. This ability to engage the court actively in policy discourse enhances the legal powers of the state administration, and involves the court more deeply in the politics of the moment than if it were restricted to entering into cases involving existing legislation.

The Courts and Issues of Hawaiian People

In contrast with this degree of in-group influence, but equally consistent with the state's political culture, the Hawai'i Supreme Court's interpretations of a number of important property rights cases have departed radically from the jurisprudence of most other state high courts. The Court's justices have, in a number of interesting cases, abandoned precedent and relied for guidance on ancient Hawaiian custom and tradition.

By July 1969, with the appointment of Bert Kobayashi by then-Governor John Burns, all members of the Hawai'i Supreme Court had been appointed by Burns. The governor reportedly told his appointees not to feel bound by territorial precedents if they felt those precedents were inappropriate for Hawai'i and did not recognize its special character. The governor's position was supported by Hawai'i state law. In particular, Section 1–1 of the Hawai'i Revised Statutes states: "The common law of England, as ascertained by English and American decisions, is declared to be the common law of the state of Hawai'i in all cases, except as otherwise expressly provided by the Constitution or laws of the United States, or by the laws of the state *or fixed by Hawaiian judicial precedent or established by Hawaiian usage*" (emphasis added).

Carol S. Dodd has put this in perspective by observing that, "To suggest the prior body of Anglo-American law is not sacrosanct comes close to heresy in some legal circles; to act upon that suggestion is even more damnable."[27] Nevertheless, not following that prior body of Anglo-American law is precisely what the Hawai'i Supreme Court has done on several important occasions. Again, to cite Carol Dodd: "Through a series of decisions stretching from the late 1960s through the next decade, Hawai'i's Supreme Court would show a willingness to defy the existing body of Anglo-American case law. In rendering its decisions in these cases, the court recognized the validity of both native Hawaiian and Anglo-American tenets of jurisprudence. At points of unresolvable conflict and contradiction between the two cultures, the court often would leap backward in time to draw upon precedents and traditions of Hawaiian culture."[28]

In the first, and perhaps most important, case that illustrated this new orientation, *Palama v. Sheenan,* the court unanimously upheld a lower court ruling that based modern property rights on ancient Hawaiian rights to use land. This 1968 ruling affirmed a decision to allow right-of-way privileges originating in old Hawaiian laws and practices.[29]

In 1973, the Richardson court handed down *McBryde Sugar Company v. Robinson.*[30] *McBryde* involved a dispute over surface water to the Hanapepe River and two of its tributaries on Kaua'i. Prior to *McBryde,* Hawai'i water law recognized three types of water rights. The first were "appurtenant," rights that based the amount of water attached to a piece of land on what was used when it was converted to private ownership. The second type were "prescriptive rights," those rights acquired by virtue of the water being used over a specific period of time. Finally, so-called "surplus waters," constituted a residual rights category for the rest of the water in a river. Hawai'i court decisions, supported by precedents on the mainland, had firmly established the private nature of water rights in the state.

The court's *McBryde* decision was one of the courts "most significant and controversial,"[31] and had the effect of standing Hawai'i water law on its head. Using precedent derived from the time of the monarchy, the court concluded that the grant of water rights by kings had been limited to need, and that all other water was reserved for public use. The court declared, consequently, that in Hawai'i all flowing surface waters belong to the state. The justices abolished the concept of prescriptive rights and of surplus water, and prohibited the transfer of appurtenant rights.

Equally far-reaching, in a series of cases that came to be called the Shoreline Boundary Cases, the Hawai'i Supreme Court found that the seaward boundary of property in dispute would be determined by the vegetation line or the line of debris left by the sea and not, as was common practice in the rest of the country, at the mean high-tide line as determined by the U.S. Coast and Geodetic Survey. The decision was based in part on "tradition, custom and usage in old Hawai'i" and the fact that the chief justice "felt that no Hawaiian king would deny his subjects access to beach frontage for any number of public uses."[32]

Other more recent cases illustrate the willingness of the Hawai'i courts to rely on Hawaiian traditions, and also illustrate a disposition of the Hawai'i Supreme Court to hand down controversial decisions justified by few mainland precedents, but which support prevailing values and policy objectives in the state. For example, in 1994, the Court upheld the right of the City and County of Honolulu to condemn leasehold property under condominiums and to then sell that land to lessees. (For more on this issue, see chapter 11.) That decision, later was upheld by the federal Supreme Court, is unusual and the Hawai'i high court's willingness to uphold it is significant.[33]

The orientation of the Richardson court has been controversial. One camp, represented by former bar association presidents Clinton Ashford and Dan Case, has argued the Richardson court, in particular, had an "activist agenda," an agenda that produced "radical decisions" that have been harmful to the people of Hawai'i.

As evidence of this harm they cite the decisions on ocean boundaries, water rights, and a move "toward expansion of the rights of Native Hawaiians, and perhaps others, to enter upon and use private property" for gathering and cultural practice.[34] This latter refers to the *Patch* decision in which the Supreme Court has ruled that current land owners are subject to access claims by Native Hawaiians in the pursuit of historical cultural practices. (These issues are discussed in more detail in chapter 11.)

Former Justice Richardson denies the allegation of activism, suggesting, in this particular instance, that Ashford and Case have mistaken activism for the peculiarities of the law applicable to Hawai'i by both constitutional structure and legislative fiat.

> Concerning traditional and customary Hawaiian law . . . Hawaii Supreme Court rulings over the last 30 years have not been 'activist.' They have interpreted the laws written by Hawaii's people through their Legislature and Constitutional Convention. Correct interpretation is not judicial activism. Ironically, Ashford and Case (conclude) by calling on Hawaii's current Supreme Court to adhere to 'traditional standards and rules.' That's exactly what my court insisted upon—decisions based on standards and values time-honored

and traditional *in Hawaii*. This also has been the hallmark of the Supreme Court since my tenure as chief justice.[35]

This Richardson Court commitment to building a body of law on Anglo-American common law *and* principles carried forth from the kingdom clearly makes Hawai'i unique. That commitment also permits Justice Richardson to endorse court decisions that would be considered activist in most places, while arguing that, in the context of what is traditional and accepted in Hawai'i, they are not.

INTERPRETING THE HAWAI'I COURTS

The Richardson Court spanned 16 years, more than enough time to make a lasting imprint on legal philosophy and the judiciary. It was followed by Supreme Courts headed by Herman Lum and then William Moon. Interpretations of the court following the Richardson era have tended to make it out as more passive, a care-taker rather than an agenda setter, and as concerned about efficiency as establishing clear judicial policy.[36] This conclusion is shared by David Kimo Frankel in an issue of the *University of Hawai'i Law Review* devoted to assessing the court in the ten years following Richardson's retirement.[37] Frankel made these points.

First, the post-Richardson court internally tends to avoid conflict and in general to defer to administrative agencies, giving them broad authority to act. It also typically allows the legislature to act without judicial interference.

Second, the court acts to protect labor, but does not give the same level of protection to the environment. This reflects the Democratic party orientation of the court, and that fact that labor is that party's most enduring constituency.

Third, the court's more conservative tendency is most evident in land use and tort decisions. During this period, however, the rights extended to criminal defendants have increased.

Fourth, the Hawai'i Supreme Court is failing to provide adequate protections to politically powerless groups. It has demonstrated less social conservatism than the United States Supreme Court, which in this period was rejecting the civil rights claims of the politically powerless, environmental groups, the poor and homosexuals. For example, in some areas the Hawai'i court has moved to broaden individual rights, especially from intrusion by the police, and by protecting individuals from arbitrary government action.

But it also has shown a conservative streak in electing not to protect certain public and group rights, denying various environmentalist claims, repeatedly failing to expand Hawaiian rights in contested cases, and through acts such as refusing to sanction write-in voting.

Finally, the court has been ambivalent about clearly articulating or forcefully conveying its own positions. It has shown this by relying on memorandum opinions that do not set precedents and do not illuminate the law.

Frankel's summary of court positions may point to tensions in the changing social-political environment that help to shape up the court's positions. For those whose frame of reference is the national economy and society, especially when viewed in property terms, the Hawai'i court still can be criticized for its radicalism, for straying from the dominant climate of jurisprudence in the other states, and for making too much of "localism."

For those who identify most strongly with values characteristic of Hawai'i and things Hawaiian, the court, while respected for its occasional bias toward "local" concerns such as the ocean and water-rights disputes, is becoming more of a force of conservatism, one that weighs in too heavily on the side of established social and political arrangements, against the interests of the less powerful.

Two issues with which the court has struggled reveal these contrasting orientations. The *Baehr v. Lewin* case, which is discussed in chapter 5 with the same-sex marriage amendment, offered the high court an opportunity to consider the question of gay rights and, in particular, to decide whether Hawai'i's constitution affords homosexuals the same standing as heterosexuals. *Baehr v. Lewin* raised the legality of the state withholding marriage licenses from same-sex couples. The Supreme Court's 1993 decision denied the state this power, forcing it to either convince the justices that a compelling reason existed for refusal of the licenses, or change the constitution.

On the face of it, this decision seems to suggest the "liberalness" of the Hawai'i" Supreme Court. That was the conclusion reached in other parts of the country.[38] From another perspective, however, the court elected to take a very conservative position in relation to Hawai'i's strong constitutional protections of personal privacy and due process.

Danielle Kie Hart, a visiting faculty member at the University of Hawai'i's Richardson School of Law, argues that even though the justices came to the right conclusion by not accepting the state's denial of licenses, they did so for reasons that are both wrong and potentially harmful.[39] By her analysis of court proceedings, the justices did not support the privacy claim that homosexuals, as much as heterosexuals, have a right to marry. They found, instead, that the couples' sexual orientation was not relevant, and that the Department of Health had erred "on an equal protection basis in spite of, rather than cause of, their homosexuality."[40]

This judicial reasoning constitutes, for Hart, a betrayal of the plaintiffs and the constitution. She contends that "if the majority had undertaken a principled analysis of plaintiffs' claims based on their sexual orientation . . . it would have been compelled to find under Hawaii's constitution that plaintiffs had a fundamental right to marry their partners."[41] She continues on to argue that, in this failure to act, two things have happened. The court has limited the privacy rights protected by Article I, section 6 in the state's Bill of Rights. Perhaps of even greater long-run significance, the Hawai'i Supreme Court has ignored the broad language used by the framers of the amendment and, in so doing, taken "an extremely conservative and narrow approach to fundamental rights analysis under Hawaii's constitution."[42]

The second area in which this tension between radicalism and conservatism is found is how the court addresses complex Hawaiian rights and sovereignty issues. Efforts to place the court in a major policy-making role with respect to Hawaiian concerns, either to endorse Hawaiian claims for restitution or to defend Western property rights against such claims, surface here, and are nicely illustrated by matters affecting the Bishop Estate, the state's largest private landowner.

As noted in chapter 2, the estate was established in 1884 by the will of Bernice Pauahi Bishop. The will gives the Supreme Court responsibility for filling vacancies, and from the beginning they have been appointed by justices of the Hawaiian nation, the republic, the territory, and the state. The estate's size and influence have meant that it reflected the economic and political relations of the times, and changing times have brought different kinds of appointees.[43]

When sugar was dominant, trustees were tied directly to the industry, and they and plantation owners could make land deals that benefited sugar and drove up estate land values. When sugar declined in importance, then trustees were well-connected professional trust and land managers. After World War II, land was starting to be developed for non-agricultural purposes, and trustees were linked to land developers. And when, starting in the 1970s, a changing political scene brought public policy initiatives that might threaten the estate, appointees became directly involved to the public policy process. (In 1998, for example, one of the five trustees was a former speaker of the house, and another, the board's chair, was former president of the senate.)

Throughout these times, the connections have, on the one hand, leveraged the power of the estate and, on the other, put it under the influence of individuals whose interests seemed far removed from serving Kamehameha Schools and its students, the trust's designated beneficiaries. In August 1997, an essay charging that the trust's relationship to its beneficiaries had fundamentally been broken received heavy media attention. The authors of "Broken Trust," all well-known in the community, included a sitting U.S. District Court judge and a former Intermediate Court of Appeals judge, the former principal of the Kamehameha Schools for Girls, a respected Hawaiian minister, and a university faculty member specializing in trust law.[44]

Their essay concluded with several dramatic recommendations, including creation of a strategic planning process for the endowment and the school, investigation of trustee conduct, changes in the rules for trustee remuneration, and limitation of trustee terms. One of the recommendations spoke directly to court responsibilities by recommending creation of a blue-ribbon commission to set criteria and procedures for selecting trustees.

The Supreme Court justices, in the ensuing months, struggled over how to respond to what had become a political firestorm. On December 20, they issued a statement that removed them from the responsibility of appointing trustees to any trust and assigned it to the probate court.[45]

The majority's decision reflects their intention to protect the court from further harm that might accompany continued participation in a highly visible and very conflictual process. The justices desire to protect the court, however, had to be weighed against arguments rejecting such a change as a betrayal of responsibilities to the will and to the Hawaiian people.

The legal case against change, made, among other places, in a dissenting opinion, was based on the Supreme Court's role being a provision of Bernice Bishop's will, as well as concerns that this delegation of authority would create a precedent for other unwarranted revisions of the will. Native Hawaiian groups, with the sole exception of the Native Hawaiian Trail Lawyers Association, argued, sometimes passionately, against the court removing itself. They believed that removal would break the court's often-sympathetic connection with the Hawaiian community, while simultaneously reducing that community's influence over trustee selection. In confronting the social and political arguments, the justices took the unusual step of meeting with groups of Hawaiians before reaching their decision.

The justices offered several reasons for their decision. They noted, in response to arguments that the will's terms were being violated, that there was no probate court when the will was written. Had a probate court existed, appointments would been given to it since it subsequently was created to handle duties relating to wills and trusts. The justices noted, in support of this position, that today the Hawai'i Probate Court appoints masters to conduct reviews of the fiscal and organizational management of the Bishop Estate. The justices downplayed concerns about bad precedents, observing that there had been other departures from the will's terms over the years. They contended that some of these changes—the shift from separate schools for boys and girls to a single, gender-integrated school, and hiring teachers who were not Protestant—were more dramatic, yet no harm appears to have resulted.

The justices responded to Native Hawaiian fears of abandonment by affirming their belief that the Bishop Estate "ultimately belongs to the Hawaiian people." They recommended that representatives of respected indigenous Hawaiian organizations be given the authority to design and implement the trustee selection process, even though the formal appointment would be made by the Probate Court.

The decision, ending more than 110 years of formal involvement with the affairs of the Bishop Estate, is likely to succeed in removing the Supreme Court from the center of controversy about estate governance. The court's credibility may be helped by coupling the justices exit with greater involvement of Native Hawaiians. It is unlikely, however, to prevent the court from being thrust into difficult conflicts involving Native Hawaiian concerns.

As the largest owner of residential leasehold properties in windward and east O'ahu, the estate once publicized its preference to retain these properties, renegotiate their terms at prevailing market rates, or invest capital, bound only by the judgment of the trustees. The leasehold conversion law, described earlier, not only forces the estate to relinquish title to the land, but to do so in compliance with the terms established by court-appointed arbiters.

The estate changed its appeal during the mid-1990s' conflicts over lease renegotiations and fee conversion prices. Using an extensive advertising campaign, it attempted to mobilize Native Hawaiians and their sympathizers by arguing that fee conversion is an attack on Hawai'i land rights, equal to the losses suffered in the *Mahele* of the 1850s. Thus, trustees—primarily representatives of the Democratic establishment—find themselves in conflict with the party's constituency of individual homeowners, while the court—often itself seen as a creature of establishment politics—is drawn into issues that pit Hawaiian factions against government in their efforts to expand Hawaiian land rights. Here the court cannot avoid entanglement in the question of how much the Office of Hawaiian Affairs should be compensated for the state's use of ceded lands, the hundreds of thousands of acres of former crown lands that were entrusted to the state at the time of admission.

Court involvement with Native Hawaiians also may come with calls to interpret Bernice Pauahi Bishop's will with respect to its designated beneficiaries. The will stipulated that the trust created by the will should generate income to be used for the education of "the children of Hawai'i." It did not, however, define who were "the children of Hawaii," and the first board of trustees simply established a practice of limiting enrollment in estate-supported schools to children of Hawaiian and part-Hawaiian ancestry. As the value of the trust grows, questions about the will's proper beneficiaries may become more significant, and more conflictual.

The fates of the Native Hawaiians and the court will continue to be joined, and their linkages remain an important element in Hawai'i's political life. What comes out of the relationship for Hawaiians or for others, will depend to a great extent on the direction in which the court evolves in the context of its own history as well as the state's changing social-political landscape.

CHAPTER EIGHT

Executive Power

Hawai'i's chief executive shares many characteristics with the governors of other states. At the same time, consistent with the state's institutional evolution and political culture, the Hawai'i executive branch and the governor embody centralized power and the dominating presence of state government to a degree not found in most other states.

The governor's power comes from several sources, but the role played in budgetary matters and the capacity to define public issues and forge responses are particularly important. Even with these powers and a legislature dominated by his own party, the governor must deal with an administrative structure that is resistant to change from any source. This is nowhere better illustrated than in efforts at reform and reinvention.

ORGANIZATION OF THE EXECUTIVE BRANCH

The business of the state is carried out in the executive branch by seventeen departments. As indicated in chapter 5, Hawai'i's constitution was strongly influenced by the public administration movement of the 1950s, a movement whose members were convinced that government efficiency depended on ensuring the governor an effective span of control. The conventional wisdom of the day held that no more than twenty departments should make up a state executive. The rule seemed sound for Hawai'i because the appointment of boards and commissions had been a common vehicle for resolving tensions between the executive and the legislature. During the territorial period, this led to a proliferation of such entities, which had to be "cleaned up" at the time of statehood.

This process has continued since 1959, although in slightly different form, with the proliferation of specific agencies attached directly to the offices of the governor and the lieutenant governor. Under Governor Cayetano, efforts were spent—again—to reorganize the executive branch in the name of efficiency, an undertaking discussed at the end of the chapter.

Spending that occurs within the executive branch accounts for about 98 percent of all government expenditures. Of the major functional expenses estimated for fiscal year 1999, the largest, at 39 percent, is for salaries. Others, in order, are for human service programs (15 percent, of which two-thirds is for Medicaid), debt service (13 percent), retirement and health plan benefits (both 7 percent).[1]

The departments of Hawai'i state government can be categorized into three groups, based either on function or size. Table 5 lists these departments by the total size of their budget, percentage of the overall state general fund budget, and the number of employees. As is true for other states, most of these have grown partly by acquiring functions not directly related to their constitutionally established purpose. Often this has resulted in duplication or overlap between agencies. An example of this is environmental protection, for which at least six departments have responsibilities.

The Service Departments

The departments that control budgets, purchasing, and personnel are likely to be powerful in a centralized system. In Hawai'i, these functions belong to Budget and Finance, Accounting and General Services, and Human Resource Development. Each of these, along with the Attorney General, have responsibilities and authority that touch all the other departments.

The Department of Budget and Finance (B&F) plans and administers the state budget and develops programs for improving the general management and financial management of state agencies. No reorganization of a state agency can be done without the participation and approval of B&F. The budget of this department is large, as seen in table 5, because it includes the operating expenses for the department, payments for the state's debt service, and the health-benefit payments for all state employees.

B&F's role in designing and implementing the state's budget has made it the most powerful of these three powerful agencies. Its director has been a formidable figure in recent administrations, closely associated with the governor. The director's decisions have tremendous impact on what departments and programs may or may not do. Under Governor Waihe'e, B&F's director, Yukio Takemoto, became a symbol of decision-making based upon

Table 5: State Departments, General-Funded Budgets, and Number of Employees

Department	Total Funds Fiscal Year 1997–98	Percentage of State General Funds	Number of Full-Time Employees 1998
Accounting and General Services	161,042,333	3.6	1,002
Agriculture	23,479,342	0.4	345
Attorney General	56,804,878	0.7	561
Budget and Finance	1,292,750,409	27.5	384
Business, Economic Development and Tourism	103,700,698	1.1	256
Commerce and Consumer Affairs	36,721,943	0.08	409
Defense	14,142,107	0.25	232
Education	881,539,380	24.3	17,387
Governor	3,795,774	0.1	65
Hawaiian Home Lands	6,747,356	0.04	130
Health	610,294,104	8.9	5,986
Human Resources	21,224,340	0.5	120
Human Services	1,137,643,180	17.5	2,268
Labor	269,388,425	0.5	743
Land and Natural Resources	49,821,116	0.9	746
Lieutenant Governor	3,615,507	0.09	51
Public Safety	127,369,410	4.2	2,128
Taxation	16,621,934	0.5	353
Transportation	466,136,066	0.0	2,383
University of Hawai'i	495,204,079	8.7	5,842
Totals	5,779,542,381		41,391

Sources: For budget information, Department of Budget and Finance, Department Allocations, 1998; for number of employees, Department of Human Resource Development.

Note: The left column is all expenditures on operations and includes federal and special funds. It does not include capital investment funded by bonds. The Department of Transportation is funded almost entirely out of other accounts, primarily the gas tax and federal allotments. The middle column is percentage of specifically state general fund appropriations from all sources that go to each department.

insider, old-boy connections, and was forced to resign to counteract the public perception of corruption and abuse in that administration.

The Department of Accounting and General Services (DAGS) administers the state's accounting and auditing system, and manages state property and purchasing activities. It is also responsible for record management. Among the other services it provides are maintaining and operating state buildings and public school facilities, operating the state's central government mail and messenger service, and directing the planning, design engineering, and construction of public works projects.

Because DAGS is involved in everything from the most routine kinds of purchases to the letting of multi-million dollar contracts, its director and staff have been powerful, and susceptible to errors of judgment in making awards to the administration's political allies.

The Department of Human Resource Development, called the Department of Personnel Services until 1995, operates the state's personnel management and civil service systems. These complex systems, especially so when combined with the public sector collective bargaining agreement, often are experienced as frustrating challenges for the individual departments *and* the central administration. Both struggle to make appointments in a timely manner through a bureaucratic maze rich with the historical protections given to Hawai'i's public sector employees. Until attempts were made to decentralize decisions in the early 1990s, virtually everything relating to hiring, promoting, and training was funneled through the time-consuming review and approval processes of this department.

The fourth service department, the Attorney General (AG), is important, but normally not as powerful on a day-to-day basis as the three just described. The AG is the state's chief law-enforcement officer. The department provides legal services to state agencies and employees, represents the state in court, and conducts civil and criminal investigations. As the chief law-enforcement officer, the AG prosecutes criminal offenses and maintains a system of identification of criminal suspects and prisoners. In Hawai'i, the AG also gives advisory opinions to state agencies on the constitutionality of legislative actions, and interprets the outcomes of citizen balloting in elections. Finally, the office provides security measures for the state capitol and the governor's residence at Washington Place.

The year 1998 proved an exception to the AG's less powerful presence. The governor gave the office responsibility for investigating charges of misconduct and mismanagement made against trustees of the Bishop Estate. This involved the AG in a very public fight with lawyers of the state's most powerful and well-connected landed trust over issues of great importance to the Hawaiian community and to the networked interests connected to the multi-billion dollar estate, resulting in trustee resignation or dismissal.

The Money Departments

A second group of departments consists of the "big" departments, those with large service clienteles, and through which flows the bulk of the state budget. These are the Department of Education, Department of Health, Department of Human Services, and Department of Transportation.

In March 1995, the Department of Education (DOE) employed 19,125 persons (17,041 full time and 2,084 part time, or 40.6 percent of all state employees). Its size results from being the only department in the nation to control all primary and secondary public education statewide, resulting in responsibility for some 180,000 students. DOE also maintains and services the statewide library system.

DOE administers the school and library systems, but policy making is vested in an elected board of education, consisting of thirteen members, ten of whom are from the City and County of Honolulu, with one each from the counties of Hawai'i, Maui and Kaua'i. The board develops and implements policies through the superintendent of education and the state librarian, both of whom it appoints.

The Department of Health (DOH) is formally responsible for coordinating, planning, and executing health programs to protect and improve the physical and mental well-being of the population. The department enforces public health laws and administers programs that deliver a wide range of health services. Historically, the size of the department grew from its administration of the thirteen state hospitals. As a result of actions of the 1995 and 1996 legislative sessions, the state hospitals are operated by a separate State Hospitals Corporation, a quasi-public agency designed to permit the hospitals to compete more effectively in the changing market for health care.

Hawai'i has been a national leader in creating a health-care system that provides access for most of its population. In a broader and less formal sense, its health policy is not located administratively within the Department of Health, but shared with other agencies. For example, the Prepaid Health Care Act of 1974, which mandates that most employers provide health-care coverage for employees who work in excess of 19 hours a week, is administered by the Department of Labor. Medicaid, a joint federal and state program that since 1994 has been organized into Hawai'i MED-QUEST—a capitated, managed care program—is administered by the Department of Human Services. DOH retains responsibility for the provision of mental health services. In the governmental component of health care, as well as other areas, such as environmental affairs, this diversity of administration results in lack of coherence in policy and its implementation.

The Department of Human Services (DHS) historically has operated all state welfare programs and Medicaid, offering assistance to people unable to provide for themselves. Programs include providing shelter, financial assistance, medical assistance, rehabilitation, and food stamps. Through these various programs, millions of federal and state dollars are transferred to more than 100,000 beneficiaries.

As just noted, DHS is heavily involved in the many dimensions of health care and welfare reform. MED-QUEST, the state's Medicaid program, stems from a waiver from the federal Health Care Financing Administration. This waiver permits states to experiment with alternative methods of providing Medicaid as a vehicle for achieving higher levels of quality and lower costs. MED-QUEST, which was implemented in July 1994, was necessitated by the continued rise of spending under Medicaid and the pressures produced by that spending on the state budget. As a capitated managed care program, it spends a predetermined amount for each beneficiary, as opposed to the fee-for-service program that it replaced, which paid providers for services performed at stipulated rates.

In some ways like DHS, the Department of Transportation (DOT) is a relatively small department that moves large amounts of money from the public to the private sector. The department is charged with the planning, design, building, and operation of highways, airports, harbors, and other transportation facilities. Most of the funds available to the department come from designated revenue sources.

Smaller, Specific Function Departments

The remaining state departments are smaller, either in the size of personnel required to perform their functions, or in their overall budgetary impact. Two departments, Public Safety (DPS) and Business, Economic Development and Tourism (DBEDT), have increased in size either because their operational activities have grown or because their number of functions has expanded. The former is the case with DPS, the latter with DBEDT.

The Department of Public Safety operates a high-security prison on O'ahu as well as community correctional facilities on each of the islands.

Paralleling trends in the rest of the United States, its size has increased as the percentage of the population incarcerated has grown. These changes often have been painful, accompanied by disputes with communities over where new prisons might be located, and intense organizational pressures. Hawai'i prisons have experienced overcrowding for years. In 1985, the American Civil Liberties Union won a consent decree against the state after filing charges of violations of prisoner civil rights, resulting in court-ordered enforcement of improvements in prison conditions.

DBEDT engages in a wide variety of activities designed to create or increase economic activity. The department's history reflects the unsettled conflict between economic growth and planned development and is, to a degree, an indicator of changes in political culture. It began as an office for business and economic research. Later, in conjunction with the state's far-reaching land-use planning system adopted in the 1960s, it became the Office of Research and Planning. In more recent years, responsibilities shifted toward business promotion and marketing. With the addition of a tourism role in the late 1980s, the department's work overlapped with the Hawaii Visitors Bureau, a private promotional entity heavily supported by state funds, to develop and implement marketing strategies. Under the activist regime of Governor Waihe'e, the department expanded, maintaining offices in various foreign cities, especially in Asia, where the administration hoped to establish or improve business relationships. Also during the Waihe'e administration, statewide planning functions were taken over by the governor's Office of State Planning, whose director became a powerful figure supporting or resisting specific economic development activities. That brought a title change from being the Department of Planning and Economic Development to the Department of Business and Economic Development. In 1996, the Office of State Planning was disbanded and its planning functions re-located to DBEDT.

The remaining departments, Land and Natural Resources, Labor and Industrial Relations, Hawaiian Home Lands, Taxation, Commerce and Consumer Affairs, Agriculture, and Defense, represent the application of broad state regulatory powers. Budgetarily, they are relatively small compared to others. but their impact often is significant.

The Department of Land and Natural Resources (DLNR) plays a critical role in how the state positions itself in relation to general land use. It also deals with aquaculture development, aquatic resources, small-boat harbors, historic preservation, the state park system, water resource-management, and some environmental issues. During the Waihe'e administration, William Paty, who had served as the governor's campaign manager, was named director of DLNR, an indication of the centrality of this department to the overall mission of that administration.

The Department of Labor and Industrial Relations administers the federal occupational health and safety laws, handles workers' compensation claims, coordinates employment information, and oversees unemployment benefits. It also is the implementation site for the state's Prepaid Health Care Act.

As chapter 4 details, the history of the Department of Hawaiian Home Lands is a sorry one. It stands as a vast disappointment of hopes that the state and federal governments would provide homesteads for Hawaiians, as stipulated by federal legislation in 1921. Although this situation began to change during the Waihe'e administration, over its life the department has been denied the funds to build infrastructure to render the lands it controls suitable for habitation. The department is among the smallest in state government.

The Department of Taxation collects all revenues destined for state coffers. Because the excise tax, a tax on business transactions, is such a significant source of revenue for the state, the department has had to adapt to the complex nature of business transactions in a global economy. For example, many firms doing business in Hawai'i are located in other places, and the department must send its auditors to the mainland and abroad to ensure that the state is receiving payment on these tax obligations. The Transient Accommodations Tax, essentially a hotel room tax, is collected by the department and distributed to the counties, as are other taxes, such as fuel and liquor, gathered and disbursed to designated funds. Real property taxes are levied and collected by the counties.

The Department of Commerce and Consumer Affairs regulates large industries such as insurance, banking, and cable television, and is frequently the focal point of lobbying. In 1998 it oversaw more than 45 boards, commissions and programs that license technical and professional groups, ranging from barbers to architects. It also represents consumer complaints against business practices. These regulatory powers, potentially vast, are often highly contested as business groups seek to limit the reach of the department into their affairs, and consumer and clientele groups seek more aggressive enforcement. The department often takes on the personality of its administrative director with respect to its degree of activism.

The Agriculture Department is less visible and influential. Like the Department of Land and Natural Resources, it is run by an appointed board. Historically, research for sugar and pineapple was done by those industries, such as through the Hawai'i Sugar Planters Association, or by means of extensive programs created on their behalf at the University of Hawai'i, especially the College of Tropical Agriculture and the Pineapple Research Institute. A small department, it now serves some advisory and regulatory functions, and provides marketing assistance to agricultural producers.

The Department of Defense oversees the Hawaii National Guard, most of the funding for which comes from the federal Department of Defense. It also coordinates civil defense, and provides some veterans services.

One other major budget claimant, the University of Hawai'i, is, at least officially, no longer a department of the state. A constitutional amendment in 1978 granted the university limited autonomy. The legislative acts that followed in the mid-1980s gave the university the ability to make purchasing agreements outside the purview of DAGS, and to prepare a budget free from the detailed oversight of B&F. In effect, the governor and B&F treat the university budget as a lump-sum item, the size of which they control, but not its distribution. Legislative Act 161 of the 1994 session gave the university the right to retain its tuition income beginning in fiscal year 1995. In the 1998 legislation, the governing board and campus administrators received significantly more authority to manage internal affairs.

This new independence was motivated by the assumption that increased flexibility would permit the university to operate more cost-effectively, thus reducing its allocation from the state's general fund. Leaders from the corporate sector also hoped that more freedom from the rules governing other state agencies would enable the research campus at Manoa to become a more active participant in revitalizing the state's flagging economy by embracing academic entrepreneurialism. The acts providing greater autonomy to the university, coupled with the pragmatics of budget and collective-bargaining politics and the sheer size of the institution in a small economy, assure that disputes over the degree of real autonomy will remain a feature of the university's relation to elected officials.

HAWAI'I'S GOVERNORS

Hawai'i has had five governors since it became a state. The first, William Quinn, was its only Republican. Quinn was the final territorial governor, appointed by President Dwight D. Eisenhower in 1958. A "New" Republican, he was also a New Dealer able to distance himself from his party and find ways to work with a Democratically controlled legislature. He ran successfully in 1960 against the Democratic tide and defeated John Burns by 4,000 votes to become the state's first elected governor. In that campaign, he proposed elimination of the sales tax on food, more personal income tax exemptions, greater unemployment benefits, and distribution of public lands to Hawai'i citizens on a fee-simple basis.

Quinn focused on converting the territorial government into a state government. He helped to design the new state capitol with its distinctive Pacific aesthetic, and helped to establish the Neighbor Islands as tourist destinations for post statehood development. He failed in a proposal to sell 145,000 acres of state land to help meet the housing shortage, losing out to the Democrats land reform agenda. He called his land program, without a sense of irony, "the second mahele."

John Burns, his successor, is undoubtedly the defining figure in the postwar period. A former policeman, Burns was a principal organizer of the Democratic Revolution of 1954 and architect of the drive to statehood. He decisively beat William Quinn in 1962 to win the new state's first four-year term. As governor, his style became one of consensus making. ("Any damned fool can take a stand.") Burns prided himself on working with diverse groups to create some degree of harmony from conflicting interests. He came to be more of a behind-the-scenes player over the years, powerful but not visible, and was affectionately referred to by some as "the Great Stone Face" or "the Great White Father."

Burns was a consistent voice for Hawai'i's non-Caucasian underdogs, and his policies supported organized labor and the emerging Asian-American middle class. In the economic arena, he promoted expansion and diversification. He wanted the islands to benefit from an influx of capital, and tried to create a climate more favorable to development. He supported policies that encouraged the "fullest and best use" of land in conjunction with this, and called those wary of the growth of mass tourism short-sighted and closed minded. Burns was a strong advocate of improving access to quality primary and secondary education, and creating a second-to-none university open to all of Hawai'i's residents, not just the cream of the educational crop.

George Ariyoshi was first elected to public office in 1954, the youngest to come in on the Democratic tide. An attorney with good connections to the business community, Ariyoshi served in the state legislature for 16 years. He was not a leader in that body, and his candidacy for the lieutenant governorship in 1970 was a surprise. Embraced by Burns and his administration, he became the nation's first Japanese-American governor when illness forced Burns to resign in 1972. He then was elected to three full terms. By the time he left office in 1986 he had been in public office for thirty years.

Ariyoshi's careful, socially conservative, and non-strident style of leadership, captured by his 1982 campaign slogan, "Quiet but Effective," was consistent with the values of Japanese-Americans. He looked for ways to protect the islands' distinct culture and open spaces. He favored orderly development and believed in planning. A fiscal conservative, Ariyoshi kept a tight rein over the state treasury, in the process shrinking support for the University of Hawai'i, which had been a centerpiece of Burns' vision of a modern Hawai'i.

John Waihe'e III, also an attorney and a graduate of the first University of Hawai'i law school class, entered public life through his role as a delegate to the 1978 constitutional convention. Possessing a forceful and charismatic personality with a social activist orientation, he ran for lieutenant governor in 1982 after serving only one term in the legislature. His independent path to public office, as well as his short legislative tenure, put Waihe'e outside the inner circle that had remained intact since the re-emergence of the Democratic party in 1954. In 1986, with the belated support of the Democratic Establishment, he became the first part-Hawaiian governor in the United States.

Waihe'e's activist government was defined by a variety of social and economic initiatives, such as making Hawai'i the health state, developing geothermal energy, and building a space-launching facility, for which he was a chief spokesperson. He increased spending on public education, worked to have more affordable housing built, promoted laws that make government more accessible, and sought to protect the environment through land banking. Waihe'e did much to advance the cause of justice for Hawaiians, including beginning a process for settling disputes over ceded lands revenues and resolving the illegal use of lands in the home lands trust.

His administration, unfortunately, appeared unable to stop some members of the old guard he had brought in from using government for their private purposes. By the end of this two terms, when he joined the local office of a prestigious national law firm, opinion polls suggested the public remembered these abuses more than his initiatives.

The most recent in Hawai'i's line of ethnic firsts, Ben Cayetano is the only governor of Filipino ancestry in the nation's history. He became governor in 1994 after spending eight years as John Waihe'e's lieutenant governor. Also an attorney, he was elected to the state House in 1974, then moved to the Senate in 1978, where he became chairman of the powerful Ways and Means Committee. In the Senate, he gained a reputation as outspoken, a party maverick, and loyal to his political allies. Cayetano's relationship with the Waihe'e administration, and with the governor himself, was ambivalent, and his candidacy in 1994 was not greeted with enthusiasm by many of the party's core members.

The new governor's outspokenness about the budget shortfall he discovered on taking office brought a favorable response from much of the public, but was unsettling to many accustomed to more private and discrete ways of dealing with such issues. He surprised those grown comfortable with more guarded and opaque decision-making by recruiting openly for appointed positions in his administration. Action-oriented and less patient than earlier governors to legislative sensitivities, he stepped on toes. Donna Ikeda, chair of the Senate Ways and Means Committee and a member of the governor's party, once publicly accused him of "acting like a dictator" by proposing programs for cutback and elimination without seeking advice of the legislature.

During his first term, he devoted a great deal of his time to searching for the means to restore economic momentum. Cayetano looked for state policies to become more business friendly, but without betraying Democratic party commitments to fairness for employees. As part of the same process he encouraged new ways of thinking about the role of government in Hawai'i, orientations that emphasize government's role as a facilitator rather than a regulator.

Cayetano was re-elected in 1998 in a close race against Republican Linda Lingle, the mayor of Maui. He won despite the poor economy, relying heavily on his image of being closer to local people, and benefiting from the higher standards of conduct that characterized his first administration.

POWERS OF THE HAWAI'I GOVERNOR

Scholars who study governors often rank them according to their strength, measured in terms of the number and scope of their formed powers. Governors typically have the authority to make appointments, to prepare and deliver to the legislature a state budget, to veto legislative actions, to issue executive orders, and to command the state National Guard. Governors exercise oversight of the judiciary through their appointment of judges. They also have the authority to pardon or to grant clemency. Equally important, outside the range of formal powers, governors, by virtue of their de facto leadership of their political party and the state government apparatus, have the capacity to establish and push an agenda within the legislature.

Appointment Powers

The Hawai'i governor has direct responsibility, with the advice and consent of the senate, for appointing department heads and other executive department members, as well as hundreds of other positions, many serving as unpaid members of boards and commissions. Illustrating this, within the Department of Commerce and Consumer Affairs, numerous such boards and commissions oversee specific economic activities. There is, for example, the Board of Massage, which examines applicants and issues or revokes licenses for those who want to be massage therapists. Of the five members of this board, two must represent the public, and the other three must have three years of experience as a licensed massage therapist. The Board of Massage is appointed by the governor with the advice and consent of the Senate.

On a broader scale, the governor appoints members to the Land Use Commission and the University of Hawai'i Board of Regents, bodies that have direct responsibility for either the oversight of very large budget items or the approval and enforcement of important policy issues.

The Centrality of Budgetary Power

Among the governor's powers, none is more important to the day-to-day, year-to-year operation of state government than that granted by Article 6 of the state constitution. This article gives the governor authority to submit a budget to the legislature, a power effected by Act 37 of the Hawai'i Session Laws. In the complexity of modern government, the authority to frame a budget for legislative review and enactment gives substance to the overall state policy agenda. It also embodies decisions about what matters and what will be absent from that agenda. The significance of this point is revealed in what occurs during the state's periodic budget emergencies.

There have been three budget "crises" since statehood. The first, brought about initially by a shipping strike, occurred during 1971, and its effects extended through 1974. During this period, the growth in state revenues dropped from an annual increase of over 9.6 percent to about 6.5 percent for one year before returning to normal.[2] Between 1982 and 1985, a variety of causes led to another slow down in state revenues.

The third and most severe budget crisis began in 1994. Governor Cayetano announced that the state was experiencing a major revenue shortfall in his January 1995 State of the State address. The context for this surprising announcement is contained in a widely circulated story in which the newly elected governor and his lieutenant governor, Mazie Hirono, were reviewing the draft of the intended speech on a Sunday afternoon about nine days before its scheduled delivery. They were visited by the just-appointed director of Budget and Finance, Earl Anzai, who announced that he had examined the budget submitted by the outgoing Waihe'e administration and discovered the state was facing a large and immediate budget shortfall. The news was so dramatic and far reaching that the governor threw away his intended speech and began writing another organized around the budget crisis.

The story illustrates three aspects of the impact of budgeting on the policy process and the role of the executive in controlling that process. First, Director Anzai's revelation set the agenda for state government for at least the next four years. After that day, virtually every act of state government was dominated by budgetary considerations. The budget became a rationale for initiating reorganization, not only in small agencies but also in large departments, such as the Department of Health and the University of Hawai'i. In August 1995, about six-hundred state employees lost their jobs.[3] The Department of Human Services cut benefits to client groups, most particularly those receiving state-funded general assistance.

The second lesson from the budget crisis that began in 1994 is the role it gave to the budget director. In normal times, the person in this position is close to the governor, the first among equals in the governor's cabinet. In such times, that is, when the budget grows a certain amount year by year, B&F influences the behavior of the executive branch by setting limits to budgetary requisitions through the governor's budget message to departments, and by prioritizing departmental budget requests to enforce those limits. Nevertheless, it is the departments that generate the substantive requests, whether for more employees to perform a given task (e.g., monitor state parks), or more money to serve an entitlement clientele (e.g., Medicaid and general assistance).

Things change in a condition of budgetary shortfall. Budgets are cut by B&F and department heads are required to determine how those cuts are to be apportioned among their programs. This action dominates the policy process. Under these circumstances, the director of B&F becomes the most powerful person in the administration. No new programs can be developed without the director's permission; the director and the governor determine which programs are to be subject to review and possible cutback or elimination; and the director is the figure through whom appeals must go for an adjustment to the cuts. As a department head remarked in June 1996, "No one does anything in this administration without Earl's okay."[4]

The third lesson is what this anecdote reveals about the budget process itself. How is it that one administration could prepare a budget to be presented for an upcoming legislature, only to have that budget and its assumptions fundamentally rejected only days into the subsequent administration, especially when the only persons who change at B&F are the director and appointed deputies?

To understand this, it is necessary to know some things about how the Hawai'i state government budget is put together. When Governor Cayetano announced that his budget director had told him the state was in the midst of a significant shortfall, two reasons were given: first, the state was spending too much; and second, tax collections were less than projected, a result of the continued economic downturn.

The Waihe'e administration, as knowledgeable about the revenue estimates from the Council on Revenues as was Anzai when he became budget director, had chosen to create and make ready for submission to the subsequent legislature a required six-year financial plan that embodied much more optimistic revenue assumptions. The gap between the Waihe'e spending levels and the Cayetano administration's more pessimistic income projections led to the cuts proposed in the spring of 1995.[5] In short, using the very same data, the Waihe'e administration, including all of the analysts at B&F, chose not to see a crisis, while the Cayetano administration saw the necessity of declaring one of such severity that it would completely dominate any policy agenda produced by the administration or the legislature.

Crises aside, during "normal" times, the governor has remarkable powers over the expenditure side of the budget. The constitution provides the authority to withhold funds appropriated by the legislature, a power that extends to all state entities, except the Judiciary and OHA.[6] This power, when the governor chooses to exercise it, can render irrelevant the efforts of departments to build a creditable set of budget recommendations to pass B&F and legislative scrutiny. The governor is able, in fact, to reverse legislative intent.

The rationale for executive restriction is the requirement to produce a balanced budget, but the governor and his agent, B&F, have great discretion in achieving that balance. Department heads can appeal their cuts either to the governor or to the budget director, but if those two hold firm, they have few options beyond complying with the restrictions, or leaving state government.

Other effects can be gained through the power of the governor to speed release of funds from the capital improvement budget (CIP). Using the CIP budget in this way can also work as a form of administrative reallocation of spending and priorities vis-à-vis the legislature. Legislative authorization for CIP projects extends for three years. If the administration does not release a project's funds during that three-year period, the project returns to the legislature for reallocation, where, of course, it must then compete—once again—for priority place with every other project on the list. The governor and B&F can, in effect, re-order legislative priorities.

The Power to Initiate

As the most visible public figure in the state, and the chief executive presiding over the large and far-flung apparatus of state government, what the governor decides to attend to or ignore can have enormous repercussions. The governor's sustained commitment to solve a particular social problem can marshal resources and, if the work is successful, bring political benefits. It also can have political downsides if the publicly announced goal with which the governor is now identified is not achieved. Thus, on the one hand the governor has the power to define what is, and isn't, important and get an issue on the public agenda. On the other, issues once highlighted can take on a life of their own and, in so doing, reduce the effective power of the governor. In investigating the Bishop Estate, Governor Cayetano was uniquely in a position to make a public issue of a problem that had lain beneath the surface of Hawai'i's public life. The consequence of his actions is that the estate and its relationship to politicians, Hawaiians, and the larger community will never be the same. The governor's role in re-kindling the state's economy in 1997 produced less favorable results. The most visible of his proposals, a tax package designed to restart the state's economy, did not make it through the legislature. Its rejection clearly was a defeat for the governor; a defeat handed him in an election year by his own party.

Other Executive Powers

The governor is also the commander in chief of the state's armed forces and is empowered to call out these forces to maintain law and order and protect the population. In cases of emergency or natural disaster, the governor may order the National Guard to render assistance or, if the National Guard is under active federal service, organize and maintain a volunteer Hawai'i State Defense Force. The governor also may use the commander in chief powers to summon the National Guard to aid in suppressing civil unrest. In September 1978, Governor George Ariyoshi called out the National Guard in response to a demonstration of Native Hawaiians and their supporters at General Lyman Field in Hilo, who were protesting the state's use of Hawaiian homes land for the airport without paying a rental fee.

Finally, the governor may also, at his discretion, grant pardons and clemency.

LIMITATIONS ON EXECUTIVE POWER

Examining the basis of a governor's power invites attention to limitations on that power. It is commonplace in public administration to observe that a structural tension exists between civil service employees and those chosen, either by election or by appointment, to lead them. Civil service employees, especially where, as in Hawai'i, civil service is overlaid with an enveloping public sector collective bargaining agreement, have something equivalent to tenure in their jobs. They also are the repository of the "expert knowledge" of an organization—the basis for their professional status. Their appointed leaders have limited terms and often lack the professional knowledge base of a given department. The governor's appointees typically have been chosen through some combination of general administrative capability and payback for political favors.

The permanent staff of a department, agency, or bureau often is reluctant to endorse the agenda of a new administration, viewing that agenda in part as the product of the political moment, a moment that may not—in the staff's view—coincide with the long-run interests of the organization. The result can be—and often is—an administrative system that is sluggish in following its elected and appointed leaders.

There are no known ways of measuring the comparative responsiveness of public bureaucracies to elected and appointed leadership. Given the pervasiveness and significance of informal relationships described in chapter 3, if there were such a measure, Hawai'i's probably would well fall on the less responsive end. Some of the state's governors have tried to increase their influence within the bureaucracy by enlarging the number of non-civil service (or "exempted") employees. That aside, because the conflict is so embedded in the structure and so amplified by Hawai'i's cultural characteristics, Hawai'i's governors must rely for their success or failure on the ability to build coalitions and to exercise influence through persuasion.

COMPARATIVE STATE EXECUTIVE POWERS

Is Hawai'i's governor unusually powerful? Most people who have studied the Hawai'i executive have thought so. As James Wang puts it: "[A] study of gubernatorial politics in Hawai'i is in many ways a study of highly centralized power in the executive office. . . . Hawaii . . . concentrates an enormous amount of political power in the person who occupies Washington Place."[7]

A study of governors conducted by the National Governors' Association used six indices to compare formal powers. By examining a governor's tenure potential (restriction on reelection), appointment powers, budget-making power, the ability of the legislature to change the governor's budget, the veto power, and the governor's strength in the legislature, the National Governor's Association ranked the formal authority of the governors from very strong to very weak. The rankings appear in table 6. By these measures, Hawai'i has a strong, but not uniquely strong, executive.

The key to the power of the Hawai'i governor is the combination of a range of formal authority that would rank that office toward the high end of the scale of gubernatorial power, and this person's role in a system that is itself highly centralized. Hawai'i's governor does not have to share power with the mayors of large cities within the state or with powerful boards of supervisors in large counties. Because of this, it is unlikely any governor in the United States equals the overall capacity to influence the policy that will prevail in important areas such as education, transportation, health, and environmental protection as the governor of Hawai'i.

THE LIEUTENANT GOVERNOR

Hawai'i elects only two officials statewide, the governor and the lieutenant governor. Candidates for these offices run as a team during the general election, ensuring that they will always be of the same party. In Hawai'i, as in most states, the lieutenant governor's best-known function is to be in the wings should the governor become incapacitated, die, or otherwise vacate the office. The lieutenant governor also becomes governor when the governor is out of the state, something that brings very little power because lieutenant governors are not likely to make serious decisions in the governor's temporary absence.

The lieutenant governor frequently stands in for the governor at events, especially if they have a good working relationship, and heads special projects or task forces assigned by the governor. For Lieutenant Governor Mazie Hirono, these have included chairing the Governor's Advisory Council on Airlines Relations and the Task Force on Science and Technology. Most of these don't provide very much visibility and political benefit, but there can be exceptions. Ben Cayetano began a low-cost after school child

Table 6: Comparison of Formal Powers of the Governor

Very Strong	Strong	Moderate	Weak	Very Weak
Maryland (27)	Connecticut (24)	Alabama (22)	Maine (19)	Texas (16)
Massachusetts (27)	Louisiana (24)	Alaska (22)	Montana (19)	N. Carolina (16)
	Colorado (23)	Iowa (22)	New Hampshire (19)	S. Carolina (14)
	Florida (23)	Ohio (22)	New Mexico (19)	
	Hawai'i (23)	Pennsylvania (22)	Virginia (19)	
	Michigan (23)	Arizona (21)	Nevada (18)	
	Minnesota (23)	Delaware (21)	Washington (18)	
	New Jersey (23)	Idaho (21)	Mississippi (17)	
	N. Dakota (23)	Indiana (21)	Oregon (17)	
	S. Dakota (23)	Kansas (21)	Rhode Island (17)	
		Oklahoma (21)	Vermont (17)	
		Tennessee (21)		
		Wyoming (21)		
		Kentucky (20)		
		Missouri (20)		
		Wisconsin (20)		

Source: Office of State Services, "The Institutionalized Power of the Governorship: 1965–1985" (Washington DC: National Governors Association, 1987.

care program for working parents when he was John Waihe'e's lieutenant governor. That initiative got him into the public's eye and was a source of future campaign material.

The lieutenant governor's office is responsible for officially recording all legislative and gubernatorial acts; maintaining a current listing of the administrative of state departments and agencies; the sale and distribution of legislative journals, session laws, and Hawaii Revised Statutes; processing name changes; and maintaining copies of the announcements and agendas of public meeting held by state departments and agencies.

Until 1995, the largest substantive concern of the lieutenant governor's office was to supervise elections. Criticism that the electoral function was too important to be placed within an administrative arena controlled by a partisan official resulted in creation of a separate Office of Elections. Between 1995 and 1998, the personnel attached directly to the lieutenant governor's office, as opposed to offices adminstratively under it, such as the Campaign Spending Commission, the Office of Information Practices, or the Office of Elections, dropped from 22 to 11.[8]

Historically, vice presidents and lieutenant governors have enjoyed limited power. John Nance Garner, FDR's first vice president, once remarked that the vice presidency was "not worth a warm pitcher of spit." Tom Gill, a former Hawai'i lieutenant governor under John Burns, said the lieutenant governor's office is "a nonsense job."[9]

Gill's comment reflects both the institution and his particular situation. In 1966 he defeated Kenneth Brown, Burns' choice for lieutenant governor, in a bitter primary contest. For the next four years, he was frozen out of the corridors of power. On the other hand, Mazie Hirono, the state's second female lieutenant governor, established a good working relationship with Ben Cayetano and was given policy responsibilities that drew upon her previous experience in the legislature. As lieutenant governor under John Waihe'e, Cayetano, in addition to establishing the A-Plus after-school care program, convened a high-profile review of public education. Clearly, the influence of a lieutenant governor varies and is a function of the latitude provided by the governor.

In Hawai'i, the lieutenant governor's office has been a good path to the governorship. Ben Cayetano used his second-in-command position as a springboard to that office, waiting to make his bid until Waihe'e's mandatory retirement after two terms. The man he succeeded, John Waihe'e, in turn, sat through one term under George Ariyoshi before making his run. Before him, George Ariyoshi had been the lieutenant governor under John Burns, succeeding him when he was forced by poor health to resign from office. Thus, in each of the last three administrations, beginning in 1970, and irrespective of the relationship between governor and lieutenant governor, when there is no incumbent running, the lieutenant governor has become the governor.

In contrast to this, when lieutenant governors have attempted to use their office as a base from which to overturn their bosses, they have lost. In 1970,

Tom Gill was defeated by incumbent John Burns. In 1982, Jean King was turned back by Governor George Ariyoshi.

Government reform has been on the executive agenda since the beginning of the administration of John Waihe'e in 1986. It was initiated by the influence of the national conversation about the desirability of "reinventing" government—itself a mix of competing aspirations to both improve and reduce government—more than from a sense of crisis. Waihe'e's second term included a number of proposals to re-think structure and re-make organizational cultures. Few made the transition into the Cayetano administration.

With the advent of the Cayetano administration in January 1995, state government, especially the executive branch, became the object of more focused pressure for change. This pressure came from sources more familiar in other states: indications of the public's sense that taxes are too high, and strident small-business complaints that they are bedeviled by a hostile regulatory environment. The pressure also came from the new governor's instincts to forestall potential threats from the "big government" foes on the small but growing political right, as well as his interpretation of his options for handling the on-going fiscal crisis.

The governor's office was a good place to begin to respond. It is under his control, and it would symbolize the chief executive's willingness to "share the pain" and "do more with less."

The core of the governor's office is relatively small, about 70 in 1998, and consists of a staff directly serving the governor. This core is composed of the chief of staff, executive assistants, a director of communication, a press secretary, a legislative coordinator, staff support, Neighbor Island liaisons, and related positions.

From 1986 to 1993, in the administration of John Waihe'e, the personnel attached to the governor's office grew from 83 to 228, an increase of 175 percent. This growth reflected a number of special programs that had become attached to it. These included the Executive Office on Aging, Office of Affirmative Action, Governor's Agriculture Coordinating Committee, Office of Children and Youth, Office of Collective Bargaining, Office of State Planning, Statewide Volunteer Services, and Office of Special Projects.

In 1995, the attorney general issued an opinion that these programs could not be treated as permanent fixtures. The opinion gave Cayetano leverage to act. The governor's staff developed an agenda to change from service delivery and administrative planning to strategic planning. The set of specialized programs would be replaced by a staff whose purpose was to deal with important long-range issues. Consistent with contemporary ideas about organizations, the new staff would remain small, deliberately multi-disciplinary in composition, and team-oriented, with an emphasis on the ability to shift focus and respond quickly to emerging issues.

Other attempts at re-arranging relationships have been less successful. Under pressure from his legislative party to respond to the fiscal crisis, in 1995 the governor and his staff proposed a reorganization and consolidation of the executive departments aimed at integrating functions and eliminating duplication. The three departments dealing with the business community—Commerce and Consumer Affairs, Planning, Economic Development and Tourism, and Agriculture—would be merged into one or two. The three providing support services to other agencies—Budget and Finance, Accounting and General Service, and Human Resource Development—would be integrated. The last proposal was modified by the legislature to exclude the possibility of merging Budget and Finance with Accounting and General Services, out of fear that the director of such a department would be too powerful.[10] None of these changes had been made by the start of the governor's second term, and by then the momentum for them seemed to have disappeared.

The Meaning of Reform

Despite the thinking reflected by changes made in the office of the governor, in Hawai'i, "reform" to date has, by and large, meant improving existing systems rather than changing the way things are done in a more fundamental way. This does not mean that there have been no efforts at transformation, but it does mean that they have not gone very far. Initiatives to shrink the size of state government through reductions in the executive branch agencies illustrate the challenges.

Table 7 lists changes in executive branch position counts during the Cayetano administration.

These data show that several departments reduced their total positions, some substantially, although the 3.8 per cent increase in the Department of Education resulted in an overall 4.9 per cent drop.

A different picture emerges when the focus is shifted to actual employees, rather than positions. According to data from the Department of Personnel Services for the same years, 572 employees were affected by cuts in positions, but, of these, only 145 actually lost their jobs. Most of those termi-

Table 7: Changes in the Size of the Executive Branch, 1994–1998

Department	Full-time Equivalent* Positions June 30, 1998	Change since December 31, 1994 (percentage)
Accounting and General Services	1,006	+10.5
Agriculture	348	–23.9
Attorney General	554	+1.0
Budget and Finance	386	–45.7
Business, Economic Development and Tourism	257	–19.0
Commerce/Consumer Affairs	410.2	–6.6
Defense	233.6	–5.9
Education	18,518.1	+3.8
Governor's Office	68.4	–69.6
Hawaiian Homelands	132.2	–4.2
Health	6,138	–6.1
Human Resources	120	–27.7
Human Services	2,271.5	–5.0
Labor and Industrial Relations	766.9	–17.5
Land and Natural Resources	750.4	–7.0
Lt. Governor	52.5	–22.3
Public Safety	2,113.5	–3.8
Taxation	353	–13.8
Transportation	2,392	–1.5
University of Hawai'i	6,456.2	–17.2
Totals	43,355.6	–4.9

Source: State of Hawai'i, Department of Human Resource Development, cited in Rob Perez, "It's My Job," *Honolulu Star-Bulletin*, October 13, 1998, p. A-9.
* Full-time equivalent refers to one person working a 40-hour week. Since two or more part-time employees may occupy one full-time equivalent position, these figures differ from the total number of employees. In general, for a department to hire an employee, it must have available a full-time equivalent position.

nated had their positions for less than two years. The vast majority affected, 427, were either placed in other vacant positions, or displaced somewhere else.[11]

The act of displacing another employee, referred to as "bumping," illustrates the challenge to reforming government in Hawai'i. Bumping is a provision of the collective bargaining agreement. It stipulates that an employee with more than two years of service whose position is eliminated has the contractual right to fill another vacant position, or to take the job of another person within their bargaining unit, as long as the person whose job has been eliminated meets the minimum job qualifications.

The rationale for bumping is that it protects individuals who have invested more of themselves in public employment. The organizational consequence, however, is that downsizing in any specific unit means that, throughout the system, less qualified workers may take the jobs of those with better qualifications and more experience. This exchange of personnel occurs without any input from co-workers, managers, or even department directors. Moreover, there will be no cost savings to the transferred employee's new unit since he or she retains the previous compensation, even if the move is to a lower paid position.

Bumping provides a good indicator of how Hawai'i's interwoven civil service and collective bargaining systems act as a brake against making substantial changes in the way government operates. Civil service and collective bargaining are based on differing principles and historically have had an uneasy relationship to one another. Civil service systems are a legacy of the last decades of the nineteenth century when the patronage system began to be replaced by principles of merit. The collective bargaining system originated in the struggles between management and labor, which resulted, after the mid-1930s, in an expanding set of rules designed to protect the right of workers.

When civil service and collective bargaining co-exist in the same system, as they do in Hawai'i, there is conflict between whether the principle of merit or the principle of seniority will dictate what is done in specific areas of the workplace.[12] In most cases, also as in Hawai'i, collective bargaining comes to dominate. The result is that changes of almost any kind that affect efficiency and performance in the public sector must have the consent of union officials. While this can happen, as it has in the Department of Labor and Industrial Relation's efforts to develop a team-based system, union approval can be a major stumbling block to reform if the conditions for cooperation are not right.

New issues are getting on the public agenda in Hawai'i. These issues are about whether government has become too big and too costly, and if the rules by which government operates have turned it inward, away from public purposes. Such concerns, common in most places on the mainland, are relatively new in Hawai'i.

The best answer to the question of the whether government has grown disproportionately appears to be: it depends. By some measures, it clearly has. Between 1988 and 1995, years that include the high-growth period prior to the state's economic downturn, state expenditures increased at an average annual rate of 12 percent.[13] State government employment increased by about 32 per cent between 1986 and 1993.[14] This particular increase, however, must take into account that state employment includes the Department of Education, and that during this period schools were adding faculty and staff to accommodate school-age population increases.

Other measures for this earlier period factor in changes in Hawai'i society, and the results look a little different. The 1993 ratio of state government employment to civilian employment, 11.5 per cent, was higher than it had been since 1970, but it was nearly that high several times in the 1970s. State and county employment was 14.3 per cent of civilian employment in 1993, an increase over the 1986 figure of 13.2, but a reversal of a 15 year decrease in that ratio, when the 1978 figure was 14.9 per cent of the civilian employment.

Statistics that cover only the years of the state's downturn suggest a decline in the size of state government. In 1995, state government spent a total $5.922 billion, but by 1998 this had dropped to $5.907 billion. When federal funds are excluded, expenditures dropped from $5.227 billion to $5.030 billion. These figures would reflect an even larger decrease if the 4 percent inflation over those years was taken into account. Finally, the ratio of state expenditures to gross state product peaked at 17.3 per cent in 1994, and dropped to 14.5 per cent by 1997.[15]

In the final analysis, reaching consensus on whether Hawai'i's government has become too large is probably not possible, and not terribly important. The opinion that government is too big, no matter what its size, is consistent with what many Americans have held since the founding of the republic. What is different in Hawai'i is that this perspective was not represented over most of Hawai'i's history, including the period of the last forty-five years, but it now is. The challenge in the islands is how to balance old and new views on what government does and how it does it.

In his January 1999 State of the State address, Governor Cayetano declared that his first term had convinced him changes in government are necessary. He now saw that the system is rigid, inflexible, and unresponsive, at a time it needs to encourage innovation, hard work, and adaptability. He proposed repealing the existing Civil Service System by June 30, 1999, in order to initiate changes. At the same time, he did not advocate reducing the size of government nor its workforce, and remained consistent in rejecting programs that are at the expense of workers or "try to bring workers down."[16]

Even in these bounded terms the advocacy of reform contributed to an earthquake within the governor's majority party. Two of his most important and visible cabinet officers, Attorney General Margery Bronster and the Budget and Finance director Earl Anzai, were rejected by the Senate in spring 1999 legislative reconfirmation hearings. The surprise decisions resulted in a huge public outcry, rich in threats for later retaliation at the ballot box.

Reform was not the sole reason for rejection of either; the attorney general, for example, lost some support for her agressive pursuit of the Bishop Estate trustees and for what a few saw as her poor management skills. Their overthrow clearly was connected to reform, however. The attorney general had made it clear that she was open to efforts to privatize some government functions, and the director of Budget and Finance had repeatedly warned of the possible need for layoffs in the public sector.

Embedded in these developing conflicts over government reform, bureaucratic rigidities, and the role of the unions, are important tensions between creating organizations that are more flexible and efficient, and maintaining administrative agencies that treat their employees fairly and are committed to public purposes. Responses to these tensions have brought a modest reduction in size of the state workforce, but this has been done with reluctance rather than celebration. Moreover, changes have not been accompanied by strong pressures to devolve authority to county government. This suggests, at least in the near-term, the governor will not be the source of radical reforms, and what reform that does take place is unlikely to diminish the power of the governor's office, or greatly reduce the responsibilities or resources of executive departments.

CHAPTER NINE

Legislative Process

There is no better place to see the dominance of the Democratic party, or witness the political culture of Hawai'i, than the state legislature. Democrats have so controlled this body that it makes greater sense to think of its own members as constituting more than one party. The absence of competition has resulted in the formation of dissident groups within the party that, though less visible, have many of the characteristics of opposition parties. Lack of official party competition also has contributed to the power of presiding officers and committee chairs.

The way the legislature does its business is heavily influenced by the web of relationships that connect its members. These relationships are based on a combination of shared personal values and styles, common outlooks on social issues and the role of government, and brokering for positions of influence.

The legislature, or course, goes about its business within a larger context. As an institutional force within a centralized governmental system, it is both impacted by and reflective of this centralization. What it does, or does not do, can have a large impact. At the same time, it is generally less powerful than the governor with whom, even though of the same party, it may substantially disagree. The legislature has produced few leaders whose influence extends beyond what they can do during its sessions, and none that have rivaled the stature of the governor. Because Hawai'i is typified by the centralization of both private and public power, often its legislation has echoed the organized voices that dominate Hawai'i's political economy.

THE LEGISLATURE AFTER 1954

The legislature occupied a privileged place in Island political life for a time after the 1954 elections. As Tom Coffman observes in *Catch a Wave,* "The young Democratic warriors who in 1954 had captured the legislature were not only politicians but popular heroes."[1] During this period, the legislature was the driving force for passage of the social agenda that constituted the core program of the new Democratic party. (See chapter 6 for a summary of this program.) The party produced a number of well-know leaders, men who, as Coffman notes, played "an inordinate role in relation to the Executive branch." Most of these leaders had left the legislature by the 1970s, and the executive was once again ascendant.

The existence of a powerful monarch prior to formation of the first legislature almost ensured that, from their earliest times, the history of legislatures in Hawai'i would be a frustrating contest of power with these strong executives. The legislature had real power during the kingdom only when outsiders sought to employ it as a vehicle to oppose the monarchy. Even the apparent contrary case, the legislature of the constitution of 1852 in which universal suffrage provided for a strong popular voice against the king, was the product of an emergent *haole* political class. The interests of that class were benefited through its members' tutelage of Hawaiians, in what were essentially American style political institutions. This sense of being overshadowed, and the history of tension, sometimes open conflict, with a strong executive branch, are carried into the current life of the state legislature.

THE CONTEMPORARY STATE LEGISLATURE

The primary formal powers of the Hawai'i legislature are to make laws and policies to confirm certain officers appointed by the governor, and to amend the constitution. It performs other functions that are related to these, including conducting legislative audits and other oversight duties, as well as appropriating and approving the state budget.

Hawai'i spent about $22 million, or 0.4 percent of total state government expenditures, on its legislature in 1996. This placed it 2nd nationally in expenditure per capita, substantially behind Alaska and slightly ahead of Rhode Island, also small population states.[2]

Laws are initiated and passed only by the legislature because, at the state level, there is neither initiative nor referendum. Constitutional amendments proposed by the legislature must be put before voters for their approval.

The legislature is organized as a bicameral body that meets annually for 60 days, beginning on the 3rd Wednesday in January. A new state budget is dealt every other year, with the intervening session devoted to supplemental budget items. Special sessions of up to 30 days may be called by the governor, who until 1968 exclusively had that authority, or by the chief officers of each chamber, with the written request of two-thirds of their members.

Although Hawai'i has had a bicameral legislature for almost all of its history, a unicameral system has been considered at each constitutional convention. A single chamber was advocated to improve legislative efficiency and save taxpayer money, but the argument never garnered sufficient support to be given to voters. The 1978 constitutional convention delegates did propose lengthening sessions to 75 days, but voters rejected the idea, largely in response to sentiment that it would no longer be a "citizen legislature." The idea continues to arise each time legislative work is not finished in the allotted time. In the 13 sessions between 1980 and 1992, it failed to meet closing deadlines 11 times.[3] Extensions of up to 15 days may be granted by the governor, who until 1968 had the sole authority to do this, or by presiding officers of each chamber upon the written request of two-thirds of their members.

The legislature consists of a Senate with 25 members elected from 25 districts for staggered four-year terms, and a House of Representatives with 51 members elected from single-member districts for two-year terms. A person must be 18 years of age, a state resident for not less than three years, and a qualified voter in the district from which election is sought to be eligible to hold office in the Hawai'i legislature. Senators and representatives were paid $32,000 annually in 1998. Given Hawai'i's high costs, these salaries are, at best, barely adequate to support only a modest standard of living; hence, most legislators have other full-time occupations.

There are no term limits for state legislators, and there is no means by which they can be recalled by voters. The issue of term limits has surfaced in session, but citizen groups have not pushed hard for them, and legislators don't show much enthusiasm. Their low priority may reflect high turnover rates. According the National Conference of State Legislatures, from 1987 to 1997, the Senate had an 84 percent turnover, and the House an 82 percent change in membership.[4]

Each house creates its own rules, establishes its own committees, and elects its own officers. The presiding officer in the Senate is its president; in the House of Representatives it is the speaker. The speaker and president, respectively, get an additional $3,000 and $5,000 annually above the base salaries. Both are elected by the caucuses of their party. The Senate and the House also elect a successor to their presiding members, a vice-president and vice-speaker, who assume the leadership duties when the president or speaker is absent.

The president and speaker have similar functions and formal powers.

These include: (1) chairing the meetings of their respective houses; (2) maintaining order in the chamber; (3) controlling and routing the flow of business and communications in their respective chambers, including the assigning of bills to committees; (4) clarifying rules and deciding on questions of order; and (5) other duties required by law or the rules of their respective houses.[5] The president of the Senate and the speaker of the House derive their day-to-day influence—influence that makes them unquestionably the most important members of their respective bodies—from their ability to route and control the flow of business and communication within their respective chambers, particularly the ability to appoint committee chairs and members, and to assign bills to committees.

More than 3,500 bills are submitted by members in a normal legislative session. Of course, not all of these are given the same consideration. Those drafted by the administration and submitted on its behalf by the House speaker or the Senate president "by request" typically get a fuller hearing. Other "important" bills gain attention because they come out of the legislative policy process or are championed by sponsors who hold powerful legislative positions.

Many legislators are candid in admitting they have virtually no way to "stay on top" of the legislative agenda. As a part-time legislature meeting for only three months, and with a permanent staff of only 105 in the house and 66 in the senate (each member in both chambers has one year-round office manager, with other permanent staff belonging to leadership, major committees, and support services), legislators survive by focusing on a narrow slice of the legislative agenda.

This necessity is at no point more evident than in the waning hours of the session. The most politically critical issues are dealt with by conference committees in an immense rush and bustle that candid members acknowledge reduces much of the legislative process to a shambles, often empowers committee chairs and marginal members alike, and too frequently generates a product that is a surprise to even to the participants. Sessions are extended because important legislation is not completed within the designated time, or because mistakes are made in the closing rush and some important part of the legislative package requires fixing.

Critics of legislative procedures find fault with this frenzied process on two major grounds. The first is the opportunity it provides for important decisions to be made "behind closed doors"—outside of public, or even other legislators', scrutiny. As noted above, members themselves not infrequently are shocked to learn what "they" have passed. The second criticism is the increased likelihood that poor legislative judgment will be the result of such haste and confusion.

Legislative Committees

The work of legislatures in general, and the Hawai'i legislature in particular, is carried out primarily through its committee system. Bills, when introduced, are assigned by the speaker or the president to the appropriate committee for deliberation. All bills must be evaluated by both a policy committee and, if there is a fiscal impact (as is usually the case), by either the Senate Ways and Means Committee or the House Finance Committee. When approved by the appropriate committees, the bill is referred back to the main chamber and voted on by all House or Senate members as a whole. The process is repeated once the bill has passed one chamber and is moved on to the other. If the bill passes both houses, it is then sent to the governor for his signature or veto. Conference committees are appointed from the membership of each house should the bills that pass the chambers differ. Differences between the two versions of the bills are then negotiated. If agreement can be reached, the result is voted on by each house and submitted to the governor.

The size and composition of committees vary from session to session. Committee structure and function change as issues rise and fall in importance. Consequently, the standing committees—committees that are permanent throughout the session and not ad hoc for a specific bill or issue—may vary in size and number, and their names may change from session to session. For example, in 1981 the Senate had 16 standing committees, and the 1998 Senate had 10. Table 8 demonstrates the difference in legislative emphasis between these two sessions.

Although these shifts are meaningful in terms of how work is organized, and how many opportunities are available to be chair, the packaging and repackaging of committee subject-matter is less important in the long run than the political process by which both members and specific bills are allocated to particular committees.

Power among the Committees

The requirement that all subject-matter committee bills with money implications be passed on by the Senate Ways and Means or House Finance Committee makes them, and their chairs, far and away the most powerful committees. In general, however, the chairs' control over any bill referred to their committees makes all committee chairs powerful. Once referred, a bill

Table 8: Hawai'i Senate Standing Committees, 1981 and 1998 Sessions

1981 Session

Agriculture
Consumer Protection and Commerce
Ecology, Environment and Recreation
Economic Development
Education
Government Operations and Intergovernmental Relations
Health
Higher Education
Housing and Hawaiian Homes
Human Resources
Judiciary
Legislative Management
Public Utilities
Tourism
Transportation
Ways and Means

1998 Session

Commerce, Consumer Protection, and Information Technology
Economic Development
Education
Government Operations and Housing
Health and Environment
Human Resources
Judiciary
Transportation and Intergovernmental Affairs
Water, Land and Hawaiian Affairs
Ways and Means

is the virtual property of the chair, who has the authority to amend, gut, refer, or bury a bill. Only under extraordinary circumstances can a bill be referred out of committee without the concurrence of its chair. The assignment to committees and the selection of committee chairs is, not surprisingly, a basic source of conflict.

The committees and their chairs also are important because a huge amount of work must be accomplished in a short amount of time. Staff are assigned to individual members as well as to committees. Committee chairs have both, to which they can assign legislative tasks, thereby significantly enhancing their control over information, and their power. Some of these staff, the full timers of the leadership offices and the money committees for example, will be among the most knowledgeable in the process. Others, including part-time staff employed only for the duration of the session, volunteers, and students working for credit, also can come to play an extraordinary role in comparison to their relative lack of knowledge and status in the political process.

LEGISLATIVE PARTIES

As is true for other American legislatures, the lens of political parties and the discipline that party competition provides, or doesn't provide, in the legislative process, offers a good way of understanding Hawai'i's legislative dynamics. (See chapter 6 for more on the place of parties in Hawai'i's political life.)

Some political scientists hold that some degree of effective competition between the parties is the central marker of a functioning party system.[6] States across the nation are described as being modified one-party Republican, two-party, modified one-party Democratic, or one-party Democratic. In states such as Hawai'i, for all practical purposes, there is very little interparty competition.

The Democratic party has controlled the Hawai'i legislature for forty-five years, as table 9 shows. About 79 percent of the members of the legislature were members of the Democrats Party in 1997, the smallest majority in more than a decade. Despite widespread expectations of change, and a larger number of more closely contested races, the same numbers held for the 1999 legislature. As a consequence, all major decisions affecting what is done, or not done, by·the legislature are controlled by members of the Democratic party or, possibly, by a coalition that includes Republicans, but is dominated by dissident Democrats.

How much does party competition really matter? Party competition has long been held to be an important component of democracy.[7] In one-party states, the most important politics, that is, the bargaining and competition among and between interests, goes on within a party, organized through and around its various factions. Such states are characterized generally by "liberal" and "conservative" factions within the dominant party. Under these circumstances, voters often find it difficult to distinguish between various factions, and the party label ends up rewarding most legislators irrespective of factional allegiance.

In Hawai'i, to make matters even more complicated for voters, the legislative factions themselves often are not clearly arrayed along a liberal-conservative dimension, and the basis of the factions may shift from election to election. Throughout the 1970s and 1980s, those held to be the "conservatives" were often referred to as the "Burns Regulars" (or later the "Ariyoshi

Table 9: Political Party Composition of the Hawai'i Legislature since Statehood

	No. of Demo	No. of Repub	Total Rep	% of Demo	% of Repub	No. of Demo	No. of Repub	No. of Other	Total Sen	% of Demo
1959*	33	19	52	63%	37%	16	9		25	64%
1960	33	18	51	65%	35%	11	14		25	44%
1961**	34	17	51	67%	33%	11	14		25	44%
1963	40	11	51	78%	22%	15	10		25	60%
1965	39	12	51	76%	24%	16	9		25	64%
1967	39	12	51	76%	24%	13	10	2	25	52%
1969	39	12	51	76%	24%	16	8	1	25	64%
1971	34	17	51	67%	33%	16	8		24	67%
1973	35	16	51	69%	31%	17	8		25	68%
1975	35	16	51	69%	31%	18	7		25	72%
1977	41	10	51	80%	20%	18	7		25	72%
1979	42	9	51	82%	18%	18	7		25	72%
1981	39	12	51	76%	24%	17	8		25	68%
1983	43	8	51	84%	16%	20	5		25	80%
1985	40	11	51	78%	22%	21	4		25	84%
1987	40	11	51	78%	22%	20	5		25	80%
1989	45	6	51	88%	12%	22	3		25	88%
1991	45	6	51	88%	12%	22	3		25	88%
1993	47	4	51	92%	8%	22	3		25	88%
1995	44	7	51	86%	14%	23	2		25	92%
1997	39	12	51	76%	14%	23	2		25	92%
1999	39	12	51	76%	24%	23	2		25	92%

Sources: State of Hawaii, Journal of the House of Representatives; Journal of the Senate; House of Representatives, Chief Clerk's Office; Senate Clerk's Office.

*These are the figures for the Thirtieth Legislature of the Territory of Hawaii. Admission to statehood did not occur until August 16, 1959. By that time the territorial legislature had met. However, the First Special Session of the Hawaii State Legislature convened August 31, 1959, to October 22, 1959. The first legislature of the state of Hawai'i convened in 1960.

**Election of legislators occurs every odd year, so the party composition of the legislature should not change in even numbered years, pending a death, resignation, or impeachment of a member. In such a case, a new member is appointed by the governor from the same party as the outgoing member, so the party composition of the legislature would not change.

boys"), and although they have gone by many labels, the "liberals" were called the "Mink" or "Gill" Democrats. This can change in specific sessions. The proposal to allow gambling, either in restricted areas or off-shore on tourist ships, brought together some of the strongest conservatives and liberals, without regard to party. During the same session, the controversy over whether to permit same-sex couples to marry divided social conservatives and liberals.

In this shifting context, the label "conservative" usually refers to a more right-of-center approach to government. It also means those who had survived in elected office for longer periods of time, who tend to oppose a more active role for citizens, such as through the power of initiative, because of its potential threat to their continued tenure. "Liberal" references concern with internal reform and larger, more transformative social agendas.

Do these local labels share meanings with their national counterparts? Sometimes. For example, in the elections to Congress in 1994 and 1996, Orson Swindle, the Republican candidate who had been Ross Perot's national campaign director in 1992, was heavily supported by the national Republican party in his contest against incumbent Democrat Neil Abercrombie. Swindle's campaign went to great lengths to characterize Abercrombie as a "tax and spend liberal," a depiction that had brought success to Perot and to Republicans in their electoral battles during this period. Swindle generated far more competition in the contest than often has been the case for Hawai'i Congressional incumbents, who frequently had been virtually unchallenged. At the same time, the effort to link this contest to national ideological identifiers was not very successful because there was no real counterpart in Hawai'i legislative contests.

The exception to this disconnect between national and local terms of reference appears to come when contests focus on "style" issues: issues having to do with the relative status of social groups. The 1996 elections for the state legislature were influenced by the style issue of same-sex marriage, with those opposed to it being identified as conservatives and those in favor being labeled liberal. Most incumbent legislators who lost seats that year were associated with a "pro" same-sex marriage position, which opinion polls showed the electorate had identified as a "radical" position relative to the conservative stance supporting "traditional" marriage.

In summary, then, Hawai'i voters in legislative districts would, on most issues, be hard pressed to identify their representative as liberal or conservative, or to associate these labels with the two parties, but on some issues these categories can be meaningful.

ASSESSING THE STRENGTH OF LEGISLATIVE LEADERS

The power of a legislative leader is difficult to calculate. One indication of relative strength is the degree to which a leader is challenged from within his or her party, something, as we will see below, that occurs with relative frequency among the Democrats' legislative party.

Where power comes from is another matter. One source is their ties to the power structure of the external community, such as to unions, corporations, or other well-organized and well-resourced entities. The Bishop Estate is a good case in point.

The estate has not always gotten what it wants in the legislative arena, but its long-term influence there is unquestioned. The vehicle for influence is ties to legislative leadership. Richard "Dickie" Wong, a powerful O'ahu legislator who served four terms in the House (1967–74) and in the Senate (1975–92), moved effortlessly from his thirteen years as Senate president to Bishop Estate trustee. Henry Peters, another Democrat from Wai'anae, had an even shorter journey, having been appointed to the estate while serving as speaker of the House. The Peters case is an interesting one because it shows the limits on the projection of external power into the legislature.

Peters was elected to the state House of Representatives in 1974, and became House Speaker in 1981. In 1984, he was appointed to the Board of Trustees of the Bishop Estate. Although widely regarded as very powerful, some felt that, since many of the estate's diverse interests are impacted by legislative business, being both trustee and House Speaker was inherently a conflict of interest. Peters did not. He argued that if a legislator could also be a banker, why couldn't he be trustee of the state's largest landowner.

In making his defense, Peters observed that other influential legislators before him had done the same thing. In particular, he named four men who had been either the chief officer of the House of Senate and at the same time a Bishop or Campbell trustee, or the vice president of a Big Five firm, and another who had been a state senator and a Bishop trustee.[8]

Peters was not re-elected as House Speaker in 1986, the vote reflecting legislator's concern about the appearance of a conflict of interest.

Beyond this obvious base in external relationships, the sources of power in the legislature are complex and not easily defined. It is here that the loose structural dynamics of the Hawai'i legislature, contributed to by the absence of strong parties, are most on display.

Sometimes the more visible legislators, like Wong and Peters, hold its formal offices, serving as the party leaders in the two bodies or chairing its most important committees. Other times, however, powerful leaders operate behind the scenes, working through networks that transcend the legislature while symbolizing the importance of Hawai'i's relational political culture.

Nadao Yoshinaga, who served in the legislature from 1955 to 1974, was such a figure.

Yoshinaga was widely recognized as the paramount figure in the legislature, and often was referred to as its "godfather." Like that cultural icon, Yoshinaga was noted not only for the legislation he influenced, but also for the development of his "boys," promising figures trained through their involvement in the legislature's committee structure. On the basis of that training, and their association with Yoshinaga, they moved, in time, to other important positions in state government. Often this was to the Department of Budget and Finance, from which they equally often moved out into various departments as administrative or financial officers. Keeping with the godfather metaphor, members of this group are sometimes termed the "finance Mafia" to refer to their loose, but useful, interrelationships.

It is also the case that sometimes Hawai'i legislative leaders are less than they seem. David McClung, who served as Senate president from 1966 to 1974, began the decade of the 1970s as a high-profile, influential leader, from which position he appears to have over-reached in efforts to extend his grasp. His misstep was complicated by declining health and personal troubles, and his influence waned within a short period of time.

In 1993, Senate President James Aki faced federal charges that he had acted improperly with respect to private lands he owns on the Wai'anae Coast. Although he denied any wrong doing, Aki, who had been the compromise coalition candidate of dissident forces in the Senate, subsequently was defeated in his 1994 Senate president bid by Norman Mizuguchi, closely associated with the Waihe'e bloc of Democrats.

LEGISLATOR CHARACTERISTICS

The occupations of state legislators can shape a variety of legislative predispositions. Nationally, by occupation, attorneys are most likely to be found in legislative bodies, followed by business owners, full-time legislators, educators, businesspersons, realtors, and homemakers.[9] At the same time, the occupations of legislators vary significantly from state to state and region to region.

Hawai'i's legislature is not representative of the general public in the state on many measures, more so on others. A 1990 survey reported by James Wang found that lawyers constituted only 9 percent of the house and 20 percent of the senate, a surprising result given the popular view that attorneys are always the dominant legislative group. Wang's own survey of the 1994–95 session learned that over 30 percent of legislators were full-time; no union officials had been elected; 8 percent had lived in Hawai'i for less than 9 years, while 25 percent were born in the islands; 88 percent had a college degree or better; and 55 percent earned at least $45,000 a year.[10] In terms of gender representation, Hawai'i has much less the number of female legislators than expected were the percentage to match the state population. For example, there were only eight women in the 51-member House, and five women in the 25-member Senate in the 1997–98 sessions.

According to an early 1990s study, there were a little more than six times as many educators in the legislature as in the state's population. The number of legislators with agricultural jobs was very close to the corresponding percentage of those employed by agriculture in the state. Ethnic diversity was, and is, much greater in the islands' legislature than in the rest of the country. This mirrors the state's heterogeneous population. With the exception of African-Americans, the most under-represented groups at that time were labor-unions members and government employees. Hawai'i had about 5 percent of the number of labor-union employees in its legislature as would be anticipated based on the number of labor-union employees in the general population. And there were no government employees.[11]

THE ROLE OF COALITIONS

It is common for one-party dominated legislatures to operate through some form of coalitional structure since effective political competition is within the party. These coalitions have been loose and shifting during the period of Democratic party dominance, reflecting changes occurring in the broader social context of the islands as well as changing personalities within the legislature. Unlike the coalitional structures of some well-known one-party systems, for example, in the Japanese Diet during the long reign of the Liberal Democratic party, in which each coalition had a definable status and formal leader, Hawai'i's Democratic coalitions have been less easily identifiable and more susceptible to change from one election to another.

The coalition of Neighbor Island legislators is an important exception to this. Numbering seven in the Senate and thirteen in the House, the needs of their rural constituents are different from than those of urban Honolulu, and they have a common interest in not being overwhelmed by O'ahu concerns. It is an enduring coalition that, while occasionally broken by specific issues, often has resulted in them having influence over legislation or leadership out of proportion to their numbers.

This is the exception, however, and for years the tone of legislative politics has been set by shifting alliances. These commonly form as challenges to the dominant coalition's leadership, and are mounted by dissatisfied and marginalized individuals or groups.

In the 1996 election, a number of high-profile legislative leaders were "punished" by the electorate for their positions on specific issues, such as same-sex marriage or the reform of no-fault automobile insurance. Donna Ikeda, Senate Ways and Means Chair, and Milton Holt, a powerful inside player in the Senate, were among those defeated. Norman Mizuguchi, the president of the Senate during the previous session, survived a significant primary challenge by unknown Diane Ho Kurtz, winning by a relatively narrow electoral margin. In the House, the speaker survived a close contest for his seat, but there were no upsets of the same magnitude as in the Senate.

Not unexpectedly, organizing the Senate following the 1996 election proved a matter of intense negotiation. The tension over the substantive issues of same-sex marriage and no-fault auto insurance was addressed through demands that the legislature be reformed to free it from the negative effects of its leadership structure. Norman Mizuguchi was re-elected Senate president, but only on the condition that the Senate standing committees be co-chaired, a clear effort on the part of dissident members to assure their greater participation in the legislative process and to reduce what they viewed as the arbitrary power of committee chairs. This was the boldest step the Hawai'i Senate had ever taken to rein in the power of its leaders.

Action in the House was more anti-climactic. A coalition, primarily of younger Democrats, had been meeting to discuss the possibility of unseating Speaker Joe Souki, contending that he had become too autocratic in running the House. The organizers spent much of the previous year shaping their agenda and building a large enough coalition to win the Speakership. They ultimately fell short by one or two votes when, because of their position on the same-gender marriage issue, some of their members failed to win re-election. Speaker Souki then allocated committee assignments on a "normal" basis after the typical meetings and bargaining with the various factions. All three of the critical committee chairs of the previous legislature were retained by their former occupants, and some members of the coalition that had attempted to unseat Souki were excluded from committee chairs and seats on key committees.

SHIFTING COALITIONS AND THE PROSPECTS FOR REFORM

Former Representative James Shon participated in the pre-session discussions about unseating the House Speaker in 1996, but then narrowly lost his own bid for re-election. His reflections on his years in the Hawai'i state legislature provide some interesting, and rare, insights.[12]

In Shon's view, personal relationships dominate the legislative process, something not surprising given the traditionalistic element in Hawai'i's political culture. The unwritten rules that operate in the House favor acting privately and with discretion, and disapprove of being very revealing about how things work. "No one wants to look bad, and open public opposition or debate is bound to make someone look bad."

The most important issue to Shon was that the party had lost its way, its popular image increasingly that of a group of inside deal makers who had disconnected from their constituents and their public mission. In 1996 a group of legislators, out of sight of the media, circulated thought pieces and met in a process aimed at forging a broad reform agenda. By early September there was enough support to take over leadership of the House and implement their program. Then came the general election of 1996, or what Shon calls "Black Tuesday." To his way of thinking, many people missed its significance. It was not just that "a few liberals who supported controversial issues like same gender marriage were thrown out . . . more fundamentally, the election crippled the reform movement in the House."

LEGISLATIVE SUPPORT SERVICES

Several offices located within the legislative branch provide services to the legislature and the state. The Office of the Legislative Auditor conducts audits of transactions, programs, accounts, and performances of state and county governments and agencies. These audits are designed to uncover any unauthorized or illegal use of state funds and to assess in general terms whether, and how efficiently, these departments and agencies are fulfilling their legislative mandates.

The state auditor is appointed by a majority of each house in joint session for a term of eight years. All auditors since the inception of the office in 1959 have enjoyed the respect of the legislature, and the office is seen as relatively free from partisan influence that might induce it to soft pedal its investigations or use them to of strike out at its enemies. The auditor's studies of state departments and major programs have been extensive and critical. The reports, which appear about bimonthly, often draw groans from administrators, perhaps an indication of the relative effectiveness of that office, whose purpose is, of course, to act as a watchdog for the legislature.

The five-member State Ethics Commission is administratively within the office of the Legislative Auditor. The Ethics Commission was created to address conflicts of interest in public office. It was the first in the country to apply to all employees, officials, and members of boards and commissions by constitutional provision. The fact that its conflict of interest rules do not apply to legislators who regularly are faced with conflicts is a notable exception to its coverage.

The commission, acting through an executive director whom it appoints, also administers the financial disclosure laws—prescribing the forms and procedures that public officials and employees fill out to indicate their financial interests. Members of the commission are appointed by the governor from lists of persons provided by the Judicial Council.

The job of the executive director of the Ethics Commission is a delicate one. The director and the commission have great potential power, power that the legislature is reluctant to cultivate by providing the commission with many enforcement teeth. A constant dynamic prevails in which the commission and its director seek broader authority to meet its mission, and the legislature drags its collective feet.

The Legislative Reference Bureau (LRB) is the legislature's research arm. With the responsibility for drafting bills, providing research and a reference service, the LRB is an important source of information for legislators—particularly in a part-time legislature like Hawai'i where legislators have funds only to support small, personal, permanent staffs. The LRB's director is appointed for a six-year term by a majority of each house of the legislature in joint session, and may be removed by a vote of two-thirds of the members in joint session.

Finally, there is the Office of the Ombudsman. Ombudsmen are independent public officials with powers to investigate citizen complaints against the actions of public agencies. Hawai'i, in 1969, was the first state to establish what political scientist Larry Hill calls a "classical ombudsman," one that is appointed by the legislature, and independent.[13] Today, four other states—Nebraska (1971), Iowa (1972), Alaska (1975) and Arizona (1996)—have them. The Hawai'i ombudsman owes its existence to the efforts of one person, Herman Doi, a former head of the Legislative Reference Bureau who served as the first ombudsman for 15 years.

The Office of the Ombudsman takes complaints about state and county agencies as well as the Office of Hawaiian Affairs. It may subpoena witnesses and force persons to testify before hearings as well as compel the production of papers and documents related to matters under investigation. Although the ombudsman has no formal power to implement the office's findings, it can, after a reasonable time, issue a report of recommendations to the governor, the legislature, or the public. Some believe the office has failed to live up to its potential of making state and county agencies more responsive to the public's they serve. Currently, for example, about 40 percent of its inquiries, but not of its working cases, are provided by prisoners, for whom it is a major window of appeal. At the same time, over its life more than 100,000 citizens have contacted the office, and it has begun investigations of 65,000 complaints filed with it.

THE PARTICULAR IMPORTANCE OF REAPPORTIONMENT

The legislatively controlled Reapportionment Commission deserves special attention because of the impact of its decisions. Article IV, Section 1 of the Hawai'i Constitution, adopted in 1968, specifies that 1973, 1981, and every tenth year thereafter are to be reapportionment years. The Reapportionment Commission is created by the appointment of two members each by the president of the senate, speaker of the house, a designated member of the minority party of the senate, and a designated member of the minority party of the house. A ninth member, serving as the chairperson of the commission, is then selected by the eight appointed members.

The Reapportionment Commission's job is to devise and recommend to the legislature a reapportionment plan. To gauge the importance of reapportionment to Hawai'i, it may be useful to digress briefly to recall some of the 'history of legislative apportionment in the United States. Any representative political system requires a mechanism for assigning legislative members to constituencies. In the Congress, members of the Senate represent states, and members of the House represent districts based on population. For most of our history, many states followed what has come to be known as the "federal plan" wherein state representation followed, to varying degrees, the method of representation used for Congress. This meant that, in some states, House members were elected on the basis of population in districts distributed throughout the state, whereas the upper chamber was elected on the basis of some larger geographic unit—usually counties.

As growing populations became more highly concentrated in some counties, those states that based one house on jurisdictions soon came to have ''malapportioned'' legislatures. These imbalances meant that some constituents were getting ''more representation'' in the legislature than others.

Jurisdictional apportionment was challenged in the federal courts, on the basis that citizens from some districts lacked the equal protection of the law. The United States Supreme Court, up to the early 1960s, had dismissed these challenges as involving a ''political question'' in which the Court would not become involved (terming the issue at one point, a ''political thicket''). The proper remedy, from the Court's perspective, lay with state legislatures. In *Baker v. Carr,* a 1962 Tennessee case, the Court changed its position.[14] It ruled that the question was a justiciable issue, and not a political matter, and remanded the case to the lower courts for resolution. In two opinions, two years later, the Court found that *both* houses of state legislatures must be apportioned on the basis of equal population within districts. In *Reynolds v. Simms,*[15] the Court found that the principle that ''one man's vote should be equal to another's'' should be extended to state senates. Chief Justice Earl Warren, a former California governor, remarked, ''Legislators represent people, not trees or acres.''[16]

In Hawai'i, the constitution of 1950 apportioned 60 percent of senatorial districts to the Neighbor Islands and 40 percent of the districts to O'ahu. In response to *Reynolds v. Simms,* the 1968 Constitutional Convention proposed, and the voters later approved, the Reapportionment Commission (see chapter 5).

The commission formulated a reapportionment plan based upon the following guidelines:[17]

1. No district shall extend beyond the boundaries of any basic island unit (county);
2. No district shall be so drawn as to unduly favor a person or political faction;
3. Except in the case of districts encompassing more than one island, districts shall be contiguous;
4. Insofar as practicable, districts shall be compact;
5. Where possible, district lines shall follow permanent and easily recognized features, such as streets, streams, and clear geographical features, and when practicable, shall coincide with census track boundaries;
6. Where practicable, representative districts shall be wholly included within senatorial districts;
7. Not more than four members shall be elected from any single district;
8. Where practicable, submergence of an area in a larger district wherein substantially different socio-economic interests predominate shall be avoided.

Reapportionment has brought some changes to the legislature. The most important, apart from stress on specific legislators who are forced to run in unfamiliar areas because of new district boundaries, is the impact on Neighbor-Island representation. Earlier rules governing representation made it easier for them to have power beyond their population base, and to control key positions. The 1968 reapportionment plan took five house seats from the Neighbor Islands and gave them to new districts on O'ahu. Neighbor Island legislators remain influential—the Speaker of the House in the 1996 legislature was from Maui, and five of 19 house committees were chaired by Neighbor-Island legislators in that same session—but their influence is no longer based on favorable apportionment.

Finally, as Jim Wang observes, the commissions that have met in 1973, 1981, and 1991 have not been completely immune from shaping electoral districts in ways that favor one party over the other.[18] He points to a case of gerrymandering on the Big Island in which the 1973 commission created an unusually large representative district, apparently to dilute the power base of a previously safe Republican.

INTEREST GROUPS IN THE HAWAI'I LEGISLATURE

The weakening of political parties in Hawai'i has meant that they have been less able to perform the function of articulating interests and placing them within the complex agendas of legislative politics. As this has happened, these activities have increasingly come to be performed by interest groups.

Jim Wang's study of government in Hawai'i listed five types of interest groups that historically have been active in the legislative process: labor, business associations, professional groups, ethnic and minority associations, and public interest groups. Within these categories, we can observe changes as the economy and social relations change. For example, among business groups, the Big Five companies are less powerful than they once were, a shift shared by the sugar and pineapple industries. Construction continues to be a "big player," as are financial institutions, the tourist industry, and the various factors that make it up. On balance, labor remains influential, although by the 1990s strength shifted from private sector labor organizations, especially the International Labor and Warehouseman's Union, to public sector organizations (especially the Hawaii Government Employees Association and the United Public Workers). On specific issues, other industries can be highly effective in the pursuit of their own interests, including but not limited to the insurance industry, the medical industry, and plaintive attorneys.

In *Group Power,* Carol Greenwald supplies a useful general inventory of legislative lobbying activities, most of which are also seen in Hawai'i,[19] First and foremost, lobbyists are an important source of information—particularly in non-professional legislatures. Information is often delivered informally, for example, through meetings, or more formally in testimony during hearings. In many cases, lobbyists will actually draft versions of bills to be introduced into the legislature.

It is important to acknowledge that some of the most important lobbyists working a legislature are those from the administration who bring to the process all the informational and persuasive resources of their departments and agencies. Many executive branch agencies in Hawai'i designate specific individuals whose most important responsibilities are to "liaison" with the legislature. These lobbyists are often as formidable and effective as those from outside government. They have the additional advantage of usually being from the same political party and being well-known personally to legislators, something especially significant in Hawai'i's political culture of interpersonal relations.

Lobbyists also may assist in raising money for legislators by attending their fund-raisers or assisting in the sale of fundraising tickets (a form of making campaign contributions). They may participate directly in campaigns by organizing members of the interest group in the legislator's district, often evidenced by generating letters from constituents, or by providing advertising. In the raucous fight over automobile insurance reform during the 1995 and 1996 legislatures, State Farm Insurance Company, a major player in this insurance market, took a leading role in the battle by frequently publishing large newspaper ads and television commercials. This was an unusually direct role for a commercial participant to take in lobbying a legislative issue. More common is the creation of a "front" organization, an organization named in general and agreeable terms to which groups with a direct interest in an outcome can give money and personnel support without necessarily revealing the extent of their participation. Industry coalitions of this sort have been created in previous auto-insurance reform efforts, as they have been in fights over development.

Another relatively new wrinkle in lobbying by advertisement is the approach taken in recent years by the Bishop Estate in its long battle over leasehold conversion. Beginning about 1994, the estate began running newspaper ads and television commercials conflating the issue of conversion of some of its residential leaseholds to private ownership with Hawaiian sovereignty, attempting to make the point that any alienation of estate land was simultane-

ously a loss to the Hawaiian community in general. The equation of a particular interest with the general community interest is characteristic of much
political advertising.

Most lobbying, however, is more subtle and informal. The vast proportion of what elected officials do escapes public view. Much new legislation
and many refinements in existing legislation receive very little, if any, attention from anyone other than those directly involved in the legislation. This
creates an environment conducive to quiet, subtle, and behind-the-scenes
lobbying. As Carol Greenwald writes, lobbyists "stress pleasantness and
competence . . . [a lobbyist should be] . . . well prepared and informed . . .
convince the official of the issue's importance to him and his constituency or
in terms of the public interest . . . smile till your face aches."[20]

The Influence of Contemporary Interest Groups

In 1997, a total of 110 labor unions and associations, of which 98 were affili-
ated with the AFL-CIO, counted a membership of 170,399 persons. This
amounted to approximately 23 percent of the private sector labor force, and
51 percent of public sector workers.[21]

Chapter 5 pointed out that one of the unusual features of the Hawai'i Constitution is the right conferred on public employees to bargain collectively.
The Hawaii Government Employee's Association (HGEA) is the largest public employee union with 22,519 members in 1997, followed by the United
Public Workers, with 11,933. Both are a major presence in Hawai'i politics,
although it is slowly becoming a less powerful presence than it once was.[22]
Other public employee unions include the Hawaii State Teachers Association, University of Hawai'i Professional Assembly, the State of Hawaii Organization of Police Officers, and the Hawai'i State Fire Fighters Association. Each either threatened a strike action or took one during the 1990s.

Among private sector unions, the Teamsters and ILWU, as indicated
above, remain important in part through their organization of tourist industry
workers, as do the construction unions. On several occasions in the past decade, construction unions have joined forces with industry interest groups to
conduct pro-development demonstrations at the state capitol.

A second group, identified using Jim Wang's categories, was business associations. These associations include the general chambers of commerce,
as well as the Japanese, Chinese, and Filipino chambers of commerce that
have been established on each of the islands. In addition, there are business
associations representing various industries, such as the Construction Indus-

try Legislative Organization, the Hawaii Sugar Planters Association, and the Hawaii Hotel Association. These groups do not incorporate all of the influence exercised by the business community. In areas such as health care, for example, the Hawaii Medical Services Association (HMSA), Kaiser Hospitals, and the Health Care Association of Hawaii, representing non-state hospitals, are influential in framing issues and indicating possible support or opposition throughout the industry.

Virtually every profession is represented by its own interest group. Within the medical community, for example, many physicians belong to the Hawaii Medical Association, just as most dentists belong to the Hawaii Dental Association. However, as these professions have become more involved in the political process and as their associations have developed "stands" on important public issues, the professional community has splintered, with new associations forming to pursue particular policy issues. In this same way, the Hawaii Federation of Physicians and Dentists was created out of groups opposed to movements toward managed care in both medicine and dentistry, and supports the retention of the "fee for service" system of direct reimbursement for services rendered to patients. The health care environment is also well populated by advocacy groups that lobby the legislature for continued support for particular beneficiaries of public policy, such as the mentally ill or abused spouses.

Architects are well-organized and since statehood have been frequently identified with sizable financial support for political candidates. Architects and architectural firms are frequently the largest campaign contributors to both gubernatorial and Honolulu mayoral campaigns.[23] Their presence in these campaigns is testament to the importance of public sector development contracts to the profession.

All ethnic minorities in Hawai'i have formal associations, but they alone don't tell the story of how such groups are organized in the community, where ethnic identification is often also organized through religious or community associations. Wang notes that, as a rule, these groups operate behind the scenes, using neither the mass media nor lobbyists to influence public policy, but rather working quietly on behalf of the interests and members of their group. Hawai'i is a small, relationship-oriented community; when one wants to find access to the process, it usually does not take much asking among associational or affiliational groups to find someone who knows a given legislator well enough to gain a hearing.

Consistent with developments discussed in chapters 4 and 9, Hawaiian groups have become much more active, and seemingly effective, in lobbying the legislature. Although this takes a variety of forms, the ability to mobilize a sizable number of committed supporters on short notice has resulted in more frequent public displays, which in turn make use of media coverage and public sympathy for their cause. For example, large, vocal turnouts at the state capitol during the 1997 and 1998 legislative sessions squashed, at least in the short term, any actions, proposed by anxious land developers and budget-conscious legislators, that would have changed earlier judicial decisions on concerning use of or compensation for ceded lands.

Finally, Wang identifies "public interest" groups as the fifth major type that operates in Hawai'i. Examples of public interest groups are Common Cause (the self-styled citizens' or consumer lobby), the American Civil Liberties Union, and various environmental groups, such as the Nature Conservancy, Life of the Land, and the Sierra Club. The public interest groups have in common the pursuit of collective goods—benefits that are available to society at large.

In an effort to update Wang's mid-1970s analysis, we undertook a survey in October 1993 of Hawai'i House and Senate members. All legislators were sent a questionnaire titled "Legislative Influence Poll" in which they were requested to identify the group, or types of groups, that they thought most influential in the Hawai'i legislative process. Each was asked to rank those groups from one to ten, with one being the most influential. Twenty-five of the legislators responded, a respectable response rate of 33 percent for a survey of this type.

In many respects, these survey results are close to those found by Wang, but some significant differences emerged. In terms of the frequency of identification, within the top five groups or types of groups designated by the legislators, the most often-named group was labor unions. Labor unions were identified more than three times as often as the next highest category. The second category was business and industry, followed by the executive branch or department heads, public interest groups, senior citizens' groups, financial institutions, representatives from human service organizations, large land estates, and community groups.

To some extent, this ranking is an artifact of the categories used by legislators. When comparisons are made across all ten groups, labor unions remain number one. If, however, all groups that have some business activity are summed, which means including tourism, the insurance industry, and the health industry, then the classification of "business and industry" rivals unions as the most identified source of lobbying activity.

There is another reason to question the influence of unions, especially in the period since the survey was taken. It seems evident that the power of private sectors unions has diminished as the place of sugar and pineapple in the economy has shrunk and the service sector has grown. This is symbolized by the fact that their membership has dropped from 21 percent of the workforce in 1986 to 16 percent in 1996.[24]

Public union membership has remained constant over the same period, at around 51 percent of the public sector workforce. These figures, however, may disguise changes in the political environment that affect the capacity of union lobbyists to create or derail policy. These changes include greater agreement that government costliness and inefficiency are a drag on economic recovery, as well as the arrival in Hawai'i' of the national reinvention movement.

Activity in the 1998 legislative session is indicative of the changing status and legislative influence of public sector unions. Several Democrat House members introduced a bill that would have radically altered the collective bargaining agreement. Among its provisions were limitations on the scope of what is negotiable in contract bargaining, with the idea of restricting those terms to issues closer to wages and fringe benefits and excluding conditions of work; the use of end-of year savings as performance incentives, thus getting around exclusive reliance on the seniority system; exclusion of supervisors from union contracts; and de-coupling the state and counties during contract negotiations so that each would reach its own agreements. The introduction of legislation with these provisions by members of the majority party a few years earlier would have been virtually unthinkable. Although in 1998 the bill was not a serious contender for passage, its introduction by Democratic legislators in a gubernatorial election year reflects a significant change.

Returning to the survey results, the number of times that the executive branch and/or department heads are identified as being influential lobbyists is of special interest. This reflects the centralization that characterizes Hawai'i state government and the influence that such centralization vests with the executive branch. In the life of the legislator, responding to the influence of the executive branch almost equals dealing with the private sector.

In contrast to the Wang summary, our survey respondents rarely (only twice, in fact) identified ethnic and minority associations as having any influence on the Hawai'i legislative process, and they only slightly more frequently—four times—identified professional groups as having such influence.

Who Are the Lobbyists and How Are They Controlled?

Under Chapter 97 of the Hawaii Revised Statutes, those conducting business with the legislature are required to register with the Hawaii State Ethics Commission. The Hawai'i Revised Statutes define lobbying as "communicating directly or through an agent, or soliciting others to communicate with any official in the legislative or executive branch, for the purpose of influencing any legislative or administrative action."[25] If an individual is paid or receives any kind of compensation for his or her lobbying services, and spends more than five hours a month lobbying, or spends more than $275 in any six-month period on lobbying, then that individual is required to register as a lobbyist with the Ethics Commission. In addition, lobbyists are required to report expenditures and contributions incurred in the process of lobbying. This does not apply to individuals acting on their own behalf, who don't make expenditures or contributions associated with their lobbying.

Lobbying registration requirements in Hawai'i provide us with a snapshot of those involved in the business of lobbying the legislature. As of June 1993, there were 246 individual lobbyists registered with the Ethics Commission, representing 182 organizations. Many lobbyists registered as representing only one interest. In most of these cases, these are employees of those organizations. Gary Rodrigues, executive director of the Hawai'i State AFL-CIO, is an example of such a lobbyist. Others, commonly referred to as "professional" lobbyists, registered as representing numerous interests. For example, Jon Okudara represented Aloha Airlines, Alpack (Pepsi Cola), BHP Petroleum, Coca-Cola Bottling Company of Honolulu, Mauna Lani Resort, the Nature Conservancy of Hawai'i, Oahu Transit Group, Oceanic Cablevision, Sears, Roebuck and Company, Sukamoto Holding Corporation, and Teachers Insurance and Annuity Association.

Companies are also required to report to the Ethics Commission how much they spend lobbying the legislature. The annual amount reported varies with the issues on the legislative agenda. Between May 1996 and March 1997, part way through the 1997 session, insurance, oil, and tobacco companies were the biggest spenders.[26] Insurance companies, worried about reforms of the no-fault system, officially spent $180,000 on lobbying. Tobacco firms, which keep local law offices on retainer to protect their interests, reported that almost $100,000 was directed to fending off cigarette-tax hikes. Oil companies allocated about $130,000 in a fight over whether they could own and operate their own retail stations in Hawai'i.

Although the registration requirements provide citizens a way to keep track of who's lobbying for whom, and, to a degree, how much money is being spent, it is noteworthy that federal, state, or county officials or employees are specifically exempted from the registration and reporting requirements in the Hawaii Revised Statutes.

WHAT DOES IT ALL MEAN?

The effects of the concentration of political power, so much a characteristic of Hawai'i political life, are readily apparent in the legislative process. Power is concentrated in the Democratic legislative leadership and in a relatively few influential standing committees, most notably the two money committees. Further, while politics in Hawai'i is sufficiently individualistic and the parties sufficiently weak to forbid the existence of a party-driven "machine" of the sort sometimes seen in other states, the legislative agenda is driven by the constitutionally powerful governor. The executive branch holds many of the cards in the governmental process, including the advantages of extensive, year-round staffing and a vast superiority in information gathering and analysis. Legislators regard executive branch officials as among the most important figures lobbying them for action, and there is no question that the package of administration bills does much to drive the overall legislative agenda.

Finally, while interest groups are plentiful, they also are relatively concentrated, reflecting the homogeneity of the Hawaiian economy. As a consequence, there is less competition among groups than in more economically heterogeneous states. With fewer groups competing for power, it is easy for power to be focused, both in the legislative and the executive branch. This is reinforced by the political culture described in chapter 3, a dominating political party and a minority party whose members are anxious to occupy the positions from which they have been excluded, and a centralized government. The result is a legislature that historically has not responded quickly, and sometimes not at all, to external forces, especially those that lie outside the boundaries of familiar political influence, and has had difficulty creating coalitions capable of sustaining significant reform.

CHAPTER TEN

Local Government, Hawai'i Style

Under the "Dillon Rule," set forth in an Iowa Supreme Court decision in 1868, all local governments are creatures of the state in that they possess only those powers given directly to them by state government. As numerous observers have pointed out, the kinds of creatures that have been created vary a great deal.

In Hawai'i, there is less local government than anywhere in America. In stark contrast to states where the counties, cities, towns, townships, districts, and other jurisdictions number in the hundreds, or even thousands, there are only four in Hawai'i. Each of these is a county, and none existed until the first decade of this century.

This unique situation is a direct reflection of the state's history. Consistent with that history, throughout the twentieth century, the status of these few "local" governments has been the subject of an on-going tug-of-war with a succession of elected and administrative state officials.

In recent years, demographic shifts toward the re-population of the Neighbor Islands have strengthened long-standing attempts to increase the authority of country governments or create municipalities capable of raising taxes and controlling land use within their boundaries. As questions about the desirability of more "home rule" are debated over the coming years, Hawai'i will continue as a novel American orientation toward blending centralized authority and democratic politics.

LOCAL GOVERNMENT'S PAST IN A CENTRALIZED STATE

Although the Kingdom of Hawai'i, as it evolved in the nineteenth century, had very little formal local government, it was not entirely absent. The 1840, 1852, 1864, and 1887 constitutions created some local responsibilities in such areas as education and roads. Beginning at least as early as the 1840s, attempts were made to formalize local government and establish Honolulu and similar-sized towns on other islands as legal municipalities. These efforts were opposed by foreigners, as well as some Hawaiians in a position to influence government policy. Both argued it would cost too much for a government already concerned about its finances, create confusion and undermine the king's authority, and give Hawaiians responsibilities for which they were unprepared.[1] As a consequence, while centralized authority developed in the direction of a constitutional monarchy, few parallel institutions evolved locally.

Leaders of the republic viewed decentralization as contrary to their desire to consolidate public authority while leaving the plantation owners free to run their businesses as they saw fit. Consequently, by annexation, the few functions that once were local responsibilities had been appropriated by the government, by then re-located to Honolulu. The issue of local governance, however, did not cease to be of concern and by the late nineteenth century was an issue around which the emerging political parties organized.[2] Its significance as a rallying point was heightened by Neighbor Islanders who believed their interests were ignored by the distant and "foreign" central authority on O'ahu.[3]

The territorial Organic Act, approved by Congress in 1900, specified that "the legislature may create counties and town and city municipalities within the Territory of Hawaii." The key words "may create" reflected a tug of war over the charter's contents. The tension was between those in Hawai'i who wished to control the apparatus of government until such time as broader participation was more acceptable, and those in Washington who believed the fact of its being American meant the new territory must have government closer to the people.

In the islands, Republicans and Democrats competed against the Home Rule party and for the Hawaiian vote by also advocating local government. At the same time, some members of both these parties were concerned about local government's implications. Republican Sanford Dole, the first territorial governor, warned against actions that "might upset the balance of the territory" and "impose local government on communities that did not desire it."[4] According to Joseph Maguire, Republican interest in a moderate form of local government was based almost entirely on the desire to undermine the Home Rule party. After it disappeared and Republicans gained control of the legislature, "Republican interest in home rule became submerged."[5]

The federal commission that visited Honolulu in 1902 to observe the territory's system of governance embodied Washington's encouragement of local government. The committee expressed surprise and concern at the extent to which the structure they saw resembled what had existed under the monarchy.[6] Their findings were reflected in the conclusion that: "These interesting, intelligent and absolutely loyal people, the native Hawaiians, [need to be brought] under the vitalizing influence of republican representative government."[7] Committee members suggested that if some form of local government was not established in the islands, they might be forced to revise the Organic Act's language to make it less discretionary, a prospect that horrified the local oligarchy.

Attempts were made in the 1903 legislature, controlled by the Home Rule party, to establish both municipal and county government. Governor Dole vetoed the Municipal Act as in conflict with both the constitution and the proposed County Act. The County Act was ruled unconstitutional by the territorial Supreme Court that interpreted the assigned taxing power to be inconsistent with the Organic Act.

The next territorial governor, George Carter, offered the modest proposal that local representation begin with two or three experiments in municipal government, suggesting that Honolulu, Hilo, and possibly Lahaina on the island of Maui would be good locations. This was never acted on by the legislature, which instead passed a revised County Act over Carter's veto. Because the legislature was not able to overcome a veto of legislation granting counties property-taxation powers, those were kept by the territorial government, with their revenues allocated to the counties. Looking at the form local government had taken, the editor of a local newspaper declared that the legislature "had passed a county act that no more constituted county government, as it is known on the Mainland, than a king constitutes a kingdom."[8]

COUNTIES IN THE TERRITORIAL PERIOD

The four counties created by the County Act covered the populated islands of the chain. Maui County included Maui and the sparsely populated islands of Lanai and Moloka'i, and Ni'ihau was part of Kaua'i, while Hawai'i and O'ahu counties were coterminous with each of those islands.[9] O'ahu County was designated to include the uninhabited islands in the archipelago to the northwest of Kaua'i. Because of the size and importance of Honolulu on O'ahu, that county was re-named the City and County of Honolulu in 1907.

The three rural counties of Kaua'i, Hawai'i, and Moloka'i were each governed by a board of supervisors and looked a great deal like Mainland counties in the territorial period. The City and County of Honolulu had characteristics that resembled a municipality, but in contrast to the election or appointment of a supervisor as head of the board, on O'ahu a mayor had veto power over the board's actions and made appointments with its consent. The counties' major functions were police, fire, water, road construction and maintenance, sewage, rubbish, and the construction and maintenance of certain public buildings, parks and playgrounds. Each county elected a corporate attorney, sheriff, clerk, auditor, and treasurer.[10]

Reflecting their dominance in the territory, county councils were controlled by Republicans. On O'ahu, between 1905, when the first council was elected, and the Democratic Revolution of 1954, 19 of 25 councils had a Republican majority.[11] Despite concerns expressed about the dangers of decentralized government, the new offices that accompanied county government represented an important resource. As a source of patronage, they helped the Republican oligarchy obtain and then retain the loyalty of Native Hawaiian voters in the decades Hawaiians constituted a demographic majority.[12] Indicative of this, in the 1920s, Hawaiians were more heavily represented in the City and County of Honolulu than in either the territorial or federal governments. For all levels of government, they constituted 44 percent of public employees, but in Honolulu Hawaiians were 65 percent.[13]

Representation in country government would change by the end of the territorial period, in response to the shift from a Republican to a Democratic regime. After 1954, Hawaiians would gradually be displaced by Japanese Americans and other Asians from positions that had provided some consolation for other losses.

The life of the counties was defined in clear patterns by the end of the territorial period in 1959. These patterns included the dominating presence of Honolulu, which contained 80 percent of the state's population; factional struggles for leadership within the Democratic controlled county councils; unclear or conflicting responsibilities between the counties and the state; increases in population, especially on O'ahu, that brought more demands for services; and the continuing hope that county government would be given more autonomy. Within these patterns, county government remained much the same, poised ambiguously between its tentative origins and an uncertain future.

CONTEMPORARY COUNTIES

The state's population was almost 1,200,000 by 1997, and the City and County of Honolulu had grown from about 500,000 thirty years earlier to 870,857.

Reversing a long-term pattern, the other counties had begun to grow at a faster rate, with Hawai'i county's population reaching 141,458, Maui county 118.864, and Kaua'i 56,423.[14] In 1995, the counties together had expenditures totaling $1,392,297,000 and employed 16,450 people. Honolulu dominated both of these categories with expenditures of $934,131,000 and a workforce of over 11,000.[15]

The coming of statehood in 1959 had brought prospects of some changes in the status of the counties. Unlike the Organic Act, the Hope Chest Constitution of 1950, crafted to demonstrate the islands' commitment to democratic principles, specified that the legislature *must* create county governments. These counties would be permitted to devise charters of self-governance, although there were no provisions for broad taxing powers. The creation of other political sub-divisions, namely cities and towns, remained optional.

The City and County of Honolulu, in 1959, became the first of the newly chartered governments. Its most noteworthy feature was the strengthened position of an elected chief executive through creation of a strong-mayor system. The mayor became the only elected administrative officer; supervised all the executive departments, including budget, finance, civil service, and the corporation council; presided over an office that had attached to it the managing director as well and the director of information and complaint; made appointments with concurrence of the council; was able to move monies between departments; and had authority to recommend government re-organizations.

The other three counties were influenced by developments in Honolulu. Each formulated a charter after receiving legislative authorization in 1963. The 1968 constitutional convention, reacting to the state Supreme Court decision in *Fasi v. City and County of Honolulu*. which held that a county charter has the same standing as a statute and may be amended by legislature, delegated more authority to the counties to decide structure and organization. This strengthened the county charters, but the court also reaffirmed that the state controlled the allocation of powers and functions between state and counties.

After 1968, each county adopted a mayor-council form of government to replace the board of supervisors. All of the counties have undertaken charter reviews periodically since then.

County mayors are all elected for four years, with the mayors of Honolulu, Hawai'i, Kaua'i and Maui counties limited to two terms, or eight years. Kaua'i is the only county that has no term restrictions on council members, but the restrictions vary from county to county. All of the county charters have provisions for recalling the mayor, and all but Kaua'i allow for the recall of council members. Each permits lawmaking or charter revision by initiative, and Maui, Hawai'i and Kaua'i all provide for referendums on county laws.

Changing county responsibilities have brought replacement of the five officials elected at the turn of the century with a larger number of department heads appointed by the mayor and approved by the council. The major exception to this are the prosecuting attorneys, who are elected to four-year terms in each county but Maui, where the office is appointed.[16]

Representation

The county councils have struggled with the form representation should take, and in particular whether it should be through at-large, single-member, or multiple-member election districts. One issue provoking strong differences of opinion is whether it is better to expect a council member to be responsive to the concerns of a fixed geographic area, such as that defined by a council district, or to act on the basis of his or her understanding of what is best for the county as a whole. Another concern is the state's diversity. Is it is better to have a system in which, in a society as ethnically heterogeneous as Hawai'i's, smaller coalitions of voters are able to elect representatives, as under multiple-member districts? Or is it preferable to hold a single elected official accountable for what county government does or does not do?

Recent histories in two of the counties illustrate this issue.[17] Hawai'i county's seat is Hilo, a town located on the rainy east side of the island. Hilo developed with the growth of sugar plantations and shipping in the nineteenth century. Even before the 1960s, a split had developed with those living on the drier west side. More attractive to tourists, and the site of non-sugar related population growth, people living in Kona felt that the concentration of power in Hilo resulted in an unfair distribution of resources. Largely in response to this issue, the county's first charter commission considered three proposals for council representation. The first would have created two multi-member districts, the east side getting six representatives and the west three. A second would have had nine at-large districts, with no residency requirements. The third was for three at-large districts with no residency requirement, and six at-large who must reside within the boundaries of the island's six historic divisions.

The last of these three proposals finally was selected by voters in 1968. After adoption, the adequacy of representation remained a source of contention for many who felt that even though a person resided in their area, the election was being determined by the higher concentration of votes from Hilo. In 1990, a charter amendment created nine single-member districts and specified residency as a requirement to stand for election to the county council.

The other illustration is from the City and County of Honolulu, a jurisdiction dominated by the city that spreads along O'ahu's southeastern shore. As a way of balancing urban and rural interests, from 1959 to 1968 council members were elected from six at-large districts and three single-member rural districts. The corporation council ruled this arrangement unconstitutional under the federal Supreme Court's 1964 one person, one vote rule, and the county was forced to adopt nine single-member districts on an interim basis.

The 1972 Charter Commission attempted to reinstitute a combined at-large and district system that could pass constitutional muster. Those opposed to it argued that at-large representation was unfair to high-density areas; and that people in single districts had developed relationships with their representatives that resulted in the representatives being better informed and more accountable. On the basis of these objections, the commission's recommendation was defeated by voters, and Honolulu became one of only a few cities over 500,000 to elect its council representatives entirely from single-member districts.[18] The single-member versus at-large question again surfaced on the general election ballot in 1980, and voters reaffirmed their preference for single-member districts.

The Dynamics of County Government

Since the 1950s, county governments have been dominated by individuals elected on the Democratic party ticket.[19] Despite this, councils more often than not have been characterized by intense and sometimes bitter in-fighting. Conflicts reflect, in some cases, the differing institutional responsibilities accorded mayors and councils, and in other instances they are contests of personal ambition. Frequently, they involve arguments over whose interests are being represented in high pay-off areas such as zoning and land use.[20] The struggle over council leadership in the City and County of Honolulu became so complex and debilitating that at one point in the 1970s, the council tried to resolve the problem through a planned rotation. Each Democrat member was to serve as chair for six months according to a fixed protocol. This failed after a short time, and a compromise candidate became council chair.

What goes on in the counties in many ways resembles patterns found at the state level: power struggles reflect the factionalism commonly accompanying party hegemony and loss of a unifying mission. At the same time, the relatively small number of patronage appointments and the fact that the state exerts so much control over policy development and fiscal matters has meant that state and federal power holders and interest groups have been less interested in influencing what goes on in local government.[21]

Honolulu is, to some extent, an exception. In population terms, Honolulu was the fortieth largest county but the eleventh largest city in the United States in 1996.[22] Because land ownership in the county is so highly concentrated, with one-third controlled by federal, state, and county governments, and another third owned by three private estates, any decisions affecting land use are consequential. Economists La Croix and Rose contend that, "Both the extent of government ownership and the concentration of private ownership are unparalleled in the United States."[23] In addition, none of the mayors of those other counties is viewed like Honolulu's as a rival to the visibility and influence of the state's governor.[24] These factors, together with the county seat being located adjacent to the state's capitol, means that Honolulu departs from patterns otherwise shared by the counties.

One such departure is the comparative size of the workforce, one sufficiently large to offer enough higher level job opportunities to present significant patronage opportunities.[25] In the years after statehood, adoption of the civil service system, especially its merit provisions, was resisted explicitly because of its anticipated negative impact on patronage opportunities.

The greater availability of capital improvement projects also makes Honolulu's government of more interest to private sector firms involved with capital improvement projects. Frank Fasi, one of a number of Honolulu mayors re-elected to several terms since the county was established, held office for all but four years between 1968 and 1994. As the city's responsibilities and revenues grew, he was able to build campaign war chests whose funds exceeded the escalating costs of mayoral campaigns and several tries at the governorship. His contributions came primarily from firms, such as architects and building contractors, seeking capital improvement business with the city and county.

Honolulu's strong-mayor system makes the chief executive the key player in county government. The mayor is the pivotal relationship for all the department heads and, as a consequence, is the recipient of most of the help for re-election that is derived from city personnel. While this pattern holds to varying degrees in the other counties, the scope of the campaigns and the size of government means the tie between public resources and re-election occurs at a higher level in Honolulu.

Under Mayor Fasi, it was common knowledge that department heads, all of which have been appointed positions since the charter of 1959, were expected to work on behalf of election campaigns. Their work often consisted of obtaining contributions from private sector firms by offering or withholding the promise of contractual work with the county.

A variation on this pattern occurred in 1994. The Fire Department was historically a valuable source of personnel for organizing community events during campaigns. The mayor dismissed the fire chief because of the chief's refusal to promise support for his re-election, replacing him with someone willing to do so. When Fasi resigned to run for governor, the former managing director, who had succeeded him in the special election, attempted to appoint a man who had been loyal to him during the campaign. During the confirmation process, disgruntled firemen, many of whom had supported other candidates, complained about the nominee's favoritism in department appointments. A public outcry ensued, leading to the defeat of the nominee and establishment of an independent Fire Commission.

COUNTY-STATE RELATIONS

Unlike differences found between the counties, there is little variation among them in their functional relationship to the state. As might be expected from the top-down manner in which institutions have evolved, state government performs many of the functions handled by towns, cities, and counties in locations where government emerged from local communities. Perhaps the most noteworthy of these is public education. The responsibility for almost everything from kindergarten to grade 12 belongs to a single elected Board of Education whose policies are administered through the statewide Department of Education. Other functions that belong to the state include the public library system; the courts; prisons and detention centers; airports and harbors; and all public sector collective bargaining involving both state and county employees.

Some functions are shared between state and county jurisdictions. These include public housing, water management, hospitals, parks, and land-use planning. In some functional areas, this is, at worst, only a minor nuisance, but in others, where the stakes are higher, such as housing, land-use planning, or the development of water resources, there is recurring conflict.[26]

The functions left to the counties include fire and police protection, the sewer system and sewage treatment, refuse collection and disposal, public golf courses, mass transit, motor-vehicle registration and issuance of drivers licenses, liquor control, and the prosecution of traffic and criminal charges.

Within the context of this comparatively short list of functions, there is an on-going tug-of-war between the counties and the state over the degree of autonomy the former should have in meeting their responsibilities. As John Kincaid observes, there has been "almost a century of experimentation and of pulling and tugging between state and local officials. . . . Although virtually every state has experienced such pulling and tugging, the situation in Hawaii has been more acute in many respects because the counties are so constitutionally and fiscally dependent on the state."[27]

Most state constitutions give exclusive taxing authority to their legislatures. Many of these bodies have used their authority to grant local governments the power to levy taxes on sales as revenue sources. The argument is that local revenue capability permits local governments to plan, as well as to rely less heavily on property taxes.

An average of approximately 45 percent of all county revenues came from real property taxes in 1995.[28] Property taxes constituted 83 percent of their tax collections and 57 percent of their total own-source revenues, proportions that have remained relatively constant over a number of years. In that same year, departmental earnings from fees and charges comprised 20 percent of total revenues, and 26 percent of county generated funds. State grants accounted for just over 9 percent of county income, and federal grants equaled slightly less than 8 percent.[29]

County officials are frustrated by the lack of diversity in their funding base, as well as their fiscal dependence on the state. Honolulu Mayor Jeremy Harris observed in 1995 that, "unlike almost every city in the country our almost sole source of income is property taxes. Instead of having a diversity of revenue sources, about 50 percent of our total revenue comes from property taxes."[30] This opinion was shared by the state's Tax Review Commission in 1989, which wondered whether the revenue system made sense for the responsibilities they hold.[31]

Mayor Harris went on to argue that Honolulu suffers not only from a narrow revenue base and dependence on the state, but is in the odd position of subsidizing state government. This subsidy occurs through the 4 percent general excise tax the city and county pays on purchases; the forfeitures and fines, including traffic fines, it must expend resources to collect, but then turn over to the state's general fund; and a waiver from property taxes given by the state to public utilities in exchange for "in lieu" fees, that also go into the state's general fund. By the mayor's accounting, these rebated revenues taken together cost the city and county about 10 percent of total income.[32]

Property Taxes

The counties' heavy reliance on property taxes leaves local government vulnerable to cyclical patterns in property values. Between 1970 and 1980, the post-statehood increase in population, coupled with planning policies restricting housing development, caused property-tax revenue to more than double on O'ahu and triple in the other counties.[33] This changed in the early 1990s. The housing inventory had increased and the wave of Japanese investment in commercial and residential properties had passed. The result was a plateauing and then a substantial decrease in property values and, therefore, county revenues. The City and County of Honolulu faced a budgetary shortfall of between $120 million and $180 million at the end of 1998, largely as a result of this.[34] As this has happened, the mayors' coordinated annual pilgrimage to the state capital to beg legislators for more revenue-raising authority, or, at a minimum, no decrease in state contributions to the counties, has taken on heightened urgency.

The property tax's central role and efforts to change fiscal relations between the counties and the state both have a long history. The property tax was first levied in 1839 on both land and personal property. The tax on land was repealed for a short time, but revived in the mid-1850s as the legal status of land changed. Personal and property taxes were an important revenue source for the kingdom, and provided two-thirds of the republic's income.[35]

Property taxes comprised one-half to four-fifths of tax receipts for territorial government prior to the establishment of a gross-income tax in 1930, following which its relative contribution declined.[36] After 1911, all property-tax revenues were given to the counties to finance their operations. Because the functions for which the counties are responsible are so truncated, this tax historically has been among the lowest in the nation.[37]

From its inception, the property tax was centrally administered, both in the kingdom and in the territory. In the twentieth century, the centralization of assessments was justified, despite the fact all revenues generated by them went to the counties, because they are more likely to be handled in a professional and unbiased manner by the state than by county offices. Proponents of this position pointed to instances of unstable or politicized tax assessments in mainland counties.[38]

County officials argued against centralized administration of the property tax, contending that their offices were just as professionally oriented as the state's, their employees only requiring appropriate training. Perhaps of more importance, they suggested that the state tax-office in Honolulu was too distant and disinterested, its officials inherently unable to make the appropriate adjustments that knowledge of the context would permit.[39]

In recent years, after decades of struggle between the counties and the state over control of property-tax administration, and especially the key function of property assessments, the arrangement has come to look more like the rest of the country. The 1978 constitutional convention initially voted to transfer all authority related to the property tax to the counties, an action consistent with the development of the new county charters. This was opposed by the Hawaii Sugar Planters Association and the Pineapple Growers Association, both of whom were pursuing their historic interest in favorable tax assessments, something they felt better positioned to achieve through the state. The change was also resisted by the powerful International Longshoreman's and Warehouseman's Union, whose officials were concerned that contract negotiations on each island might be influenced by different assessments. In addition, others simply argued for the principle of uniformity in assessments across the counties.[40]

As a result of this lobbying, elements of the transfer of authority were delayed for eleven years by a requirement that the counties agree on uniform policies and methods of assessment. On November 7, 1989, this stipulation of uniformity expired and each county was finally in a position to be "more flexible, and perhaps more creative, in adapting its real property tax system to local needs and preferences."[41]

State Support of Counties

Greater flexibility did not solve the problem of excessive reliance on the property tax, nor of dependence on the state for a larger revenue base. The role of state grants in the county budget illustrates this. In 1992, these grants constituted about 10 percent of all county revenues. By 1995, they dropped to around just over 9 percent. There is considerable variation across the counties. Grants from the state constituted only 4.3 percent of Honolulu's budget, but 16 percent of that for Maui and 32 percent for Kaua'i county.[42]

Before 1965, money was distributed to counties by the state via tax sharing, especially from general excise tax revenues. In that year, Act 155 was passed to make it more difficult for the state to mandate county responsibilities without providing a means to fund them. It also had the effect of reducing the base amount going to all the counties and changing the distribution ratio between them. Over the years, this amount was altered several times, reflecting the state's desire to maintain control over what it gives the counties as well as the irritation of some state legislators who saw the counties demanding greater grants-in-aid while at the same time they were considering lowering the property tax rate. Between 1976 and 1986, state contributions declined by 18 percent, despite the fact that state revenues more than doubled.[43] In 1980, the cost of all grants in aid to counties was only 1 percent of the state's total operating budget.[44]

In 1990, through Act 185, the legislature decided that counties would receive 95 percent of the state's transient accommodations tax, a tax levied primarily on hotel rooms. These monies are placed in a special fund and then distributed to the counties by the state's director of finance. Envisioned for use primarily in tourism and infrastructure development, in practice the counties have directed some to both operating and capital costs.

Regular skirmishes have occurred in the years since the state adopted this method of funding the counties. Beginning in 1991, for example, state revenues began to fall as the economy slowed. At the same time, the state faced strident demands to improve the educational system, deal with Medicaid funding shortages, and maintain levels of social services initiated during the preceding expansion. Prior to the start of the January 1993 legislative session, the director of the Department of Budget and Finance proposed upping the state's share of the transient accommodation tax (TAT) from 5 percent to 30 percent, something that would have cost the counties millions of dollars in revenue, without providing relief from existing responsibilities. The state argued, against strong objections by the mayors, that because the money would be used to resuscitate tourism, on which everyone was dependent, all of the counties would be benefited fiscally.

In 1997, again in response to expected tax revenue shortfalls, state legislators proposed reducing the county portion of the TAT in exchange for monies collected from uncontested traffic fines and public utility taxes. County income from these sources would be capped, however, at whatever was received from the TAT in 1994–95. At other times legislators also have used the threat of reductions in the tax on TAT to prevent counties from implementing tax policies with which they or their constituents disagree, such as raising real property taxes on hotels.

Seeking Broader Fiscal Authority

The counties' heavy reliance on property taxes, together with concerns about levels and continuity of revenues from the state, have fueled repeated efforts to broaden their authority to raise money. Unsuccessful arguments for this authority were made during the formulation of the 1950 Hope Chest Constitution and in subsequent constitutional conventions. The legislature consistently has been unwilling to permit development of new revenue sources. For example, in the 1995 session, bills were introduced to let counties increase traffic fines and keep the difference between the new receipts and what goes to the state from present charges; impose a gross receipts tax on the telephone utility, that is currently exempted; allow counties to levy a value-based, versus weight-based, tax on automobiles; and permit counties to collect fees for regulating time-share condominiums. As in earlier years, these proposals failed, losing out to concerns over abuse and the argument for straightening out areas of overlapping functions before altering tax policies.[45]

Fiscal pressures on the counties have increased in recent years. They arise from the fiscal plight of state government, an increase in Neighbor Island tourism, population growth, declining real-property assessments following the late 1980s boom years, and federal and state environmental mandates.[46] In this context, John Kincaid points out that, "Nearly every statewide body . . . that has examined the state-local system and that has not been directly beholden to the state legislature, governor, or judiciary has recommended forms of increased functional and/or fiscal authority for Hawaii counties."[47]

Improving County Government

The likelihood that greater fiscal authority will be given to the counties is uncertain at best. Studied opinions in favor of delegated authority will have to contend with the more powerful interests favoring centralized control of fiscal policy. The revenue constraints that reached Hawai'i state government in the early 1990s, and will continue through at least the turn of the century, will aggravate these limitations.

In the meantime, the counties will be compelled to search for ways to make the best use of the revenues they have. One vehicle for doing this is privatization. The counties have taken the lead in attempting to make greater use of private contractors to perform public services, such as refuse collection. These efforts have created conflicts with public sector unions, whose leaders and members worry that job losses will follow. In response to these opposing interests, the 1998 legislature passed a bill that permits a short-term experiment in managed competition. The compromise exempts government contracts with private vendors from civil service and collective bargaining laws, while ensuring that no public sector jobs will be lost to the new agreements.

Restructuring is another way in which the counties might deal with their fiscal pinch. The case of the city and county of Honolulu provides an example of how difficult this can become if the changes are driven by fiscal crisis.

Mayor Jeremy Harris saw his county's fiscal position continuing to erode as a consequence of falling property tax revenues and the state's withholding of a portion of the transient accommodation tax. To deal with this, he proposed a reorganization. Since it would involve the merger of several city and county departments, and therefore required a change in the city and county charter, the mayor called for the convening of a charter commission. At this point things became very complicated.

One of the departments he wished to merge was the Board of Water Supply. His proposal to join it to the Department of Public Works was greeted with terrific resistance. The resistance was from employees who worried that the mission of the semi-autonomous agency would be undermined, and from individuals who believed the mayor's real agenda was to get his hands on the revenues the board generated from water and sewage fees.

The resistance was strong enough to force the mayor to amend his reorganization plan in order to get the five city council votes needed to convene a charter commission. Getting those votes, in turn, resulted in a re-alignment of coalitions on the council, and a new council chair.

Commission's membership is decided on jointly by the mayor and the council chair, with the mayor deciding who serves as chair. After the commission began its work, its chair, a well-known small businessman, resigned, contending that the newly elected chair of the city council was usurping the commission's autonomy. His replacement was someone favored by the council chair, a reflection of the on-going collision between the chair and the mayor. Meanwhile, the League of Women Voters brought suit against the mayor for not allowing the required amount of time to pass between the work of a review commission and the submission of its proposals to voters.

Despite the struggle, Mayor Harris was able to get most of what he wanted in the end. Voters approved all five of the charter amendments aimed at making the City and County of Honolulu more efficient and cost-effective in the November 1998 election.

HOME RULE

It is worthwhile to explore the prospects for other forms of local governance in the light of the experience of Hawai'i's counties. As noted at the beginning of this chapter, although the Hawaiian Kingdom was a centralized system of governance, there was a degree of district-level self-governance over roads and education. Even this did not carry over into the republic, a fact that seems incongruous with the New England origins of those who established it.[48]

On the American mainland, home rule commonly refers to the power of self-governance given to local jurisdictions by state constitutional provision.[49] In Hawai'i, it has had somewhat different meanings. In the period after 1900, one usage referred to making the counties more independent of the territorial government. The other meaning focused on creating smaller units, including more counties and cities and towns within existing counties.

Consistent with strengthening county government, at various times, beginning in the 1930s, the counties sought to change their status by getting the federal Congress to amend the Organic Act. Honolulu has been the most aggressive county over the years in trying to obtain more autonomy by working through the Hawai'i legislature to alter its relation with the state.[50] With respect to creating smaller units of governance, both the island of Lanai and the leeward side of the Big Island have at different times tried to become counties. Pressure for some form of home rule increased on O'ahu after World War II as clusters of communities sprouted and their residents asked for services. Residents of these communities, which would have been towns on the mainland, organized, unsuccessfully, to have their own government.[51]

Although the "1954 Democrats" were much more sympathetic to decentralization than the Republicans they replaced, remarkably little has occurred in the subsequent forty years. The Hope Chest Constitution of 1950 referred to home rule in a vague manner that left its form and degree to the discretion of future legislatures. In line with its constitutional provisions and the orientations of the new Democrats, the 1955 legislature provided for the appointment of a charter commission that, in turn, led to the revised charters summarized earlier in this chapter.

Local Government, Hawai'i Style

One observer of state-local relations has noted that Hawai'i can be seen simultaneously as ahead of many states and out of step with most.[52] This seeming paradox results from the historically high levels of involvement by the state in county affairs, a degree of integration from which many states could benefit. Simultaneously, local governance in Hawai'i is unusually weak and dependent on the state, despite the fact that the only form it takes is county government. The result has been that every commission established since statehood to study some aspect of this issue has "to a greater or lesser degree, recommended increased local self-government."[53]

Despite these recommendations, the closest thing to government below the counties remains the system of Neighborhood Boards on the island of O'ahu. The boards were established in 1972 through a revised Honolulu charter that included appointment of a Neighborhood Board Commission. The commission's establishment was consistent with national efforts at community development occurring in the early 1970s, such as the Model Cities Program and the Office of Economic Opportunity.[54]

The commission's nine members are appointed by the mayor and city council. Its function is to assist in forming and maintaining the up to 32 Neighborhood Boards that are specified in the commission's plan. The Neighborhood Boards themselves are different from community associations found in many places. They are legally recognized bodies under the city and county. By law, they have elected members, receive funds and staff support, and are obliged to follow commission rules regarding such things as frequency of meeting and report filings.

Neighborhood Boards typically deal with concerns particular to their local context. These include capital improvement projects, community planning, and changing service requirements. Their meetings frequently are attended by legislators and administrative officers wishing to get a sense of community opinion. For some public agencies, such as the county Department of Parks and Recreation, these visits are required. Not uncommonly, the boards are the organizing point for a local issue, and the concerns mobilized and focused by them are taken seriously.

At the same time, board decisions are, by statute, unofficial and advisory. The motivation for the boards may have been to increase citizen participation through decentralization, but they were established only on O'ahu. Their creation did not entail the city and county giving away any authority over policy or resources, and avoided any conflict with existing state powers. Boards' inability to control resources leaves them vulnerable to interpretation as more symbolic than substantial.

The Prospects for Change

The most likely force in promoting devolution of greater authority to county government, and perhaps even incorporating cities and towns, is changing demographic patterns. The most important of these is the redistribution of population to the Neighbor islands where separation by distance and ocean channels helps make a centralized system controlled from Honolulu seem unresponsive to growing local needs. It is hard to predict whether this population shift will change the balance of public institutions toward local and away from the state. The principles of fairness, coordination, and efficiency, in combination with specific private and bureaucratic interests that see themselves benefited by a centralized system, may serve to keep change at a symbolic level. Even if re-balancing occurs, uncertainty remains over whether the result would be a political society that is more fully democratic.

Two questions lie behind this issue. In the light of how they have evolved in the territorial and post-statehood periods, to what extent do Hawai'i's county or neighborhood government offer avenues to invigorated citizenship? Turning it the other way around, can the state-dominated governmental structure with which Hawai'i is most familiar learn to be more responsive to highly varied local interests and encourage greater public participation?

Introducing greater flexibility in a centralized system rather than creating more local government is one way of responding to this unsettled balance between local control and social fairness. Perhaps such an experiment could lead to needed clarity on the key issue of which public functions are best handled by what level of government. Doing this, however, is challenging. A conflict that occurred over economic development and community integrity points to some of the complexities.

In his first State of the State address to the legislature in January 1987, Governor John Waihe'e announced he wanted a launching facility for small to medium-size commercial and scientific missiles completed within five years.[55] The designated site was in the district of Ka'u on the Big Island, a rural area with two small towns and a population of about 4,400. The Ka'u location was supported by the owners of C. Brewer and Co., one of the oldest firms in the islands and a former member of the Big Five oligopoly. C. Brewer management was anxious about the depreciating value of company lands as sugar became less viable and good alternatives failed to materialize. Their connections to the legislative and executive branches in Honolulu helped get state officials sufficiently interested in this business alternative to establish an Office of Space Industries, hire a "space czar," and spend millions of dollars promoting what came to be referred to as the "space port."

The Ka'u district was a plantation society dominated by C. Brewer until after the Second World War. As sugar began to spiral downward, retirees and people looking for an alternative style of life began to move into parts of the area, primarily around the town of Na'alehu where one of the district's two mills had earlier shut down. The result was that the plantation workers who agreed with, or were not willing to publicly object to, company plans were counterbalanced by a growing population of new arrivals and long-term resident Native Hawaiians. This coalition feared that the spaceport, which might soon double the district's population, would be foisted upon them without their input.

Over the next several years, the state paid for an expensive public relations campaign aimed at convincing Ka'u residents that the space port would be good for them. Residents who disagreed had no local jurisdiction through which to organize their interests, even though it appeared that those against or concerned about the project may have substantially out-numbered those in favor. Resistance was focused through hearings held in association with an Environmental Impact Statement, and through forums conducted by state representatives.

The mayor and county council played a relatively minor role in the drawn-out conflict. One reason was the knowledge that Ka'u district interests would be mixed with interests island-wide, especially those in more densely populated Hilo, where the project was seen as an economic benefit with few locally felt costs. Of equal importance was the state's overwhelming power to act in this area.

Despite the millions spent by the state, the project never reached the construction stage. Failure to find a private company willing to make even an informal commitment to participate was a key factor. This hesitancy was based upon strict business calculations, calculations that invariably included discomfort with anticipated community resistance.

If county government had greater authority to act in this area, would the community's interests have been taken into account more than they were? Would the state have elected to be as forceful in promoting the project if it had to deal with district or town governments able to speak officially on behalf of their constituents? Perhaps most important, if the community had a vehicle through which its members' concerns about economic viability and community preservation could be formally negotiated, would such forcefulness even have been needed?

This case points to several issues surrounding the development of viable local jurisdictions. The most compelling reason for local governance, in Hawai'i and other places, is that it provides authoritative channels for communities to deal with the issues most immediate to them. These issues include the desirability of zoning changes, the adequacy of parks, neighborhood environmental problems, and whether to accept the siting of such things as half-way houses or spaceports. Communities are sensitive to these and similar issues long before they are even on the radar screen of broader jurisdictions. Moreover, by their closeness to the social and cultural context of which the issues are a part, local communities begin with some valuable knowledge, knowledge an outsider could only try to learn.

Creating and sustaining these authoritative channels for local communities has fiscal and political culture implications. Any kind of government costs money, administratively and for the services it provides. How much are local residents in Hawai'i willing to pay, especially if services turn out to be more expensive because they can't match the lower cost per unit the state derives from its larger scale of operation? Equally important, how much tax revenue will existing jurisdictions be willing to give up to compensate for the delegation of responsibilities to local governments? Given that counties historically have been neglected fiscally, it is likely that pressure to share revenue sources with local governments will be directed at the state. The state's traditional reluctance to share revenues, as well as the well-established pattern of reducing support for the counties during fiscally tight times, suggest that, even if formal authority is granted, it will be a substantial challenge to obtain adequate and consistent revenues.

Government at the community level also will be shaped by the political culture of which it is a part. Providing a voice on issues of concern to a broad range of community members requires a political culture compatible with that purpose. The degree of compatibility is likely to vary significantly from place to place.

Residents must see themselves as participants, and government must welcome their active involvement. Neither of these qualities is likely to be supported by the political culture of the rural Big Island communities described in the preceding case. That political culture is heavily traditionalistic, molded by the way in which local culture has encountered the overwhelming presence of C. Brewer and Co. For decades, C. Brewer was the dominant employer and virtual owner of the plantation town of Pahala. Its orientation was heavily paternalistic, and what company officials decided was best for the community is what was done. Those officials saw the spaceport as the best way to generate economic activity in the face of sugar's decline, and resistance to its siting was the first significant expression of disagreement with the company's view of the community's future.

The political culture of this area, and those similar to it that are scattered across the islands, will present serious obstacles, at least in the short term, to establishing local governance that is broadly representative and highly participatory. In those circumstances, the stresses resulting from divergent expectations about government and citizen roles may be substantial.

Other communities might be made of political cultures with a blend of traditionalistic, moralistic, and individualistic outlooks that is more congenial to vibrant local governance. This will be true of places on O'ahu that have, for example, a large number of urbanized professionals, such as the town of Kailua on the windward side of the island or the "second city" of Kapolei in its central plain. It also will apply to other less urban settings on O'ahu and to rural Neighbor Island towns that mix retirees, refugees from congested Honolulu, former plantation workers and Native Hawaiians, such as Hale'iwa on O'ahu , Kamuela on the Big Island, Makawao on Maui, and Hanalei on Kaua'i.

As this suggests, local governance is likely to reflect the complex mosaic that is the reality of the islands, in some instances providing a supportive environment for political institutions and practices treated as commonplace in parts of the United States, and in others rejecting them almost as if they were foreign.

CHAPTER ELEVEN

Continuities in Public Issues

Many of the important challenges and opportunities that present themselves to Hawai'i's public life may appear to be new, but, in fact, have a long history. The most important of these deal with the issues of Native Hawaiians, the islands long struggle to find balance in their relationship with the outside world, and the preservation of Hawai'i as a special place. Others issues that are central to Hawai'i' society, and have re-surfaced throughout this book, emerge within these three broad themes, including the matter of economic and political centralization and the different ways in which change might occur.

ISSUES FOR HAWAIIANS

The prospects for Hawai'i's indigenous people has been an issue since the missionaries and businessmen first arrived in the islands. Their decline was obscured during the nineteenth century behind the creation of a society influenced by Hawaiian culture but dominated by outsiders. A redefinition of their relationship with the federal government has been significant in more recent times (see chapter 4). Within the state, the claims of indigenous people for restitution are likely to remain at the center of public discourse until there is a settlement acceptable to both Hawaiians and non-Hawaiians.

Many people living in the islands believe that amends must be made for a profound injustice done to Hawaiian people. This belief is held by groups that may be harmed by settlements involving substantial land or money. It can be seen in the answers of residents to survey questions asking whether Hawaiians deserve more restitution for the overthrow of their nation than the Department of Hawaiian Home Lands and the Office of Hawaiian Affairs can provide. In that 1993 survey, 46 percent of Caucasians, 41 percent of

Japanese-Americans, and 53 percent of Filipinos thought greater restitution was warranted.[1]

Many of the state's prominent elected officials publicly acknowledge an injustice occurred. Governor John Waihe'e ordered the flag at the state capitol be lowered to half-mast in observance of the one hundredth anniversary of the monarchy's overthrow in January 1993. In the fall 1994 campaign, future governor Ben Cayetano stated that, if elected, he would turn over Washington Place, the Governor's official home, to Native Hawaiians.[2]

Not surprisingly, Hawaiians share this sentiment for redress. Eighty-three percent responded that Hawaiians deserve some form of reparation, in land or in money, for the overthrow in a 1995 survey. Questions that focused specifically on attitudes toward self-determination showed that 85 percent had heard of sovereignty, and 53 percent favored some form of the idea. If that form preserved Hawaiian culture, 84 percent of the Hawaiians surveyed indicated they would support it.[3]

Self Determination and Sovereignty

In a November 1995 survey of individuals self-identified as Hawaiians, 45 percent felt that a form of sovereignty is inevitable, 36 percent believed it will never happen, and 17 percent were uncertain.[4] These views on the prospects for self-determination probably are matched by a similar diversity of opinion in the general population. They reflect uncertainty about the direction, or combination of directions, Hawaiians' calls for justice will or should take.

One direction they might take is toward constitution making and formation of a sovereign, twenty-first-century Hawaiian nation. Several distinct models of self-governance had coalesced by the 1990s. Grouped under the label "sovereignty," each features the return of land to a governmental authority controlled by Native Hawaiians. In some cases, the lands are located in the ceded lands trust, and in others they comprise all of the Hawaiian archipelago.

The most far-reaching sovereignty model proposes an independent nation of Hawai'i, one that will establish its own relations with other countries, including the United States.[5] Some of its advocates foresee it to be open only to those of Hawaiian heritage, or perhaps with birthright in the islands, while others suggest citizenship might rest on an individual's willingness to commit to the new nation and its cultural priorities. One version of an independent nation uses some of the islands, or ceded lands on different islands, as its base. Another version envisions protection of a Hawaiian land base under the United Nations. This could adopt the status of "free association" now held by former members of the Trust Territory of the Pacific.

Another model of self-governance, referred to as a nation within a nation, follows the path taken by many Native American tribes. The new entity would exist inside the American governmental system and be obligated to follow rules that apply to other sub-national jurisdictions. For example, it would not be possible to establish foreign relations, or, if no other form of gambling was permitted in the state, to establish gambling as a source of revenue. Native Hawaiians would select the form of government within the new nation, as well as the rules about membership, police powers, and businesses licensing. In this model, the scope of authority to tax would be a key issue.

A third form of self-governance, called a state within a state, would use existing or modified institutional formats to control resources, especially the land, for Hawaiian people. The most likely existing structure is the Office of Hawaiian Affairs (OHA).

OHA was established by the 1978 constitutional convention as a state agency that is independent of the other branches of government, an unusual arrangement. Its purpose is to provide for "accountability, self-determination, methods for self-sufficiency through assets and a land base, and the unification of all native Hawaiian people."[6] This agency's budget in 1999 was $7.7 million, or about one percent of state appropriations.[7]

OHA holds title to property set aside in trust for Native Hawaiians. In a state within a state arrangement, it would manage the ceded lands already entrusted to it—lands that constitute almost one-half of the state's total acreage, perhaps disbursing the benefits that derive from these lands on the basis of decisions by representatives Hawaiian voters had elected.

Some concrete, but contested, steps have been taken toward debate and adoption of a model of self-governance. The 1993 state Legislature, in conjunction with the 100th anniversary of the overthrow of the Hawaiian Nation, created the Hawaiian Sovereignty Advisory Commission to provide advice on issues relating to self-governance. The council, consisting of twenty Hawaiians appointed by the governor, scheduled a plebiscite for November 1994 for the purpose of asking, "Shall a process begin to restore the sovereign Hawaiian Nation." That date was pushed back to November 1995. Subsequently re-named the Native Hawaiian Elections Council, it too was forced to cancel the second vote and re-schedule for September 1996.

The cancellations, revised name, and subsequent change of question resulted in part from the state's declining fiscal resources, but also reflected conflicts among Hawaiians over who should organize the debate about sovereignty.[8] The council focused intense disagreements within the Hawaiian community. Some Hawaiian leaders argued passionately that no state-sponsored entity, including OHA and the Commission, would be able to move beyond status quo interests to meaningfully reverse earlier betrayals. The strongest opposition was organized by *Ka Lahui* Hawai'i, a Native Hawaiian organization whose members saw themselves as the legitimate basis of a future Hawaiian government. For *Ka Lahui*, the state-supported plebiscite was "The Final Theft."

Those supporting the plebiscite believed its more conservative revised question—"Shall the Hawaiian people elect delegates to propose a Native Hawaiian government?"—offered the best vehicle for initiating a process that would engage most Hawaiians—not only the most vocal Hawaiians—in a discussion of their collective future. (A poll conducted at about the time the 1995 plebiscite would have been held indicated most Hawaiians agreed with the plebiscite's proponents, by a margin of 66 percent to 20 percent, with 11 percent undecided.)[9]

The third vote scheduled did take place in September of 1996, though preceded by opposition attempts to stop it through court intervention. About 82,000 ballots were mailed to eligible individuals in Hawai'i and on the mainland. Of these, 49,000, or about 59 percent, were not returned. Among the 33,000 sent back that could be counted, 22,194, or about 74 percent, voted for a constitutional convention, and just over 8,000, or 27 percent, voted against it.

A new body, *Ha Hawai'i*, was formed after the election outside of state government to replace the Hawaiian Sovereignty Elections Council. *Ha Hawai'i* organizers, former council members, sought to raise funds for a convention to debate Native Hawaiian government. They searched for ways to cover the costs, expected to be in the neighborhood of $3–5 million, by looking at different combinations of funding from private donations, state government, and an OHA whose Board of Trustees now included the influential former head of *Ka Lahui*.

Hawaiian Legal Rights

The expansion of collective legal rights is a second direction for Hawaiian claims.

Article 12, Section 7, adopted by the 1978 Constitutional Convention, specifies the state must protect all customary and traditional Native Hawaiian rights. As chapter 7 summarized, subsequent case law created by decisions of the State's Supreme Court has infused Hawaiian customs into Western property law, especially regarding access to shorelines, historic gathering sites, and water resources.

The court declared, in 1982, that gathering rights on land are determined by practices that occurred historically in a specific area (*ahupua'a*), as long as it was undeveloped and there was no harm to the property. Ten years later the court extended this beyond the immediate site of traditional practices to include access rights to the area. The 1995 high court decision in the *Nansay* case on the Big Island specified that those preparing to develop land must consider protected rights in their development plans.[10]

At play in these decisions are the contrasting orientations of control—that is, the right to exclude—and public trust—the community's right to use and maintain—embedded in these cultures. Proponents of Native Hawaiian legal rights argue that in the islands fee title is less exclusive a determinant of land use than in mainland settings, and that such use should take into account Native cultural practices.

Supporters of a Western law understanding of private property contend an illegal judicial "taking" is occurring, with dangerous consequences. An attorney for a corporation attempting to build a hotel on 450 acres where contemporary Hawaiians practice aspects of traditional culture put it this way: "It throws a lot of what we understood to be established property law in Hawai'i into a state of some confusion. There's going to be a lot of conflict that arises out of this."[11] For the spokesperson of an national organization whose avowed goal is protection of the rights of property owners, "court rulings adverse to private property rights in Hawaii are a major threat to individual liberties and economic prosperity in the state."[12]

Reparations

Another direction for redress is reparations; compensation in land or money that does not include, or includes only minimally, a system of self-governance. One vehicle for this is the Homelands Trust. A settlement was negotiated in 1995 specifying that the state will pay the Department of Hawaiian Home Lands $600 million over 20 years. This amount represents compensation for the state's breaches of the Trust's terms. These breaches consisted of removing land from the Trust, or using Trust lands without compensation. The compensation, along with the federal land exchanges discussed in chapter 4, has helped, but not reduced the thousands of long-standing requests for homestead parcels.

The other vehicle for a reparations-like settlement is in relation to the enormous Ceded Lands Trust. The Ceded Lands Trust has been, and will remain, at the center of Native Hawaiians changing relations with state government and the evolving movement to, as one Native Hawaiian put it, deal with the fact that, "the children of the land are strangers in their own land."[13]

When land was converted to a fee-simple basis through the Mahele in the 1850s, King Kamehameha III (Kauikeaouli) divided up the approximately 2.5 million acres he controlled. The government was assigned 1.5 million acres (usually referred to as public lands) and 1 million was designated for him and his heirs (referred to as crown lands). Between the time this division was made and the overthrow of the Kingdom in 1893 approximately 600,000 acres of public lands were sold or leased, largely to non-Hawaiians. That remaining, totaling approximately 1.8 million acres, or slightly less than one-half of all the lands in the island chain, was claimed by the Republic and then turned over to the federal government. In 1920, about 188,000 acres were put into the Hawaiian Home Lands trust by means of the federal Hawaiian Rehabilitation Act.

At statehood the federal government gave 1.4 million acres of the Ceded Lands Trust to the state to be administered. The rules specified that, among other purposes, they must be used for the benefit of Hawaiians. A 1978 constitutional amendment mandated formation of the Office of Hawaiian Affairs in order to better the conditions of Native Hawaiians. The legislation creating the agency two years later also specified that 20 percent of the income from ceded lands be earmarked for that department.[14]

After 1980, in compliance with a Constitutional Convention amendment and subsequent enabling legislation, the state paid OHA $2–3 million a year from ceded lands revenues. During this period the state and OHA engaged in difficult negotiations over whether this amount was adequate. The State agreed in 1993 to pay OHA a lump sum of $131 million, and $7 to $8 million annually.

Ceded lands revenues became a more pressing issue for the state in July 1996 when Circuit Judge Daniel Heely ruled the state must pay back to OHA revenues for 15 prior years. The Chairman of OHA at the time, Clayton Hee, estimated these payments, plus interest, would come to about $300 million. Others suggested that the figure would be higher, perhaps significantly so depending upon how revenues are calculated.[15] Their estimates ranged from

$595 million to $1.2 billion. Director of the Department of Budget and Finance Earl Anzai, responding to these higher figures, stated in a Circuit Court affidavit that the repayment would "leave uncertainty as to the soundness of the state's financial position." In less formal language, state officials expected this could "break the state's economic spine."[16]

The State Attorney General appealed Judge Heeley's decision to the state Supreme Court in the fall of 1996. After hearing the oral arguments, the justices requested that representatives of the state and OHA attempt to negotiate a settlement. This included the stipulation that if unsuccessful, then the Court would make the decision.

Although the legislature decided not to become involved in questions about back payments, it did act in relation to future payments to OHA for the use of ceded lands. The 1997 legislature first decided to freeze annual payments to OHA at $15.1 million. It then asked for a complete inventory of ceded lands throughout the state. Finally, the legislature created a five-person task force, composed of two OHA and three state representatives. The task force was given until the middle of 1999 to propose a compensation amount to the legislature. Failing to do that, the annual payment would be set at $15.1 million.

Social and Political Dynamics

Any proposal Hawaiians make for self-governance will have to be worked out not only with residents and state government, but federal authorities as well. As noted by Senator Inouye, "Should consensus be reached among Native Hawaiians on a model of sovereignty, and the people of Hawaii concur, and the United States, through Congress approve, we may finally see the restoration of the sovereignty of the native Hawaiian people."[17]

The 1995 survey of Hawaiian attitudes, referred to above, showed a range of divisions on matters directly related to self-determination. For example, 37 percent indicated they were better off today than if the monarchy had not been overthrown, while 33 percent expect they would be ahead if it still existed. Forty-three percent believed a Hawaiian nation's land should be distributed to its citizens, while 42 percent thought it should be controlled and developed for the benefit of its citizens.[18]

The differences suggested by these and similar findings can be substantial. For some, secession from the United States, or even local self-governance, is unfathomable. Others contend that state and federal laws do not apply to them, and have refused to carry state-issued drivers licenses or use state license plates. An unknown number have declared that they are no longer subject to state or federal taxation, and a few of these have tried to bring charges against various public officials.

Beyond differences of opinion on the substantive questions of American allegiance and national self-determination, there are important disagreements among Native Hawaiians over how to organize. Although a great deal of coordination and collaboration occurs among the dozens of sovereignty groups that exist statewide in 1999, leaders have fought intensely with one another, defining positions that leave little room for compromise. Some of the worse conflicts have taken place among the nine trustees of OHA. In 1998, for example, two disputing factions were unable to agree on an interim replacement for a deceased trustee, forcing a reluctant governor to make the choice for them. The effects of this kind of rancorousness are seen in 1995 survey results showing large numbers of Native Hawaiians think there is too much infighting, too little effective leadership, and declining chances for unity.[19]

The question "Who is Hawaiian?" is another important matter for Hawaiians. The answer to it has been a source of conflict since at least 1921 when eligibility was established for benefits under the Homestead Act.[20] Representatives of the Hawaiian Sugar Planters Association argued that only full-blooded Hawaiians should qualify, a rule that would have greatly reduced the number of beneficiaries. All those who identified themselves as Hawaiians at the hearings, including territorial delegate Jonah Kuhio Kalaniani'ole, testified there should be little or no "blood quantum" test. The resulting compromise of 50 percent has remained for initial eligibility to homestead lands.[21] It was adopted by the state in 1980 to determine how OHA may use monies generated from ceded lands.

Since its founding OHA has conducted two plebiscites to learn what its constituency thinks the definition should be. Most of those expressing an opinion are less than one-half Hawaiian by blood, and it is not surprising that the results of both plebiscites supported changing the rule to require only some Hawaiian inheritance.

Today the agency has two different ways of deciding who is Hawaiian. To vote in elections, which determines who sits on the governing board and decides how monies shall be spent, one need have only a trace of Hawaiian blood. To receive those resources, one must possess 50 percent blood quantum.

These differing rules in part reflect strategy—the number of people with 50 percent Hawaiian blood is declining due to intermarriage, thereby raising concerns about the future of OHA's base of influence.[22] The rules also reflect concerns about fairness. If a Hawaiian is anyone descended from the kingdom, more will gain from the wealth of ceded lands. However, enlarging the number of beneficiaries inevitably means each claimant will get less. As one Hawaiian leader put it, that policy "will take the little that was given to the few and stretch it to cover the many."[23]

The matter of who is Hawaiian leads to a third question facing Native Hawaiians: what is Hawaiian culture in the contemporary world? George Kanahele, an Hawaiian educator, observes that "the modern Hawaiians [are] a vastly different people from their ancient progenitors. Two centuries of enormous, almost cataclysmic change imposed from within and without have altered their conditions, outlooks, attitudes, and values. Although some traditional practices and beliefs have been retained, even those have been modified. In general, today's Hawaiians have little familiarity with the ancient culture."[24]

The cultural identity of contemporary Hawaiians is subtle, complex, and often unclear. Many were raised in a social and political context that rejected Hawaiian ways and defined Hawaiians as inferior, except as their culture was packaged for the consumption of tourists. As a consequence, it was common to conceal "Hawaiianess," something relatively easy to do in a society so full of people of mixed ethnicity. When Hawaiian culture experienced a re-birth, and even came to be portrayed as superior to Western and Asian cultures, individuals who began to reclaim their Hawaiian past were faced with what it would mean to them. What is traditional Hawaiian culture in the context of a modern society? How will adopting it impact on the rest of their lives, especially those things they value in an individual rights, consumer-oriented society?

Survey results reflect uncertainty about the answer to these questions. As noted earlier in the chapter, 84 percent of part Hawaiian respondents indicated they would support some form of sovereignty if it "preserved Hawaiian culture." At the same time, only 20 percent would opt for monarchy in any form.[25] This, together with similar findings, suggests the contemporary image of Hawaiian culture does not include facets once central to it, as was the monarchy and associated authority, symbols, and rituals.

Most contemporary Hawaiians value traditional music, language, arts and sea faring skills, but many, probably most, also are wedded to the citizenship rights, social equality, and material culture that are part of modern society.[26] Though marginalized, they also lived in and around mainstream institutions. It is not surprising then that, as was true for Asian immigrants, many of the state's indigenous people value their culture *and* are American nationalists. Drawn to aspects of traditional culture, they simultaneously embrace the rights and protections enjoyed under the federal and state constitutions.

Although justice for Hawaiians is a prominent public issue today, it is bounded as a topic in electoral politics. Candidates do not run for office, except for the Office of Hawaiian Affairs, offering their positions on Hawaiian self-determination or reparation or rights. No gubernatorial candidate campaigns on what he or she will do to resolve an issue affecting Hawaiians, or their relationship to non-Hawaiians. This partly reflects the messages sent by members of the Hawaiian community to let Hawaiians resolve their own problems. It also means that concerns about the implications of a sovereignty solution have not reached a critical point among non-Hawaiians. If and when they do, the terms of the discussion will, in one way or another, be changed.

HAWAI'I'S STRUGGLE WITH DEPENDENCE

External resources have been used to do things otherwise not possible locally since not long after the arrival of Captain Cook, At the same time, concerted efforts have been made to avoid relinquishing control to interests seen as foreign to the nation, republic, territory or state. Though successively characterized as being in everyone's interest, each set of relationships has brought differentiated rewards and costs to individuals and groups. There is little reason to expect this will be different in the future.

Energy needs provide one graphic way to illustrate the state's reliance on the outside world. Despite efforts to reduce dependence by developing geothermal, biomass, wind and solar energy, garbage to energy, and even turning to high-grade coal, more than 90 percent of the state's energy comes from imported oil, mostly from sources outside the United States. This compares to an average of around 40 percent for the rest of the country.[27]

Data on imports and exports provide an even more revealing snapshot. In 1993, the state's percentage of total imports making up the gross state product (GSP)—that is, goods and services brought in as a proportion of the total value of goods and services—was over 60 percent, having risen from 45 percent in 1973.[28] On the other side of the ledger, of all fifty states, in 1990 Hawai'i had the smallest dollar figure—$179 million—of exports originating from its own resources (that is, not including tourism).[29] At the same time, the ratio of *total* exports—that is, when tourism is brought into the picture—to GSP was 57 percent, having risen from about 40 percent ten years earlier. In comparison, the national ratio of exports to the total economy was

10 percent, and even that had doubled in recent decades.[30] Finally, a Bank of Hawaii analysis revealed that, during this same period, total exports plus federal defense expenditures in the islands made up about 70 percent of GSP. This placed the Hawai'i economy in the top five internationally in the ratio of exports to imports to gross domestic product.[31] Hawai'i's economy, in short, far more than that of other states, is reliant on forces that lie outside its boundaries and over which it has virtually no control.

The Specter of A New Kind of Plantation Economy

These data suggest the specific form dependence takes. Tourism dominates the Hawai'i economy. It accounts for roughly 30 percent of the state's personal income and more than 40 percent of employment.[32] This industry's role is what explains the difference noted, at the end of the previous section, between having the nation's lowest figure in originating exports, and an exports to total goods and service ratio almost five times above the nation-alaverage.

Elected officials and the general public have expressed, for a number of years, discomfort with over-dependence on visitors. A survey taken in the relatively prosperous late 1980s suggested residents felt that tourism was a net gain to the state, but even then it was seen as, "time to stop building new hotels" because of tourism's contribution to the cost of living, traffic congestion, and crime.[33] Through the 1980s and into the 1990s, officials repeatedly expressed concern about vulnerability to downturns on the mainland, competition from new exotic-sounding tourist destinations outside the United States, and transportation disruptions.

Tourism's dominance brings other concerns. It is a service industry that pays lower wages and offers little occupational mobility. In 1991, the higher paying professional and technical positions comprised only 5.2 percent of jobs in the tourist industry in comparison to almost 17 percent for the state as a whole. With respect to the chances for upward movement, 3.9 percent of individuals were in managerial positions in comparison to 13.4 percent for all other occupations, a problem compounded by the fact that tourism facilities owned by foreign companies, as are a high proportion, may be more inclined to bring in their own management personnel.[34]

Concentration in the hands of external owners, a significant percentage of whom are foreign, is another characteristic of the state's major industry. By the end of 1991, more than 65 percent of all hotels were owned by foreigners, and 61 percent of the these were Japanese investors.[35] On Maui, over 80 percent was foreign-owned. Although substantial selling has occurred by the

Japanese since then, often it has been to other non-Hawai'i owners, and the overall pattern continues.

External control of tourist facilities is a reflection of other ways in which the state's economy has been penetrated by international actors. Of the former Big Five sugar factors, only two remain locally owned. Money from outside the state, much of it foreign, owns office towers in the center of Honolulu, the state's largest shopping centers, fast-food and supermarket chains, insurance companies, department stores, agricultural property, and prime commercial property.

Yet, clearly, not all concerns are economic. A great deal has to do with control and the power to shape Hawai'i society. There is no question that a large number of lawyers, real estate brokers, and well-connected local advisers have made lots of money helping global investors enter the Hawai'i economy. There are differences of opinion about their role in helping outsiders exercise influence over local affairs. Some argue there have been surprisingly few attempts to shape policy by lobbying elected officials and administrative agencies.[36] Others see alarming continuities in being "Islands under the influence" of powerful external forces, with the 1980s and 1990s merely the latest stage in Hawai'i's economic and political dependence.[37]

The control issue raises the question of how much the islands are being transformed in ways that respond to external interests, but are not good for most people who live in Hawai'i. It highlights the possibility of a new colonialism, in which the controllers of capital reward local elites for helping to extract wealth from those areas in the islands offering the greatest opportunities for profit.

For some observers, the average person's circumstances—living within a single-industry economy heavily penetrated by outsiders, and a centralized political apparatus under their influence—raise the specter of a new plantation economy. In the words of one descendent of plantation life, "Today, while plantations have declined significantly in size and influence, and the Big Five are gone or greatly reduced in importance, more Hawai'i residents continue to feel the powerlessness and exploitation of plantation life."[38]

HAWAI'I AS A SPECIAL PLACE

Public opinion research indicates that a high proportion of residents experience contemporary Hawai'i in similar ways. These shared perceptions are complex, blending the sense that Hawai'i maintains a historic identity as a special place with fears it is becoming just like everywhere else.

A February 1996 statewide survey of 807 residents, summarized in table

Table 10: Resident Perceptions of Life in Hawai'i

Issue	Percentage
Feel less safe than a few years ago	66
Experience workload as heavier than a few years ago	46
Feel a lot more stressed than a few years ago	67
Think Hawaii has become just like any other place	45
Think people of different racial and ethnic backgrounds get along better than other places	83
Think Hawaii will be a good place to raise their children	69
Think aloha spirit is important in how people live	87

Source: Greg Wiles, "Despite Economic Worries, People Feel Aloha in Islands," *Honolulu Advertiser*, February 25, 1996, p. A-1.

10, found that an overwhelming majority believed that racial and ethnic harmony continue to exist in the islands. About seven of ten expected Hawai'i will be a good place for their children to be raised, and almost nine of ten believed the "spirit of aloha" remains alive and well. At the same time, compared to a few years ago, people felt less safe, saw themselves working harder, and experienced higher levels of stress. About half agreed, "Hawaii has become just like any other place in America; it's no longer special," a response indicating that for many people who live there "Hawai'i" is an image packaged for tourists, and not a direct experience in their day-to-day lives.

The complex sense of what makes Hawai'i unique to its residents and a source of allure to visitors has always competed with other realities. "Paradise" had its thorny underside for the nineteenth-century adventurers who came to do business in the islands and decided to remain, for the hundreds of thousands of immigrant laborers who fought to cut out a place for themselves in their adopted society, and for the descendants of Native Hawaiians who watched their traditional home slip out of their control. Today, a constellation of realities, some with roots deep in the past, and others relatively recent in origin, challenge the sense that Hawai'i is "someplace special."

Shifting Demographics

Between 1980 and 1990, the state's population increased by 143,538 to reach 1,108,229. Over 78 percent of this was accounted for by births.[39] After July 1990, according to the U.S. Census Bureau, the state's population increased at about the national rate of 6 percent, reaching 1,183,723 in July 1996.

Table 11: Hawai'i's Changing Ethnic Mix, 1970 and 1992

Ethnic Group	1970 Population	1970 Percentage	1992 Population	1992 Percentage
Total	773,632	100.00	1,138,866	100.00
Hawaiian	7,967	1.0	9,118	0.8
Part-Hawaiian	124,224	16.2	211,630	18.6
Mixed, non-Hawaiian	60,770	7.9	209,831	18.4
Caucasian	255,437	33.0	265,211	23.3
Chinese	29,966	3.9	52,611	4.6
Filipino	61,240	7.9	119,256	10.5
Japanese	207,379	26.8	224,800	19.7

Source: Hawai'i State Department of Health, Hawaii Health Surveillance Program. Groups not reported in the tables constitute less than 2 percent of the population.

Changes in the remarkable ethnic diversity that may be the islands' most distinctive feature are contained within these growing numbers. Between 1970 and 1992, the portion of the population that is Caucasian and Japanese dropped substantially (table 11). Those labeling themselves Caucasian remain the most numerous group, but they have shrunk from 33 percent to just over 23 percent. In contrast, individuals designating themselves as non-Hawaiian mixed ethnicity have increased from 7.9 percent to 18.4 percent, while part-Hawaiians have grown from 16.2 percent to 18.6, and Filipinos have jumped to 10.5 from 7.9 percent.

These changing demographics, although emphasizing a quality prized in the islands, also contain challenges. One challenge relates to shifts in the age distribution. Hawai'i's population is growing at both ends of the age scale, but increases among the elderly are by far the most dramatic and socially significant. Between 1990 and 1994, the number of residents between ages 15 and 19 grew by 5,000, from 73,100 to 78,1000. Residents 70 to 74 years of age went from 32,800 to 39,300, a gain of 6,500 during the same period. Around 11 percent of the state's population in 1990, people 65 and over are expected to constitute about 15 percent by 2015 and 20 per cent by 2020, a reflection, in part, of the fact that Hawai'i has the longest average life span of any state in the United States.[40]

Hawai'i's elderly live at home at a much higher rate than anywhere else in the country. Approximately 77 percent of those 65 and older were estimated to live with family or friends in 1980, in comparison to the national average of about 28 percent.[41] This mirrors the high priority given to family and relationships. It also reflects economic realities and, relatedly, the absence of viable alternative arrangements. In 1999, there were only a handful of publicly supported assisted living facilities throughout the state, although on O'ahu the city and county have been active in building subsidized housing for low-income elderly. The first private for-profit apartment complex, so popular in areas of the United States that have concentrations of senior citizens, was built in 1998, with projected costs far out of reach of most residents. Hawai'i had a ratio of 14.4 nursing home beds per 1,000 person 65 and over 1989, compared to the United States' average of 52.8 beds per 1,000.[42]

These circumstances contrast sharply with Hawai'i's self-description as the "health state." That image is made up of its low rates of infant mortality, illness and death from heart disease and cancer; longer life expectancy; and lead in putting together a system of universal medical care access.[43] Despite this, in the mid-1990s a growing number of experts declared the aging of the state's population a looming crisis that would have widespread repercussions. Medical costs are an obvious worry, especially where there are few intermediate care options. The cost of housing has forced many younger people into smaller living spaces, unsuitable for accommodating aging parents. The state's extended fiscal crisis and the pressure to prioritize investment in prisons and schools, makes it less likely that, at least in the foreseeable future, more public facilities will be built. Many of the elderly, in turn, find themselves having to relinquish or creatively re-finance their homes in order to supplement fixed incomes that fail to keep up with costs.

A second challenge, related to changing demographics, is the out-migration of residents, especially those viewed as social and economic assets. Between July 1990 and July 1996, more residents moved out of Hawai'i than came to it from other states, and between 1995 and 1996, the total number leaving exceeded even those immigrating from other countries.[44] Reflecting the depth of the issue, a 1995 survey estimated that 12 percent of residents planned to move away from the islands in the following twelve-month period, up from 3 per cent at the end of 1994.[45]

The kind of resident the state may be losing is what is most striking about these data and estimates. A large number of secondary school graduates attend mainland universities, especially those graduating from several of the state's best private schools. Due to the increased opportunities that present themselves after college graduation, and the lower cost of living in most parts of the country, many never return. The result has been that the state experiences the loss of its most promising youth to other places, like the post-statehood period when the Neighbor Islands experienced a loss of their most talented youth to the greater options and economic opportunities available in

urban Oʻahu. A university economist, after studying the out-migration patterns for graduates of the state's most prestigious private secondary school,
concluded that "Hawaii may very well have a brain drain problem like that
commonly found in third world countries."[46]

Economic Realities

The relative absence of class distinctions plays a role in making Hawaiʻiʻ a
special place beyond the role played by ethnic tolerance. Such distinctions,
created and reinforced by growing discrepancies in wealth, would threaten
the social openness so valued in the islands.

Income distribution is an indicator of differences in wealth, although it is
not the same thing as total wealth, which includes assets such as property and
other financial assets. The GINI index is a well-known measure of income inequality. A GINI index value of zero indicates complete equality, while 1.0
reflects a situation in which one person or family has all the income.[47]

The index for Hawaiʻi typically has shown less income inequality than
the national average, but it has fluctuated over the decades. In 1929, it was
slightly below its 1990 value of .519, reflecting somewhat greater equality in
the earlier period. By statehood, consistent with enfranchisement through
education and an expanding economy in the post-ear period, the figure
dropped to .426. Income inequality gradually increased afterwards, and between 1970 and 1990 it grew 18 percent. These changes were slightly less
than what occurred nationwide, where inequality grew 23 percent over the
same period.

There is an indication that the index for Hawaiʻi has again dropped since
1990; that is, it appears that income has become somewhat more evenly distributed. According to a study by the Department of Business, Economic
Development, and Tourism, the GINI index for 1994 was 0.380, a slight
movement from the 1989 figure of 0.395.[48] Hawaiʻi continued to have less
inequality than the United States as a whole, for which the figure was 0.456
in 1989.

This suggestion of relative income equality is countered by the economic
facts of life for many residents. At the center is the disparity between the high
cost of living and personal incomes. This imbalance forces a large number of
people to work more than one job, and results in a high proportion of families
in which both parents work. In 1994, 65 percent of children under 18 had both
parents or their only parent in the labor force. Sixty-three percent of women
were employed in 1990, a figure that was both the highest in the nation

and up 13 percent from 1970.[49] Because of this, the state's comparatively high national ranking in per capita income can be misleading, since it is based on higher levels of multiple employment. Job loss, the common indicator of an economic downturn, is disguised when someone's loss of a second job—even though he or she is dependent on it to make ends meet—is not reflected in official statistics.

The difference between the cost of living and income has other effects. A 1992 report estimated that 8 percent of the population were "hidden homeless," while 28 percent were three or fewer paychecks from losing their place of residence.[50]

As many as one-third of Hawai'i children may be latchkey kids, left on their own between the time school is out and a parent returns home from work. It was estimated in 1990 that almost 20 percent of children were below the poverty level if they had only one parent. For mothers with children under five, the figure climbed to 41 percent. This was a particular problem since the number of mothers who were, or were likely to become, single had increased. Nearly 1 in 4 children were born out of wedlock in 1990, compared to 1 in 10 in 1970. Births to single teens increased from 6.5 percent of all births in 1980 to 7.9 percent of all births in 1993, with higher jumps on the Neighbor Islands.[51]

Gender and ethnicity contribute to economic inequalities. Women have been over-represented in lower paying job categories, and have earned less across all job categories. They were estimated to earn $.65. for every dollar earned by a male in 1990.[52] In 1991, women held only 9.1 percent of corporate directorships for the top 50 Hawai'i companies.[53] Women occupied only 13.9 percent of the high-level administrative positions in Hawai'i's state and county governments, according to a survey conducted by the Center for Women in Government in 1990. This was the lowest percentage of all fifty states, four points lower than even the traditionally patriarchic Utah.[54]

Despite Hawai'i's deserved reputation as a ethnically integrated society, an individual's ethnicity appears to affect their economic position. Japanese males and all Caucasians are over-represented in higher status and better paying executive, administrative and managerial jobs, according to census data. Filipinos and Hawaiians, on the other hand, appear as operators, fabricators, and laborers significantly out of proportion to their numbers in the population.[55]

The Natural Environment

If any single thing makes Hawai'i special, it is the natural environment. It is a continual source of celebration in the popular songs of Native Hawaiian artists, and it is the warmth of the climate and the beauty of the land and surrounding ocean that draws so many visitors. Not surprisingly, Hawai'i and Honolulu are at the top of the national "green' lists of environmental quality.

Kirk Smith, formerly an environmental scientist at the East-West Center, observed that as seen in national rankings done in recent years Honolulu's environmental quality is unsurpassed.[56] These rankings are based on measures of water and air pollution, toxic and other waste, automobile fuel efficiency, community and worker health, and facilities producing chemical carcinogens. Honolulu is not only first, but there is often a large gap between first and second in these areas.

It is not surprising that population increases and economic growth put pressure on the Hawai'i environment. The 1993 estimate that 7,971,338 people visited Waikiki beach, a relatively narrow section of sand no more than one mile long, illustrates this pressure. In the same year, 2,310,864 dropped in to Hanauma Bay, a sheltered cove on O'ahu that offers snorklers excellent fish viewing.[57]

These pressures have raised concerns in a number of areas, of which waste management, endangered species, and water resources are both illustrative and significant.[58] Hawai'i has been a pioneer in converting garbage to energy through a facility known as H-Power. H-Power, located in urban Honolulu, takes trash that otherwise would find its way to the landfills and converts it into electricity, thus reducing dependence on imported oil. Despite its success, H-Power has proven more expensive than expected, strains the city/county budget, throws toxic chemicals into the air, and creates an annual residue of 600 tons of waste for alternative disposal. In addition, it can only postpone the future crisis of locating viable new landfills on densely populated O'ahu.

Hawai'i is rich in animal and plant species found nowhere else in the world, as noted in the opening chapter. More than 97 percent of its native flowering plants, non migratory land birds, insects, and land snails are found nowhere else. Since contact with the West, about one-third of the islands' endemic bird species have disappeared. Today, Hawai'i has more animal and plant extinctions, and likely extinctions, than any other state.[59]

The main source of water on the densely populated island of O'ahu is the underground aquifers that collect rain water filtering down to them through ground soil and lava rock. (The largest of these is the Pearl Harbor aquifer.) Prior to 1879, when a well was first used to tap into the aquifer system, Honolulu was served by streams draining off the nearby mountains.[60] Wells proliferated after 1879, the net effect being recurring water shortages and a falling water table.

The Honolulu Sewer and Water Commission was established in 1925, soon restricting private water development and capping abandoned wells. By the 1930s, the water table rose for the first time since the 1880s. As Honolulu grew, the Board of Water Supply, 1929 successor to the commission, looked for water sources outside the urban area. The board had expanded its search across the Ko'olau mountains to the rainier windward side by the 1960s, moving water through a system of transmountain tunnels and dikes.

These demands conflicted with traditional users of stream water. The first check on the board's authority came in the 1970s from a taro farmer named Rapun in a windward valley. He successfully argued that stream diversion to supply residential or plantation users made his farming impossible and therefore conflicted with rights conferred in provisions of the Mahele in 1848. The court ordered a partial restoration of stream water.

The Rapun case and a court decision in 1973, declaring that all natural flowing water belonged to the state, made water an issue at the 1978 constitutional convention. Convention delegates gave control of water development to the state. In 1987, after many difficult meetings, a water code was established, for administration by a six-member Commission on Water Resource Management.

The city-county board and the state commission have subsequently fought over the lines of their authority. For example, in 1992 the Windward side of the island of O'ahu, which the board wanted to continue to develop for other uses, was designated a management area from which withdrawals would be restricted. The commission decided in 1997, after hearing heated arguments and counter-arguments, on a plan to allocate water no longer being used by O'ahu sugar growers between development interests in the central plain and taro farmers on the windward side.

In the 1990s, demands have increased statewide from Native Hawaiians for preservation of water used in sustainable, small-production agriculture. On the island of Moloka'i, for example, there has been a difficult, and sometimes violent, conflict over the parceling of water between resort hotels at its west end and subsistence farming on Hawaiian Homelands.

These issues focus on the question of where water will be found to meet expected population growth. Some will be derived from reclamation of water used by former sugar plantations. Other water may come from private land owners, such as the Bishop Estate, developing sources on their land and dedicating it to the city or state as part of their own development plans. Even with these options, the use of seawater and construction of desalinization facilities may be a necessity in the somewhat longer term.

Whatever the pressures on its environment and natural resources, Hawai'i gives surprisingly little organized attention to environmental matters. Various ratings place the state below the national average on measures of commitment. One, conducted in 1987, put it behind other states in trying to protect groundwater, reduce hazardous wastes, and manage solid wastes. It was ranked 49th in 1987 in dealing with military hazardous wastes, a significant issue given the Department of Defense's presence in the islands. And in 1990, Hawai'i was ranked 46th in environmental spending as a percent of the state budget.[61]

Consuming Paradise

Competition for tourists in an increasing competitive global market, as well as the greater challenge to maintaining the picture of Hawai'i as a remote tropical paradise, have led to new marketing strategies. The emphasis, in the late 1990s, is on the islands as a great place to shop. This identity, always implicit in the message to the visitor, is aimed especially at Asian tourists. Asian tourists, on average, spend more than those originating in North America or Europe, but they have shown signs of lessening interest in Hawai'i's romantic image.

The new face of paradise is supported by multiplication of high-end stores that cater to well-heeled visitors. The Ala Moana Shopping Center, the state's largest shopping mall, is one of the best places to see this change. Because it is located not far from Waikiki, it always has drawn non-resident shoppers. Historically, however, their presence was far out-weighed by "locals" who, because it was the first and for a number of years only shopping complex, saw the center as their place.

By the late 1990s, Ala Moana Shopping Center had transformed itself to cater to rich residents and well-to-do foreigners, in the process becoming almost a foreign land to lower and middle income locals. Symbolizing this shift, in 1998 Nieman Marcus joined a fleet of high-priced specialty stores selling merchandise that often makes little sense to local consumers. Liberty House, once the centerpiece of the mall, in that same year declared bankruptcy, and its owners wondered publicly if they had made a mistake in abandoning their traditional base of local customers.

DISTINGUISHING GROWTH FROM DEVELOPMENT

Non-economic concerns bring into prominence another important historic and contemporary issue: the difference between economic growth and social development. Hawai'i experienced tremendous economic growth after statehood, but many questioned who benefited from it, and whether its less desirable byproducts were concealed or ignored. Even if there is success in vitalizing Hawai'i's economy through diversification, perhaps by means of some form of private-public collaboration, the general benefits to a sustainable quality of life are uncertain.

Measuring what is meant by "social progress" is a key challenge in attempting to given attention to both economic and social improvement. The standard measure of economic success is increases in the total production of goods and services, represented by the gross state product. Some other non-economic indicators are available, in particular changes in environmental conditions, such as air and water pollution, or species loss. Apart from these, and despite widespread acceptance of the concept of sustainable growth, there has been remarkably little work done to specify and give authority to other indicators, indicators that would permit movement beyond an historic American assumption that equated progress with increases in gross production numbers.

Oregon Benchmarks is a pioneering effort to define success in terms of an expanded mix of social and economic indicators. Established by law in 1989 with the creation of Oregon Shines and the Oregon Progress Board, Oregon Benchmarks is a statewide effort that defines and then collects data on a range of baselines, or "benchmarks." Once established, changes are tracked on specific benchmarks targeted as important areas for improvement.

Initiatives similar to Oregon Benchmarks had, by 1997, been undertaken in six other places.[62] Five of these efforts were located in Florida; Iowa; Minnesota; Santa Clara Valley and San Jose, California; and Jacksonville, Florida. The sixth was in Hawai'i.

The Hawai'i benchmarking project began in 1992, inspired by a visit from the former director of the Oregon Progress Board, the statewide planning body for Oregon's work. Known as *Ke Ala Hoku,* a Hawaiian phrase meaning "charting the course," this project's organizers relied heavily on the statements of a cross-section of thousands of Hawai'i youth to first define a set of 13 critical issues, for each of which was created a desired result, called an outcome; a measure of movement toward the desired results, called an indicator; and a benchmark, a time-specific target for moving toward the goal using the indicator.

Indicators were created in each of these areas, after which they were re-formed into six focus areas, which together had 58 critical indicators. These areas, with examples of critical indicators for them, are listed in table 12.

Table 12: *Ke Ala Hoku* Social Indicators

Area	Outcome	Indicator
Aloha spirit	All people feel and live the Aloha spirit	People who live "aloha" Preservation of sacred sites
Healthy natural environment	Hawai'i actively pursues the preservation, protection, and enhancement of distinct ecosystems with natural healthy habitats	Water quality Human crowding Soil erosion
Safe, nurturing, social environment	Children and youth feel safe from violence and drugs in schools Hawai'i has safe home environments where all family members are free from harm There is a reduction in youth gang involvement	Community and school safety Children with after-school care Gang involvement
Thriving, diverse and sustainable economy	Income parity is increased Hawai'i is a competitive, diverse, affordable and fair business climate for consumers and businesses All individuals and families can meet their basic needs	Multiple job holdings Diversification of the tourism market Home ownership
Educated citizens	People are lifelong learners	Adult literacy Early childhood education Information technology for education
Vital civic life	Citizens participate to ensure an informed, effective, and ethical government	Perceived quality of life Satisfaction with public leadership Community-based planning and decision-making

Ke Ala Hoku represents, among other things, an effort to provide a new answer to a very old question: what would social *and* economic development look like in Hawai'i? It addresses the challenge facing the state to find ways to promote sustainable businesses that are compatible with environmental and cultural values, oriented to a mix of local and export markets, capable of being established outside of urban O'ahu, and able to pay sufficiently high wages and salaries. From the perspective of its work, a decline of tourism may be something of a blessing by encouraging new ways, like that found in *Ke Ala Hoku,* in which to think about the question.

CHAPTER TWELVE

Images of the Future of Paradise

Hawai'i has been a national leader in endeavoring to anticipate, and perhaps shape, its future. In 1970, eleven years after admission to statehood, the legislature created the Conference on the Year 2000. The publicly funded event pulled together hundreds of participants from across the state and resulted in a widely distributed report summarizing what had been concluded in the deliberations. State government, in particular the state Judiciary, subsequently has incorporated futures research methods as part of its work. Helping to set the tone for this orientation, the University of Hawai'i is the home of the Hawai'i Research Center for Futures Studies, established by the state legislature. James Dator, a well-known futurist and head of the center, was for many years secretary general and president of the World Futures Studies Federation. In 1996, Dator and others began planning for a statewide conference on Hawai'i in the year 3000.

Two more recent projects, in this context, are especially relevant to understanding current images of the state's future. A. A. Smyser, a former editor of the *Honolulu Star-Bulletin,* one of the state's two largest newspapers, in 1988 published *Hawaii's Future in the Pacific—Disaster, Backwater or Future State?*[1] The study, a result of his work as a fellow at the East-West Center, projects five alternative futures for the next 20 to 30 years.

"Backwater" is one of the scenarios. It is distinguished by the state's shrinking relationship with the outside world. By becoming, or deliberately making itself, less attractive, the number of people who wish to reside, visit, or invest drops dramatically. This, in turn, leads to a lower gross state product and fewer resources for education and social services, as well as diminished support for cultural activities.

In "The Third World," the state's population continues to grow, and external investment and new businesses are actively courted. Environmental standards are neglected to create incentives for investment. Little is done to control who benefits from new wealth and, as a consequence, the disparity between rich and poor grows. This leads to the marginalization of much of the population. In Third World fashion, an elite enjoys access to scarce land, desirable housing, quality health care, and dominates public policy.

"Nostalgia" is another scenario that Smyser thought attractive, but unrealistic. In it, the state is able to parlay strong, environmentally friendly standards into long-term wealth. Public policy discourages in-migration. Self-sufficiency is emphasized through support of small-scale farming and fishing, and by means of geothermal, solar, and wave-based energy. Tourism is limited to what can be supported without destroying local communities or local culture.

The image Smyser liked most he labeled "The Future State." (He also considered, and rejected, calling it "Special Place" or "Geneva of the Pacific.") Environmental quality, natural beauty, and cultural diversity are used to create and sustain an active position in the international economy, in particular as an economic and cultural hub of the Pacific. The state attracts enterprises capable of making use of its natural resources while at the same time sustaining them. Public policy promotes businesses that pay middle-income wages to local residents. There is ethnic harmony and a diverse range of cultural activities.

Symser's least desirable future, "Disaster Scenario," could be created through the failure of any of the others. In it, control is lost to outsiders, many of whose interests do not coincide with those of the state's long-term residents. Tourism is over-exploited and declines. The environment is destroyed. Hostilities increase between ethnic groups. Because of a decreased tax base, public services, including education, are cut back severely.

Hawai'i 2020

The conclusions of another project on Hawai'i's future were published in May 1996. Titled *Hawai'i 2020*, it was based on focus-group discussions with about one-hundred opinion leaders, primarily from O'ahu, and including members of the Native Hawaiian community.[2] The groups were formed around a set of social issues, such as education, business, and the economy; Hawai'i's place in the world; and cultural relations. Each met several times.

These two works overlap, especially in the emphasis on race relations and social harmony. At the same time, the scenarios making up *Hawai'i* 2020 reflect images that developed in the eight years since publication of *Hawai'i's Future in the Pacific*.[3] The prominence of Native Hawaiians and their culture is one of the most noticeable of these changes. Another is the role of local communities in determining the quality of life. Although pivotal in the *Hawai'i* 2020 scenarios, both of these were virtually absent in the earlier visions.

The *Hawai'i* 2020 images reflect many of the themes tying together this book, including the direction that will be taken by historically centralized public authority; the character of ethnic relations and political culture; the position of Native peoples; the pattern of relationships with outsiders; and the continued identity as someplace special.

In the *Hawai'i* 2020 future, individuals live in decentralized communities. Strong families are supported by those communities, with the assistance of locally controlled, publicly supported centers. Information technology is used to increase government responsiveness by allowing easier electoral participation and joining citizens to informed public deliberations. There is a high degree of ethnic group intermingling and cooperation, but individual cultures maintain their traditions. The state has a viable place in the global economy, especially in the Pacific and Asia regions. Business life, including the tourist industry, reflects non-economic values, and the local economy is able to provide a satisfying degree of self-sufficiency. Injustices to Native people have been settled by an autonomous land base and fiscal resources. At the same time, the values of Hawaiian culture are prominent in day-to-day relationships of all kinds. Finally, the islands retain their specialness, characterized by residents' tolerance, cooperation on behalf of shared goals, and reverence for the environment.

CONVERTING IMAGES TO REALITY

Taking time to think clearly about alternative futures is part of the task of creating a society attractive to most residents. In that regard, Hawai'i is doing well.

There is, however, a great distance between a group of citizens, no matter how broad-based, imagining a future, and concerted movement toward it.

The challenge of charting a course to the future in the real world is illustrated by a highly visible debate that took place in 1998. Chapter 8 noted the governor's role in sponsoring the Economic Revitalization Task Force (ERTF), and the failure of its more important elements to survive the legislative session. A good-for-business orientation[4] is embodied in the ERTF's proposals to abolish the Land Use Commission, most likely making it easier to rezone land for development; reduce worker's compensation benefits; make greater use of the University of Hawai'i as an economic, as opposed to educational asset; privatize some government functions; and introduce public-private competition for service delivery.

The ideological shift is consistent with the re-emerging Republican party and an emphasis on the political culture of individualism. It is more complicated in relation to the Democrats. Governor Cayetano, trying to deal strategically with what he saw as a fiscal emergency while also taking away some fuel for a Republican resurgence, embraced proposals that would have been anathema to most of the party 25 years earlier. They came into direct conflict with those whose orientation was still primarily the social justice agenda, proving to be such a stress point within the legislative party that, in the end, the governor's program suffered a very public rejection.

The premise that Hawai'i has been inhospitable to business and economic development is a central feature of the new orientation. Those who hold this position commonly refer to Hawai'i as something akin to an over-regulated, bureaucratic hell. This conclusion has some basis. However, just as beneficiaries and supporters of the social justice ideology had to deal with questions that accompanied overly concentrated power, the future promised by the new ideology raises its own questions.

First, there is the matter of the degree to which Hawai'i is in fact Business Hell. If it is, one must wonder how the tourist industry continued to expand in Waikiki long after many people began to wonder, out loud and in legislative forums, if it was in the state's economic interest to have such a dense concentration of hotels. More to the point, rather than dismissing Hawai'i as Business Hell, it makes more sense to recognize it is also a place that has adopted specific policies that affect business but reflect important social values. From this perspective, businesses are responsible for their own success and failure within the set of rules of the game, as long as those rules are applied fairly and consistently. As one small business owner put it, "There are numerous communities throughout the United States and the world that have much higher taxes and equally as complex land-use regulations as Hawaii. Businesses in those areas, like businesses everywhere, adapt and live within the structure and laws of the community in which they are based. If they can't make it, they leave and someone else takes their places. It is really pretty simple."[5]

Second, experience makes clear that the interests of small businesses and large corporations are often quite different. While government regulations may be one of the enemies of small business, another often are large businesses. Small businesses in Hawai'i face the often overwhelming challenge of large mainland firms with deep pockets. The result can be substantial consumer savings if competition is sustained in that market, but it also means the closure of many once profitable businesses and the loss of local ownership.

The third question about the good-for-business orientation focuses on the degree to which government action, on behalf of either large or small businesses, matters. As chapter 4 made evident, the state is subject to the workings of the evolving global economy and its supra-national actors. Governments everywhere have become reactive, struggling with the now familiar pattern of rapid capital flows; once local firms finding greater profit margins in settings that require lower wages and lack health and safety regulations; shrinking tax resources to deal with increasing social demands; and a diminished sense of control over their society's economic destiny. Hawai'i decision-makers, as a result of these forces, could claim little credit for the earlier increase in Japanese tourism and investment, and in the late 1990s there is not much they can do about the diminished Japanese presence. Nor can they be responsible for the ripple effects on the islands of sudden withdrawals of capital in other Asian counties in 1997.

HAWAI'I'S CAPACITY TO CREATE A DESIRABLE FUTURE

Chapter 3 proposes that, at the beginning of the 1990s, Hawai'i seemed to be headed in two different directions, each consistent with the state's history, but in tension with one another. One direction was toward greater institutional openness and multiple centers of power. The other was toward privileged insider relationships. These two paths, which have co-existed, are what has created the islands uniquely as at once highly progressive and like a traditional, Old Boy dominated society in the American south.

New forces are shaping the state as it approaches the turn of the century. Where before these two paths seemed the most likely, now others seem possible. The contest between the social justice and good-for-business agendas suggest what these might look like.

Which path is taken, and whether it is chosen or adapted to, will depend upon how several difficult issues are handled.

1. Decentralization and Responsive Governance. Accomplishing the devolution of public authority to support forms of governance closer to residents' communities means facing forces in tension with one another. On one hand, the virtual absence of local structures is an opportunity. There are no entrenched bureaucracies or interest groups to dislodge at this level. This relatively clean slate permits a design process that can glean what has been learned from experience in other places. Some of this experimentation is already occurring as communities devise local control over education, medical facilities, policing, and small-scale economic development.

On the other hand, there is much less concrete experience with local governance in Hawai'i than elsewhere, and there are good reasons for some kinds of centralization. Some support is found in specific interests, inside government and out, that benefit from jobs or policies. But apart from that, the role the centralized system has played in creating fairness—such as the even distribution of resources to schools in a variety of socio-economic settings —and the noteworthy legacy of public-regarding policies, reviewed in chapter 6, creates other support for centralization. Retaining what the state's historic system does well while embracing new forms of local governance will be a concerted effort extending well beyond any single administration.

2. Economic and Cultural Viability. Avoiding the cultural homogenization that comes with global marketing and global workplaces is of particular importance in the islands, as images of the future suggest.

Hawai'i may be successful in managing its roles in the international economy by encouraging local markets, and by agreeing to be more selective about who is allowed to do business in the islands. This may help to preserve the islands as a special place in cultural and environmental terms, but it also is likely to bring a cost in net wealth.

Internationally, there is intense competition to attract culturally and environmentally friendly businesses that pay good wages. The more restrictions that are placed on what is an acceptable business enterprise, the less likely a location, especially one as physically removed as Hawai'i, is to attract capital. The long-term question, then, is whether the state is willing to assume that risk, or more specifically, what it will take for those who most benefit from global investment to redefine their interests. Equally fundamental is how the consequences of any self-imposed restraint can be distributed evenly so as to avoid increasing material inequalities in a society uncomfortable with such differences.

3. Resolving Hawaiian Sovereignty. There is not now, and there is unlikely to be, a single Hawaiian voice describing what a Hawaiian society should look like. Yet, a large majority of the state's citizens, including many of its elected officials, believe an injustice has been done to Hawaiians. For them, some restitution is in order.

Despite this broad sympathy, if their efforts go well, at some point sovereignty's direction will be specific enough to affect identifiable property, business, and cultural interests. It is not possible for any kind of sovereign entity to be created over the staunch opposition of a large number of non-Hawaiians, especially those with economic or political power. In this regard, the recommendations of the Economic Revitalization Task Force, composed primarily of the heads of large businesses, are noteworthy. It made no specific proposals about Hawaiian claims and self-determination. The task force did pointedly suggest, however, that resolution of the issue is vital for the state's economic future, and urged that representatives of labor, business, government and the community come together with Native Hawaiians to find a mutually acceptable solution.

It is equally clear that the movement of Hawaiians has developed politically to the point that residents cannot expect to exist in a harmonious society without responding in substance to their demands. The question is what kinds of compromises must be made, and whether solutions that emerge from these compromises will earn sufficiently broad acceptance among Hawaiians and non-Hawaiians.

4. Creating Public Space. The revitalization of community and expansion of civic participation is partly an issue of creating commitment and pathways for action. It is also a practical matter of how much time and energy are available.

Thirty years ago, the slower, more personal pace of life in the islands, including Honolulu, was luxuriously different from many other places. Urbanization, in combination with the cost of living, has resulted in a dramatically increased pace for large portions of the population. As the data presented in chapter 11 show, in the 1990s it is normal for a Hawai'i family to have both parents employed, too frequently with one working two or more jobs. Add to this the commute through congested highways and obligations to extended families of uncles, aunts, and cousins, and little time is left for public activities.

The public spaces in the average person's life—the time and energy available to share concerns outside of work and family—must be enlarged if Hawai'i's future is to be made of vibrant communities and involved citizens. Without such an expansion, these efforts will be left to a circumscribed group of the financially successful and retired, or those employed to lobby for particular interests, far too small a portion of the population to meet a definition of community.

This book has argued that Hawai'i is distinguished by bringing together long-term in-group control and a remarkable array of public-regarding policy, making it seem like a progressive traditional southern state, a social-political combination that may not co-exist anywhere else in the country.

It is appropriate to conclude this look at an American state and a Pacific society by suggesting that its first goal and greatest challenge are the same: to become more pluralistic while protecting those elements of political culture that have produced so many policies of broad public benefit. Meeting this goal will not be easy given the persistence of historic patterns, or the pressures of global economic competition.

Often a crisis, a problem that makes normal responses irrelevant, can provoke actions that otherwise would not have been considered. The challenge of restructuring the economy may present one such opportunity. Responding to it can be an incentive to think anew about the relationship between government responsibilities and community resourcefulness, a desirable balance between creating an environment for business and preservation of an Island culture, and the differences between growth and development.

The demands being made by Native Hawaiians also present an opportunity. Embodied in these demands are deep-seated values that support more autonomous communities and open, face-to-face relationships; the acceptance of difference; and a deep appreciation for Hawai'i as a special place. Viewed in this way, modern Native Hawaiians, whose culture has been so influential in shaping contemporary Island society, may provide the opportunity to move in directions not possible in other places.

CHAPTER THIRTEEN

Suggestions for Further Reading

The works suggested below will take the interested reader more deeply into many of the areas explored in this book. This is a starter list, and much that is worthwhile does not appear here. Most of the titles are revealing of their content. Some references are accompanied by comment.

DATA SOURCES

Business Trends. Bank of Hawai'i. A regular publication providing data and interpretation on issues relating to the state's economic performance.

Government in Hawai'i. Tax Foundation of Hawai'i. The Tax Foundation is a government monitoring organization. This publication provides valuable, current information on the sources, spending, and fiscal health of state and local government. Until recently an annual publication, it now appears less often because of budget constraints.

Ke Ala Hoku Project. "Critical Indicators Report—1997–98." Honolulu: Hawai'i Community Services Council, 1997. A compilation of sometimes hard-to-find data on social and economic issues, collected in association with efforts to establish community benchmarks.

Native Hawaiian Data Book '98. Honolulu: Office of Hawaiian Affairs. The Office of Hawaiian Affairs publishes this to familiarize policy makers, administrators, and the general public with the conditions and needs of Native Hawaiians. Much of the information appears in other sources, but this publication pulls the data together in one place and offers interpretations of what they mean.

State of Hawai'i, Office of the Auditor. This office produces a series of reports each year on different aspects of state government. The reports often explore issues of concern to legislators, but there is a broader motivation for the work. The *1995 Annual Report* listed the themes that seemed to run through that year's 34 reports. These themes included the clarity and purpose of public agencies, limiting and streamlining government, and the potential for positive change. The following pages contained reflections on the success that agencies of state government were having in making effective use of electronic information systems, pairing what was hoped for with these systems against what actually seemed to be happening.

State of Hawaii Data Book. The legacy of well-known former state statistician Robert C. Schmitt, this is an annual issue of the state Department of Business, Economic Development, and Tourism. It contains a wealth of information, usefully divided into sections and accompanied by an index. The *Data Book* is also available on the World Wide Web at http://www.hawaii.gov/dbedt/. This site also contains tables that are updated in-between publication of the hard copy.

HISTORY

Edward Beechert, Buo V. Lai, and Doug Munro. *Plantation Workers: Resistance and Accommodation*. Honolulu: University of Hawai'i Press, 1993.

Tom Coffman. *Nation Within—The Story of America's Annexation of the Nation of Hawai'i*. Kaneohe HI: EPICenter, 1998.

Gavan Daws. *Shoal of Time: A History of the Hawaiian Islands*. Toronto: Macmillan, 1968.

Lawrence H. Fuchs. *Hawaii Pono: A Social History*. New York: Harcourt, Bruce and World, 1961. The best-known interpretation of Hawai'i's evolution from 1900 to 1960. This and the work above by Gavan Daws are informative and highly readable.

Hawaiian Journal of History. Scholarly studies of periods or events in Hawai'i's past.

Ralph S. Kuykendall. *The Hawaiian Kingdom*. Vol. 1, *1778–1854: Foundation and Transformation*. Vol. 2, *1854–1874: Twenty Critical Years*. Vol. 3, *1874–1893: The Hawai'i Kingdom*. Honolulu: University of Hawai'i Press, 1938–67. This is a three-volume set that has been a basic reference for the history of the period covered. Perhaps less influential because of newer works that raise questions about the Western framework the author brought to his study, it remains a valuable resource.

Mari J. Matsuda. "Law and Culture in the District Court of Honolulu, 1844–1845: A Case Study of the Rise of Legal Consciousness." *American Journal of Legal History* 32, no. 1 (January 1988): pp. 15–41.

Riley M. Moffat and Gary L. Fitzpatrick. *Surveying the Mahele*. Honolulu: Editions Limited, 1995. A detailed and engaging look at how the great mid-nineteenth-century land division was implemented.

Theodore Morgan. *Hawai'i: A Century of Economic Change, 1776–1876*. Cambridge: Harvard University Press, 1948.

Oral History Project. Center for Oral History, Social Science Research Institute, University of Hawai'i at Manoa.

HAWAIIANS

Michael Kioni Dudley and Keoni Kealoha Agard. *A Call for Hawaiian Sovereignty*. Honolulu: Malo Press, 1991.

Michael Kioni Dudley. *A Hawaiian Nation I: Man, Gods and Nature*. Honolulu: Na Kane O Ka Malo Press, 1990.

E. S. C. Handy and M. K. Pukui. *The Polynesian Family System in Ka'u, Hawai'i*. Tokyo: Charles E. Tuttle, 1972. An interesting look at the way Hawaiians lived that serves to remove stereotypes about traditional society.

Alan Howard. *Ain't No Big Thing: Coping Strategies in a Hawaiian American Community*. Honolulu: University of Hawai'i Press, 1974. An interpretation by an anthropologist of how contemporary Hawaiians relate to a non-Hawaiian world on O'ahu.

Lilikala Kame'ekeihiwa. *Native Land and Foreign Desires*. Honolulu: Bishop Museum Press, 1992. This book and the works by Jocelyn Linnekin and Kehaulani Kealoha-Scullion represent a newer wave of scholarship about Native Hawaiians and their history. They are revisionist in questioning the perspective on which previous histories have been based, particularly Western and male. There are also within these works important differences on the role Hawaiians and Hawaiian played in what happened to their society and culture. Kame'ekeihiwa and Kealoha-Scullion are both part Hawaiian, with Ph.D.s from the University of Hawai'i.

Kehaulani K. Kealoha-Scullion. "The Hawaiian Journey: Out of the Care of Identity, Images of the Hawaiian and Other." Ph.D. Diss., University of Hawai'i at Manoa, December 1995.

Jocelyn Linnekin. *Sacred Cows and Women of Consequence*. Ann Arbor: University of Michigan Press, 1990.

Marshall Sahlins. *Anahulu: The Anthropology of History in the Kingdom of Hawai'i*. Vol. 1, *Historical Ethnography*. Chicago: University of Chicago Press, 1992. A remarkable anthropological study of a section of the island of O'ahu held by Ka'ahumanu, the most influential wife of Kamehameha I.

Sahlins weaves together discoveries from this area with an interpretation of changes occurring in the larger Hawaiian society in the early nineteenth century.

David F. Stannard. *Before the Horror: The Population of Hawai'i on the Eve of Western Contact*. Honolulu: University of Hawai'i at Manoa, Social Science Research Institute, 1989. Stannard's book served to foster a more scholarly debate about the size of the Hawaiian population at contact and therefore the magnitude of devastation through disease over the next decades.

CULTURE AND CULTURAL RELATIONS

Michael Haas, ed. *Multicultural Hawai'i—The Fabric of a Multiethnic Society*. New York: Garland Publishing, 1998.

E. S. Craighill Handy. *Cultural Revolution in Hawai'i*. Honolulu: American Council Institute of Pacific Relations, 1931.

Dorothy Ochiai Hazama and Jane Okamoto Kamejii. *Ohage Sama De: The Japanese in Hawai'i, 1885–1985*. Honolulu: Bess Press, 1986.

Bernard L. Hormann and Andrew W. Lind. "Ethnic Sources In Hawai'i." *Social Process in Hawai'i* 29 (1976). A well-regarded collection of writings about Hawai'i's ethnic groups, this was reissued in 1996 through the efforts of Professor Peter Manicas.

Andrew W. Lind. *An Island Community: Ecological Succession in Hawai'i*. Chicago: University of Chicago Press, 1938.

Milton Murayama. *All I Asking for Is My Body*. Honolulu: University of Hawai'i Press, 1959.

Eleanor C. Nordyke. *The Peopling of Hawai'i*. 2nd Ed. Honolulu: University of Hawai'i Press, 1989.

CONTEMPORARY SOCIAL, POLITICAL, ECONOMIC AFFAIRS

Tom Coffman. *Catch A Wave: A Case Study of Hawai'i's New Politics*. Honolulu: University Press of Hawai'i, 1973.

George Cooper and Gavan Daws. *Land and Power in Hawai'i*. Honolulu: Benchmark Books, 1985. An extraordinarily detailed account of what happened after the Democratic Revolution of 1954, when land reform changed to land development.

Carol S. Dodd. *The Richardson Years: 1966–1982*. Honolulu: University of Hawaii Foundation, 1985. A look at the working of the Hawai'i Supreme Court, which rendered decisions in land cases that many saw as radical but which have shaped subsequent Hawaiian laws relating to the intersection between Hawaiian rights and private property rights.

Kathy E. Ferguson and Phyllis Turnbull. *Oh, Say, Can You See?: The Semiotics of the Military in Hawai'i*. Minneapolis: University of Minnesota Press, 1999.

Noel J. Kent. *Hawai'i: Islands under the Influence*. 2nd Ed. Honolulu: University of Hawai'i Press, 1993.

Anne Feder Lee. *The Hawaii State Constitution—A Reference Guide*. Westport CT: Greenwood Press, 1993. A detailed review and interpretation of how and why the Hawaiian state constitution has changed over four decades. The first section provides a nice review of Hawai'i's historic constitutions.

Ira Rohter. *A Green Hawai'i: Sourcebook for Developmental Alternatives*. Honolulu: Na Kane O Ka Malo Press, 1992.

Randall Roth, Ed. *The Price of Paradise*. 2 vols. Honolulu: Mutual Publishing, 1992–93. These volumes contain short essays addressing different issues thought to trouble island residents. The books were intended to generate greater public dialogue in a political culture the authors thought discouraged open discussion.

Zachary A. Smith and Richard C. Pratt, Eds. *Politics and Public Policy in Hawai'i*. Albany NY: SUNY Press, 1992.

Social Process in Hawai'i. A somewhat regular product of the University of Hawai'i at Manoa Department of Sociology, this publication continues a tradition of doing good social and political analysis of Hawai'i issues.

James C. F. Wang. *Hawai'i State and Local Politics*. Rev. Ed. Hilo HI: Wang Associates, 1998.

Theon Wright. *The Disenchanted Isles: The Story of the Second Revolution in Hawai'i*. New York: Dial Press, 1972.

Notes

CHAPTER ONE

1 See Richard W. Hazlitt and Donald W. Hyndman, *Roadside Geology of Hawai'i* (Missoula MT: Mountain Press, 1996), chapter 1.

2 All of these places that lie to the north of the island of Kaua'i, inhabited only by rich populations of sea mammals and birds, fall within the jurisdiction of the City and County of Honolulu, technically making it the longest county in the nation.

3 *The Atlas of Hawai'i*, 2nd ed. (Honolulu: University of Hawai'i at Manoa, 1983).

4 It is popular to claim that the islands of the Hawaiian chain are the most remote on the planet. That is true, but only with some qualifiers. As retired state statistician Robert Schmitt put it: "Hawaii is the most remote, large populous, demographically significant land mass or group of islands in the world." Will Hoover, "All Alobe—All of Us," *Honolulu Advertiser*, November 10, 1997, p. A-1.

5 Richard J. Tobin and Dean Haguchi, "Environmental Quality in America's Tropical Paradise," in Zachary A. Smith and Richard C. Pratt, eds., *Politics and Public Policy in Hawai'i* (Albany NY: SUNY Press, 1992), p. 124.

6 David F. Stannard, *Before the Horror: The Population of Hawai'i on the Eve of Western Contact* (Honolulu: Social Science Research Institute, University of Hawai'i at Manoa, 1989).

7 *State of Hawai'i Data Book 1993–1994* (Honolulu: Department of Business, Economic Development and Tourism, 1994), pp. 18 and 174.

8 Robert Gardiner, "Can We Limit the Size of Our Population?" in Randall Roth, ed., *The Price of Paradise*, vol. 1 (Honolulu: Mutual Publishing, 1992), p. 18.

9 Robert C. Schmitt, "Historical Statistics of Hawai'i," State of Hawai'i, Department of Planning and Research, 1962, p. 15; *State of Hawai'i Data Book 1997*, pp. 105 and 213. See also *State of Hawai'i Data Book 1991–1992*, p. 12. Note that the

figures for 1993 are for stays of one night or longer, while the earlier data are for two days or longer.

10 *State of Hawai'i Data Book 1997*, p. 17. See also Richard Kosaki, "Hawai'i," in Leroy Hardy, Allen Heslop, and Stuart Andersen, eds., *Reapportionment Politics* (Beverly Hills: Sage, 1981), p. 87.

11 *State of Hawai'i Data Book 1997*, p. 22.

12 *State of Hawai'i Data Book 1993–1994*, pp. 338 and 339. Susan Hooper, "Gap Narrows Between Mainland, Hawaii Prices," *Honolulu Advertiser*, November 1, 1997, p. A-1. See also "Scanning Hawai'i: Forces for Change in the 1990s," Hawai'i Community Services Council, 1993, p. 33.

13 *State of Hawai'i Data Book 1997*, p. 362

14 *State of Hawai'i Data Book 1997*, p. 120; Shannon Tangonan, "Isle Property Crime Up," *Honolulu Advertiser*, December 4, 1994, p. A-3; Rod Ohira, "Hawaii's Crime Rate Continuing to Decline," *Honolulu Star-Bulletin*, September 26, 1997, pp. A-1(14).

15 *State of Hawai'i Data Book 1997*, pp. 37–39.

16 "1995 Market Facts, All about Business in Hawai'i," *Pacific Business News*, p. 5; "Cost Makes Isle Teachers Lowest Paid," *Honolulu Advertiser*, November 26, 1995, p. A-32. Karen Peterson, "Students Feel Safer in Hawaii," *Honolulu Advertiser*, October 14, 1998, p. A 1(7). On school violence, see Deane Neubauer, et. al., *Ke Ala Hoku Issues Paper* (Honolulu: Hawai'i Community Services Council, 1996), p. 17.

17 *State of Hawai'i Data Book 1997*, p. 94. The national average for private school attendance is about 11 percent. John P. Dolly, "Why Are the Test Scores of Public School Children So Low," in Roth, *The Price of Paradise*, 1:211–17.

18 "Scanning Hawai'i," p. 12; *State of Hawai'i Data Book* 1997, p. 47.

19 For an analysis of the impact of centralization on policy in the field of education, see Maenette K. P. Bentham and Ronald H. Heck, "Political Culture and Policy in a State-Controlled Educational System: The Case of Educational Politics in Hawai'i," *Educational Administration Quarterly* 30, no. 4, (November 1994): pp. 419–50.

20 "Sourcebook 1997," *Governing*, 8, no. 5 (February 1995): p. 34.

21 "Sourcebook 1997," p. 30; see also "A Comparative Review of Hawai'i's Fiscal System, 1965–1981," Working Paper No. 2 (Honolulu: Tax Review Commission of Hawai'i, February 1984).

22 *State of Hawai'i Data Book 1997*, p. 242.

23 "Ranking the 50 States," *Governing* 8, no. 5 (February 1995): p. 33.

24 "1995 Market Facts, All about Business in Hawaii," *Pacific Business News*, p. 5;

Advisory Commission on Intergovernmental Relations, "Significant Features of Fiscal Federalism, Vol. 2," (Washington DC: September 1993), pp. 196–99. It is important to remember these figures are contextual and comparisons between states can be misleading.

25 Marc L. Schulhof, "Taxing Geography," *Kiplinger's Personal Finance Magazine*, October 1998. See also Richard S. Miller, "Hawai'i Isn't Tax Hell and Should Publicize It" (letter to the editor), *Honolulu Star-Bulletin*, September 30, 1998, p. A 12.

26 For the case that Hawai'i taxes are too low, see Jerome G. Manis, "Hawai'i Taxes Are Too Low," *Honolulu Weekly*, January 21–27, 1998, p. 3.

27 State Department of Budget and Finance.

28 State of Hawai'i, Department of Human Resource Development. This does not include casual hires. The total number employed full-time by state government is calculated in different ways and there are disagreements on the correct figure. Other counts are both lower and higher. David Waite, "Size of the State Work Force Remains a Mystery," *Honolulu Advertiser*, June 18, 1995, pp. A-1(2). See also *State of Hawai'i Data Book 1997*, pp. 284 and 286.

29 "The Changing Workforce."

30 "The Changing Workforce."

31 *State of Hawai'i Data Book 1997*, pp. 183 and 185.

32 *State of Hawai'i Data Book 1993–1994*, pp. 191 and 283. These figures are estimates.

33 James Mak, University of Hawai'i at Manoa, Department of Economics, Personal interview, September 19, 1995. Estimates vary. Some cite higher percentages. C.f. James Mak, "Tourism and Hawai'i's Economic Development," (paper presented at Japan-Hawai'i Resort Development Workshop, Honolulu, October 21–22, 1991), p. 1. In addition, if resident tourism is included these figures are a few percent higher. For one slightly lower, see "Hawaii's Economy," *Economic Report*, vol. 45 (Honolulu: Bank of Hawaii, April 1996), p. 6.

34 Officially there are five counties in the state, but one of these, Kalawao, is an administrative device through which the Department of Health runs Hansen's Disease Colony at Kalaupapa on Moloka'i.

35 Noel J. Kent, *Hawai'i: Islands under the Influence*, 2nd ed. (Honolulu: University of Hawai'i Press, 1993), p. 187. Statement made by writers of a Hawai'i state plan in 1977.

36 For the argument that intercollegiate sports "sends [a] message that Hawaii is equal," see Jim Donovan, "Should UH Stop Trying Be [*sic*] a Big-sports Powerhouse?" *Honolulu Advertiser*, August 30, 1998, pp. B-1(4).

37 For an interesting review of historic and contemporary images of Hawai'i as paradise, see Paul F. Hooper, *Elusive Destiny: The International Movement in Modern Hawaii* (Honolulu: University of Hawai'i Press, 1980), chapter 2.

38 Elvi Whittaker, *The Mainland Haole: The White Experience in Hawaii* (New
York: Columbia University Press, 1986), p. 19.

39 Whittaker, *Mainland Haole*, p. 19.

40 Francine du Plessix Gray, *Hawai'i: The Sugar Coated Fortress* (New York: Ran-
dom Press, 1973), p. 121.

41 Whittaker, *Mainland Haole*, p. 45.

CHAPTER TWO

1 For a debate over interpretations of the history of Hawaiians, see Robert M. Rees,
"The Fight for Hawaiian History," and David Stannard, "The Fight for Hawaiian History, Part II," in the April and August 1996 issues of *Honolulu Magazine*.

2 Whittaker, *The Mainland Haole*.

3 Marion Kelly, *Demography of the Hawaiian Islands* (Honolulu: Bernice P.
Bishop Museum, Bulletin 233), p. 290.

4 Robert H. Stauffer, "Holy Quest, the Puritan Americanization of Hawai'i,"
M.A. thesis, University of Hawai'i at Manoa, August, 1980, p. 69; Marshall
Sahlins, *Historical Ethnography* (Chicago: University of Chicago Press, 1992,
pp. 29–30.

5 Stannard, *Before the Horror*. Population rise before contact is controversial.
Some scholars suggest population peaked centuries before Cook's arrival, shrinking due to climatic change, pressures on resources, and perhaps disease introduced by earlier visits from Japanese or Spanish.

6 cf. Gananath Obeyesekerer, *The Apotheosis of Captain Cook: European Myth-
making in the Pacific* (Princeton: Princeton University Press, 1992); Marshall
Sahlins, *How Natives Think* (Chicago: University of Chicago Press, 1995).
Obeyesekerer argues against Hawaiians initially mistaking Cook for the god
Lono. To Sahlins, suggesting Hawaiians would not have seen Cook as *akua* is a
reverse ethnocentrism that imposes valued Western thinking where it is not
needed to justify the ways of an indigenous culture.

7 Dorothy Ochiai Hazama and Jane Okamoto Kamejii, *Okage Sama De: The Japanese in Hawai'i, 1885–1985* (Honolulu: Bess Press, 1986).

8 Gray, *Hawai'i: The Sugar Coated Fortress*, p. 30.

9 Patricia Nelson Limerick, *The Legacy of Conquest: The Unbroken Past of the
American West* (New York: W.W. Norton, 1987), p. 217.

10 Succession in the Hawaiian Kingdom was from the monarch to the son or daugh-

ter of a designated marriage. In the absence of children, a blood relative could be named to inherit the crown.

11 Ralph S. Kuykendall, *The Hawaiian Kingdom*, 3 vols. (Honolulu: University of Hawai'i Press, 1938–67), 1:65.

12 Theodore Morgan, *Hawai'i: A Century of Economic Change, 1776–1876* (Cambridge: Harvard University Press, 1948), pp. 124–25. Linnekin's study, among others, rejects the conclusion that Hawaiians were unwilling to work hard on a sustained basis. The issue was the terms and conditions of work, not Hawaiian character. See Linnekin, *Sacred Cows*, p. 218.

13 Andrew W. Lind, *An Island Community: Ecological Succession in Hawai'i* (Chicago: University of Chicago Press, 1938), p. 55.

14 Lind, *An Island Community*, pp. 147–49.

15 Kuykendall, *The Hawaiian Kingdom*, 1:179.

16 Lind, *An Island Community*, p. 55.

17 Lind, *An Island Community*, p. 58.

18 Kuykendall, *The Hawaiian Kingdom*, 1:170.

19 Stannard, *Before the Horror*, pp. 45–46. See also Eleanor C. Nordyke, *The Peopling of Hawai'i*, 2nd ed. (Honolulu: University of Hawai'i Press, 1989), chapter 11.

20 Kuykendall, *The Hawaiian Kingdom*, 1:156–57.

21 Lilikala Kame'ekeihwa, *Native Land and Foreign Desires* (Honolulu: Bishop Museum Press, 1992), p. 197.

22 Kame'ekeihwa, *Native Land*, p. 197.

23 Kehaulani K. Kealoha-Scullion, "The Hawaiian Journey: Out of the Care of Identity, Images of the Hawaiian and Other," Ph.D. dissertation, University of Hawai'i at Manoa, December 1995.

24 Kame'ekeihwa, *Native Land*, p. 207.

25 For a detailed study of these changing relationships and their impact on the morale of *maka'ainana* see Marshall Sahlins, *Anahulu: The Anthropology of History in the Kingdom of Hawai'i*, vol. 1, *Historical Ethnography* (Chicago: University of Chicao Press, 1992); Kealoha-Scullion, "The Hawaiian Journey."

26 Sumner La Croix and James Roumasset, "The Evolution of Private Property in Nineteenth Century Hawai'i," University of Hawai'i at Manoa, Department of Economics, October 1988; Marion Kelly, "Changes in Land Tenure in Hawai'i, 1778–1850," M.A. thesis, University of Hawai'i at Manoa, June 1956, p. 138.

27 Kuykendall, *The Hawaiian Kingdom*, 1:216.

28 Davianna McGregor-Alegado, *Roots of Hawaiian Resistance*, M.A. thesis, University of Hawai'i at Manoa, 1979, p. 8.

29 Kame'ekeihwa, *Native Land and Foreign Desires*, pp. 295–98.

30 Linnekin, *Sacred Cows*, p. 204.

31 Stauffer, "Holy Quest," p. 33. In 1865 legislation was passed to make crown lands inalienable. Both King Kauikeaouli and King Alexander Liholiho had begun to sell them off to deal with their cash shortages. After 1865 these lands came under a Board of Commissioners of Crown Lands.

32 Kuykendall, *The Hawaiian Kingdom*, 1:292.

33 Kuykendall, *The Hawaiian Kingdom*, 1:293.

34 Stauffer, "Holy Quest," p. 38.

35 Theon Wright, *The Disenchanted Isle: The Story of the Second Revolution in Hawai'i* (New York: Dial Press, 1972), p. viii. See also Morgan, *Hawai'i: A Century of Economic Change, 1776–1876*, pp. 136–39.

36 Lawrence H. Fuchs, *Hawai'i Pono: A Social History* (Harcourt, Brace & World, 1961), p. 16.

37 Andrew W. Lind, "The Immigration of South Sea Islanders," *Social Process in Hawai'i* 29 (1982): p. 46.

38 Kuykendall, *The Hawaiian Kingdom*, 2:181.

39 The United States government had passed a Chinese Exclusion Act in 1882.

40 Edwin G. Burrows, *Hawaiian Americans: An Account of the Mingling of Japanese, Chinese, Polynesian and American Cultures* (New Haven: Yale University Press, 1947).

41 Dennis Ogawa and Glen Grant, *To a Land Called Tengoku* (Honolulu: Mutual Publishing, 1985), p. 7; Fuchs, *Hawai'i Pono*, p. 107.

42 Kuykendall, *The Hawaiian Kingdom*, 2:168.

43 Fuchs, *Hawai'i Pono*, p. 29. Universal suffrage already had been restricted in the constitution of 1864 during the reign of Kamehameha V.

44 Schmitt, "Historical Statistics of Hawai'i," p. 8.

45 Wright, *The Disenchanted Isles*, pp. 12–13.

46 Fuchs, *Hawai'i Pono*, p. 33.

47 Roger Bell, *Last among Equals* (Honolulu: University of Hawai'i Press, 1984), p. 35; Kent, *Hawai'i: Islands under the Influence*, p. 57.

48 Kent, *Hawai'i: Islands under the Influence*, pp. 60–61; Bell, *Last among Equals*, p. 24.

49 Fuchs, *Hawai'i Pono*, prologue.

50 Gavan Daws, *Shoal of Time: A History of the Hawaiian Islands* (Toronto: The Macmillan Co., 1968), p. 312.

51 Limerick, *The Legacy of Conquest*, p. 114.

52 Fuchs, *Hawai'i Pono*, p. 251.

53 Gray, *Hawai'i: The Sugar Coated Fortress*, p. 75.

54 Kent, *Hawai'i: Islands under the Influence*, p. 80.

55 Kent, *Hawai'i: Islands under the Influence*, p. 73. Native Hawaiians earlier had been deprived of voting rights under the constitution of 1864, the king arguing that popular participation would be the ruin of the monarchy and the nation.

56 Daws, *Shoal of Time*, p. 294.

57 Fuchs, *Hawai'i Pono*, pp. 157–58.

58 Fuchs, *Hawai'i Pono*, p. 159.

59 Daws, *Shoal of Time*, p. 313.

60 Daws, *Shoal of Time*, p. 297.

61 Daws, *Shoal of Time*, p. 297.

62 Although the original act called for 200,000 acres to be dedicated to Hawaiian homesteading, that agreement was not fulfilled until 1994, when the state turned over an additional 16,000 acres.

63 Fuchs, *Hawai'i Pono*, p. 174.

64 Fuchs, *Hawai'i Pono*, p. 258.

65 Fuchs, *Hawai'i Pono*, p. 259.

66 Burrows, *Hawaiian Americans*, p. 27.

67 Fuchs, *Hawai'i Pono*, pp. 207–12. For a critical analysis of the shifting relations between those who worked on the plantations and their owners or managers, see Edward D. Beechert, *Working in Hawai'i—A Labor History* (Honolulu: University of Hawaii Press, 1985).

68 Limerick, *The Legacy of Conquest*, p. 117.

69 Kuykendall, *The Hawaiian Kingdom*, 2:147.

70 Gray, *Hawai'i: The Sugar Coated Fortress*, p. 66. See also, Fuchs, *Hawai'i Pono*, p. 55, for more detailed comparisons.

71 Fuchs, *Hawai'i Pono*, p. 116.

72 Andrew W. Lind, "Immigration to Hawai'i," *Social Process in Hawai'i* 29 (1982), pp. 9–20. See also Nordyke, *The Peopling of Hawai'i*.

73 Nordyke, *The Peopling of Hawai'i*, p. 194.

74 Nordyke, *The Peopling of Hawai'i*, p. 188.

75 Andrew W. Lind, "Racial Block Voting in Hawai'i," *Social Process in Hawai'i* 21 (1957): p. 16.

76 Daws, *Shoal of Time*, p. 316.

77 Fuchs, *Hawai'i Pono*, p. 357.

78 Gray, *Hawai'i: The Sugar Coated Fortress*, p. 81.

79 Fuchs, *Hawai'i Pono*, p. 54.

80 Fuchs, *Hawai'i Pono*, p. 130.

81 Lind, "Immigration to Hawai'i," p. 17.

82 Wright, The *Disenchanted Isles*, p. 175.

83 The eulogy was written by Robert Fukuda for Edward Nakamura. Both were

prominent figures in Hawai'i's postwar public and political life. Diane Yukihiro Chang, "Eulogizing the Late, Great Ed Nakamura," *Honolulu Star-Bulletin*, October 3, 1977, A-18.

84 Wright, *The Disenchanted Isles*.

CHAPTER THREE

1 Cindy Keiko Kobayashi MacKey, "Out of Rebellion: The Politics of Identity and the Japanese in Hawai'i," Ph.D. dissertation, University of Hawai'i, May 1995, p. 37.

2 Gray, *Hawaii: The Sugar Coated Fortress*, p. 84. For more detailed information see Fuchs, *Hawaii Pono*, pp. 412–13. See also Bell, *Last among Equals*, for a review of the statehood process.

3 Wright, *The Disenchanted Isle*, chapter 16.

4 Tom Coffman, *Catch a Wave: A Case Study of Hawaii's New Politics* (Honolulu: University Press of Hawai'i, 1973), pp. 50–51.

5 Carrie Takenaka, "A Perspective on Hawaiians," Hawai'i Community Foundation, 1995, p. 2; Michael Kioni Dudley and Keoni Kealoha Agard, *A Call for Hawaiian Sovereignty* (Honolulu: Malo Press, 1991).

6 This and the demographic information which follows can be found in Takenaka, "A Perspective on Hawaiians," pp. 2–6; *State of Hawai'i Data Book 1993–1994*, pp. 38 and 40; and Dudley and Agard, *A Call for Hawaiian Sovereignty*.

7 Takenaka, "A Perspective on Hawaiians," p. 7.

8 A. Didrick Castberg, "Crime and Justice in Hawai'i," in Zachary A. Smith and Richard C. Pratt, eds., *Politics and Public Policy in Hawai'i* (Albany NY: SUNY Press, 1992), p. 210.

9 Takenaka, "A Perspective on Hawaiians," p. 20.

10 Mele A. Look and Kathryn Braun, "A Mortality Study of the Hawaiian People, 1910–1990" (Honolulu: The Queens Health System, 1995). See also Walter Wright, "Hawaiians Rank No. 2 Nationally in Cancer Death Rate," *Honolulu Advertiser*, May 2, 1996, pp. A(2).

11 There are many interesting interpretations of traditional Hawaiian culture. See, for example, Michael Kioni Dudley, *Man, Gods and Nature* (Honolulu: Na Kane O Ka Mal Press, 1990); E. S. C. Handy and M. K. Pukui, *The Polynesian Family System in Ka'u, Hawai'i* (Tokyo: Charles E. Tuttle, 1972); Kelly, *Demography of the Hawaiian Islands*; Alan Howard, *Ain't No Big Thing: Coping Strategies in a Hawaiian American Community* (Honolulu: University of Hawai'i Press, 1974); and Kame'ekeihiwa, *Native Land and Foreign Desires*.

12 For interpretations of how Hawaiians adapted to the growing power of others

groups, see Howard, *Ain't No Big Thing*; Edwin G. Burrows, *Hawaiian Americans: An Account of the Mingling of Japanese, Chinese, Polynesian and American Cultures* (New Haven: Yale University Press, 1947); Fuchs, *Hawai'i Pono*, pp. 81–83.

13 For summaries of this history, see George S. Kanahele, "The New Hawaiians," *Social Process in Hawai'i* 29 (1982): pp. 21–31; Luciano Minerbi, "Native Hawaiian Struggles and Events: A Partial List, 1973–1993," *Social Process in Hawai'i* 12, no. 35 (1994): pp. 1–14.

14 Fuchs, *Hawaii Pono*, pp. 87–92, 104.

15 Fuchs, *Hawaii Pono*, pp. 87–92; Gray, *Hawaii: The Sugar Coated Fortress*, p. 66.

16 Fuchs, *Hawaii Pono*, p. 91.

17 Wen-Shing Tsang and Walter Char, "The Chinese of Hawaii," in Tsang, McDermott, and Maretzki, eds., *People and Cultures in Hawaii*, University of Hawai'i at Manoa, Department of Psychiatry, School of Medicine, 1974, p. 25.

18 Fuchs, *Hawaii Pono*, p. 86.

19 Lind, *Hawaii's People*, p. 100.

20 Miriam Sharma, "Labor Migration and Class Formation Among Filipinos in Hawaii, 1906–1946," in *Labor Immigration under Capitalism: Asian Workers in the United States Before World War II* (Berkeley: University of California Press, 1984), p. 603.

21 Danilo F. Ponce, "The Filipinos of Hawaii," in Tsang, McDermott, and Maretzki, eds., *People and Cultures in Hawaii*, p. 602.

22 Sharma, "Labor Migration and Class Formation among Filipinos in Hawaii," pp. 585–586.

23 Bienvenido D. Junasa, "Filipino Experience in Hawaii," *Social Process in Hawai'i* 29 (1982): pp. 97, 104.

24 Gray, *Hawaii: The Sugar Coated Fortress*, p. 73.

25 Ponce, "The Filipinos of Hawaii," pp. 36–37.

26 Gray, *Hawaii: The Sugar Coated Fortress*, p. 73.

27 Genevieve Correa and Edgar C. Knowton Jr., "The Portuguese in Hawaii," *Social Process in Hawai'i* 29 (1982): pp. 56–59.

28 Fuchs, *Hawaii Pono*, pp. 56–59.

29 Wright, *The Disenchanted Isle*, p. 61.

30 The lower figure is from Edward Beechert, "Labor," in Michael Haas, ed., *Multicultural Hawai'i—The Fabric of a Multiethnic Society* (New York: Garland Publishing, 1998), p. 170. The 90,000 figure is from James Okahata, *A History of the Japanese in Hawaii* (Honolulu: The United Japanese Society of Hawaii, 1971), pp. 78–79.

31 Fuchs, *Hawaii Pono*, chapter 4; David Kinzie and Edward Furukawa, "The Japanese of Hawai'i," in Tsang, McDermott, and Maretzki, eds., *People and Cultures in Hawaii*, p. 57. MacKey argues that the story of the unity of Japanese cultural roots is overstated. MacKey, *Out of Rebellion*, pp. 54–57.

32 For a moving depiction of traditional and transitional immigrant Japanese cultural and intergenerational struggles over values and conduct, see Milton Murayama, *All I Asking for Is My Body* (Honolulu: University of Hawai'i Press, 1959).

33 Fuchs, *Hawaii Pono*, p. 116. See also Ronald Takuki, *Pau Hana: Plantation Life and Labor in Hawaii, 1835–1920* (Honolulu: University of Hawai'i Press, 1983).

34 See MacKey, *Out of Rebellion*, pp. 70–74.

35 Eileen H. Tamura, *Americanization, Acculturation, and Ethnic Identity: The Nisei Generation in Hawaii* (Chicago: University of Illinois Press, 1994), p. 237.

36 Burrows, *Hawaiian Americans*, pp. 63–64.

37 Yasama Kuroda, "Public Opinion and Cultural Values," in Michael Haas, ed., *Multicultural Hawai'i—The Fabric of a Multiethnic Society* (New York: Garland Publishing, 1998), pp. 144.

38 This is not to argue that they are absent, but that they are less tightly drawn. For example, on O'ahu Waipahu is predominately Filipino. The Wai'anae coast and Waimanalo are heavily part Hawaiian. There are a number of ethnic communities in rural parts of the Neighbor Islands, such as the Hawaiian village of Miloli'i on the Big Island and the largely Filipino plantation town of Hanapepe on Kaua'i.

39 Andrew W. Lind, "Race and Ethnic Relations: An Overview," *Social Process in Hawai'i* 29 (1982): p. 138.

40 Bernhard L. Hormann, "The Mixing Process," *Social Process in Hawai'i* 29 (1982): p. 119.

41 Lind, "Race and Ethnic Relations," p. 149. The 1992 figure is taken from the Hawaii Health Surveillance Program, Hawaii State Department of Health.

42 Lind, "Race and Ethnic Relations," pp. 138–39.

43 Wayne S. Wooden, *What Price Paradise: Changing Social Patterns in Hawaii* (Washington DC: University Press of America, 1981), p. 22. See also Lind, "Race and Ethnic Relations," pp. 130–50.

44 Wright, *The Disenchanted Isle*, p. 255; Lind, *An Island Community*, p. 298; Lind, *Hawaii: Last of the Magic Isles*, p. 100.

45 Lind, "Race and Ethnic Relations," p. 141.

46 Lind, *Hawaii: Last of the Magic Isles*, p. 97.

47 C.f. Noel J. Kent, "The End of the American Age of Abundance: Whither Hawai'i?" *Social Process in Hawai'i* 35 (1994): pp. 179–94.

48 C.f. Robert Stauffer, "Real Politics," *Honolulu Weekly*, October 19, 1994, pp. 4–6.

49 For an example of this orientation in a highly respected history of the islands, see Fuchs, *Hawaii Pono,* p. 449.

50 George Cooper and Gavan Daws, *Land and Power in Hawai'i* (Honolulu: Benchmark Books, 1985).

51 C.f. Eric Yamamoto, "The Significance of Local," *Social Process in Hawai'i* 27 (1979): pp. 101–15.

52 Bernhard L. Hormann, "The Haoles," *Social Process in Hawaii* 29 (1982): p. 121. Sociologists use the concept of secondary socialization to refer to the process that a group goes through in dealing with the dominant society's reaction to it.

53 Jonathan Y. Okamura, "Aloha Kamaka Me Ke Aloha Aina: Local Culture and Society in Hawai'i," *Amerasia Journal* 7, no. 2 (1980): p. 122.

54 Okamura, "Aloha Kamaka Me Ke Aloha Aina," p. 135.

55 Haas and Resurrection, eds., *Politics and Procedure in Contemporary Hawaii,* p. 32; see also Wooden, *What Price Paradise,* chapters 2–4.

56 Haas and Resurrection, *Politics and Procedure in Contemporary Hawaii,* p. 39.

57 The use of moralistic, traditionalistic, and individualistic to interpret political culture is found in Daniel J. Elazar, *American Federalism: A View from the States,* 3rd ed. (New York: Harper and Row, 1984).

58 The Manoa campus of the University of Hawaii provides an interesting example of these conflicting impulses. On one hand, it has been treated as an important public resource to which as many people as possible should have access. On the other hand, much of what happened on the campus has been tightly controlled by those in public office, often for very narrow purposes such as placing members of the in-group in good jobs. See David Yount, *Who Runs the University* (Honolulu: University of Hawai'i Press, 1996).

59 For a review of the relations between these ethnic groups prior to and during the 1954 "Revolution," see Wright, *The Disenchanted Isle.*

60 Fuchs, *Hawaii Pono,* p. 426.

61 See Cooper and Daws, *Land and Power in Hawai'i.*

62 See Cooper and Daws, *Land and Power in Hawai'i,* chapter 3. See also Coffman, *Catch a Wave,* pp. 50–60; G. Kem Lowry, "Evaluating State Land Use Control: Perspectives and Hawaii Case Study," *Urban Law Annual* 18 (1980): pp. 85–125.

63 Cooper and Daws, *Land and Power in Hawai'i,* pp. 6, 8.

64 MacKey, *Out of Rebellion,* p. 201.

65 Tamura, *Americanization, Acculturation, and Ethnic Identity,* p. 14.

66 Coffman, *Catch a Wave,* p. 10.

67 Coffman, *Catch a Wave,* p. 64.

68 "American Democracy in Hawai'i: Finding a Place for Local Culture," *University of Hawai'i Law Review,* 17, no. 2 (fall 1995): pp. 609–16.

69 "American Democracy in Hawai'i," p. 630.

70 Jonathan Y. Okamura, "Why There Are No Asian Americans in Hawai'i: The Continuing Significance of Local Identity," *Social Process in Hawai'i* 35 (1994): pp. 171–73.

71 The interpretations that follow are based on David Hagino, "Palaka Power," unofficial monograph, 1979 (library acquisition date). This document was created to prepare a selected group of individuals to assert their influence at the 1978 Constitutional Convention.

72 Kevin Dayton, "Cayetano's a Changed Leader the Second Time Around," *Honolulu Advertiser*, December 6, 1998, pp. A(20).

73 C.f. Tamura, *Americanization, Acculturation, and Ethnic Identity*.

74 These generalizations, while pointing to important differences in the values and behavior of members of cultural groups, have to be used carefully. For example, the advent of a market society has produced many non-whites who display all the trappings of an individualistic culture in business relations but maintain more traditional relational values in other parts of their lives.

CHAPTER FOUR

1 Bell, *Last among Equals*, p. 33.

2 Kent, *Hawai'i: Islands under the Influence*, p. 89.

3 Lind, *An Island Community*, p. 302.

4 Bell, *Last among Equals*, p. 133.

5 Bell, *Last among Equals*, p. 134.

6 Fuchs, *Hawai'i Pono*, chapter 6.

7 Fuchs, *Hawai'i Pono*, p. 154.

8 *State of Hawai'i Data Book 1997*, p. 280.

9 Edwards, "1994 Federal Tax Burden by State," p. 3. This is eighteenth if the District of Columbia is included.

10 *State of Hawai'i Data Book 1997*, p. 280. *Federal Expenditures by State for Fiscal Year 1994* (Washington DC: Bureau of Census, March 1995), p. 51.

11 *Government in Hawai'i* (Honolulu: Tax Foundation of Hawai'i, 1996), table 12; Department of Budget and Finance, Office of the Director.

12 *State of Hawai'i Data Book 1997*, p. 510. As a sign of the time, in 1994 the 99-year-old Hawai'i Sugar Planters Association changed its name to the Hawai'i Agricultural Research Corporation.

13 C.f. Pete Pichaske, "Price Support for Sugar Seen as 'Scandal,'" *Honolulu Star-Bulletin*, August 15, 1995, pp. A-1(6).

14 *State of Hawai'i Data Book 1997*, pp. 279–80.

15 Ann Markusen, Peter Hall, Scott Campbell, and Sabina Dittuco, *The Rise of the Gunbelt: The Military Re-mapping of Industrial America* (New York: Oxford University Press, 1991).

16 Pete Pichaske, "Spending by Military is a Hawai'i Boom," *Honolulu Advertiser*, July 18, 1995, pp. A-3(8).

17 *State of Hawai'i Data Book 1993–1994*, p. 249.

18 *Honolulu Advertiser*, November 16, 1992, p. A-2. Part of the property held by the Department of Defense consists of ceded lands.

19 *State of Hawai'i Data Book 1995*, p. 459; State Department of Business, Economic Development and Tourism, Resources Center.

20 Will Hoover, "Airport '97—From Lei's to Cops," *Honolulu Advertiser*, October 26, 1997, E-1(4).

21 First Hawaiian Bank, "The Airline Industry and Hawai'i," *Economic Indicators*, January/February 1993, pp. 2–3.

22 Tina Raminez, "Foreign-Born Population Here Keeps Growing," *Honolulu Advertiser*, August 26, 1995, p. A-6.

23 For a critique of the military presence in the islands, see the pamphlet "Re-thinking the Military in Hawai'i," authored by Kathy Ferguson and others and funded by the Office of Women's Research at the University of Hawai'i at Manoa.

24 "Costly, Long Delayed,—But Done," *Honolulu Advertiser*, December 11, 1997, pp. A-1(8).

25 Editorial, *Honolulu Advertiser*, July 2, 1994, p. A-9.

26 See James Dooley, "Convicted Drug Dealer Calls Self 'Bait' in Probe of State Officials," *Honolulu Advertiser*, August 28, 1995, p. A-4.

27 Pete Pichaske, "GOP's Congressional Clout Deals Hawai'i Some Hard Hits on Funding," *Honolulu Star-Bulletin*, August 30, 1995, p. A-9.

28 Pete Pichaske, "Spending by Military is a Hawai'i Boom."

29 Jim Specht, "Proponents of Reform Run into Inouye," *Honolulu Advertiser*, July 6, 1993, p. A-5. Inouye told plantation employees at the announcement ceremony on Kauai that "We're concerned about agriculture and we're not going to let you die." Jan TenBruggencate, *Honolulu Advertiser*, April 14, 1998, A-1(2).

30 *State of Hawai'i Data Book 1995*, p. 193.

31 "Ranking the 50 States," pp. 32–33; "State Yearbook 1993," *Governing* 6 (July 1993): p. 43. Data vary for years 1990 through 1994.

32 In 1997 Nevada dropped out of the consortium, but Alaska and Guam agreed to join.

33 Graves and Zdanovich, "An Initial Case Study," p. 3.

34 *Foreign Investment in Hawai'i Interim Report II*, State of Hawai'i, Office of State Planning, May 1991, p. 8.

35 Bank of Hawai'i, "Another Look at Japanese Investment in Hawai'i," *Business Trends*, January/February 1991, p. 1.

36 Kenneth Leventhal, *1993 Japanese Investment in U.S. Real Estate* (Los Angeles: Kenneth Leventhal and Co., 1994).

37 Bank of Hawai'i, "Another Look at Japanese Investment in Hawai'i," p. 2.

38 Graves and Zdanovich, "An Initial Case Study," p. 9.

39 Graves and Zdanovich, "An Initial Case Study."

40 Frank Fasi, "Standing Up to Japan," talk to Harvard Business School Club of Honolulu, December 13, 1989, pp. 6 and 8.

41 Typical of Hawai'i's complex cultural and political life, the former mayor's wife is part Japanese.

42 Kenneth Leventhal, *1993 Japanese Investment in U.S. Real Estate*; Kenneth Leventhal, *1994 Japanese Investment in U.S. Real Estate* (Los Angeles: Kenneth Leventhal and Co., 1995).

43 Kuykendall, *The Hawai'ian Kingdom*, 3:305.

44 Paul F. Hooper, *Elusive Destiny: The International Movement in Modern Hawai'i* (Honolulu: University of Hawai'i Press, 1980), p. 6.

45 Fuchs, *Hawai'i Pono*, p. 27.

46 Kuykendall, *The Hawai'ian Kingdom*, 3:312.

47 Hooper, *Elusive Destiny*, p. 162; Wright, *The Disenchanted Isle*, p. 239.

48 Hooper, *Elusive Destiny*, p. 165. The Office of International Relations was dropped as part of re-organization cut-backs in the Cayetano administration.

49 Hooper, *Elusive Destiny*, p. 171.

50 A. A. Smyser, *Hawai'i as an East-West Bridge* (Honolulu: East-West Center, 1990), p. 58.

51 Smyser, *Hawai'i as an East-West Bridge*, pp. 4–5.

52 Hooper, *Elusive Destiny*, p. 136.

53 See Ben Fenney, *From Sea to Space* (Honolulu: University of Hawai'i Press, 1992) for a review of the cultural and historical significance of these voyages.

54 "Native Hawaiian Federal Funding," *Honolulu Advertiser*, January 17, 1995, p. A-2.

55 This trust is one of two important Native Hawaiian land trusts. The second, the ceded lands trust, is discussed in chapter 11.

56 *Native Hawaiian Data Book '98* (Honolulu: Office of Hawaiian Affairs, 1998), p. 180. The number of people waiting is somewhat unclear because some appear on lists for more than one kind of lease. Total applications, which continue to increase, were about 28,000 at the end of 1995. Since the administration of part-Hawaiian Governor John Waihe'e, more money has gone to the Homelands Department to provide the roads, water, and electricity that makes these lands habitable.

57 Public Law 103–150, 103rd Congress of the United States of America, First Session, approved November 23, 1993.

58 These differing interpretations are seen in the *Congressional Record* statements of two U.S. senators. Slade Gorton, R., Washington: "The logical consequences of this resolution would be independence." Senator Daniel Inouye, D., Hawai'i: "To suggest that this resolution is the first step toward declaring independence for the state of Hawaii is a painful distortion of the intent of the authors." Ann Botticelli, "Sovereignty, the Road Ahead," *Honolulu Advertiser*, November 28, 1995, p. A-2.

59 Mike Gordon, "Hawaiians Need Unity, Akaka Says," *Honolulu Advertiser*, November 22, 1998, p. A-27.

60 For a review of this issue, see Haunani-Kay Trask, "*Kupa'a Aina*: Native Hawaiian Nationalism in Hawai'i," in Zachary A. Smith and Richard C. Pratt, eds., *Politics and Public Policy in Hawai'i* (Albany NY: SUNY Press, 1992), pp. 253–55.

61 Yasmin Anwar, "Hawaii Agency Gets 900 Acres," *Honolulu Advertiser*, September 1, 1998, A-l(2). Stuart M. Benjamin examined the status of Hawaiians from a legal perspective in "Equal Protection and the Special Relationship: The Case of Native Hawaiians," *Yale Law Journal* 106, no. 3 (December 1996): pp. 537–612. He observed that Hawaiians have never been constituted as a group in the same way as "Indian tribes," the crucial difference being that whether one is Hawaiian or not is based upon ethnic and blood quantum, rather than political or tribal considerations.

62 Bundy Bakutis, "Native Fishing Zone Created," *Honolulu Advertiser*, August 10, 1998, B-1(4).

CHAPTER FIVE

1 Carl Brent Swisher, *American Constitutional Development*, 2nd ed. (New York: Houghton Mifflin, 1954), pp. 9–10.

2 Carl J. Friedrich, *Constitutional Government and Democracy: Theory and Practice in Europe and America* (New York: Ginn & Co., 1950), pp. 122–23.

3 Kuykendall, *The Hawaiian Kingdom*, 1:133.

4 Kuykendall, The *Hawaiian Kingdom*, 1:166.

5 Kuykendall, *The Hawaiian Kingdom*, 1:153–54.

6 Kuykendall, *The Hawaiian Kingdom*, 1:160.

7 Kuykendall, *The Hawaiian Kingdom*, 1:168–69.

8 Kuykendall, *The Hawaiian Kingdom*, 1:228.

9 Kuykendall, *The Hawaiian Kingdom*, 1:266.

10 Kuykendall, *The Hawaiian Kingdom*, 2:115.

11 Kuykendall, *The Hawaiian Kingdom*, 1:267.

12 James C. F. Wang, *Hawaii State and Local Politics* (Hilo HI: James C.F. Wang), 1982, p. 9.

13 Kuykendall, *The Hawaiian Kingdom*, 2:119–20.

14 Ralph S. Kuykendall, *Constitutions of the Hawaiian Kingdom*, papers of the Hawaiian Historical Society, no. 21 (Honolulu: Hawaiian Historical Society, 1940), p. 31. On these points, see also Lee, *The Hawaii State Constitution: A Reference Guide* (Westport CT: Greenwood Press, 1993), p. 4.

15 Lee, *The Hawaii State Constitution*, p. 4.

16 Kuykendall, *The Hawaiian Kingdom*, 2:131–32.

17 Kuykendall, *The Hawaiian Kingdom*, 2:133.

18 For example, universal suffrage, rejected by the 1864 constitution, was restored in 1874, just before the death of King Lunalilo.

19 Merze Tate, *The United States and the Hawaiian Kingdom* (New Haven: Yale University Press, 1965), p. 58.

20 Tate, *United States and the Hawaiian Kingdom*, p. 93.

21 Tate, *United States and the Hawaiian Kingdom*, p. 115.

22 Kuykendall, *The Hawaiian Kingdom*, 2:117.

23 Kuykendall, *The Hawaiian Kingdom*, 3:603.

24 Sylvester K. Stevens, *American Expansion in Hawaii: 1842–1898* (New York: Russell and Russell, 1945), p. 271.

25 Fuchs, *Hawaii Pono*, p. 168.

26 Women were not enfranchised to vote in the territory until 1930, when Congress amended the Organic Act for that purpose.

27 Fuchs, *Hawaii Pono*, p. 154

28 Lee, *The Hawaii State Constitution*, p. 7.

29 Lee, *The Hawaii State Constitution*, p. 9.

30 John Kincaid, *Hawaii's State-Local System: Developments in Basic Parameters of Fiscal and Functional Responsibilities* (Washington D.C.: U.S. Advisory Commission on Intergovernmental Relations, 1989), p. 6.

31 Norman Meller, *With an Understanding Heart: Constitution Making in Hawaii* (New York: National Municipal League, 1971), p.5.

32 Taken from Lee, *The Hawaii State Constitution*, p. 10.

33 Much of this interpretation of the 1968 constitutional convention is taken from Meller, *With an Understanding Heart*, and Lee, *The Hawaii State Constitution*, pp. 11–15.

34 Wang, *Hawaiian State and Local Government*, p. 32.

35 Meller, *With an Understanding Heart*, p. 148.

36 The statehood constitution had specified a 60-day session every other year, with a 30-day budget session in-between.

37 Richard Kosaki, "Constitutions and Constitutional Conventions of Hawaii," *The Hawaiian Journal of History* 12 (1978): p. 124.

38 Lee, *The Hawaii State Constitution*, p. 16.

39 The ethnic backgrounds of the 1978 convention are less well studied. These data are based on Anne Feder Lee's estimates.

40 Norman Meller and Richard S. Kosaki, "Hawaii's Constitutional Convention— 1978," *National Civic Review* 69 (1980): p. 251.

41 Lee, *The Hawaii State Constitution*, p. 20.

42 Lee, *The Hawaii State Constitution*, p. 21.

43 Robbie Dingman, "Unions Sue to Block Convention," *Honolulu Advertiser*, November 26, 1996, p. A-2.

44 Source of these data is Lee, *The Hawaii State Constitution*, p. 20, and for more recent figures, the Legislative Reference Bureau.

45 This issue, which has generated so much heat, is more complex than most people who have an opinion on it are willing to admit. For example, under existing Hawai'ian law it is permissible for an opposite-sex couple to marry, even though both partners are homosexual.

46 Hawaii Revised Statute 572–1 (1994 Supp.)

47 The case was renamed *Baehr v. Miike* when Lawrence Miike replaced John Lewin as director of the Department of Health.

48 H.B. 118, 19th state legislature.

49 Jean Christensen, "Funds Pouring into Same-sex Marriage Fight," *Honolulu Advertiser*, September 10, 1998, p. B-1(4).

CHAPTER SIX

1 James V. Hall, conversation with author, March 1996.

2 Gerry Keir, "Ariyoshi Gets 56% OK, Lawmakers Get Low Grades," *Honolulu Advertiser*, December 22, 1981, p. A-4; Jerry Burris, "Voters Cool on Officials," *Honolulu Advertiser*, May 20, 1978, p. A-1.

3 For research describing and interpreting the anxieties, resentments, and cynicism of American voters, see E. J. Dionne Jr., *Why Americans Hate Politics* (New York: Simon and Schuster, 1991).

4 Mike Yuen, "52% Believe Government Is Dishonest," *Honolulu Star-Bulletin*, August 19, 1998, pp. A-1(8).

5 Peter Rosegg, "Voters: Local Politics Rotten? Yes. How to Fix It? Well. . . ," *Honolulu Advertiser*, August 3, 1994, p. A-1.

6 Rosegg, "Voters: Local Politics Rotten?" p. A-2.

7 Wright, *The Disenchanted Isle*, p. 189.

8 Mary Adamski, "Voter Turnout Was Second Lowest in Hawaii History," *Honolulu Star-Bulletin*, November 5, 1998, p. A-8.

9 *State of Hawai'i Data Book 1993–1994*, p. 217. See also Ronald Brownsteen, "Political Survey Finds 3rd Party Idea is Gaining," *Los Angeles Times*, September 21, 1994, pp. A-1(16).

10 First Hawaiian Bank, "Hawai'i Voter Turnout and the Economy," *Economic Indicators*, September/October 1994, p. 1.

11 Chiwio Hayashi, et al., "The Fourth Attitudinal Survey of Honolulu Residents, 1988," (Tokyo: Institute of Statistical Mathematics, 1988), p. 121.

12 Bill Daly, "Ethnicity and Hawai'i's Voters (and related matters)," (Honolulu: Voter Contact Services, October 19, 1990), pp. 8–9.

13 Diane Blair, *Arkansas Politics and Government* (Lincoln: University of Nebraska Press, 1988), p. 98.

14 Robert M. Rees, "A Consensus of Cronies," *Honolulu Weekly*, September 13, 1995, p. 5.

15 Wang, *Hawai'i State and Local Politics*, p. 160.

16 Wang, *Hawai'i State and Local Politics*, p. 163.

17 Kuykendall, *The Hawai'ian Kingdom*, vol. 3.

18 Fuchs, *Hawai'i Pono*, p. 158.

19 C.f. Fuchs, *Hawai'i Pono*, pp. 319–22.

20 For a detailed study of this period, see Paul C. Phillips, "Hawai'i's Democrats, A Study of Factionalism," Ph.D. dissertation, University of Hawai'i at Manoa, 1979; Paul C. Phillips, *Hawai'i's Democrats: Chasing the American Dream* (Washington DC: University Press of America, 1982).

21 Kent, *Hawai'i: Islands under the Influence*.

22 Norman Meller, "Centralization in Hawai'i: Retrospect and Prospect," *American Political Science Review* 52 (March 1958): p. 105.

23 Robert M. Kamins, "The Month the Clock Stopped," University of Hawai'i at Manoa, Legislative Reference Bureau, 1955, p. 19; Daniel W. Tuttle, "Politics in Paradise," University of Hawai'i at Manoa, Department of Political Science, 1955.

24 Craig Gima, "Astrologer Wins GOP's Nine-candidate Race to Challenge Inouye," *Honolulu Star-Bulletin*, October 26, 1998, p. A-14.

25 On this point in relation to the party's liberal faction see Wang, *Hawai'i State and Local Politics*, chapter 4.

26 Ian Lind, "Architects and Engineers Provide Bulk of Democratic Funds," *Hawai'i Monitor* 3, mo. 1 (December 1992): p. 2

27 Mike Yuen, "Heen to Challenge Gill for Party Chief," *Honolulu Star-Bulletin*, April 30, 1998, p. A-3.

28 Lind, *Hawai'i's People*, p. 94.

29 Lind, "Racial Block Voting in Hawai'i," p. 19. John Digman and Daniel Tuttle, "An Analysis of Oahu's 1956 City-County Election," University of Hawai'i at Manoa, Department of Government and Psychological Research Center, April 15, 1959; John Digman, "Ethnic Factors in O'ahu 1954 General Election," *Social Process in Hawai'i* 21 (1957); Wang, *Hawai'i State and Local Politics*; Michael Haas, "Politics," in Michael Haas, ed., *Multicultural Hawai'i—The Fabric of a Multiethnic Society* (New York: Garland Publishing, 1998).

30 Okamura, "Why There Are No Asian Americans in Hawai'i"; Coffman, *Catch a Wave;* Dan Boylan, "Blood Runs Thick: Ethnicity as a Factor in Hawai'i's Politics," in Zachary A. Smith and Richard C. Pratt, eds., *Politics and Policy in Hawai'i* (Albany NY: SUNY Press, 1992); Peter Rosegg, "The—SSShhh—Ethnic Vote Factor," *Honolulu Advertiser*, September 11, 1994.

31 Rosegg, "The—SSShhh—Ethnic Vote Factor," pp. 1(4).

32 Michael Haas, "Comparing Paradigms of Ethnic Politics in the United States: The Case of Hawai'i," *Western Political Quarterly* 40, no. 4 (December 1987).

33 Rosegg, "The—SSShhh—Ethnic Vote Factor," p. 1.

34 Boylan, "Blood Runs Thick," pp. 67–69.

35 The Democrats became more explicit in this accusation in the campaign's hectic last days. Their leaders took to the airways to argue that a cartoon by a popular local humorist that was linked to a Republican web site depicted local people as stupid, thereby revealing Republican prejudices.

36 Kevin Dayton and Ken Kobayashi, "Undecided Voters Key to Election," *Honolulu Advertiser*, November 1, 1998, p. A-1.

37 Boylan, "Blood Runs Thick," pp. 67–69.

38 Ken Kobayashi and William Kresnak, "GOP Rally Shakes Up Democrats," *Honolulu Star-Bulletin*, November 21, 1998, p. A-1; and Kevin Dayton, "Lingle Shows Drawing Power," *Honolulu Advertiser*, September 20, 1998, p. A-8.

39 Chiwio Hayashi, et al., "The Fourth Attitudinal Survey of Honolulu Residents, 1988," pp. 246–47.

40 Chiwio Hayashi, et al., "Toward the Development of Statistical Analysis for the Study of Comparative Cultures," An Attitudinal Study of Honolulu Residents (Honolulu: University Press of Hawai'i, 1980), pp. 38–39.

41 Dionne, *Why Americans Hate Politics*.

42 Ronald Brownsteen, "Political Survey Finds 3rd Party Idea is Gaining," *Los Angeles Times*, September 21, 1994, p. A-1(16).

43 For analysis of the decline of political parties in Hawai'i see Boylan, "Blood Runs Thick," pp. 67–80.

CHAPTER SEVEN

1 Estimate for FY 1999. State Department of Budget and Finance.

2 These categories are suggested by Lester Cingcade, who for many years was chief administrator of the Judiciary under Chief Justice William Richardson.

3 For a detailed study of the influence and changing role of women in Hawaiian society, see Jocelyn Linnekin, *Sacred Cows and Women of Consequence* (Ann Arbor: University of Michigan Press, 1990).

4 For interpretations of the *kapu* system in the context of traditional Hawaiian society, see George Hu'eu Sanford Kanahele, *Kū Kanake Stand Tall: A Search for Hawaiian Values* (Honolulu: University of Hawai'i Press, 1986) and Kame'ekeihiwa, *Native Land and Foreign Desires*, chapter 2.

5 Kanahele, *Kū Kanake Stand Tall*, pp. 44–45.

6 Kame'ekeihiwa, *Native Land and Foreign Desires*, p. 81.

7 Kuykendall, *The Hawaiian Kingdom*, 1:168–69.

8 Kuykendall, *The Hawaiian Kingdom*, 1:169.

9 Kuykendall, *The Hawaiian Kingdom*, 1:268.

10 Wang, *Hawaii State and Local Politics*, p. 464.

11 Wang, *Hawaii State and Local Politics*, p. 469. Total workload for the Supreme Court is made up of primary cases and supplemental proceedings made within those cases.

12 State of Hawai'i, The Judiciary, *Annual Report*, July 1, 1994, to June 30, 1995, p. 2; and July 1, 1996, to June 30, 1997, p. 28.

13 State of Hawai'i, The Judiciary, *Annual Report*, July 1, 1994, to June 30, 1995, p. 3.

14 State of Hawai'i, The Judiciary, *Annual Report*, July 1, 1993, to June 30, 1994, p. 8.

15 State of Hawai'i, The Judiciary, *Annual Report*, July 1, 1996, to June 30, 1997, p. 35.

16 State of Hawai'i, The Judiciary, *Annual Report*, July 1, 1993, to June 30, 1994, p. 15.

17 State of Hawai'i, The Judiciary, *Annual Report*, July 1, 1994, to June 30, 1994, p. 17.

18 State of Hawai'i, The Judiciary, *Annual Report*, July 1, 1996, to June 30, 1997, p. 43.

19 Carol S. Dodd, *The Richardson Years: 1966–1982* (Honolulu: University of Hawai'i Press, 1985), p. 113.

20 Norman R. Luttbeg, *Comparing the States and Communities: Politics, Government, and Policy in the United States* (New York: Harper Collins, 1992), p. 298.

21 Wang, *Hawaii State and Local Government*, p. 487.

22 Dodd, *The Richardson Years*, p. 27.

23 Richard A. Watson and Rondal G. Downing, *The Politics of Bench and Bar: Judi-*

cial Selection under the Missouri Non-Partisan Court Plan (New York: Wiley, 1969).

24 For an excellent review of this problem see Creel Froman, *The Two American Political Systems* (Englewood Cliffs NJ: Prentice-Hall, 1984) See particularly chapters 3 and 5.

25 C.f. Stuart S. Nagel, "Political Party Affiliation and Judges' Decisions," *American Political Science Review* 55 (December 1961): pp. 843–50; and Sheldon Goldman, "Voting Behavior on the U.S. Court of Appeals Revisited," *American Political Science Review* 69 (June 1975): pp. 491–506.

26 *Judicial Review of Legislation in Ten Selected States* (Bloomington: Indiana University, Bureau of Government Research, 1943), as reported in William J. Keefe and Morris S. Ogul, *The American Legislative Process: Congress and the States*, 8th ed. (Englewood Cliffs NJ: Prentice Hall, 1993), p. 444.

27 Dodd, *The Richardson Years*, p. 54.

28 Dodd, *The Richardson Years*, p. 54.

29 50 Hawaii 298, 440 P. 2d 95 (1968).

30 *McBryde Sugar Company v. Robinson*, 54 HAW 174 (1973), *Rehearing*, 55 HAW 260, sert. denied, 47 U.S. 976; enforcement enjoined 441 F. Supp. 559 (D. Hawaii 1977).

31 Lee, The *Hawaii State Constitution*, p. 167.

32 Dodd, *The Richardson Years: 1966–1982*, p. 63.

33 Melissa Vickers and Linda Hosek, "City Scores on Leasehold," *Honolulu Star-Bulletin*, February 18, 1994, p. A1.

34 Clinton Ashford and Daniel Case, "No Order in Stare Court," *Honolulu Advertiser*, August 4, 1996, p. B-3.

35 "Did 'Richardson Court' Rewrite Hawaii Law? Former Chief Justice Says No," *Honolulu Advertiser*, September 1, 1996, p. A-4.

36 Williamson B. C. Chang, "Reversals of Fortune: The Hawaii Supreme Court, the Memorandum Opinion, and the Realignment of Political Power in Post-statehood Hawai'i," *University of Hawai'i Law Review* 14, no. 2 (summer 1992), pp. 17–56.

37 David Kimo Frankel, "The Hawai'i Supreme Court: An Overview," *University of Hawai'i Law Review* 14, no. 1 (summer 1992), pp. 5–16.

38 C.f. "The New Gay Struggle," *Time*, October 26, 1998, pp. 31–44.

39 Danielle K. Hart, "Same-Sex Marriage Revisited: Taking a Critical Look at *Baehr v. Lewin*," *George Mason Civil Rights Law Journal*, forthcoming 1999.

40 Hart, "Same-Sex Marriage Revisited," p. 8.

41 Hart, "Same-Sex Marriage Revisited," p. 36.

42 Hart, "Same-Sex Marriage Revisited," p. 137.

43 See Brian Sullam, "Bishop Estate—the Misused Trust," *Hawaii Observer*, special report, 1976, pp. 12–13.

44 "Broken Trust," written by Gladys Brandt, Walter Heen, Samuel King, Monsignor Charles Kekumano, and Randall Roth, first appeared in the *Honolulu Star-Bulletin* on August 9, 1997.

45 The only other trust now affected by the decision is that of King William Charles Lunalilo.

CHAPTER EIGHT

1 State of Hawai'i, Department of Budget and Finance.

2 Deane E. Neubauer, "Arts and Science after Statehood," in Robert Kamins and Robert Potter, eds., *Malama Malama: A History of the University of Hawai'i* (Honolulu: University of Hawai'i Press, 1998).

3 Because of rules in the civil service and collective bargaining systems, few employees actually left state employment.

4 Personal communication.

5 Deane E. Neubauer, "Hawai'i Budgeting 1995: An Early Look," Roundtable on Budgetary Processes in the Thirteen Western States, Western Political Science Association Annual Meeting, Portland, Oregon, March 16–18, 1995.

6 Stone, *Policy Paradox and Political Reason*.

7 Wang, *Hawaii State and Local Politics*, p. 366.

8 Office of the Lieutenant Governor, November 1998.

9 Wang, *Hawaii State and Local Politics*, p. 415.

10 Mike Yuen, "Downsizing Government Left in Hands of Administration," *Honolulu Star-Bulletin*, April 24, 1996, p. A-3.

11 Perez, "It's My Job," p. A-9.

12 See Joel M. Douglas, "State Civil Service and Collective Bargaining Systems in Conflict," in *Contemporary Public Administration*, David H. Rosenbloom et. al., eds. (New York: McGraw-Hill, 1994), pp. 262–80.

13 Chris Grandy, "Taming the Growth of State Government," unpublished memorandum, Research and Economic Analysis Division, Department of Business, Economic Development, and Tourism, fall 1998.

14 This analysis is taken from Chris Grandy, ". . . and Maybe Government Didn't Grow Much, After All," *Honolulu Advertiser*, September 29, 1994, p. A-11. Grandy was on the faculty of the Department of Economics at the University of Hawai'i–Manoa when this was written.

15 Grandy, "Taming the Growth of State Government."

16 William Kresnak, "Gov. Cayetano Charts Second Term," *Honolulu Advertiser*, November 5, 1998, p. A-1(6).

CHAPTER NINE

1 Coffman, *Catch a Wave*, p. 85.

2 National Conference of State Legislatures, cited in *Governing*, February 1998, p. 40. Percentage figure is from State Department of Budget and Finance.

3 Lee, *The Hawaii State Constitution*, p 89.

4 Cited in William Kresnak, "Action on Term Limits Unlikely," *Honolulu Advertiser*, December 28, 1997, p. A-19.

5 Legislative Reference Bureau, *Guide to Government in Hawaii*, 9th ed. (Honolulu: State of Hawaii, 1989), p. 2.

6 Much of the material for this section is taken from V. O. Key Jr., *Southern Politics in State and Nation* (New York: Knopf, 1949). Key, in describing one-party Southern states, wrote, "The South really has no parties" (p. 229).

7 C.f. Robert A. Dahl, *A Preface to Democratic Theory* (Chicago: University of Chicago Press, 1956.)

8 Cooper and Daws, *Land and Power in Hawai'i*, p. 444.

9 The percentages, provided by the National Conference of State Legislatures, are as follows: attorneys 16 percent, business owners 14 percent, educators 8 percent, full-time Legislators 11 percent, homemakers 2 percent, businesspersons 6 percent, realtors 4 percent. *State Legislators Occupations: A Decade of Change* (Denver: National Conference of State Legislatures, 1986), p. 7. Cited in Luttbeg, *Comparing the States and Communities*, p. 227.

10 James C. F. Wang, *Hawai'i State and Local Politics*, rev. ed. (Hilo HI: Wang Associates, 1998), pp. 127–28.

11 Luttbeg, *Comparing the States and Communities*, p. 230.

12 These observations are taken from Shon's manuscript, currently under review for publication. It is tentatively titled "Inside the Capitol—Lessons in Legislative Democracy."

13 Larry R. Hill, "Institutionalizing a Bureaucratic Monitoring Mechanism: The First Thirty Years of Hawaii's Ombudsman," Paper prepared for delivery at the 1998 Annual Meeting of the American Political Science Association. The data provided here are taken from his study.

14 369 U.S. 186 (1962).

15 377 U.S. 533 (1964).

16 The second reapportionment case in 1964 was *Wesberry v. Sanders*, 376 U.S. 1 (1964), wherein the court found that congressional districts within a state had to be apportioned on the basis of population as well.

17 This is taken from Legislative Reference Bureau, *Guide to Government in Hawaii*, 9th ed., p. 3.

18 James C. F. Wang, *Hawai'i State and Local Politics*, p. 136.

19 Carol S. Greenwald, *Group Power* (New York: Praeger, 1977), p. 70.

20 Greenwald, *Group Power*, p. 70.

21 *State of Hawai'i Data Book 1997*, pp. 351; Union Membership and Earnings Data Book, 1997 ed.

22 *State of Hawai'i Data Book 1997*, pp. 321.

23 Wang, *Hawai'i State and Local Politics*, p. 129.

24 Union Membership and Earnings Data Book, 1997 ed., cited in *Honolulu Star Bulletin*, October 12, 1998, p. A-11.

25 Hawaii Revised Statutes, Section 91–1

26 Angela Miller, "Reports Identify Top Lobbyists," *Honolulu Advertiser*, April 1, 1997, p. B-1(4).

CHAPTER TEN

1 Donald D. Johnson, *The City and County of Honolulu: A Governmental Chronicle* (Honolulu: University of Hawai'i Press, 1991), p. 25.

2 Johnson, *The City and County of Honolulu*, pp. 28–29.

3 Johnson, *The City and County of Honolulu*; Fuchs, *Hawai'i Pono*, p. 160.

4 Joseph Maguire, "A Study of Local Government Processes in the City and County of Honolulu," M.A. thesis, American University, 1965, p. 27.

5 Maguire, "Study of Local Government Processes," p. 31.

6 Maguire, "Study of Local Government Processes," p. 28.

7 Johnson, *The City and County of Honolulu*, p. 36.

8 Johnson, *The City and County of Honolulu*, pp. 44–45.

9 A fifth county, Kalawao, was created for the Hansens disease colony on Moloka'i and administered by the Department of Health.

10 Robert M. C. Littler, *The Governance of Hawai'i* (Palo Alto: Stanford University Press, 1929).

11 Johnson, *The City and County of Honolulu*, p. 392.

12 Fuchs, *Hawai'i Pono*.

13 Littler, *The Governance of Hawai'i*, pp. 74–80.

14 *State of Hawai'i Data Book 1997*, p. 57.

15 *State of Hawai'i Data Book 1997*, pp. 264, 332.

16 Wang, *Hawai'i State and Local Politics*, pp. 565–67.

17 Wang, *Hawai'i State and Local Politics*, pp. 546–56.

18 Wang, *Hawai'i State and Local Politics*, p. 551.

19 Since a charter amendment was approved in the November 1992 election, all elected offices in the City and County of Honolulu are, officially, non-partisan.

20 Wang, *Hawai'i State and Local Politics*, pp. 575–82.

21 Maguire, "Study of Local Government Processes," p. 102.

22 "State Yearbook 1993," *Governing* 6 (July 1993): pp. 43, 50.

23 Sumner La Croix and Louis Rose, "Government Intervention in Honolulu's Land Market," University of Hawai'i at Manoa, Department of Economics, Working Paper No. 91–17, August 1991, p. 4.

24 In 1978 the state adopted a constitutional amendment requiring the mayor to resign from this office to run for another. Many felt it was specifically aimed at reducing the power and resource base of Mayor Fasi.

25 Johnson, The *City and County of Honolulu*, chapter 11.

26 Wang, *Hawai'i's State and Local Politics*, pp. 654–657.

27 John Kincaid, "Hawai'i's State Local System: Development and Basic Parameters of Fiscal and Functional Responsibilities," in *Intergovernmental Fiscal Relations in Hawai'i* (Honolulu: Tax Review Commission of Hawai'i, November 1989), p. 6.

28 Property taxes as a percent of total revenues ranged from 22.4 for Kaua'i County to 57.6 for Hawai'i County in 1995. Honolulu was 44.2 percent. Tax Foundation of Hawaii, *Government in Hawaii, 1996*, tables 24–27.

29 Tax Foundation of Hawaii, *Government in Hawaii, 1996*, tables 24–27.

30 A. Kam Napler, "City of Debt," *Honolulu Magazine* 31, no. 7 (January 1995), p. 21.

31 "Report of the Tax Review Commission," (Honolulu: State of Hawai'i, December 1, 1989), p. 51.

32 Napler, "City of Debt," pp. 21 and 22.

33 Wang, *Hawai'i State and Local Politics*, p. 631.

34 The picture is somewhat different for Maui County, where the island of Maui has not fared as poorly in the 1990s slump.

35 Y. S. Leong and Robert M. Kamins, "Property Taxation in the 50th State," *National Taxation Journal* 14 (March 1961): pp. 59–60. The tax on personal property shrank until it was eliminated in 1948.

36 Leong and Kamins, "Property Taxation in the 50th State," pp. 59–60.

37 Leong and Kamins, "Property Taxation in the 50th State," p. 611 In 1991 the state's property taxes per capita placed it 35th among the 50 states. Advisory Commission on Intergovernmental Relations, "Significant Features of Fiscal Federalism, Vol. 2," (Washington DC, September 1993), p. 196.

38 Leong and Kamins, "Property Taxation in the 50th State," p. 64.

39 Leong and Kamins, "Property Taxation in the 50th State," p. 64.

40 Wang, *Hawai'i State and Local Politics*, p. 644.

41 Kincaid, "Hawai'i's State Local System, " p. 12.

42 Tax Foundation of Hawaii, *Government in Hawai'i, 1995*, tables 24–27.

43 Gregory G. Y. Pai, "Property Tax Reform in Hawai'i," paper presented at the Annual Conference of the Hawai'i State Association of Counties, June 24, 1988, p. 7.

44 Wang, *Hawai'i State and Local Politics*, p. 650.

45 For a review of this history see Wang, *Hawai'i State and Local Politics*, pp. 650–53.

46 See Kincaid, "Hawai'i's State Local System," p. 14.

47 Kincaid, "Hawai'i's State Local System, " p. 13.

48 Richard Kosaki, "Home Rule in Hawai'i," University of Hawai'i at Manoa, Legislative Reference Bureau, 1954, pp. 29–31

Forty-eight states have county-level governments. Of these, 40 provide the option of adopting home rule charters. Jonathon Walters, "Cry, the Beleaguered County," *Governing* 9, no.4 (August 1996): p. 35.

49 Kosaki, "Home Rule in Hawai'i," p. i.

50 Kosaki, "Home Rule in Hawai'i," pp. 33–40.

51 Kosaki, "Home Rule in Hawai'i"; Maguire, "Study of Local Government Processes," pp. 17–18.

52 Kincaid, "Hawai'i's State Local System," chapter 2.

53 Kincaid, "Hawai'i's State Local System," p. 13.

54 Rodney Funakoshi, "Community Adoption of Innovations: Honolulu Neighborhood Boards," M.A. thesis, University of Hawai'i at Manoa, 1977, p. 13.

55 This material is taken from Richard Pratt, "Saving Ka'u," in *Occasional Papers in Political Science*, University of Hawai'i at Manoa, vol. 3, no. 2, August 1989, pp. 14–22.

CHAPTER ELEVEN

1 Jerry Burris, "Islanders Support Hawaiian Cause," *Honolulu Advertiser*, November 22, 1993, pp. A-1(4).

2 Some people reacted to Waihee's dramatic gesture as an irresponsible, even traitorous, compromise of national sovereignty. Once elected, Cayetano moved away from his pledge not to occupy Washington Place, permitting him to avoid the question of exactly who would receive it.

3 Mark Matsunaga, "Owed Payment for Overthrow," *Honolulu Advertiser*, November 20, 1995, p. A-1(2); Mark Matsunaga, "Sovereignty Views Varies with What's to Be Gained, Cost," *Honolulu Advertiser*, November 25, 1995, pp. A-1(2). This survey was of 400 individuals statewide who, in a telephone interview, self-identified themselves as "Hawaiian."

4 Matsunaga, "Sovereignty Views," pp. A-1(2).

5 For a summary of sovereignty proposals see Dudley and Agard, *A Call for Hawaiian Sovereignty*.

6 From constitutional convention proceedings, as reported in Lee, *The Hawaii State Constitution*, p. 177.

7 State Department of Budget and Finance.

8 For an interpretation of this process, see Robert M Rees, "A Conspicuous Absence," *Honolulu Weekly* 5, no. 46 (November 15, 1995): p. 4.

9 Matsunaga, "Sovereignty Views," pp. A-1(2). The survey asked, "Shall the nation of Hawaiian people elect delegates to propose a Native Hawaiians government?"

10 *Kalipi vs. Hawaiian Trust Co.* (1982);*Pele Defense Fund vs. Paty* (1992); *Public Access Shoreline Hawai'i vs. Hawai'i County Planning Commission and Nansay Inc.* (1995).

11 Janice Otaguro, "Islander of the Year: Mahealani Pai," *Honolulu Magazine* 30, no. 67 (January 1996): p. 34.

12 David White, "Property Rights Now Threatened," *The Honolulu Advertiser*, January 26, 1997, B-5.

13 George S. Kanahele, "The New Hawaiians," *Social Process in Hawai'i* 29 (1982): p. 22.

14 The 20 percent figure derives from Section 5(f) of the Admission Act, which defined five uses for ceded lands. "The betterment of the conditions of Hawaiians" was one of them. The others were improving education, broadening farm and home ownership, making public improvements, and providing lands for public use.

15 The method of calculation is complex and subject to interpretation. For example, if only half of a revenue source sits on ceded lands, should OHA receive the required 20 percent of all its revenues, or one-half of that 20 percent?

16 Greg Barrett, "OHA Seeks Land Settlement," *The Honolulu Advertiser*, January 28, 1997, p. B-1; Alan Matsuoka, "The Ceded Lands Ruling—Will It Break the Bank?" *Honolulu Star-Bulletin*, January 13, 1997, p. A-5.

17 Greg Barrett, "Debate over Sovereignty Looks beyond Islands," *The Honolulu Advertiser*, August 26, 1995, p. A-1 (6).

18 Mark Matsunaga, "Owed Payment for Overthrow," *Honolulu Advertiser*, November 20, 1995, p. A-1(2); Mark Matsunaga, "Hawaiian Nations Mustn't Live Apart, Poll Majority Says," *Honolulu Advertiser*, November 22, 1995, pp. A-1(2).

19 Pat Omandam, "No Consensus on Sovereignty," *Honolulu Star-Bulletin*, August 25, 1995, p. A-8. These results are found in a statewide survey of 821 individuals registered to vote in Office of Hawaiian Affairs elections.

20 This interpretation is taken largely from John Heckathorn, "The Native Hawaiian Nation," *Honolulu Magazine* 23, no. 6 (December 1988): p. 59.

21 The rules have been amended over the years to permit wives, children, and grandchildren who are one-quarter Hawaiian to inherit household lands.

22 One estimate shows that in 1924 individuals with 50 percent or more blood quantum comprised about 90 percent of the population of Hawaiians. By 1964 this had become less than 40 percent, and fifty years from now it is expected to be around 10 percent. Heckathorn, "The Native Hawaiian Nation," pp. 58–59; *State of Hawai'i Data Book 1993–1994*, p. 40.

23 Heckathorn, "The Native Hawaiian Nation," p. 59.

24 Nordyke, *The Peopling of Hawai'i*, p. 42.

25 Matsunaga, "Hawaiian Nations Mustn't Live Apart," pp. A-1(2).

26 Within this mosaic there are, of course, variations in which parts of traditional culture are accepted or rejected, something likely to be associated with whether the person is living an urban or rural lifestyle. This mix is likely to change as the extensive educational projects associated with self-determination continue.

27 Andy Yamaguchi, "Akaka Renews Calls for Isle Oil Reserve," *Honolulu Advertiser*, October 30, 1993, p. A-3; *All about Business in Hawai'i* (Honolulu: Crossroads Press, 1992).

28 First Hawaiian Bank, "Hawai'i: The Most Vulnerable State in the Nation," *Economic Indicators*, September/October 1993. Exports and imports in these figures include the U.S. mainland as well as foreign countries.

29 *All about Business in Hawai'i*.

30 First Hawaiian Bank, "Hawai'i: The Most Vulnerable State in the Nation."

31 Bank of Hawaii, *Business Trends*, January/February 1992. At this time Hawai'i followed Singapore, Hong Kong, and Malaysia. Consistent with Hawai'i's Asia/Pacific compatabilities, 18 of the top 20 export economies in the world are in those regions.

32 C.f. "The Labor Situation in Hawai'i's Visitor Industry" (Honolulu: Department of Labor and Industrial Relations, Tourism Training Council, November 1992); James Mak, "Non-Tourism Jobs for Hotel Rooms," Paper delivered at Pacific Regional Science Association Meeting, Cairns, Australia, July 1991.

33 Kincaid, "Hawai'i's State Local System," p. 20.

34 "The Labor Situation in Hawai'i's Visitor Industry," pp. 22–25.

35 *State of Hawai'i Data Book 1997*, p. 628.

36 James Mak and Marcia Sakai, "Is Foreign Trade Good or Bad for Hawai'i?" in Roth, *The Price of Paradise*, 1:38.

37 Kent, *Hawai'i: Islands under the Influence*.

38 Mak and Sakai, "Is Foreign Trade Good or Bad," pp. 33–39.

39 *State of Hawai'i Data Book 1994*, p. 51.

40 *State of Hawai'i Data Book* (Honolulu: Department of Planning, Economic Development and Tourism, 1996), pg. 35; Regional Projections to 2045, vol. 1, States, July 1995 (Washington: U.S. Bureau of Economic Analysis, July 1995), p.69. Some estimates of Hawai'i's population have a much higher projection, putting those 65 and over at up to 25 percent of the population.

41 Deane Neubauer, et. al., *Ke Ala Hoku Issues Paper* (Honolulu, Hawai'i: Community Services Council, December 1995), p. 5.

42 Takamura, J. and M. Seely, "Beyond Mirrors and Smoke: The Challenge of Longevity and Long-term Care," in B. Grossman and J. Shon, eds., *The Unfinished Health Agenda: Lessons from Hawai'i* (Honolulu: Hawai'i Primary Care Association, 1994)

43 Neubauer, *Ke Ala Hoku Issues Paper*, p. 76. In 1994 Hawai'i was ranked as the fifth healthiest state on a scale measuring 23 factors.

44 Sandra Oshiro, "Residents Being Lost to Mainland," *The Honolulu Advertiser*, March 20, 1997, A-1(2).

45 Susan Hooper, "Hawaii Survey Shows Increased Confidence," *Honolulu Advertiser*, March 7, 1996, p. C-1(3).

46 Walter Miklius, "If Hawai'i is Paradise, Why Do so Many People Leave?" in Roth, *The Price of Paradise*, 1:242, 243.

47 The analysis which follows is taken from First Hawaiian Bank, "Income Distribution in Paradise," *Economic Indicators*, January/February 1991, p. 1. Data are taken from the 1990 Internal Revenue Service publication of tax returns.

48 "Income Distribution in Hawaii," (Honolulu: Department of Business, Economic Development and Tourism, 2nd quarter, 1996).

49 Robbie Dingeman, "State's 63% Tops U.S. Average," *The Honolulu Advertiser*, July 7, 1996, p. A-1.

50 "Homelessness and Hunger in Hawaii" (Honolulu: SMS Research, June 15, 1992), p. 10.

51 Neubauer, *Ke Ala Hoku Issues Paper*, pp. 4, 18, and 58.

52 Data suggest that female-male income disparities have not been as great in Hawai'i as on the Mainland. See Bank of Hawaii, "Women in the Work Force," *Business Trends*, March/April 1992.

53 Coralie Chun Matayoshi, "Do Women in Hawaii Have Equal Access to Jobs?" in Roth, *The Price of Paradise*, 1:205–9.

54 "Few Women Found in Top Public Jobs," *New York Times*, January 3, 1992, p. 1.

55 Neubauer, *Ke Ala Hoku Issues Paper*, pp. 29 and 95.

56 Kirk Smith, "Are We Adequately Protecting Our Environment?" in Roth, *The Price of Paradise*, 259–93.

57 Neubauer, *Ke Ala Hoku Issues Paper*, p. 71.

58 For a review of these issues, see Tobin and Higuchi, "Environmental Quality in America's Tropical Paradise," pp. 113–30.

59 Tobin and Higuchi, "Environmental Quality in America's Tropical Paradise," p. 124.

60 This material is taken from Kevin O'Leary, "Troubled Waters: A History of Water Development on O'ahu," *Honolulu Weekly* 3, no. 6 (February 10, 1993): pp. 4–7.

61 Tobin and Higuchi, "Environmental Quality in America's Tropical Paradise," p. 127; Neubauer, *Ke Ala Hoku Issues Paper*, p. 7.

62 This information is provided by the Hawai'i Community Services Council, the lead organizer of the Hawai'i benchmarking project.

CHAPTER TWELVE

1 A. A. Smyser, *Hawaii's Future in the Pacific Disaster: Backwater or Future State?* (Honolulu: East-West Center, 1988).

2 Robbie Alm, et. al., *Hawai'i 2020* (Honolulu, May 1996)

3 These differences, of course, also reflect their authors, but emergence of the sovereignty movement and statewide discussions of greater local governance suggest it is more than that.

4 The distinction between the social justice agenda and the good-for-business orientation is not absolute but a matter of degree and emphasis. The Burns Democrats approved of about economic growth and did things to promote it. Statehood was one of them. Building the University of Hawai'i was another. The difference in emphasis is, nonetheless, clear and significant.

5 Gary Hooser, "Look to Business, Not Government, for Revitalization," *Honolulu Advertiser*, February 15, 1998, B-3.

Index

internationalism, 82–83; elitist character of, 83; Hawaiians' role in rebirth of, 83; sources of, 82

International Longshoreman's and Warehouseman's Union (ILWU), 37, 39, 42, 121, 222

Japanese: changing images of, 38; conflict over assimilation, 52, 278 n.32; conflict with plantation owners, 52; in-migration, 36; investment in Hawai'i, 80, 81–82; labor immigration, 26, 51; traditional culture, 51

Japanese-Americans: ethnic concerns, 60, 61; and future Democratic party, 137–38; place in new Democratic regime, 59; political style of, 61; voter turn-out among, 116; in World War II, 39–40, 67

"Japanese Menace" and statehood, 43

Jones Act: costs and benefits of, 73; and shipping costs, 72–73

Jones-Costigan Act, and future of sugar, 67

judges, appointment of, 148–50; "Burns method," 149; partisanship in, 149; rejections, 149–50

Judicial Selection Committee, 148–49

Judiciary: budget for, 141, 142

Ka'ahumanu, 19, 92, 143

Kaho'olawe, importance of, 85

Ka Lahui Hawai'i, 235

Kalakaua, King David, 28, 82, 97

Kame'ekeihiwa, Lilikala, 21, 22, 265

Kamehameha I, 18, 92

Kamehameha II, King (Liholiho), 19, 43

Kamehameha III, King (Kauikeaouli), 93

Kamehameha V, King (Lot), 96–97

Kanaka Maoli, 17, 46

Kapu system, 142–43; overthrow of, 19, 143, 288 n.4

Ke Ala Hoku, 252–54

Kealoha-Scullion, Kehaulani, 22

Kent, Noel, 32

Kincaid, John, 220, 224

kingdom: and foreign powers, 23, 30; effect on form of government, 92–93

Koki, Stan, 130

kuhina-nui, 92, 93, 94

Kuhio, Prince Jonah Kalaniana'ole, 33, 132, 239

Kuykendall, Ralph, 24, 94, 95, 264, 282 n.43

labor, control of, on plantation, 36

Labor and Industrial Relations, Department of, 167, 183

labor immigration, 36–37; and assimilation, 38, 39; attitudes toward, 26, 27, 32; changing images of, 38; Chinese, 26, 47; cultures of laborers, 27; Filipino, 49; Japanese, 26, 51; Portuguese, 49; South Pacific Islander, 26; as threat to haole elite, 99

labor unions: and Democratic party, 121; government reform of, 185, 224; influence of public unions on, 207–8; as interest groups, 203; size of, 205

land: changing status, 94; control of, 34, 35; corporate control of, 35; illegal "taking" of, 236; importance